ANTI-SPAM TOOL KIT

PAUL **WOLFE**
CHARLIE **SCOTT**
MIKE **ERWIN**

McGraw-Hill/Osborne

New York   Chicago   San Francisco
Lisbon   London   Madrid   Mexico City   Milan
New Delhi   San Juan   Seoul   Singapore   Sydney   Toronto

The McGraw·Hill Companies

McGraw-Hill/Osborne
2100 Powell Street, 10th Floor
Emeryville, California 94608
U.S.A.

To arrange bulk purchase discounts for sales promotions, premiums, or fund-raisers, please contact **McGraw-Hill/Osborne** at the above address. For information on translations or book distributors outside the U.S.A., please see the International Contact Information page immediately following the index of this book.

Anti-Spam Tool Kit

Copyright © 2004 by The McGraw-Hill Companies. All rights reserved. Printed in the United States of America. Except as permitted under the Copyright Act of 1976, no part of this publication may be reproduced or distributed in any form or by any means, or stored in a database or retrieval system, without the prior written permission of publisher, with the exception that the program listings may be entered, stored, and executed in a computer system, but they may not be reproduced for publication.

234567890 FGR FGR 01987654

Book p/n 0-07-223168-8 and CD p/n 0-07-223169-6
parts of
ISBN 0-07-223167-x

Publisher
 Brandon A. Nordin
Vice President & Associate Publisher
 Scott Rogers
Executive Editor
 Jane K. Brownlow
Senior Project Editor
 LeeAnn Pickrell
Acquisitions Coordinator
 Athena Honore
Technical Editor
 James C. Foster
Copy Editor
 Lisa Theobald

Proofreader
 Marian Selig
Indexer
 Valerie Haynes Perry
Composition
 Tara A. Davis, Kelly Stanton-Scott
Illustrators
 Kathleen Edwards, Melinda Lytle
Series Design
 Dick Schwartz, Peter F. Hancik
Cover Design
 Theresa Havener

This book was composed with Corel VENTURA™ Publisher.

Information has been obtained by McGraw-Hill/Osborne from sources believed to be reliable. However, because of the possibility of human or mechanical error by our sources, McGraw-Hill/Osborne, or others, McGraw-Hill/Osborne does not guarantee the accuracy, adequacy, or completeness of any information and is not responsible for any errors or omissions or the results obtained from the use of such information.

About the Authors

Paul Wolfe

Paul Wolfe is currently an independent information security consultant and author. Before that, he spent eight years in the data center industry (the source and destination of much spam), where he implemented information security policies and procedures, including secure electronic commerce and e-mail systems for small to mid-sized companies. Paul has performed information security work for Fortune 500 companies, law enforcement, and government. He has coauthored the following books: *Snort for Dummies* (Wiley, 2004), *Virtual Private Networks, 2nd ed.* (O'Reilly & Assoc., 1999), *Virtual Private Networks, 1st ed.* (O'Reilly & Assoc., 1998), *Building Web Commerce Sites* (IDG Books, 1997), *Building VRML Worlds* (McGraw-Hill/Osborne, 1997), and *The CGI Bible* (IDG Books, 1997). He served as technical reviewer for *Web Programming Secrets* (IDG Books, 1996).

Charlie Scott

Charlie Scott is an information security analyst for the city of Austin, where he helps maintain the city's network security infrastructure and policies. He sees spam as a special kind of security problem and has engineered spam countermeasures for ISP and government e-mail systems. He serves on the board of directors of Austin Free-Net, a nonprofit, community-based organization dedicated to ensuring underserved communities can access and effectively use the Internet and computer technologies. Charlie is a Certified Information Systems Security Professional (CISSP) and a Cisco Certified Network Professional (CCNP). He has coauthored the following books: *Snort for Dummies* (Wiley, 2004), *Virtual Private Networks, 2nd ed.* (O'Reilly & Assoc., 1999), *Virtual Private Networks, 1st ed.* (O'Reilly & Assoc., 1998), *Building Web Commerce Sites* (IDG Books, 1997), *Building VRML Worlds* (McGraw Hill/Osborne, 1997), *The CGI Bible* (IDG Books, 1997), *Web Programming Secrets* (IDG Books, 1996), and *The 60 Minute Guide to VRML* (IDG Books, 1995). He served as technical reviewer for *The 60 Minute Guide to CGI Programming in Perl 5* (IDG Books, 1996).

Mike Erwin

Mike Erwin is the President and Chairman of Symbiot, Inc., a risk-management company specializing in intelligent security management, risk metrics, and threat modeling. Mike is one of the original founders of Symbiot and continues to guide the company by providing organizational management, leadership, and vision. Prior to Symbiot, he thwarted spam at OuterNet, Inc., an ISP and data center company he founded in 1994, and prior to that, he served as an Internet services manager at Apple Computer. He has given conference presentations on a variety of topics, including anti-spam tactics and tools. Mike is a Certified Information Systems Security Professional (CISSP), and he has coauthored the following books: *Snort for Dummies* (Wiley, 2004), *Virtual Private Networks, 2nd ed.* (O'Reilly & Assoc., 1999), *Virtual Private Networks, 1st ed.* (O'Reilly & Assoc., 1998), *Building Web Commerce Sites* (IDG Books, 1997), *The CGI Bible* (IDG Books, 1997), *Web Programming Secrets* (IDG Books, 1996), *The 60 Minute Guide to VRML* (IDG Books, 1995), and *Foundations of WWW Programming in HTML & CGI* (IDG Books, 1995).

About the Technical Editor

James C. Foster

James C. Foster (CISSP, CCSE) is the Director of Research and Development for Foundstone Inc., and is responsible for all aspects of product, consulting, and corporate R&D initiatives. Prior to joining Foundstone, Foster was a senior advisor and research scientist with Guardent Inc. and an adjunct author at *Information Security Magazine*, subsequent to working as an information security and research specialist at Computer Sciences Corporation. With his core competencies in programming, web-based applications, cryptography, protocol analysis, and search algorithm technology, Foster has conducted numerous code reviews for commercial OS components, Win32 application assessments, and reviews on commercial-grade cryptography implementations.

Foster is a seasoned speaker and has presented throughout North America at conferences, technology forums, security summits, and research symposiums with highlights at the Microsoft Security Summit, MIT Wireless Research Forum, SANS, MilCon, TechGov, InfoSec World 2001, and the Thomson Security Conference. He is commonly asked to comment on pertinent security issues and has been sited in *USAToday, Information Security Magazine, Baseline, Computer World, Secure Computing,* and the *MIT Technologist*. Foster holds degrees and certifications in Business, Software Engineering, Management of Information Systems, and numerous computer-related or programming-related concentrations and has attended or conducted research at the Yale School of Business, Harvard University, Capitol College, and the University of Maryland.

Foster is also a well-published author with multiple commercial and educational papers and computer books. He is a contributing author of *Hacking Exposed, 4th Edition*.

AT A GLANCE

Part I	Preparing for the Fight

1	Forming Your Plan Against Spam	3
2	Goals and Criteria for Evaluating Spam Control Solutions	17
3	Methods for Mail Content Control	27
4	Anti-Spam Implementation Strategies	43

Part II	Building Your Anti-Spam Arsenal

5	Blocking Spammers with DNS Blacklists . . .	61
6	Filtering Spam with SpamAssassin	89
7	Catching Spam with SpamAssassin's Bayesian Classifier	113
8	Enhancing and Maintaining SpamAssassin . .	125
9	Configuring Popular E-mail Clients for Spam Filtering	143

v

Part III — Implementing Other Popular Anti-Spam Tools

10	Anti-Spam Clients for Windows	171
11	Anti-Spam Servers for Windows	249
12	Anti-Spam Tools for Macs	283
13	Anti-Spam Tools for Linux	307

Part IV — Stopping Spam in the Long Term

14	Know Your Enemy	327
15	Advanced Topics and Fine Tuning	345
16	Fighting Spam Defensively	361

Glossary	Definitions and Acronyms	383
A	Selected Anti-Spam Resources	387
B	About the CD-ROM	399
	Index	403

CONTENTS

Acknowledgments xvii
Introduction. xix

Part I
Preparing for the Fight

1 Forming Your Plan Against Spam 3
  A Brief History of Spam 4
    Why the Word Spam? 5
  The Basics of Fighting Spam 6
    Traditional Methods—Filtering by Keyword 6
    Open-Relays and Blacklists 6
    Advanced Methods and Why They Work 7
    Trends Forming Around Spam Legislation 8
  Developing E-Mail Policies 9
    Organizing Everything 10
    Developing an E-Mail Policy 10
    Establishing a Resource Plan (Identifying Systems) 13
    Conduct Testing and Refinement 14
  Spotting Problems Before They Happen 14
  Advanced Topics and Cross-Pollination 15
  Summary 16

2 Goals and Criteria for Evaluating Spam Control Solutions 17

The Mail Flow Architecture 18
The Digital You: Authentication and Repudiation 19
Goals of a Robust Mail Control System 20
    Restrict Access to Your E-Mail Identities 20
    Identify the Spammers 21
    Identify the Spam 21
    Select the Best Locations 21
    Select the Best Tools 22
    Select for Operational Ease 22
Bringing It All Together 22
Selecting Mail Control Components 23
    Breadth (All Forms of Mail-borne Content Filtered) 23
    Depth (Multiple Techniques Used at Multiple Points) 23
    Impact 24
    Operation 24
    Specific Criteria in Selecting Anti-Spam Solutions 24
Summary 26

3 Methods for Mail Content Control 27

Building on a Historical Basis 28
    RFC 2505—SMTP and MTA Best Practices 28
    RFC 2635—An Explanation for Why Spam Is Harmful 29
    RFC 3098—A Discussion of
        Responsible Internet Advertising 29
Analyzing Spam 29
    Analysis That Targets the Content of the Message 30
    Analysis That Targets the Sender or Intermediaries 34
    Analysis That Targets the Benefactor 39
New Approaches to Circumvent Advanced Spam Filtering 41
Summary 42

4 Anti-Spam Implementation Strategies 43

Choosing the Right Solutions 45
    Key Factors That Affect Your Decision 45
Recommendations on Solution Robustness 48
    Policy Recommendations 48
    Technical Recommendations 50
Spam Solutions Covered in this Book 51
    Subscriptions to Network-Based Blacklists 51
    Client-Based Spam Filtering 52

Server-Based Spam Systems	53
Gateway-Based Spam Systems	54
Provider-Based Spam Systems	56
Summary	58

Part II
Building Your Anti-Spam Arsenal

5 Blocking Spammers with DNS Blacklists 61

Understanding DNS Blacklists	62
Types of DNSBLs	62
Criteria for DNS Blacklists	64
Adding or Removing Entries from a DNS Blacklist	65
Choosing a DNS Blacklist	66
Mail Abuse Prevention System (MAPS)	66
How MAPS Works	67
Subscribing to MAPS	69
SpamCop	69
How SpamCop Works	70
Subscribing to SpamCop	71
Open Relay Database (ORDB)	71
How ORDB Works	72
Subscribing to ORDB	72
Distributed Server Boycott List (DSBL)	72
How DSBL Works	72
Subscribing to DSBL	73
Spamhaus	73
How Spamhaus Works	73
Subscribing to Spamhaus	74
Not Just Another Bogus List (NJABL)	74
How NJABL Works	74
Subscribing to NJABL	75
RFC Ignorant (RFCI)	75
What Makes Someone RFC Ignorant?	76
Subscribing to RFCI	78
Implementing DNSBLs Within Sendmail	78
Configuring Sendmail for IP-Based DNSBLs	79
Configuring Sendmail for Domain-Based RHSBLs	79
Implementing DNSBLs with Postfix	80
Configuring Postfix for IP-Based DNSBLs	80
Configuring Postfix for Domain-Based RHSBLs	80

	Implementing DNSBLs with Microsoft Exchange	81
	Exchange 2000	81
	Exchange 2003	82
	Summary	88
6	**Filtering Spam with SpamAssassin**	**89**
	Dossier of a Spam Assassin	90
	SpamAssassin = Spam Detective	90
	SpamAssassin Rules!	91
	SpamAssassin Scores!	91
	Killer Features	93
	SpamAssassin Gone Commercial	93
	Installing SpamAssassin	94
	Software and Hardware Requirements	94
	Before You Start	98
	Installing the Easy Way: From CPAN	99
	Installing the Less Easy Way: From Tarball	101
	Installing from the Edge: CVS	104
	Other Ways to Install	104
	Understanding SpamAssassin's Components	105
	The spamassassin Utility	105
	The Spamd Daemon	106
	The Spamc Client	106
	The local.cf Configuration File	107
	The user_prefs Configuration File	108
	Configuring SpamAssassin	109
	Per-User Configuration	109
	Site-Wide Configuration	110
	Spamd Configuration	110
	An Introduction to SpamAsssassin's Output	111
	Looking at a Message	111
	Is This the Only Option?	111
	Summary	112
7	**Catching Spam with SpamAssassin's Bayesian Classifier**	**113**
	Implementing SpamAssassin's Bayesian Classifier	114
	Looking at SpamAssassin's Bayes-Related Files	114
	SpamAssassin's Bayes Rules	115
	Automated Learning	116

	Training SpamAssassin's Bayesian Classifier	117
	Giving sa-learn Input	117
	Training with Ham	118
	Training with Spam	118
	Correcting Mistakes	118
	Bayes Database Expiration	119
	Getting Bayes Statistics	121
	Implementing Bayes System-Wide	122
	Bayesian Learning Caveats	123
	Summary	124
8	**Enhancing and Maintaining SpamAssassin**	**125**
	Creating Your Own Rules	126
	Where to Create and Modify Rules	127
	Components of a Rule	127
	Building a Rule	129
	Testing the Rule	131
	Whitelisting and Blacklisting	131
	trusted_networks	131
	whitelist_to	132
	more_spam_to	132
	all_spam_to	133
	Localizing	133
	ok_locales	133
	ok_languages	134
	Using MIMEDefang with SpamAssassin	135
	MIMEDefang and SpamAssassin	136
	MIMEDefang Requirements	136
	Using amavisd-new with SpamAssassin	138
	amavisd-new and SpamAssassin	139
	amavisd-new Requirements	139
	Using SpamAssassin as a Gateway to Another Mail Server	140
	Summary	141
9	**Configuring Popular E-mail Clients for Spam Filtering**	**143**
	Configuring Spam Filters on Eudora	144
	Watching for Spam with Eudora's SpamWatch	144
	Turning On Eudora's SpamWatch	145
	Tweaking Eudora's SpamWatch	145
	Training Eudora's SpamWatch	146

Configuring Spam Filters on Mozilla Mail	147
Mozilla's Junk Mail Controls	147
Using Mozilla Message Filters with SpamAssassin	149
Configuring Spam Filters in Outlook Express	152
Blocking Senders in Outlook Express	153
Using OE Message Rules with SpamAssassin	156
Configuring Spam Filters on Outlook	158
Configuring Outlook's Junk and Adult Content E-mail Filters	159
Using Outlook Message Rules with SpamAssassin	166
Summary	168

Part III

Implementing Other Popular Anti-Spam Tools

10 Anti-Spam Clients for Windows	171
SpamBayes	172
How It Works	172
Installing SpamBayes	173
User Knowledge and Machine Learning	174
SpamPal	183
How It Works	183
Installing SpamPal	185
Controlling the World Through Lists	188
SpamCatcher	194
How It Works	194
Installing SpamCatcher	194
Making Contact with the SpamCatcher Network	198
Lyris MailShield Desktop	203
How It Works	204
Installing MailShield Desktop	204
Manipulating MailShield to Suit Your Needs	207
SPAMfighter	212
How It Works	213
Installing SPAMfighter	213
Configuring SPAMfighter	214
SpamButcher	218
How It Works	218
Installing SpamButcher	219
Butchering Spam	220

iHateSpam	227
How It Works	228
Installing iHateSpam	228
Turning iHate to Action	229
SpamNet	231
How It Works	232
Installing SpamNet	232
Netting Spam with SpamNet	233
KnockKnock	236
How It Works	236
Installing KnockKnock	236
Knocking on a Spammer's Door	237
Knocking KnockKnock	241
POPFile	242
How It Works	242
Installing POPFile	242
POP Goes the Spammers	244
11 Anti-Spam Servers for Windows	**249**
iHateSpam Server Edition	250
How It Works	250
Installing iHateSpam	250
Hating Spam in the Enterprise	254
GFI MailEssentials	266
How It Works	266
Installing GFI MailEssentials	267
Configuring the Essentials	269
Trend Micro Spam Prevention Service	276
How It Works	276
Installing SPS	276
12 Anti-Spam Tools for Macs	**283**
PostArmor	284
How It Works	284
Installing	284
Use Your Armor!	288
POPmonitor	292
How It Works	292
Installing	292
Operating POPmonitor	295

Spamfire 297
    How It Works 298
    Installing 298
    Firing Up the Spammers 299
MailGoGoGo 302
    How It Works 302
    Installing 303
    Getting Spam to Go Go Go... 304
    Mail Gone, Gone, Gone 305
Summary 306

13 Anti-Spam Tools for Linux 307

Vipul's Razor 308
    Examining the Razor 309
    Downloading and Installing Razor 310
    Using Razor 311
Distributed Checksum Clearinghouse 313
    Welcome to the Clearinghouse 313
    Downloading and Installing DCC 314
    Running DCC 315
Bogofilter 315
    Installing Bogofilter 315
    Running Bogofilter 316
SpamBayes 317
    Installing SpamBayes 317
    Using SpamBayes 318
Quick Spam Filter 319
    Downloading and Installing QSF 319
    Running QSF 319
The SpamBouncer 321
    Installing and Configuring the SpamBouncer 321
    What You'll See 323
    A Pleasant Surprise 324
Summary 324

Part IV
Stopping Spam in the Long Term

14 Know Your Enemy 327

Profile of an "E-mail Direct Marketer" 328
    Spam Tools 328
    The Purveyors of Spam 332

Getting to Know the Product (Spam)	335
Anatomy of an E-mail Header	335
Spam Examples	339
Red Alert: Reporting Known Spammers	343
Direct E-mail	343
DNS Blacklists	344
Update Your Own Anti-Spam Tool	344
Summary	344

15 Advanced Topics and Fine Tuning — 345

The Black, the White, and the Grey	346
Roll-Your-Own Blacklist	346
Blacklisting with a Bite	346
What in the World Is Greylisting	347
The Complete MX Relay Defense	348
Defense by Disguise	349
Use Graphics Instead of Text	349
Use the HTML ASCII Equivalence	349
Use a Scripting Language (JavaScript)	350
Spam-bots and How They Work	351
Harvesting with Our Perl Reaper	353
Spam-bots Patented: the End of the World Must Be Near…	354
What Is the Robots.txt File	354
Where Can I Get More Info on Robots?	356
Siphoning a 55-Gallon Drum of Spam	356
Reversing the Spam-bot Spigot	358
The Reverse Dictionary Defense	358
The DDoS Detection Defense	359
What to Send Once You've Identified Them	359
Summary	360

16 Fighting Spam Defensively — 361

Win Before Fighting	362
E-mail Addresses	362
Challenge/Response: The Next Weird Thing	367
Future Spam-Fighting	369
Keeping Your Own House Clean	369
Open Relays	369
Securing Your Resources	372
Spyware: Another Spam Pathway	375
Pop-ups: The New Spam	375

		True Spyware	376
		Anti-Spyware Tools	376
	Summary		381
Glossary	Definitions and Acronyms		383
A	Selected Anti-Spam Resources		387
	E-mail and Spam-Related RFCs		388
	Papers, Whitepapers, and Treatises		388
	Spam and the Law		389
	DNS Blacklists		389
	SpamAssassin Resources		390
	E-mail Clients		390
	E-mail Servers		391
	Anti-Spam Client Tools for Windows		391
	Anti-Spam Servers for Windows		394
	Anti-Spam Tools for the Macintosh		394
	Anti-Spam Tools for Linux		395
	Other Tactics and Tools		396
	U.S. Government Sites Concerning Spam		397
B	About the CD-ROM		399
	How to Use the CD-ROM		400
	Anti-Spam Tools on the CD		400
	Links to Additional Tools		401
	Problems with the CD		401
	Index		403

ACKNOWLEDGMENTS

The authors bow humbly before the developers of the open-source and proprietary anti-spam tools covered in this book. Thank you for giving us such a diverse and creative arsenal for spam-fighting.

The authors would like to extend a huge "thank you" to William A. Broussard, Esq., for his tremendous assistance in interpreting the legalese of the current anti-spam legislation, as well as providing the necessary guidance in what it really means to us non-lawyers.

We would also like to extend our great thanks to James Foster for his excellent feedback and the technical direction that he provided for the final draft of this book.

Additionally, we would like extend our heart-felt thanks to Carol McClendon and Waterside Productions for representing us and our technical projects.

Of course, this book wouldn't be possible without the very professional staff of McGraw-Hill/Osborne and the work of Jane Brownlow, Athena Honore, LeeAnn Pickrell, Lisa Theobald, and a host of other people tucked away behind the scenes.

Charlie and Mike tip their hats to Paul for ruling this project.

Charlie would like to dedicate his portion of this book to his spam-fighting co-workers: Scott Brown, Paul Fiero, Ann Morse, Teri Pennington, and Clayton Stapleton. He would also like to thank his wife, Mary, for telling him when to work and when to chill for the past ten years.

Paul would like to dedicate his portion of this book to Brenda, Nikolaus, Lukas, Rayna, and Jesse, whose constant support made his work possible. He would also like to thank the men and women of the U.S. armed forces and their families for their dedication, perseverance, and sacrifice in these troubled times. Come home safe and soon.

INTRODUCTION

The three of us began our tech careers at a small local Internet service provider, where every dollar was sacred and wasting one was the equivalent of sacrilege. What we discovered then is still true today: Any way you cut it, spam wastes money. Organizations and individuals devote more time, money, and strategy to thwarting spam than to any other online problem. Even the Congress is talking about it. As of this writing, they have passed the *Controlling the Assault of Non-Solicited Pornography and Marketing Act* (or the CAN-SPAM Act, if you can believe it), and we know that those guys have more important things to do than monitor your e-mail box.

This book was written to help you thwart the assault of unwanted commercial e-mail whether you run a sizable organization's e-mail system or you're sitting at home banging your head on your keyboard, trying to sift a real e-mail message from the chaff. Within this book, you will find a thorough discussion of spam-fighting tools and technologies:

- We cover more than 30 individual anti-spam tools across three major platforms, both client- and server-based, open source and proprietary.
- We talk about the technologies on which the e-mail system is based and why that system is conducive to spam.

- We cover the four major schools of thought for fighting spam, the specific tools that demonstrate those methods, and some future spam-killing strategies coming down from on high.
- We give advice on how you should start looking at the spam problem in your organization and how to begin formulating a strategy.
- We talk about the spammers themselves: their motivation, the technology, and the methods used for filling your e-mail box with junk.
- And finally, we provide hundreds of references for further reading, a spam glossary, and a CD packed with anti-spam tools.
- As a special bonus, we give you the (widely agreed upon) first spam message ever sent on the Internet (see Chapter 1).

What we cannot teach you is how to completely eradicate spam from your life. Even with our tricked-out SpamAssassin setup, we only catch about 99 percent of the spam messages destined for our mail server. And we like to think we know what we're doing. The scary fact is that spam is here to stay. It has permeated the e-mail system, crossed over to web pop-ups and spyware, and even infects mobile phones and text pagers. Congress can't stem the tide; your Internet service provider has a marginal effect. So, it's up to you to wage your own war on spam.

Anti-Spam Toolkit is a starting place, and as such, it provides you with the basis and tools you need. Plenty of additional resources are available on the Internet itself. If you're in a bind and you need someone in your foxhole, feel free to contact us. We started a web site (*http://www.vorpalmedia.com*) to support this book and to add to the overall anti-spam effort. Check in there for anti-spam news, tool updates, and other tidbits of information. And feel free to contribute because we're fighting this war together.

PART I

PREPARING FOR THE FIGHT

CHAPTER 1

FORMING YOUR PLAN AGAINST SPAM

Anti-Spam Tool Kit

Some years back, it was suggested that in a typical e-mail box, the number of spam messages per day might eventually match the number of regular e-mail messages on a one-for-one basis. Sadly, we must report that this is already true—in fact, we "Internet old fogies" reached that milestone a few years back. Our personal ratio is currently about 30 *good* messages to around 300 *spam* messages each and every day!

Despite this exponential torrent of unwanted e-mail, almost everyone goes to extraordinary lengths to stem the spam tide. We install filters, we use blacklists, and, increasingly, we rely on advanced content analysis to help us control unwanted e-mail. An entire software industry has emerged that builds applications to assist us in holding back the flood. These applications have grown in size and number almost as rapidly as the amount of spam in our inboxes.

Not to be left out, the Internet Engineering Task Force (IETF), a think tank of core Internet founders, has also been hard at work on the problem. The Anti-Spam Research Group (ASRG) grew from the IETF's efforts to act as a clearinghouse for spam-related issues (see http://www.irtf.org/charters/asrg.html). The ASRG concluded that before global anti-spam weapons could be effective, a fundamental change in the way e-mail works was required. We liken this to the IETF's rethinking of the global Internet and the birthing of IPv6 (Internet Protocol Next Generation). And, like IPv6, it may be some time before these Internet-shaping changes take affect. It's important work, and we are glad that the task force got the ball rolling with the ASRG, but most of us need some spam relief today. That's what this book is all about.

A BRIEF HISTORY OF SPAM

Believe it or not, the first spam ever transmitted crossed the wire in May of 1978. Even more amusing is the fact that the message actually contained an advertisement and was sent in bulk to every e-mail address on the West Coast (more than 600 users). Hats off to Digital Equipment Corporation (DEC), who caught flames for sending it. Because we knew you would be curious, we've included the contents of the first recognized e-mail spam here:

```
DIGITAL WILL BE GIVING A PRODUCT PRESENTATION OF THE NEWEST MEMBERS OF THE
DECSYSTEM-20 FAMILY; THE DECSYSTEM-2020, 2020T, 2060, AND 2060T.  THE
DECSYSTEM-20 FAMILY OF COMPUTERS HAS EVOLVED FROM THE TENEX OPERATING SYSTEM
AND THE DECSYSTEM-10 <PDP-10> COMPUTER ARCHITECTURE.  BOTH THE DECSYSTEM-2060T
AND 2020T OFFER FULL ARPANET SUPPORT UNDER THE TOPS-20 OPERATING SYSTEM.
THE DECSYSTEM-2060 IS AN UPWARD EXTENSION OF THE CURRENT DECSYSTEM 2040
AND 2050 FAMILY.  THE DECSYSTEM-2020 IS A NEW LOW END MEMBER OF THE
DECSYSTEM-20 FAMILY AND FULLY SOFTWARE COMPATIBLE WITH ALL OF THE OTHER
DECSYSTEM-20 MODELS.

WE INVITE YOU TO COME SEE THE 2020 AND HEAR ABOUT THE DECSYSTEM-20 FAMILY
AT THE TWO PRODUCT PRESENTATIONS WE WILL BE GIVING IN CALIFORNIA THIS
MONTH.  THE LOCATIONS WILL BE:
```

```
TUESDAY, MAY 9, 1978 - 2 PM
   HYATT HOUSE (NEAR THE L.A. AIRPORT)
   LOS ANGELES, CA

THURSDAY, MAY 11, 1978 - 2 PM
   DUNFEY'S ROYAL COACH
   SAN MATEO, CA
(4 MILES SOUTH OF S.F. AIRPORT AT BAYSHORE, RT 101 AND RT 92)

A 2020 WILL BE THERE FOR YOU TO VIEW. ALSO TERMINALS ON-LINE TO OTHER
DECSYSTEM-20 SYSTEMS THROUGH THE ARPANET. IF YOU ARE UNABLE TO ATTEND,
PLEASE FEEL FREE TO CONTACT THE NEAREST DEC OFFICE
FOR MORE INFORMATION ABOUT THE EXCITING DECSYSTEM-20 FAMILY.
```

For those of you still wondering where you were in 1978, consider that the Internet didn't quite exist, as it was still molting out of ARPANet. This Net was peopled by an exclusive group of denizens (less than 10,000 people), who were the hard-core pioneers of early research. They were equipped with mega-expensive time-sharing computers, and they worked for large corporations and universities. DEC's invitation to check out its new system caused a lively discussion across ARPANet. Ironically, the company's blunder was even mildly defended by Richard Stallman, the father of the modern Open Source movement and architect of the GNU Foundation, upon which the Linux operating system was ultimately built.

Why the Word Spam?

Although its origins are disputed, we recollect that the use of the term *spam* came from USENET originally. For those of you who have forgotten about it already—or who just weren't involved with computers in those days—USENET is a worldwide bulletin board system by which people post messages in a public forum. The whole system is organized into thousands of categories that are layered many levels deep with subtopics. USENET discussion groups pertain to a variety of topics, from dog grooming and kite flying to esoteric technical topics.

USENET is always hopping with scholarly debates, vitriolic arguments, and outright flames—and, of course, lots of spam. A boiling pot of many Internet ideas and terms, USENET actually gave us the word *spam* to refer to any unwanted posting, solicitation, or communication on the boards.

Spam was chosen as the name for "junk" e-mail in deference to its use in an old Monty Python skit depicting a restaurant that served only dishes composed of the actual canned meat product, SPAM, which was assembled in every conceivable way (SPAM and broccoli soup, SPAM-and-jelly sandwiches, SPAM milkshakes—you get the picture). At various intervals while patrons were trying to converse, restaurant employees dressed as Vikings broke out into a song, repeating "SPAM, SPAM, SPAM…Lovely SPAM!" Clearly, the intention on USENET was to label any unwanted communications as noisy, annoying, and unrelentingly repetitious (and, some might say, tasteless).

THE BASICS OF FIGHTING SPAM

Most spam fighting is accomplished by filtering e-mail through a process that determines the probability of each message being "junk." The next several chapters cover in detail the basic methods used to filter spam; here, we've highlighted the major points of each spam-fighting method.

Traditional Methods—Filtering by Keyword

Early techniques for combating spam stemmed from the detection of keywords in the subject field of the message. For instance, use of such words as *promotion*, *advertisement*, and *refinance* became likely indicators of spam. Fledgling spam filters (often nothing more than command-line scripts) matched and filtered messages against a forbidden word list into specified mail folders for later inspection. As the amount of spam increased, so did the options for filtering it, and so did the accidental removal of real mail. Filtering as a technique was somewhat effective in the beginning, but it gradually declined with accuracy over time. Spammers got the hang of what passed by a mail filter and started using sneaky personal-sounding subjects to thwart the keyword filters. Much of the spam you see today is consistent with this approach. It's common to see subjects of spam such as: "Hello" or "RE: Our meeting last week" or even the veiled "RE: About us."

Later filtering techniques searched the entire message body for keywords, which had the desired effect of finding more spam, but at the cost of wasting precious processing time. Larger e-mail implementations send mail through several server-side filters in addition to the client-side filters. The results of this layered approach were better, but only marginally so.

Generally, as the use of e-mail increases over time, spam still manages to worm its way into our mailboxes. The amount of e-mail sent daily grows at such a pace that it makes keyword filters less and less capable in the long run. Considerable time and effort are needed to maintain the word lists, and even more time is needed to cull through the captured spam just to make sure real mail didn't slip into the captured list. This method is obviously a losing battle, and one that begat other more advanced methods for our arsenal.

Open-Relays and Blacklists

Early mail server software (failing to anticipate that people would abuse the configuration) allowed third-party forwarding of e-mail that effectively masked the origin of the sender. This gave the spammer an anonymous source and essentially free infrastructure for sending massive amounts of e-mail. Since most servers at the time were running in this *open-relay* mode, a virtual explosion of unwanted e-mail soon followed, and the race was on.

Noting this, anti-spam groups put together lists of domains, servers, and networks that allowed the open exchange of e-mail and blacklisted them through a variety of schemes. A handful of open-relay databases and quite a few blacklists were developed. Most of them provided the means to look up an offender in real-time. Spam-hunting administrators immediately configured their mail servers to check the source of every message and discard any that matched a known spam-friendly relay.

Of course, this strategy had its disappointments, too. With a strong desire to protect their anonymity, spammers gravitated toward the huge commercial Internet service providers (ISPs) to source their e-mail. While gigantic operations such as AOL and EarthLink had experienced staff and strict acceptable use policies forbidding spam, by the time they caught on that a spammer was using their network, several thousand messages were already underway and the spammer was long gone. Most ISPs are aware of spammers' methods, and few allow such users to continue using their services.

Using automation *seemed* like a good idea but turned out to be more trouble than it was worth. Programmed blacklisting couldn't protect against accidentally blocking one of these super-ISPs, which was definitely not the intended purpose of the filters. But many small shops, especially local ISPs, blocked e-mail from AOL and Hotmail, particularly because at that time the bulk of the spam flood originated from those networks. Again, there had to be a better way.

Advanced Methods and Why They Work

The spam conflict is essentially an escalating war of methods and tools. The spammers find a weakness in a system and exploit it, and the spam-fighters develop new methods and tools to thwart them. Spammers need only install the latest spam-blocking tool and alter the composition until the message passes through. Once a valid format is found, they have a limited window in which to send out as many messages as possible.

In this war, the good news is that the spam-fighters are winning by restricting the spammers to a smaller and smaller front. Spammers are reduced to finding ways around complicated algorithms and "fuzzy" logic. The bad news is that the spam-fighters' front becomes just as small, and they *have* to let legitimate e-mail through or their tool is useless.

The beauty of advanced spam-fighting methods is that they largely work as expected. State-of-the-art spam filtering relies on server software that uses a basic form of machine learning, or artificial intelligence (AI), to separate spam from "ham" (legitimate e-mail). We as humans usually have no problem separating spam from real mail, and a computer can be taught to do the same. Using machine learning, content analysis, and a continuously updated database of *profiled* spam, a mail server can recognize the difference between a legitimate message and spam. This reduces false positives (legitimate e-mail tagged as spam) and false negatives (spam in your inbox).

NOTE Just to illustrate how effective AI software is, our filters miss less than half of 1 percent of all spam sent to us, with a near perfect score in false positives (the accidental determination of a real mail as spam). Plus, since the system learns what characteristics make up a likely spam message, new formats tried by solicitors never make it to our mailbox—not even once.

AI software doesn't just look at the rank and relevance of words in the e-mail; it also takes into consideration other factors. The time of day the message was sent, the number of mail servers used to send it, the locations of those servers, and even the structure of the e-mail itself all go into the analysis. Spam has certain characteristics that are easy to identify, once a pattern has been abstracted. Many spammers use colored HTML text embedded in their messages, and most use a plethora of punctuation as attention-grabbers.

Those are dead giveaways of spam, and the AI engines easily detect them, regardless of color, size, or shape. Likewise, legitimate e-mails from over-enthusiastic coworkers or web-mail dependent relatives will make it through unscathed.

It's the spammer's message that ultimately betrays it in the end. No matter how many "hops" spammers use to cover their tracks, what kind of disguise they use to shroud the message, or even how they clone the basic elements of the message itself, it comes down to the fact that they are including some content that just doesn't belong. There's always a clue within the message, and that clue will always be found with specialized tools. Spam of the future will not be elaborate, it won't have "click to remove" links at the bottom, and it won't have a flashing red "Act Now" icon embedded in the body. Those are meta-traits of spam that will have to be abandoned if spammers want to be successful. Thus, the most advanced method for thwarting AI-based filters is a plain message, sent directly and without embellishment.

Trends Forming Around Spam Legislation

You may be wondering what laws are in the works, given the increased popularity of spam as a cheap advertising vehicle. We're sure you'll agree that spam is something that should be regulated or at least controlled enough to protect the ordinary consumer against fraud and resource abuse.

In a recent poll conducted by Harris Interactive (*http://www.harrisinteractive.com/harris_poll/index.asp?PID=424*), an overwhelming majority (74 percent) of online users are in favor of actually making spam illegal. In a similar poll of more than 1000 e-mail customers, 97 percent agreed that any random mail promoting business opportunities or pornography was spam. Further, some people are so antagonized by it that they would consider labeling jokes or humorous notes from their own friends as spam (see *http://maccentral.macworld.com/news/2003/05/26/spamlegislation*).

It's clear that one of the stumbling blocks to getting effective legislation passed is that dozens of different groups represent equally as many interests out there, and all have aggressive opinions as to how a well-rounded approach to controlling spam legally should look. However, that isn't stopping U.S. leaders from making progress. In the United States, we fully expect to see some federal laws cresting the horizon sometime within the year 2004. Most U.S. states already have laws on the books, and those that don't are a stone's throw away from adding them.

As of the writing of this book, federal policy-makers have introduced dozens of bills designed to control the distribution of rogue content, and one has actually been inked into law—the *Can Spam Act of 2003.*

The Can Spam Act is so new that its effectiveness is still unproven, but it does have some teeth. Basically, the Act requires commercial e-mail be nondeceptive about where it originates. It forbids spammers from disguising themselves using falsified names, addresses, and fake hosts, as well as prohibits the use of address harvesting programs, which spammers use to get the bulk of their targets. The Act contains some nasty enforcement mechanisms with the most serious offenders facing $6 million or more in fines.

Additionally, the Congress approved Senate bill 1052: *Ban on Deceptive Unsolicited Bulk Electronic Mail Act of 2003*, which is just one of many other bills pending consideration.

This legislation, like most of its brethren, makes it illegal to forge mail headers and for the sender to masquerade as someone else. It also has provisions making it unlawful to harvest e-mail addresses from anywhere to build lists of targets. Lastly, it harbors a hotly contested point: the *opt-out clause*, which forces the sender to provide a mechanism for the receiver to be removed from its lists. Strong anti-spam supporters, however, are in favor of an *opt-in clause*, which would require that potential advertisers somehow get permission from the e-mail receiver *before* sending the solicitation to begin with.

One of the timeliest resources for keeping up with the spam legislation efforts worldwide can be found at *http://www.spamlaws.com/*.

DEVELOPING E-MAIL POLICIES

Now that we've taken you through a basic introduction to spam and some of the issues surrounding it, we need to embark upon the first step in bolstering your e-mail posture: *policy development*. Without getting too bogged down by complexity, let's quickly review how a general security system is governed.

Security implementations are classified into common sets of rules: standards, policies, guidelines, and procedures. *Standards* represent industry-accepted norms for a particular topic (for example, a certain quality and type of encryption used to secure sensitive information such as a financial institution that may store PIN-numbers using 256-bit AES keys). *Policies* are company-specific adoptions of standards within a given environment. Our goal here is to help you establish a rudimentary e-mail policy as a starting point. *Guidelines* are commonly agreed upon methods for enacting standards and policies, but they are not rigidly enforced. Lastly, *procedures* are step-by-step instructions that detail a particular goal given a set of problems and resources.

Let's begin by developing our policy.

As with any project, the planning and organization phase is likely the most difficult to undertake, yet it is the most critical to the project's eventual success. Getting a grip on what you do with your e-mail now is key. If your e-mail is important to your livelihood, as it is increasingly becoming for all of us, knowing how you use e-mail and the tools that carry it are a clear first step.

An effective strategy for dealing with spam boils down to the following steps:

1. **Classify**   Organize your e-mail accounts.
2. **E-mail Policy**   Develop a strategy for filtering based on types.
3. **Allocate Resources**   Build a set of systems to implement the plan.
4. **Manage**   Design a testing methodology to ensure that the policy works as expected.

Organizing Everything

To help you get started, first sort your mail accounts into these six basic categories:

- **Direct Users**   Individual contributors receiving direct inbound e-mail (for example, *user@your_org.com*)
- **User Groups**   Groups of direct users (for example, *marketing@your_org.com*)
- **Role Accounts**   Sometimes handled as aliases (for example, *service_manager@your_org.com*)
- **Internal Accounts**   E-mail for private communication, not generally available to outsiders (for example, *payroll@your_org.com*)
- **Administrative Accounts**   Programmatic accounts for system maintenance and management (for example, *root@your_org.com*)
- **Lists**   E-mail processed by an automated system for mailing lists, also called an auto-responder (for example, *press_list@your_org.com*)

The basis for sorting your accounts is that each of the preceding classifications has a different policy associated with it. It's also quite possible that if you are a small shop, you may not need all of these categories. Our list is a general grouping and we recognize that many administrators may prefer alternative methods of classification. The real goal of this exercise is to develop a firm idea of the different types of accounts and how they are distributed across your user base.

Developing an E-Mail Policy

An appropriate electronic mail policy doesn't need to be a 30-page, International Organization for Standardization (ISO) compliant model of all electronic transmissions across your organization. What's important is to establish a baseline of activity that recommends actions should certain circumstances arise.

The following details a set of parameters you can use as a starting point to build your e-mail policy:

- **Publication Restrictions (Print, Electronic)**   Each group of accounts should have a policy defining how it is normally distributed. Some common publication methods include business cards, letterhead or stationery, newspaper or other print advertisements, e-mail signatures, web pages, and list-server footers.
- **Security and Confidentiality**   This policy determines the protection needed on the storage and transmission of your e-mail messages. Although encryption is more easily applied to individual messages, some accounts may require that every message be encrypted, or none. A common method is to require that all accounts conform to encrypting confidential or classified information. Many organizations are just now using encryption in general, and we expect to see a marked increase in its use as groups work to establish baseline plans such as this.

- **Expungement Window**   This establishes the length of time a particular message should be kept in storage, both locally and on the server. Although many organizations seemingly have perpetual windows for storage, we find it far more manageable to establish long windows for important or historical documents and short windows for transient accounts.

- **Forwarding and Redirection**   Certain provisions need to be addressed for most user accounts to accommodate vacation, holiday, and other forwarding requirements. Given the temporary nature of these requests, specific policies should be developed to offer these services to the user base and to control how they are implemented. Lax implementations lead to disgruntled users and hidden workarounds that may lead to unanticipated security breaches.

- **Access Privileges**   A set of administrative, managerial, and security personnel needs to be identified from a policy perspective as having legitimate authority to access other accounts when necessary. Policies should define *what* acceptable access means (for instance, when a security event is hampering the organization), *when* it can occur, and for *how long*.

- **Documentation, Authorization, and Acceptable Use Policies**   As with any effort, the demands on you to catalog, draft, distribute, and maintain the necessary documents can make up a sizable chunk of your workday. When finalizing your policy, be sure to check the Acceptable Use Policies (AUP) of any vendors, ISPs, or other information exchange partners, as often provisions exist that control how they exchange e-mail with you and what their actions will be. For example, be sure that you have appropriate procedures drafted to handle circumstances that could violate an ISP's AUP. With the rampant spread of malware, a sneaky worm could infiltrate your network one evening, and by the time you get to work the next morning, you'd find that your ISP has cut off your access, citing a failure to comply with its policy.

A practice for managing electronic mail must take into consideration several important qualities. E-mail, since it is partially server-based and partially client-based, has storage and retention requirements along with requirements for traditional transmission, access, and authentication. By applying the appropriate concentrations against the e-mail account classifications discussed earlier, you can come up with a well-sized, well-ordered system for managing e-mail.

An Example Setup

Here is an example of how a small e-mail server setup could look, which might help you build your own plan. Consider a small office of accounting and tax specialists, called *Tom and Jerry's CPA Service*. Tom and Jerry, the CPAs, employ 10 staff accountants and one administrative assistant. The firm has an on-site e-mail server (Windows 2000 Server running MS Exchange) connected via a Digital Subscriber Line (DSL). The staffers check their e-mail using the Outlook Express client and the Post Office Protocol (POP). Additionally, users can access their mail offsite by using web mail provided by the same server. Let's walk through how building a policy can help Tom and Jerry get a handle on spam.

Small Office/Home Office
(13 E-mail Accounts, One Server, One Domain)

Server:	mail.tom-and-jerry.tld and smtp.tom-and-jerry.tld
Domain:	tom-and-jerry.tld
Accounts:	13 direct users (e.g. tom@tom-and-jerry.tld, jerry@tom-and-jerry.tld)

Direct user accounts are expected to be privately published (on business cards and in signature lines), to have a low security requirement, to be able to be forwarded for up to two weeks at a time to any address (even externally), and to be limited only to the owner for normal access privileges. Additional access rights are granted to the system administrator (an employee of an outside consultant) only when specifically needed. The archive policy dictates that users may delete their own mail at any time within the six-month timeframe, but the server is required to keep a tape archive of all transactions during that time, including mail sent, mail received, and server logs.

User Groups	*sales@tom-and-jerry.tld*

The sales address is a fully published address and is implemented as an alias and forwarded to both Tom and Jerry. No temporary files should exist and no security restrictions should apply. Temporary files are often used as an interim step in processing e-mail. Generally the mail server application removes the temporary files after processing mail, but not always; sometimes temporary files are found floating around orphaned. For security reasons, we recommend performing a regularly scheduled cleanup to ensure private or sensitive e-mail isn't globally accessible by accident.

Role Accounts	*webmaster@tom-and-jerry.tld*

The webmaster role account is fully published and implemented as a separate account so that an externally contracted web-maintenance firm can access it without exposing the direct users. Given that the owner for this account is external to Tom and Jerry, Inc., a monthly audit is done to ensure that the account is complying with the company's policy.

0	Internal Accounts
0	Administrative Accounts
1	List Account (*updates@tom-and-jerry.tld*)

The updates account is an electronically published account implemented as a list server with a web front-end. Mail is archived for two years, with no associated password to check the account. Further, no security restrictions apply as the list maintained by the address is open and without moderation.

As you can see, even a relatively simple and flat organization can encounter a few twists when developing a complete e-mail policy. We encourage you to establish a philosophy similar to what we've demonstrated, as it will definitely help you later on.

Establishing a Resource Plan (Identifying Systems)

Once you have a good handle on what types of e-mail accounts you've deployed, an ideal second step is to spend some time reviewing your mail server hardware and software. Although many different platform combinations can be used to deploy your mail environment, outdated software or antiquated hardware eventually causes problems and should be avoided and replaced.

We suggest reviewing the capacity and load requirements of your system against actual performance metrics on a quarterly basis, at least. More important (and likely more time consuming) is the adoption of a regular practice of testing, updating, and reviewing the security faults that may have been discovered during the system's operation. Generally, not a day goes by that some new vulnerability or exploit isn't found somewhere on the Internet. Conducting a strong, regular review of your mail server's security posture is critical, and it should include version control, operating requirements (memory footprint, hard-drive allocation, system load averages), and proper backup procedures. Gathering metrics, proofing systems, and applying updates should be integrated into any regular maintenance and administrative tasks.

To help compartmentalize mail systems, many organization conform their server platforms along the following logical divisions:

- **Inbound E-mail Servers**   MX, "mail exchanger records"
- **Outbound E-mail Servers**   Simple Mail Transport Protocol (SMTP) services that your local client uses
- **Backup Mail Exchangers**   Additional MX entries to handle the condition when the main server is down or unavailable

Of course, it's also reasonable for a small- to moderate-sized organization to bundle these functions onto a single server, especially when only a few mail accounts exist. For the purposes of a robust e-mail policy, spam is usually controlled at one or two distinct points in the flow of mail: first, at the inbound mail gateway, which is usually where the MX records are pointing; and second, directly on the workstation retrieving the mail. Mail between servers is exchanged using SMTP and is later retrieved using Internet Message Access Protocol (IMAP) or POP (which is frequently passed over a Secure Socket Layer [SSL] tunnel to protect the credentials of the users and confidentiality of the message). Mail can be checked using a combination of these methods. For instance, web-mail systems manually read mailbox files or even perform a local connection using POP or IMAP. Basically, almost all methods use some variant of the few just described.

In our example, Tom and Jerry's one server acts as their inbound, outbound, and web-mail front-end, bundled into one easy-to-manage package. Scripting provides tape backups that meet the established archive requirements detailed in Tom and Jerry's policy, e-mail clients are qualified by Tom or Jerry personally, and it's all implemented by the system administrator.

Conduct Testing and Refinement

Any Information Technology (IT) implementation is incomplete without a testing cycle. You could probably argue that a live system like e-mail is under constant testing, but we subscribe to the concept that as changes are introduced to any complex and controlled system, a robust testing procedure should be followed that governs possible failures.

Specific to spam control, however, testing often does include the live system with live mail. The capture, containment, and control of unwanted e-mail are generally handled with a method of quarantine. We would not recommend fielding a system where spam filtering obliterates the alleged messages without any recourse. With a quarantine system, live messages can be measured against the company's policy and appropriate tweaks to the spam-fighting configuration can be made. Like any system, constant tuning should be the result of the maintenance ritual, along the timeline that is most appropriate given your setup and organizational goals. We tune our system on a weekly basis, which works nicely for our configuration and volume of traffic. Cyclical testing helps you narrow your configuration to match your goals.

SPOTTING PROBLEMS BEFORE THEY HAPPEN

The Federal Trade Commission (FTC), overseers of the public good, considers spam e-mail a scourge that's gaining popularity among the fraudsters. For more information, check out *http://www.ftc.gov/bcp/conline/pubs/alerts/doznalrt.htm*. Imagine a tool capable of sending millions of solicitations with almost no monetary investment in the hands of the pyramid schemers? We shudder at the thought. The FTC has named its "dirty dozen" scams most likely to arrive via bulk e-mail:

- **Business Opportunities**   Pyramid, multi-level marketing (MLM), or identity theft scams
- **Bulk E-mail**   Offers to sell and resell lists of e-mail accounts
- **Chain Letters**   Requests to send $1 to the five names on the list…or else!
- **Work-at-Home Schemes**   Envelope stuffing, pen assembly, jewelry construction

- **Health and Diet Scams** Pills, herbals, pharmacy, and other drug misrepresentations
- **Effortless Income** Get-rich-quick schemes
- **Free Goods and Services** Just another MLM or Ponzi scheme
- **Investment Opportunities** Crazy rates of return, offshore accounts, precious metals, penny stocks
- **Cable/Satellite Descramblers** The kits generally don't work, and use of them is illegal
- **Guaranteed Loans** Generally unhelpful lists of uninterested lenders
- **Credit Repair** Erases or cleans your credit usually in conjunction with a loan
- **Vacation Promotions** "You Won" a free vacation in Hawaii, with only a small fee to claim your prize

ADVANCED TOPICS AND CROSS-POLLINATION

With even worse goals than filling your mailbox with garbage, spammers are increasingly abusing the general public to extend their blanket of anonymity and increase their rate of solicitation. Previously, we mentioned the open-relay condition whereby spammers create two victims at once. One victim has a misconfigured mail server and acts as a spam-amplifier, sending out millions of e-mails to other recipients who angrily point back to the first victim instead of the spammer.

To combat that style of attack, many excellent resources catalog these broken mail servers across the Internet. The Open Relay Database (*http://www.ordb.org*) is currently reporting more than a quarter-of-a-million active open relays, each of which spew forth spam like an open fire hydrant. An important first step in making sure you aren't being used is to check that your IP addresses and domain names aren't listed as a known open relay. The spam promoters make extensive use of the databases, so you should become comfortable with them, too.

Even if you've eradicated all of the open relays from your network, certain holes could present themselves to spammers, allowing them to relay mail anyway. Worms, viruses, and other security flaws are increasingly exploited by spammers. One popular and still prevalent problem is the formmail.pl or formmail.cgi vulnerability. By carefully crafting a message, a spammer can send a piece of spam through your system using a fault created by one of those scripts. I'm sure you have received spam with a subject "Thank you for your submission" or something similar. These e-mails most likely came through that exploit. As we wrote this, in the last week alone, more than 50 such attempts were made against our system, with all manner of junk mail attached.

SUMMARY

In these pages, we covered a short history of spam origins, took you through the various methods used to combat spam, and built a simplified e-mail policy as demonstration. In the next chapters and throughout the rest of the book, we introduce you to the best spam-fighting strategies and tools available today. In addition to installation and configuration, we also cover each tool in a real-world, spam-fighting scenario. The *Anti-Spam Tool Kit* is your tool kit and guide to reducing spam across your mail systems.

CHAPTER 2

GOALS AND CRITERIA FOR EVALUATING SPAM CONTROL SOLUTIONS

In Chapter 1, we established that spam was a wildly growing contagion, greater in size, scope, and acceleration than most people realize. We also introduced you to a simple mail content control policy as a preparation for the introduction of anti-spam software to your systems.

In this chapter we will explore how e-mail systems are organized, track the flow of mail content through the plumbing of the Internet, articulate some goals that are consistent with filtering techniques, and (most important) develop some criteria that can be used to measure the success of those systems once they have been deployed.

THE MAIL FLOW ARCHITECTURE

Let's start by following a piece of e-mail as it swims its way through the maze of networks, eventually landing in your inbox. Figure 2-1 is a fairly complete example of the potential paths that an e-mail message might take from sender to recipient. Not all links may exist in that chain or even be encountered, but for the sake of completeness we wanted to illustrate them.

As you can see, the design of modern e-mail systems comprises many different layers, each providing a set of services and allowing for the control of content through that node. The most likely type of software to exchange e-mail is an SMTP (Simple Mail Transport Protocol) server. The most popular SMTP servers that run on the UNIX platform are sendmail, postfix, qmail, and courier. On Windows, most STMP implementations are serviced through Microsoft Exchange. By and large, mail transaction systems fall into two main categories:

- **Server or gateway systems**   Mail/Message Transport/Transfer Agents (MTAs)
- **Client or end-user mailbox systems**   Mail/Message User Agents (MUAs)

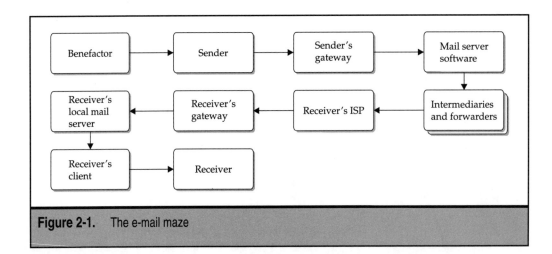

Figure 2-1.   The e-mail maze

Not coincidentally, the exchange of information between these systems falls into neat categories as well. Most mail is delivered from server to server as an SMTP message, and most mail-composing software relies on Post Office Protocol (POP), POP-over-SSL (Secure Socket Layer), IMAP (Internet Message Access Protocol), or IMAP-over-SSL as a mode for accessing your mailbox. Figure 2-2 gives you a quick visual study of how this all ties together.

When discussing how to implement e-mail filtering software through policy, it becomes clear that controls can be fitted on the clients, on the server, or on both. Additional control can be achieved by implementing systems that restrict the network protocols or filter them based on certain criteria. We cover this in more detail in the following pages.

THE DIGITAL YOU: AUTHENTICATION AND REPUDIATION

E-mail is one of the staples of modern mass communication, resplendent in its capacity to tie people together anywhere they happen to be. Even with its age and proven reliability, e-mail has long been criticized for its deepest shortcoming: the lack of any *real* authentication.

Authentication is a just fancy term that means that a verifiable, trusted way exists to determine the identity of the parties on the connection. A good analogy is a conversation on a regular telephone line (including one equipped with caller ID). Many a time we have picked up the receiver and stared cross-ways at the incoming phone number, fearful that a solicitor was preparing his script. This has a strong correlation to an e-mail coming from some unknown domain name (from the other side of the world).

What's drastically different with e-mail is that the e-mail solicitor incurs virtually no cost, either in time or in money. Add to this the near perfect anonymity of the sender, and voilà, it's a formula for the cheapest advertising vehicle on earth. Phone solicitors usually have to pay for the long distance they incur, the salaries for their personnel, the office they use to house their staff, as well as other office equipment. E-mail spammers have no such hurdles. This is one of the biggest reasons why e-mail spam is like a runaway train—and why great effort goes into combating it. Similar to our analogy of phone solicitation, junk mail and spam faxes share many common characteristics. All have limiting factors that make it impractical, unprofitable, and often illegal to pursue.

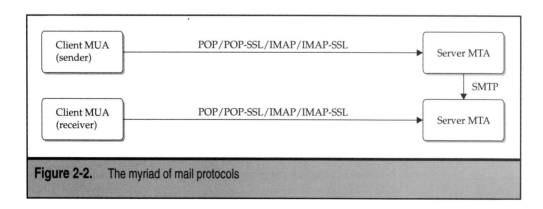

Figure 2-2. The myriad of mail protocols

However, spam e-mail is in an alien world unto itself. It is being exploited almost entirely due to the implicit trust that e-mail parties have placed with one another. The mere knowledge of someone's e-mail address is all you need to start sending messages—regardless of content, size, frequency, or even imposition. Just imagine waiting for an important phone call from a family member interspersed somewhere within a steady stream of 900 phone calls, all day and all night. Or imagine trying to find your daily mail after it has been randomly sorted into 10 boxes crammed with porno catalogs and credit card offers. Pretty disturbing, right? This identity asymmetry is even stronger than the cost asymmetry we spoke of earlier—so critical, in fact, that we hope it will be resolved in the very near future.

Lastly, we must speak to the topic of nonrepudiation. *Nonrepudiation* ensures that a transferred message has been sent and received by the parties claiming to have sent and received the message. Coming with the lack of authentication is the idea that since you don't really know who sent you that message, it's very, very easy for the sender to deny that they did it, even if they actually did. There exists well-worn protocols for providing strong authentication and nonrepudiation that give both parties the comfort of knowing that neither can claim to be something other than what it is. Future e-mail systems will not only provide verifiable authentication of the sender to the receiver well before an e-mail is ever sent, but these systems will also guard against senders who manage to slip stuff through and then renege. Efforts are even underway to restructure large servers to support these methodologies. However, the bulk of the public consider those efforts draconian and unlikely to be widely adopted.

GOALS OF A ROBUST MAIL CONTROL SYSTEM

Before evaluating specific spam solutions and their implementations, we cover the basics of evaluating a tool's capabilities in light of your overall mail filtering objectives. Put simply, the goals of deploying spam control systems fall into the same categories as deploying most IT solutions: Total Cost of Ownership (TCO) and Return on Investment (ROI). The difficulty comes in comparing the currency denominated cost figures to the more ephemeral productivity savings costs. Thankfully, the installation of new spam control software is a much easier sale to a CIO than other technology implementations, proven of course that your proposal includes eradicating all the spam in the CIO's mailbox.

Restrict Access to Your E-Mail Identities

One of the strongest and most effective goals is also the most difficult to effect: Limiting or removing a spammer's access to your e-mail identities would stop spam at its source. Of course, that's hard to imagine, given that once an e-mail address is out there, it's out there for good! While not technically implemented by any of the spam solutions detailed in the book, we want to point out that a strong e-mail publication policy *does* go far toward reducing spam in the long run. As we mentioned in Chapter 1, the most popular method for a spammer to obtain your address would be simply to lift if off a web page. So an effective strategy would be to audit and control the addresses published on your web sites.

Another way of servicing this goal is to cleanse your e-mail addresses periodically from spammers that have invaded your mailbox by using their "remove me" methods. There's still a heated debate going as to whether those links do nothing more than confirm that there is a sucker at the other end of the address. Still, until automation simplifies the process, ad-hoc removal would seem to be the only way to address this.

Identify the Spammers

We know that limiting who gets your e-mail address is difficult to do, especially when you set out against a mass of spamming organizations with questionable ethics. Even if you manage to cleanse your addresses from any given spammer's database, the sheer simplicity of incorporating another business for them is quick, painless, and cheap, and it's *not* limited by your "opt-out" request. It's possible for them to move faster than you can opt yourself out of their programs, making it a tiring game of cat-and-mouse.

Failing restrictions on the distribution of your addresses, the next best strategy is to identify the senders themselves. Of course, this, too, has its drawbacks, and the technical methods of implementing the goals associated with it largely fall to black/white listing, a strategy that we cover in greater detail shortly, and one that isn't a complete solution in itself by a long shot. We think that you will find that these goals fit the formula found throughout the entire sphere of security administration: protection through layering.

Identify the Spam

Although much of the spam-fighting software available and covered in this book relies on several techniques, it fights spam predominantly by detecting what really *is* spam. To do this, a combination of factors is generally employed: consideration of the contents of the message body, many of the characteristics within the header, and the nature of the message itself. As anti-spam implementations grow more robust, the analysis of spam boils down to what the message actually is. As with the identification of the spammer, the identification of spam must also come with a high degree of confidence for it to be a worthwhile goal.

Select the Best Locations

Another goal is to place the appropriate mail filters and anti-spam controls at strategic locations in your network. To do this, an up-to-date network map coupled with an analysis of how e-mail transits your network should be studied. The overarching goal of selecting the best location can be summarized by the least cost, smallest footprint, and least intrusive site from the possible choice of sites that you've developed. Other factors also creep into the equation, notably ease of operation, nearness to backup facilities, and impact should the planned installation suffer outages.

You should consider the balance between having too many and too few spam controls stationed about your network. Too few, and you might suffer a considerable slowdown caused by the bottleneck that was formed. Too many, and the upkeep and filter modifications become onerous for all but giant organizations with lots of staff.

Select the Best Tools

Once you've established your goals for deploying mail control software based on how your network is organized and against what kinds of spam you will likely need to configure, you can tackle the specific selection of tools.

To maximize the benefit of installing anti-spam software, pay special attention to the methods of measuring their overall impact. Some common meters are the following:

- **Qualification (Is it really spam?)** The software must be fast, accurate, and dynamic. A good way to measure the quality of your spam control solutions is to calculate a percentage of false positives and false negatives and compare the results to other possible implementations.

- **Quantification (How much does it slow down my server?)** Some tools come with measures that demonstrate how much overhead or how much load is applied to your mail systems by their implementation. Some common meters are "messages per second" or "CPU time per message," which can be used for gross comparisons. Obviously, systems that rely on computational complexity to produce better results require more time per message and ultimately load your mail systems as a result. Sites with huge mail flow should pay particularly careful attention to how a spam-fighting software impacts overall performance.

- **Quarantining (What is that, anyway?)** We expect to see a developing trend in anti-spam offerings that can not only do live capture of questionable content, but also sort it according to rules established by the administrator. This would provide for the few messages that will always exist and that are unknown and unknowable and should be considered by a human, rather than by a machine. More of an *attractive feature* than a goal, finding current solutions that sport quarantining methods should be taken seriously.

Select for Operational Ease

A fully implemented mail control system should be easy to use, fix, and update; it should provide solid reporting; and it should scale appropriately given your thoughts on installation location and capacity expectations. The ongoing operation of a system should account for a significant portion of your overall criteria weight.

BRINGING IT ALL TOGETHER

A perfect system addresses spam as unwanted content using the following process:

1. By denying the spammer ways to harvest addresses.
2. By using a *multi-node* architecture that is deployed at many levels, providing a distributed approach throughout the mail transmission path.

3. By using a *multi-mode* approach to layer different types of anti-spam software at the different points.
4. By establishing a ritual of testing, tweaking, and refinement. No system is complete without its upkeep.

SELECTING MAIL CONTROL COMPONENTS

Now that we've covered a broad set of general goals meant to guide you in your selection of an effective anti-spam solution, we turn our attention to the criteria you should use in evaluating the tools that meet those requirements. We start by offering some generalized criteria that can be used across a broad range of anti-spam solutions; then we cover some specific guidelines that you can use to narrow down your selection to a specific package or set of packages.

Breadth (All Forms of Mail-borne Content Filtered)

By using the goals defined earlier, we can classify the *location of implementation*, the *identification of the spammers*, and the *content of the spam itself* to be strategies of breadth. The term *spam* encompasses lots of territory (including instant messenger spam, digital fax spam, SMS [short message service] spam), and as the universe of anti-spam solutions mature, we will see them tackling this whole raft of additional content.

For instance, e-mail infection vectors of viruses, worms, and Trojans are being classified by newer spam filtering processes along with the normal set of "unwanted content." This hasn't gone unnoticed by the major manufacturers of anti-spam software, as many of them are rushing to add extended spam-fighting techniques to their virus-control platforms. Given the location and methods of control inherent with how virus regulation is handled, it is a natural fit for those firms to offer comprehensive and capable packages for spam control.

Whatever combination of anti-spam software you elect to deploy should take into consideration the many forms of content.

Depth (Multiple Techniques Used at Multiple Points)

As we discussed previously with our goals, to be effective, a robust mail control policy *must* be met with a variety of approaches at a variety of points in the mail transmission path. Since filtering is becoming more and more of a requirement, it's foreseeable that any given piece of mail will be met with as many as a dozen different systems along its journey, and each recipient will be spending precious computational resources to make the determination on whether or not to toss it. In short, it takes a measurable amount of computing resources to filter spam continuously (CPU time and storage, most notably). Further, a direct relationship exists between the overall load of the spam control system and the amount of e-mail traversing it.

Because of this, the installation of spam control software naturally leans toward a multi-point architecture to distribute the load across many systems and a multiple technique solution to promote effectiveness. Of course, the application of many different techniques over and over to a huge amount of e-mail can cause system degradation, so the most effective solution would be one that had low system overhead while providing many different tests to incoming mail.

Impact

The impact of an anti-spam toolset is stated simply as the *determination* of its *effectiveness*. A sustainable and viable system must be good at limiting false positives and false negatives and must provide a method of recovery should something fail. The system must be robust with reporting requirements and must provide a regular stream of complete and thorough updates (both to the software itself as well as to the rules and signatures on which they rely).

The system (based on its location of deployment in the network landscape) must also be scalable to the necessary levels of your anticipated growth and must be minimally impacting to critical network or service components.

Additionally, denial of service should be considered, as many e-mail implementations are subject to failures under a large amount of load, which could be caused by large mail bombs, long processing times, or even nonrelated system misconfigurations.

Operation

It probably goes without saying to the well-rounded system administrator, but no software should be installed without first considering the entire set of practices needed to install, configure, update, and operate it over time. All systems have operational parameters that need monitoring, and systems that provide poor reporting and inexplicable manuals, as well as those that are rushed to market with bugs, should be avoided as they may lead to more problems than they solve. Remember that your e-mail is a basic service that must be highly reliable; it should be treated with kid gloves when applying control measures such as those discussed in this book.

Spam control software is systematic in nature and is becoming more and more advanced and capable of dynamic configuration. As machine learning, behavioral analysis, and artificial intelligence start to dominate the decision-making capabilities of the software, so, too, does the complexity of maintaining these systems. Systems that "learn from doing" as well as "learn from watching" are a bit more difficult to maintain, since they are self-organizing and self-configuring. Our strong recommendation with deploying these kinds of systems is to test them in a closed or limited environment prior to major implementation.

Specific Criteria in Selecting Anti-Spam Solutions

When selecting a spam-control package, consider the following four criteria, listed in order of importance:

- Stability
- Advanced features

- Interoperability
- Ease of use

First, you want to focus on the *stability* of your entire system. Flaky, untested, or shallowly deployed systems could end up causing more harm than good. Don't beta test someone's newfangled gadget unless you know what you are getting into. Everyone has grown accustomed to the normal delivery of mail, so you have to find the right balance between getting new functionality and sacrificing normal day-to-day operations. Although some might argue for reordering these factors, and indeed, after analyzing their needs, different organizations may find another approach more appropriate, we believe this order provides a fine starting point, which can then be revised accordingly.

Stability of the Software, Service, or Hardware Manufacturer

Although it might be preferable to select products created by established and stable companies, consideration should be given to younger firms with solid advanced technologies. In fact, many of the offerings detailed in this book are distributed by start-ups.

The offering company should release updates to its software on a quarterly basis at the least. What's really important is the manufacturer's long-term commitment to quality and capability. Check out your prospective vendors, call their support lines, and ask them all a battery of tough questions. The way they deal with you pre-sale is indicative of the way they will deal with you post-sale.

Look for strong and frequent updates to filtering rules, signatures, patterns, and lists. This point can't be stressed enough. More and more, spam filtering products are only as smart as their last filter/signature update. The best idea is to select vendors that have automation that keeps your installation refreshed on a real-time basis. Hourly, daily, or even scheduled updates are also ideal, as long as the time between updates is relatively fast.

Look for healthy and positive reviews of the product and the company at consumer sites and in the press. Magazine articles and online product reviews are a fantastic source of information. They not only give you a clear picture of everyone out there offering spam solutions, but they also do a good job of comparing and contrasting the full range of features that vendors offer. We've found their classification systems helpful for understanding how one product differentiates itself from the pack.

Strong Methods and Techniques Used to Combat Spam

Often the *first* and *only* criterion used to select spam-filtering packages is the technique used by the software. Certainly better, more advanced capabilities will drive users to adopt new technologies; however, before adopting a new technology, you need to ensure the software is stable, operable, and supportable.

Some of the technologies covered in this book feature broad content-protection mechanisms, such as header, body, sender, and attachment analysis. Other products focus on the mail transmission path, analyzing where spam flows, for instance, through gateways, mail exchangers, outsourced providers, and even client desktops. Others focus on broader classifications, going beyond simple e-mail into virus protection, worm and trojan detection, and organizational policy violations.

The stronger the methods used to combat spam, the less spam you will receive and the happier you will be. Comparing and contrasting the different approaches used by each potential filtering strategy is an important objective, but still second-chair, in our experience, to overall system stability.

Interoperability

As a network grows in composition and size, the complexity of that network increases at a nonlinear rate. For small network installations, interoperability among components is not that big an issue. For larger network sites, nothing is added to the network without extensive testing to make sure everything still interoperates as expected. Thankfully, today's anti-spam packages communicate almost exclusively with mail servers and mail clients using protocols such as SMTP, POP, and IMAP; however, as more advanced features are incorporated into standard anti-spam packages, more and varied interoperations will likely be forged. In the not so distant future, content management systems, virus checkers, intrusion detection systems, and network throughput systems could act as common communication peers.

Ease of Use

Ease of use is also an important selection criterion and like all the others, a subject of hot debate as to whether it's the most important of the group. Within our definition of ease of use, we include the overall user interface, reporting capabilities, and system management. How system updates are propagated, how signatures are updated, how detailed and complete the documentation, as well as how policies need to be altered are all important and relevant topics. We've found that mature anti-spam offerings have easy-to-administer maintenance windows (which can often be scheduled in less than an hour), strong and flexible configuration parameters, and a sophisticated and knowledgeable service desk at the user's disposal.

SUMMARY

Spam is an abuse of e-mail that is architecturally and automatically "trusted" without any authentication on the front-end. There is an inherent asymmetry of identities in a mail transmission that spammers use to their advantage—that is, they know us, but we don't know them. The goals of any spam control system should be to reduce spam by limiting access of your data to the spammer to begin with, followed by a successive strategy of controlling what e-mail enters your system. The criteria for selecting anti-spam packages are based on breadth, depth, impact, and operational ease.

CHAPTER 3

METHODS FOR MAIL CONTENT CONTROL

Although no bulletproof architectural standard has emerged to restrict or regulate the sending and receiving of electronic mail, many vendors have implemented common methods of control. In this chapter we cover best practices, their corresponding strategies, and a brief technical explanation of each practice and strategy.

BUILDING ON A HISTORICAL BASIS

First, let's take a visit to the "Encyclopedia Internet," where we will find some well-drafted memorandums and position papers used to set the "unwritten" laws of the Net. These documents are referred to as Requests for Comment (RFCs). Since the Internet is a hostile, connect-at-your-own-peril kind of place, "laws" aren't really practical or technically feasible to enforce, so the best we have is the agreement of large collections of participants that could be coerced to act in consistent ways given certain circumstances.

A curious strategy for keeping order in a huge unmanageable place like the Internet boils down to the science associated with the interactions of crowds. Many RFCs are like bulletin boards that provide analysis, give support, and even make suggestions, where appropriate. Others are enforced as if they were the law of the land. Although many RFCs carry the weight of worldwide pressure for adoption, vendors are still free to implement all of an RFC or part of it, or they can ignore it entirely.

A few spam-oriented RFCs are well worth the read and give clear recommendations on how to best implement spam-reductive servers and advertise ethically. Following are the abstracts of the RFCs we found to be the best indicators from which the anti-spam technologies have drawn their basis.

RFC 2505—SMTP and MTA Best Practices

The complete RFC text can be found at *http://www.faqs.org/rfcs/rfc2505.html*. The following abstract will provide an overview of the text:

> "This memo gives a number of implementation recommendations for SMTP, [1], MTAs (Mail Transfer Agents, e.g. sendmail, [8]) to make them more capable of reducing the impact of spam(*).

> "The intent is that these recommendations will help clean up the spam situation, if applied on enough SMTP MTAs on the Internet, and that they should be used as guidelines for the various MTA vendors. We are fully aware that this is not the final solution, but if these recommendations were included, and used, on all Internet SMTP MTAs, things would improve considerably and give time to design a more long term solution. The Future Work section suggests some ideas that may be part of such a long term solution. It might, though, very well be the case that the ultimate solution is social, political, or legal, rather than technical in nature.

> "The implementor should be aware of the increased risk of denial of service attacks that several of the proposed methods might lead to. For example, increased number

of queries to DNS servers and increased size of logfiles might both lead to overloaded systems and system crashes during an attack.

A brief summary of this memo is:

Stop unauthorized mail relaying.
Spammers then have to operate in the open; deal with them.
Design a mail system that can handle spam."

RFC 2635—An Explanation for Why Spam Is Harmful

The complete RFC text can be found at *http://www.faqs.org/rfcs/rfc2635.html*.

"This document explains why mass unsolicited electronic mail messages are harmful in the Internetworking community. It gives a set of guidelines for dealing with unsolicited mail for users, for system administrators, news administrators, and mailing list managers. It also makes suggestions Internet Service Providers might follow."

RFC 3098—A Discussion of Responsible Internet Advertising

The complete RFC text can be found at *http://www.faqs.org/rfcs/rfc3098.html*.

"This memo offers useful suggestions for responsible advertising techniques that can be used via the Internet in an environment where the advertiser, recipients, and the Internet Community can coexist in a productive and mutually respectful fashion. Some measure of clarity will also be added to the definitions, dangers, and details inherent to Internet Marketing."

ANALYZING SPAM

One common element that underlies all anti-spam technology is the reliance on a relatively limited set of standards used to transact e-mail transmissions. In Chapter 2, we learned that almost all e-mail relied on the SMTP, POP, and IMAP protocols for transmission and delivery. This has evolved almost exclusively to promote and ensure the interoperability between vendors of messaging software.

Some of you may note that an obvious and ideal way to combat spam would be to rewrite the networking protocols used to send it. Certainly this would solve the bulk of the spam problem, but the engineering and deployment of such a solution at this immense scale is likely impossible. Current efforts that are well underway along these lines mainly involve the IPv6 protocol (the next generation of the common Internet Protocol). We don't want to belittle the excellent work being done in this area; rather, we'll redirect your attention to more immediate methods that lessen our collective spam intake.

Consistent with the goals we outlined in the prior chapters, we segment and present the basic technical solutions into three main categories:

- Content analysis
- Sender or intermediary analysis
- Benefactor analysis

Analysis That Targets the Content of the Message

Content analysis comes in many shapes and sizes, but it boils down to parsing the bulk of an e-mail message and analyzing the results to determine whether or not the message is spam. Early spam filtering tools were quick Perl scripts or shell scripts that often carried a great deal of overhead with them, making them impractical and sometime dangerous to use. Because of this, it was often necessary to scan only the headers of incoming mail, and often only the subject line, in an effort to minimize system load. Present day spam-fighting solutions are far more capable at not only processing every byte sent in an e-mail exchange, but also at applying advanced techniques before the message is fully spooled.

Content Analysis, Keyword, and Pattern Matching

One of the oldest and simplest approaches to combating spam involves studying the subject and body of the message itself. How many of us have gotten a box full of messages with subjects like

```
"REFINANCE Today!!!"
```

or

```
"V1agr4, Cheap from Mexico! ................ x9746."
```

Many of us have opened an innocuous looking message with the subject "Hey!" only to find a full-color advertisement, complete with flashing 36-point text and whole paragraphs of SHOUTING in ALL CAPITAL LETTERS.

Upon seeing these types of messages, many programmers have an initial inclination to set up a simple keyword filter that looks for common spam words and rejects any message that contains them. Additionally, simple patterns can also be constructed—lots of punctuation (misplaced or otherwise), strange numbers at the far end of the subject line, use of hacker jargon (*w0rdz sp3ll3d w1th numb3r5*), or even embedded HTML are usually dead giveaways.

Keyword filters are easy to set up but are fraught with false positives. We ran a regional Internet service provider (ISP) several years back, and we built a server-side filter to catch and trash e-mails that had subjects containing a series of two exclamation points (!!) or that had the word *cash* anywhere in them. Quite happily, those two content filters alone immediately reduced our spam intake by about 30 percent on the first day system-wide, and we were appropriately self-congratulatory. Of course, soon afterward, confused phone calls from our clients started coming in, complaining of lost e-mails.

For completeness sake, we make a subtle distinction between *keyword filtering, pattern matching,* and *heuristic (rule-based) filtering.* To us, keywords are the simplest case—single matches of words or phrases that cause a filter to be evaluated as true only when they make an exact match. Hence, a filter that finds the keyword *implant* in the subject would trigger an action from the spam filter. Pattern matching encompasses a broader case by mixing constant text such as keywords and variable components such as wildcard characters. For instance, the pattern *1-800-[0-9][0-9][0-9][0-9]* could represent all 1-800 telephone numbers. Lastly, these examples would be different from a rule that finds the date/time a message was sent by using the header information and calculating whether it was consistent with the claimed location of the sender. We cover heuristic filtering more in the following paragraphs.

Keyword and heuristic filtering both have the added merit of being almost the exclusive mechanisms for spam filtering until early in 2002, when advanced techniques were required to make a dent in the rampant proliferation of messages crafted by newer, smarter spamming tools.

Rule-Based (Heuristic) Filtering

One considerable advancement over simply matching words that could indicate spam is the notion of how those words are used, what they mean, and what relationship they have to each other. Heuristics are rules that can be applied to sets of data to provide an output from certain inputs. Keyword matching is the simplest case of a heuristic algorithm: if you find *ADV:* in the subject, toss it. The nice thing about rule-based filtering is that enhanced decision-making can be drawn from advanced rule construction. Several rules can be strung together to form a decision tree that effectively does multiple-pass filtering on any single given message.

Signature and Hash-Based Filtering

Signature-based filters operate by performing a calculation on each message received and comparing it to a database of known spam messages. The actual type of calculation used falls into a set of one-way transformation functions called *hashes*. A hash value is a fixed-length "signature" and is often computed using the MD5 algorithm. Long messages, those with attachments, and even those with lots of embedded HTML code all produce valid hash signatures that can be used to identify them correctly and uniquely.

One benefit of hash-based spam filtering is that the hashes are usually quite small (often only 64 or 128 bits), making them easy to manage on a moderate scale. Plus, fixed-length strings can be easily indexed and sorted, making the database operations required to handle them also fairly responsive. For a signature to be effective, it needs to be checked "on the run," as the e-mail knocks upon your server's door.

Another benefit is that large content management organizations (such as Yahoo! and Hotmail) along with the tier-1 ISPs who pass the bulk of the Internet traffic can participate in a hash signature sharing network that could potentially stop spam messages quickly for large swaths of the mail-reading public, providing nice economy of scale.

However, quite a number of problems make signature-based spam filtering not the be-all and end-all of effective e-mail control. An obvious circumvention to such filters is

> ## How Hash Functions Work
>
> Hash functions take an arbitrary length "message," which it converts into a fixed-length value, sometimes called a *key*, *hash value*, or *message digest*. Although several different popular implementations of hashes are available (SHA-1, MD5, MD4, MD2, and RIPEMD), they all rely on a few common mechanisms to perform the transformation:
>
> - Padding the end of message to a fixed number of bits
> - Segmenting of the original message into fixed blocks
> - Performing some kind of calculation (XOR, bit transformations, or arithmetic)
> - Chaining the results of one block with the results of another
> - Truncating excess bits
>
> The MD5 and SHA-1 hash algorithms are often cited and are popular implementation, but they are very sophisticated in their construction. A full exploration of these algorithms goes beyond the scope of this book, but if you'd like to explore the topic in depth, a good starting point is on the Web at *http://www.rsasecurity.com/rsalabs/faq/2-1-6.html*.

to change each message slightly and randomly, so that it technically becomes unique and therefore produces a different hash value. The security-minded reader should note that this could also be an effective denial-of-service (DoS) attack against the hash databases (even if unintentional). This is because a "single" message sent to a million people, with equally as many variants, produces a million different signatures in the database—an unworkable disproportion of anti-spam to pro-spam efforts in the long run. Also problematic is the creation, distribution, and maintenance of the signature hashes. Until a hash is added to your local mail server's signature database, that message is allowed to pass. It's often a daunting task to manage a gigantic signature database, especially given that spam gets delivered 24 hours a day. This is one of the reasons we have seen the rise of distributed, network-based services that handle the bulk of this for you. It's far easier to implement a quick lookup against an outsourcer's database of known spam than it is to build your own (and keep it running) from scratch.

Signature filtering has its place, but it's effective only if used in conjunction with other, stronger techniques to support it.

Bayesian and Statistical Filtering

Possibly extolled as being the savior of spam filtering, Bayesian-based filtering does its magic by applying statistical modeling to any form a spam message may take. As of this writing, the simplest Bayesian implementation operates by breaking a message into component parts (individual words) and applying a frequency analysis to it.

However, to make the ever-important determination as to whether an inbound message is or is not spam, this method has to have a basis for comparison. Statistical filters need a starting point, which is to say they need to have a bunch of "real" messages to calculate a baseline to begin the process. Because it's an iterative process, the spam filter has the added benefit of being constantly refined as mail flows through the system. Some implementations (such as the SpamAssassin filter) separate the known good mail into a classification they call *ham*, and they use ham to develop the groundwork for future comparisons. Others use the same method but call spam *Junk* and ham *Not-Junk*. Several tools are provided for managing this process, and we discuss them at length in Chapters 7 and 8.

One of the compelling reasons for adopting Bayesian processing for spam is that it's remarkably accurate, especially on a user-by-user basis. The more mail the filter gets to see, the more likely it will be able to develop a strong baseline, and it can do this for every user on the system independently. The accuracy of statistical filtering over rules-based

What Words Are Most Likely to Make Up a Spam Message?

According to one of our more popular e-mail accounts, the following is an excerpt of frequency counts maintained by our SpamAssassin filter after about four months of continuous use. Notice that the first few lines of the file appear to be garbage—but they're not. Statistical analysis considers anything a "word" as long as it's bracketed by spaces. Those items are part of the (usually hidden) mail header, and the way they are used is indicative of spam. What really surprised us were the several trademarks found in the top 50 spam words (including *WalMart*, *Blockbuster*, and *Starbucks*). Here's the list (with some minimal edits for readability):

```
62515 N:H*r:NNNNNNN-NNNNN
62515 H*x:Bat!
62515 H*x:Business
62515 N:H*x:vN.NNf
62515 forever!
62515 prizes
62515 Click
62517 Wal*Mart
62519 Lucky
62519 FREE
62519 YOUR
62519 Gap
62519 emailremove.asp
62522 ANYONE
62524 ALL
62524 MESSAGE
```

content filtering is pretty dramatic. If the word *free* (a heavily-weighted spam word) is used in an e-mail from a known good sender, a blind rules-based filter bounces it immediately, but a Bayesian filter allows it to pass since the overall composition of the mail conforms to what we would normally receive. As the statisticians say, "There is always a reversion to the mean." The more mail you have that looks normal, the more spam sticks out like a sore thumb.

Another strong benefit is that statistical filters are not only very accurate, but they're also very efficient. Given the method of their operation, they are capable of adapting to new techniques used by innovative spamming organizations. Really, the only way for a spammer to slip one by the filter is to have some idea of what words are already weighed high and avoid using them. This would also include using fancy colors, lots of punctuation, and web links used in other known spams, just to name a few.

Uniformly across the group of filtering techniques, Bayesian methods are among the highest rated and deserve to be one of the key components in your quest for a clean mailbox.

Analysis That Targets the Sender or Intermediaries

In this section, we introduce you to the methods of spam filtering that are based on the identity of the sender or of the relay, rather than content of the messages. As mentioned in earlier chapters, verifiable identities are almost nonexistent given the architecture of the current e-mail environment. Because of this, spam filtering that relies heavily on these techniques often produces less-than-perfect results. However, used in combination with several other control factors, filtering that takes the sender into the equation goes a long way toward providing a robust solution.

Blacklisting and Whitelisting

Blacklisting and whitelisting have become popular mechanisms for spam control over the last few years. Almost all available packages, whether they are distributed by commercial enterprises or are freeware, shareware, or open source projects, have some integrated black/whitelisting options.

Grouping known spammers into a blacklist provides an easy way to block unwanted mail content quickly and efficiently based on the sender's source. Blacklists can contain exact e-mail addresses (such as spamster@spam.tld), variants of e-mail addresses using standard wildcards or regular expressions (such as *@spam.tld, [0-9][0-9][0-9][0-9]@spam.tld, or getrichquick@*.com), or even lists of IP addresses.

Blacklists can be managed at several points along the mail data flow as well: at the receiving server, at the exchange servers, at the perimeter, or even at the user's desktop. In fact, we've seen some installations in which several sets of blacklists are installed in several places to provide multiple layers of filtering. This is a configuration that we don't recommend, since the added work required to manage, update, and isolate problems across many blacklists far outweighs the meager benefits you might enjoy. We recommend blacklists at the perimeter mail server, as close to the Internet as possible, and nowhere else. Our goal with this strategy is to reduce the processing time, resource requirements, and bandwidth needed on the front-end, before spam makes it too far into your network. As an added bonus, managing list updates, software upgrades, and live queries to blacklist organizations is better handled right at the network perimeter.

Blacklists come in two distinct flavors: shared network–based and local database–based. Given the sheer number of spammers out there and the added complexity of keeping up-to-the-minute lists effective, most blacklisters pool their resources and share them over a network with other networks to cut down the processing, load, and storage of the data. In fact, a fair number of groups hailing from the commercial sector, as well as the free one, offer live blacklisting services. We cover a large percentage of these in more detail in Chapter 5. Local database blacklists are normally found as part of a comprehensive spam-filtering suite to augment the effectiveness of their solutions.

One of the major drawbacks with blacklisting harmonizes with a theme we have established in the first two chapters of this book: validity. Organizations that rely heavily on blacklisting solutions sometimes find important servers accidentally added to the blacklist, either completely by mistake or because a spammer managed to slip spam through the gateway, rendering it labeled as a "known spammer." Blacklists have no real granularity of control and hence are very binary with their decision-making: It's either blocked completely or it's allowed without further regard. Obviously, this approach could lead to potential pitfalls on several fronts.

Another drawback with filtering based on blacklists is the acceleration of the cat-and-mouse game that is currently being played out in the market these days. For a spam to be blocked using a blacklist filter, the spammer's address needs to have already been correctly identified as being a source of spam, and (more important) it needs to have already been added to the database for the checks to be successful. Given the increased amount of spam entering the network, coupled with the increased caution being taken by spammers, the culprits are more likely to bleat out a few million messages and then move on to another IP address and network provider before the heat gets turned on to them. In years prior, they would usually stay put long enough for the anti-spam blacklist organizations to identify them and update their lists accordingly.

Since network-based blacklists are run by outside organizations, the quality of the filtering is only as good as the people running it. Keep that in mind when you select an ISP, where one of your main decision criteria is the offering of an integrated spam-filtering service as part of the entire package. From a quick survey of the market, almost every major ISP has some level of spam offering, and this could ultimately become a problem should it be poorly operated.

Lastly, we want to discuss whitelisting as a part of this section, given its reliance on the same technical methods and practices. Whitelisting is simply the exact opposite of blacklisting. A blacklist identifies senders whose transmissions are unwanted because they have sent spam on a previous occasion. A whitelist identifies known good senders that, even if they send something that could be labeled spam, should still be allowed through without filtering.

In contrast to our earlier recommendation, whitelists are normally better implemented at the end-user host level than anywhere in the server path. Users have unique requirements, and even though they may be grouped together in an organizational chart, they may still prefer to manage their local e-mail in vastly different ways. Because of this, we find it best to let each user handle his or her own whitelisting.

Challenge/Response Approaches

One somewhat burdensome method for reducing spam is to enforce an identity check as part of the initial mail handshake. By way of explanation, spam pretty much comes only from "new" addresses that haven't sent you e-mail before. Of course, there are exceptions to any rule—you've probably received mail supposedly addressed from your best friend that contained an advertisement to take advantage of a low interest rate loan, or something equally spam-like.

Because of this, methods have been devised that require new senders to follow a quick verification procedure before their mail is allowed to pass, with the risk that if they fail to register, their mail is thrown away without recourse. The current e-mail doctrine is established around an "always allow" philosophy. A nice comparison can be drawn from the network filtering field, where firewalls can be set up with either an "always allow" or "always deny" fundamental foundation.

Since e-mail doesn't have an analogous "always deny" implementation, the challenge-response architecture was created to try and remedy that deficiency. It's certainly an excellent strategy from a theoretical ground, and one that could reduce spam to almost nothing. However, the largest impediment to a quick adoption and a world of spamless e-mail is that it places a heavy burden on the sender of new mail. It's similar to an automated approach to updating a whitelist on the fly, but all of the hassle is borne by the sender alone.

Let's explain how a challenge/response transaction works: A new sender, Alice, sends some piece of mail to the receiver, Bob. Bob's e-mail server, upon failing to find Alice in his whitelist, automatically responds with an instruction mail and challenge request.

Here's an example of a challenge that's been sanitized to protect the identity of one of our clients:

```
Your e-mail message with the subject of "testing -- ignore"
is being held because your address was not recognized.

To release your message for delivery, please send an empty message
to the following address, or use your mailer's "Reply" feature.

    XXXXX-confirm-1067743565.1158.878e31@XXX.tld

This confirmation verifies that your message is legitimate and not
junk-mail.

[ This notice was generated by TMDA/0.58 (http://tmda.sf.net/),
  an automated junk-mail reduction system. ]

--- Enclosed is a copy of your message.
```

Notice that the message back to the sender makes no bones about being staged inches above the trashcan. The challenge relies on a timely response from the sender, and after the initial query is approved, the system is silent and nonintrusive. All in all, using a challenge/response in filtering out unwanted communication partners has gotten a firm following, and from the outset it seems to be on a growing track.

A big drawback with the challenge/response system, however, is that it requires a certain amount of time and effort before normal communication can take place. This becomes somewhat nasty when dealing with lots of addresses that are both new and valid. Some prime examples include mailing list administrators, persons invited to a party, or even coworkers that you have little contact with but who could likely e-mail you with a random message.

More of an impediment is that most people can't tolerate the few additional steps necessary to become "registered" with someone else's mail system. Within that group are a smaller group of people who are so incensed that they drop communication altogether.

We don't have particularly strong feelings on the matter either way. The challenge/response system is indeed quite effective, even if it takes a bit of work to get going, but we don't see it as a major player put side-to-side with Bayesian content filtering or networked shared blacklisting. One strategy for adoption is to automate the handshake, where users don't have to see the ugly underpinnings. Of course, the risk is that spammers could grow wise to the automation and re-engineer their systems to bypass a person's challenge with automated responses to satisfy the checks.

One last method that is about as effective as you can get (nearly 100 percent, minus only a fraction of a percent) is based on the challenge/response methodology. It follows the basic concept of authenticating the sender before allowing him or her to send mail, but instead of using simple untrustworthy means, it would rely on cryptographic keys to establish identity during the initial handshake. Many crypto protocols, which are extremely well-tested and many years old, rely on these protocols for much more delicate communications.

Speaking of crypto protocols, a wealth of effort is going into several fronts to assist the spam-fighting war. Probably one of the more drastic and idealistic efforts relies on changes to the network substructure that keeps the bits flowing. IPv6, once fully implemented, is designed from the ground up to provide basic authentication, authorization, and identity services right at the network layer.

Currently, network communications between peers of IP addresses are fully trusted and fully visible, and they provide no direct remediation, quality of service, or reporting functionality. IPv6 radically changes all of that, making a spammer's identity known and verified even if he or she doesn't want it to be. The real problem with IPv6 is the long and winding road that it's going to take before it becomes widely available. Some ISPs, many higher education institutions, and the bulk of the US government networks are slated to be converted in the next five years, but we don't feel too confident that effective spam solutions built on these grounds will be commonly available anytime soon.

Slowing Down Spammers

One particularly curious effort deals with the very nature of the timing of the communication between the spammer and the spamee. During the normal transit of e-mail, some usually negligible amount of time is spent handling, sorting, parsing, and either rejecting or accepting the mail. The idea is that there is a wide difference between the time spent by "normal" mail servers and those that are bulk mail senders, and this is usually highly correlative with the contents of the message being labeled as spam.

What this means is that there should be a way to slow down the spam servers to a point at which the huge asymmetry that they enjoy isn't as pronounced. Right now, the most advantageous circumstance of the spammers is that they are able to exploit the minimal amount of time and resources needed to send mass e-mails.

Think about it this way: Regular mail servers tend to send and receive about the same number of messages during the course of a normal day, whereas spam servers do nothing but send, and they do so with such great volume that in most cases they are easily identified. Most spam-sending software is measured against the others by the measure of "millions of messages per hour" that they can ultimately send. That's a lot of mail!

The implementation needed to grind the sender's server to a halt can be done via several methods, although one of the clearest examples involves a pure computational tax. It might work something like this: Upon a connection to your server by an outside party (any outside party), the receiver's server asks the sender to perform a mathematical calculation and provide the correct answer before it can continue. For the normal exchange of e-mail (numbering in the thousands per day), this is a negligible tax on resources. However, for a server that is firehosing out millions of messages per hour, a very perceivable slowdown could be experienced.

One of the sizeable hurdles with implementing a strategy based on punishing the spammer by slowing his shop down to a crawl is that the entire mail exchange protocol would have to be rewritten to accommodate the computational tax, which isn't likely to happen and is even more unlikely to gain broad enough adoption to merit its use. Add to this the fact that there is a great reliance on open relays to provide anonymity to the spammer, which factors the processing to a third-party victim and, in essence, nullifies the entire "slowdown" tactic.

Another hurdle is that most e-mail servers are implemented in software, and because of this, it's almost a given that the computational tax be rendered along with it. The workaround for the spammer is to deploy a hardware-based calculator once the code for the exact computation has been adopted. For the protocol to work, it needs to be open to inspection, alteration, and testing. Since there's a perfect visibility to all the parts of it, it is trivial for the spammers to abstract the necessary parts to hardware, side-stepping the whole goal.

The concept of slowing down the sender is a curious idea, but it's not really one that has long-term viability. It seems more like a fairly advanced workaround than a "root cause" technique to stop spam.

Micro-Payments

Another class of spam control that's based on punishing the spammer is the concept of putting a cash register in front of your inbox. We are sure that this method's got a certain appeal to most everyone. The idea is based on the fact that an e-mail account, even if seemingly entirely ephemeral, has certain costs associated with its maintenance and operation. Most people can attribute exact dollars to the equation pretty easily. After all, even "free" accounts really aren't free.

If all e-mail costs something to send, not only would the sheer volume of spam mail decline dramatically, but some sort of economic balance would be necessary for those that would inevitably remain. The idea is appealing to us, even if its implementation has the same huge looming obstacles that the challenge/response or the spammer server slowdown strategies would have.

Speaking of obstacles, the micro-payment plan has the additional complexity of needing maturity with the digital money vendors, which is clearly not present in today's markets. Further, the focus on the importance of good network security takes the lead position since the risks of being used as a spam pump by an unscrupulous spammer would cost the relaying site real money and bear real consequences of organizational liability more onerous than just financial losses.

Analysis That Targets the Benefactor

We've covered the bulk of mail filtering tactics with our exploration of content and sender analysis, and now we turn our attention to a matter that's been largely overlooked: benefactor analysis.

It's a curious thing to us that a great deal of effort has gone into leveling blame at the senders of the spam, rather than directing angst against the actual people who benefit from responses to their campaign. Someone has to hire the spam senders to begin with for the entire scheme to work. Obviously, lots and lots of benefactors out there see profit in the prosecution of sending bulk spam. We know this because we get thousands of commercial spams a day, with almost as many benefactors.

The two methods we cover here are Filters that Fight Back (FFBs) and legal approaches.

Live Back Trace, a.k.a. Filters That Fight Back

Along the same lines of attacking the spammer's back is a current consideration underway for using the spammer's own message against him. Practically every spam message has a web link in it somewhere, usually pointing back the product or service that ultimately underwrites the spam. This strategy makes use of the web link by following it but doing nothing with the results. Consider that a regular speed spam outlay could generate up to a million messages an hour. What would happen if everyone who received the spam were to click their browsers simultaneously and load the link referenced in the spam?

What would happen is what computer security experts call a DDoS attack. *DDoS* stands for Distributed Denial of Service, and it's a fancy way of saying that the coordinated effort of all of those simple requests would likely crash the benefactor's web server. It would also have the added benefit of drastically increasing the benefactor's Internet bill, possibly to the point of being quite financially punitive. We're sure that if such a system were well-formed and available today, someone who just decided to "try out e-mail marketing" once would likely never do it again.

Of course, like all things, the major drawback with this approach is that you can't just go DDoS-ing someone into oblivion without some sort of verification. Since IP addresses, and even more so e-mail addresses, are so easy to forge, it would be somewhat tragic to be the recipient of a $10,000 bandwidth invoice for spam mail that you never sent and that didn't benefit you in any way. To muddy the waters further, there's likely to be stringent penalties associated with certain Internet crimes, and Denial of Service could likely rank in the top five.

Tracking Those Responsible

Since establishing the benefactor's identity is our immediate goal, let's cover some of the more mundane and mechanical things you can do to hunt them down. First and foremost, the headers of the e-mail have precious little information pertaining to the actual underwriter of the spam. Often, it will lead you to the vicinity of the spam processing firm (which is alright if you want to employ some of the technical stratagems from above), and often it will lead you in circles or to an offshore group with an obviously fictional name.

The best tracking actually comes from the contents of the spam mail itself. To promote what they are selling or espousing, spammers need to offer you a way to get to it. They usually do this as a web link, but we've also seen a telephone number offered just as often.

Lots of important data can be had from their web links with some minimal research. For instance, a long trail of names, addresses, and phone numbers are associated with each domain in the path, all of which are potentially the ultimate benefactors of the spam. Further, doing an analysis of the raw content of their web server, identifying how and when the files were manufactured, often uncovers additional evidence directing you toward the benefactor.

The Law Will Protect Me

The most direct assaults against spammers aren't technical in nature at all. Many of the techniques we've detailed so far are largely preventative or rely on obfuscation for protection. Many opponents of spam argue that the bulk e-mail problem isn't a technical problem at all, but a societal one that needs the appropriate measure of law to remedy. However, for it to be anywhere near effective, we return to the old saw of needing to accurately establish the identity of the benefactor.

Also, the law is a very, very slippery subject, and highly charged topics such as governmental regulation of a common resource like e-mail, which effects a large segment of the American population, is bound to bring out a lot of well-funded, divergent lobbyists promoting a variety of different opinions on how best to "set the bar."

We definitely subscribe to the notion that an overriding set of laws should be in place to protect the best interests of the public. What we are worried about is a titanic struggle between giant, well-funded groups that after 20 years finally agree on a diluted basket of protections that do too little, too late, and that cost too much.

There's also the consideration that since the Internet is a world unto itself, without well-defined borders, the laws of the physical lands will be difficult to administer and easy to skirt. We see a rich and colorful nomenclature being developed to help steer the right laws onto the books, which can actually be effective in the new world in which we reside.

A great effort is going into spam control both at the state and federal levels. In 1977, Nevada was the first state to enact spam legislation, and between 1999 and 2003, at least thirty one other states have enacted laws restricting spam.

State laws, however, may be preempted by a new federal law that went into effect on January 1, 2004. The new law, known as the *Controlling the Assault of Non-Solicited Pornography and Marketing Act of 2003* or *CAN-SPAM Act of 2003*. imposes stiff monetary penalties and in some instances even jail terms. It remains to be seen whether the law will have any meaningful effect in stemming the tide of spam. Indeed, in passing the statute, Congress found specifically that "the problems associated with the rapid growth and abuse of unsolicited commercial e-mail cannot be solved by Federal legislation..." and "development and adoption of technological approaches and the pursuit of cooperative efforts with other countries will be necessary as well."

It's not likely that spammers will fear significant reprisals under the CAN-SPAM legislation. Many spam messages already violate laws regarding fraud and theft and are actionable under existing criminal laws. In passing CAN-SPAM, Congress recognized that most of unsolicited commercial e-mail messages "are fraudulent or deceptive in one or more respects." Considering the volume of spam—over one half of all electronic mail traffic—law enforcement officials simply are not equipped to track and prosecute illegal spam.

In addition to domestic laws, many foreign jurisdictions have enacted laws that attempt to thwart spammers. In December 2003, the United Nations created an initiative to address spam worldwide, although it may be years before anything tangible comes of that effort, and there is no guarantee the U.N. will have the ability to speak to the spam issue any more effectively than its member states.

Like many legal issues relating to the Internet, controlling spam also raises jurisdictional issues. Because it is often virtually impossible to determine the origin of a spam message, it is difficult to determine which jurisdiction's laws apply. And even when the spammer's location can be identified, the recipients may be located in other geographic areas, creating further jurisdictional difficulties.

In any event, for now we can't rely on the law to rid our inboxes of spam. For that, we need robust solutions based on technical offerings, such as those that we covered earlier in this chapter. Even though the law provides stiff penalties for burglary, theft, and fraud, those crimes still happen every day, including criminal activity supported by spam. Criminals manage to weigh the risks versus the penalties, and by their math it's still worth the risk. The same is true for spammers. They have little fear of the law actually catching up with them, and the amount they stand to earn is obviously enough to merit their behavior.

NEW APPROACHES TO CIRCUMVENT ADVANCED SPAM FILTERING

Throughout this book we cover the latest defensive methods for fighting spam. As we've illustrated, the more advanced anti-spam solutions become, the smarter the spammers get at building workarounds.

Given the success that Bayesian and statistical analysis has had with limiting spam, the senders have basically two big choices to combat it:

- Reduce the message to its essential parts until it slips through.
- Develop a way that the Bayesian classifier can't get a grip on the message.

We've seen activity in both arenas. We've noticed a reduction in the complexity of spam message bodies that we've seen over the past year, which suggests that the senders are not only refining their messages, but also testing them against a reference platform to see how well they fare.

To avoid the advanced filter entirely, we've seen an increase in the number of messages that have been run through a process that converts them into images (JPEGs, GIFs, TIFFs, and so on). Statistical modeling of e-mail relies on there being a significant quantity of text to analyze and compare to the baseline. Some messages we've seen have been constructed cleverly to avoid the filters by having no text whatsoever, with the exception of the header info. Of course, a preponderance of messages that all have only an image file in the body might be construed as spam, eventually applied to the model, and thus discarded.

Another advanced spamming technique falls under what we call "drive-by spamming." The near ubiquity of 802.11 wireless devices light up almost any city with free, anonymous, untracked, and unlogged access to the Internet, seven days a week, 24 hours a day. What we are finding is that successful spammers refine their message to the point of being capable of traversing the filters, and then they go for a drive one late night, find an open wireless access point, and spew out millions of spams through the unsuspecting organization that was beaconing its network.

Lastly, in a effort to stay one step ahead of the law and an angry mob of recipients, spammers are often found to be hiding behind empty shell corporations that can be easily tanked or built offshore. Often the cost of setting up a new corporation is so small and the turnaround time for the initial paperwork is so fast, that many spammers set up a corporate entity just long enough to get away with it.

SUMMARY

A variety of methods are available by which anti-spam solutions get their job done. They can be easily classified as filters that operate using the content of the message itself, filters that target the sender and intermediaries through which spam passes, and filters that target the final benefactor that had underwritten the spam to begin with. We covered a group of current practices in each category, and we even explored some of the more leading-edge technology. Without going into specific products or implementations, we covered the theoretical methods on which those solutions rely and even projected futuristic next steps in the evolution of spam-sending ware.

CHAPTER 4

ANTI-SPAM IMPLEMENTATION STRATEGIES

In the preceding chapters we covered the origin of spam, its impact to society, and the out-of-control growth that has marked its existence. We also explored the development of some plans for combating it, the beginnings of an e-mail content control policy, as well as the technical merits of the variety of methods that exist for eradicating it.

We discovered that to be effective, a strategy of "defense-in-depth" should be adopted and deployed throughout an organization. In short, this means that implementing a single defense at only one point along the mail path is generally inadequate to control an appreciable amount of spam in the long run.

In this chapter, we take what we've learned and explore some options for building the most appropriate spam control system across a broad set of circumstances, platforms, and operating systems. We briefly identify the technologies covered in depth across the remainder of this book, broken into "blacklist subscription" options, "server-based" solutions, "client-based" solutions, as well as a few "gateway-based" and "provider-based" spam initiatives.

Both gateway-based and provider-based offerings are relatively new and feature some advantageous concepts to the war on spam. Developers of gateway offerings designed them as a "bump in the wire," in line with the other raw traffic analysis gear (such as firewalls, intrusion detection/prevention, and other content gateways). Gateways are traditionally found in the DMZ or directly at the network's perimeter. For a quick diagram describing where these solutions are placed (along the other spam filtering solutions), check out Figure 4-1.

Gateway-based solutions are really just special firewalls that handle more than just spam filtering. More times than not, mail gateways could be called "general purpose content firewalls" because they often handle huge messages, strange attachments, viruses, pornography, as well as policy violations (such as the transfer of confidential or proprietary information) into or out of the network. Newer implementations even offer authentication services based on the organization's Lightweight Directory Access Protocol (LDAP) or Remote Authentication Dial-In User Service (RADIUS) protocol server (just to name a few). As the world moves more toward using stronger content control through encryption (to provide confidentiality) and authentication (to ensure identity), content analysis gateways become a robust alternative.

Provider-based solutions are equally as young and are best described as a blend of outsourced e-mail and *targeted* content filtering wrapped up into a single solution. The provider-based solutions have nice economies of scale, especially for very small organizations without the resources to staff an IT shop internally. Provider-based solutions are often more specific in nature than gateway approaches, since they focus strategically and completely on a particular area of deficiency (such as spam filtering). The most fundamental difference, however, is that they are pure outsourced solutions, resident on third-party hardware using third-party resources. They have the opportunity to provide exceptional service to a whole class of similar customers because they bulk hundreds and sometimes thousands of customers together.

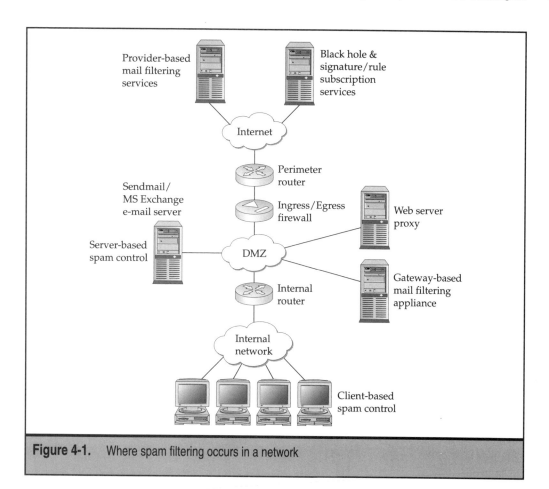

Figure 4-1. Where spam filtering occurs in a network

CHOOSING THE RIGHT SOLUTIONS

"Defense-in-depth" doesn't necessarily mean that you have to procure as many different products as you can, and then install them throughout your organization; instead it means that you cover the broadest range of filtering activities as controls during any potential spam transmission. The objective is to get the best bang for the buck with a minimum of long-term maintenance hassles using solutions obtained from stable, reputable firms.

Key Factors That Affect Your Decision

Of the factors that guide you, we consider an organization's size, architectural complexity, and ongoing support/maintenance requirements to be the most critical. There are, of course, many other equally important factors that should be taken into consideration, such as what types of training your staff has undergone, the frequency you send and receive mail, and the importance of e-mail to your organization's overall success, but size, composition, and support requirements really should be the heart of your first-pass focus.

Organization Size

As we alluded to in the introduction to this chapter, a very small organization (less than a dozen e-mail accounts) could satisfy the goal of "defense-in-depth" by considering a provider-based solution, as opposed to building, installing, and maintaining a mail server in-house. Although they are new to the scene, provider-based solutions give you several powerful advantages, including vigilant updates to software, subscriptions to a wide array of blacklisting, and quick response to malevolent mailborne viruses. We devote a whole section to a few of the leaders in the provider-based space, in-depth, at the end of this chapter.

Larger organizations (between a dozen to 100 e-mail accounts) typically have an in-house IT group and normally have a private internal network, protected by a packet filtering firewall (among other security infrastructure gear). Organizations of this size often have two or three mail servers, so that there is a division of labor across the cluster for handling the load. The first, and most likely, separation of function for server administrators is to segregate in-bound versus out-bound e-mail.

Segregation of Inbound vs. Outbound Mail Using DNS

Separation of mail flows is traditionally done using DNS and by creating an inbound exchanger preference using an MX (or mail exchanger) entry in the name server's zone configuration or database files. Additional backup mail exchangers can also be configured by stipulating several MX entries with a different numeric precedence.

```
$ORIGIN corp.tld.
        corp.tld.           IN      A               172.16.0.50
                            IN      MX      10      mail-1.corp.tld.
                            IN      MX      20      mail-3.corp.tld.
                            IN      MX      100     smtp.isp.tld.

        mail-1.corp.tld.    IN      A               172.16.1.30
        mail-2.corp.tld.    IN      A               172.16.1.31
        mail-3.corp.tld.    IN      A               172.16.1.32
```

In this example, our company (corp.tld) has three mail servers that are set up to receive inbound mail with the DNS advertised names of mail-1, mail-2, and mail-3. We've set the configuration so any mail designed for any user @corp.tld will first be sent to the server mail-1.corp.tld, then to the mail-3.corp.tld, and then to a backup at our Internet Service Provider (smtp.isp.tld). You'll note that the precedence is established using the numbers following the MX entries (10, 20, and 100)—the lowest number gets the highest priority.

Huge organizations often look similar to large organizations in that they have their own networks (often gigantic ocean-crossing wide area networks), multiple installations of servers to manage, and lots and lots of e-mail users. Because of the importance and reliance on e-mail as one of the most critical of communication functions, huge organizations devote a good deal of their IT staff and resources to making sure that mail flows properly.

Huge mail installations continue along the path of separation by dividing up the core mail responsibilities between similar sets of users, in addition to segregating the incoming from outgoing flows. Oftentimes you will see the certain departments or specific geographic divisions with separate servers handling their mail.

Support and Maintenance

As with all systems in production, maintenance is not a luxury to be taken lightly. Aim first for anti-spam solutions that play to your organization's strengths. If you are predominantly a Windows shop with Microsoft Exchange mail servers, stick to solutions built for your environment. Installing a Linux operating system with an operational mail server would be headache enough if you've never done it before. If you have the time and inclination to support a heterogeneous mail environment, however, you might find it worth your while.

As our coverage of anti-spam offerings shows, much of the same basic functionality is available across the entire group of competing anti-spam solutions, so it's a good idea to review what's out there carefully, choosing the best fit for your goals. Additionally, some vendors even offer cross-platform versions, for those die-hard types who are already hooked on a specific system.

As mentioned previously, selecting solutions that have timely updates to their software and robust rule/signature distribution mechanisms makes ongoing management considerably easier. Look for solutions that have well-written manuals, complete with easy-to-understand examples and friendly, intelligent support staff. When considering open-source solutions, look at those that have plenty of How Tos and FAQs (Frequently Asked Questions), that are actively developing and beta testing their software, and that have lively mailing lists. The open-source projects that thrive are those that have engaged developers *and* users. A little commercial backing sometimes helps, too.

You can also learn a lot about a company *before* purchasing its products by doing some investigative research. As a quick and incomplete taste of how the company conducts business, we've found that by reviewing the "troubleshooting" and "FAQ" areas of a potential vendor's web site gives you a pretty decent understanding of what problems you'll likely encounter by purchasing the product. Some vendors also host mailing lists or bulletin boards, where customers can open a general dialog on the operation of their products. We've found some of the most accurate and honest appraisals posted to bulletin boards or list servers. However, it's important to note that this is only the tip of the iceberg with corporate research. The more background checking you do, the better you will be equipped to make an informed decision. We aren't suggesting that this minimal amount of exploration is by any means complete, but it does provide a good starting point.

Architectural Considerations

One big consideration facing you is the physical architecture of your network. Selection of the appropriate tools is predicated on how mail flows into and out of your infrastructure. Look back to Figure 4-1 for a moment. Although this diagram depicts a somewhat normal network topology, lots of different configurations are out there, including yours. Having an up-to-date network map that details the major components is a *must have*. Collect it before you sit down and introduce new components, and if you have the resources (such as a lab environment or extra servers lying about) try out a few ideas *virtually* before committing to any specific solution.

Also, be sure to take into account the composition as well as architecture of your environment. Heterogeneous installations have the broadest selection of anti-spam offerings at their disposal, but they also have the most headaches. Identify what mail clients your e-mail reading public normally uses, talk with the persons responsible for the mail servers, and if you can, develop a holistic picture of how e-mail is used, before you start shopping.

RECOMMENDATIONS ON SOLUTION ROBUSTNESS

We've separated our recommendations into policy and technical recommendations. Policy suggestions are all-encompassing across an entire organization's methods of operation. They include such things as what escalation procedures should be followed and when to report spammers to the authorities, while technical recommendations cover the specific software, hardware, and architectural goals.

Policy Recommendations

As suggested previously, it's best to deploy spam-fighting software at multiple levels. Layered protection produces better results, is naturally scalable, and distributes processing requirements to specific nodes. Additionally, this approach segregates streams of traffic by destination and produces discrete systems for more granular control.

Implement strategies based on your organization's security policies first, content control policies second, and e-mail specific policies last. Since spam filtering falls under the larger domain of general content control, which in turn falls under general information security, those two groups of policies need to be scrutinized prior to the establishment of new systems. Of course, those recommendations need to be taken into consideration of your overall policies concerning development, maintenance, disaster recovery, and business continuity.

Recommendation: Report Spammers to the Authorities

Report spammers to their ISPs (using automation if possible). Many of the tools covered in this book do a good job of taking corrective action by notifying IT staff, adjusting rules/signatures, applying auto-learn statistical techniques, and blocking potential spam sources. Some packages also have features that automatically send complaint mails to the various participants that were involved with sending the spam to begin with. From a policy perspective, it's good practice to notify potentially vulnerable people that spam was sent using their systems (either knowingly or unknowingly). What's best is to find solutions that have thresholds for determining when to take action silently and when to post a notification. For instance, a nice threshold can be built based on the numeric value that most packages use to determine a message's overall "spaminess."

Recommendation: Backup, Backup, Backup

Another good policy, which was briefly covered in Chapter 1, is the need to archive old mail, especially e-mail that is determined to be spam. It is really *not* a good idea to just blindly delete anything that matches the spam criteria settings of a particular software tool, no matter how good it would feel. Because spam-filtering methods are imprecise, the archive can be used to find accidentally lost mail, as well as determine ongoing and baseline statistics for how well the system is behaving.

We would suggest a two-tiered approach to the archive of old mail and server log information. Use local hard drive space on the server to keep a recent copy of the server-specific data (log files, error reports, config files) as well as a copy of the mailbox and user-specific configuration files. This "hot backup" will come in handy for "teaching" advanced filters, such as Bayesian systems, which typically require a corpus of known-spam and known-good e-mail.

Lastly, having a long-term "cold storage" of e-mails and server configuration data, gives the mail administrator a good starting point when some catastrophic event happens that enacts the organization's Disaster Recovery Plan.

Recommendation: Audit and Review Log Information

Also important are policies that handle the management, rotation, and regular review of log files. E-mail is one of the noisiest of the "well-known" services (web, e-mail, FTP, SSH, LDAP, and so on), producing volumes of logged information. A good indication of how your spam filtering solutions are performing can be gleaned from log file audits. We recommend not only a regular review of your log files (both anti-spam and e-mail service), but also the archive of old log files, consistent with the approach we outlined earlier.

Logging and Hard Drive Requirements

For our system, which handles more than 10,000 messages and produces about 50MB of log file information per day, we keep at least a year's worth of logs, and three months' worth of archived mail. Actually, we keep a lot more than that, since the entire system is backed up to tape on a weekly basis—but those are just our "hot" backups made via an extra hard drive. We highly recommend analyzing the storage requirements for your logging scenario, as well as developing a regular recurring strategy for log file review. Some anti-spam filtering solutions have precious little in the way of logging, which makes the need to archive mail all the more imperative.

The larger an organization becomes, the more it needs to embrace policies relating to change management. Widely separated staff managing hundreds of devices across world-wide geographies typically employ systems that track the "who, what, and when" of changes to production configuration files. It's a good idea to include these systems in your plan for spam filtering, especially for blacklists, whitelists, and general configuration files.

Recommendation: Read and Review AUPs and SLAs

Another recommendation we found important is a review of your ISP's Acceptable Use Policy (AUP) for appropriateness. We use "appropriate" because some ISPs have a somewhat vindictive approach to spammers, which although admirable, may be too zealous for your operation. One of our larger scale network vendors sometimes gets a little overexcited at forged spam that erroneously cites our domain or IP address, to which it responds with a strongly worded e-mail, complete with a termination threat. Also, knowing your ISP's Service Level Agreement (SLA) as it pertains to spam and downtime is an important issue and well worth your investigation.

It's a good idea to make sure you know how your vendors respond to e-mail related incidents (even if misinterpreted). It's also good to keep the vendor's contact numbers around, including the after-hours support group, should something come up that impacts service.

Technical Recommendations

Although not critically important, we recommend running spam-filtering in combination with other content-analysis software. If you already have anti-virus or web-proxy software installed, it makes sense to explore any spam control options offered by those same vendors. Using the same hardware (and in some cases the same software) to handle these multiple tasks can serve to prevent double transmissions, save on storage needs, and ultimately reduce expensive CPU processing.

Configure spam-filtering software to check for forgeries of the sender's IP address, the sender's domain, and whether any open relays were used to exchange the mail. As we cover in Chapter 5, much of the open-relay testing is done using a live blacklist service, either as a paid-for subscription service or as a free DNS-based one. Most packages have some support for these functions, and we highly recommend using them as they can reliably reduce the amount of spam you get by as much as a third.

Likely, the best reward for your money is to select a solution with robust statistical or behavioral analysis functions. These techniques have been proven to be effective at the root problem of spam filtering: correctly identifying it. Our recommendation is not only to find a package with these features (such as Bayesian analysis), but also to base your decision around the leaders.

You should also use as much automation as possible with all of your choices. Rule development, automated signature updates, online blacklisting, statistical auto-learning, and filtering are all par for the course. In today's spam-heavy environment, with the attentions of the spam purveyors aggressively focused on side-stepping your defenses, automation isn't a luxury, it's required.

SPAM SOLUTIONS COVERED IN THIS BOOK

In this book, we tried to review a broad set of spam-filtering software solutions across many operating environments in the hopes of giving you a good idea of what choices you have out there. Some packages weren't reviewed and some were not included, but this in no way represents a lack of support for those offerings; we wanted to keep this book moderately broad, but not exhaustively so.

Subscriptions to Network-Based Blacklists

In Chapter 5, we cover a few of the more popular DNS-based blacklists. Many of the services they provide are free. Even so, we would definitely recommend sending the maintainers a donation if you find their services useful after installing it.

We found that most of the installed mail servers that we configured in our testing lab had about equal support for connecting to the blacklists (including Windows Exchange Server, sendmail, postfix, and courier).

In Table 4-1, we summarize the highlights of the different lists. For more information on each of the lists, how they differ, and the specifics of installing each, please refer to Chapter 5. Also, you might not be familiar with some of the acronyms used in the table, and Chapter 5 provides a great starting point on translating those back into English.

Features List	Open Relay	Open Proxy	Known Spammer	Dial-up Dynamic	Spam Policy Abuse	IP Based	Domain Based	Fee
MAPS NML					√	√		√
MAPS DUL				√		√		√
MAPS RSS			√			√		√
MAPS RBL	√	√	√		√	√		√
MAPS RBL+	√	√	√	√	√	√		√
SpamCop			√					√

Table 4-1. Real-time Blacklist Services Compared

Features List	Open Relay	Open Proxy	Known Spammer	Dial-up Dynamic	Spam Policy Abuse	IP Based	Domain Based	Fee
ORDB	√					√		Donation
DSBL		√				√		Donation
SpamHaus		√			√	√		Donation
NJABL	√	√	√	√		√		Donation
RFCI IP Whois					√	√		Donation
RFCI all others					√		√	Donation

Table 4-1.   Real-time Blacklist Services Compared *(continued)*

Client-Based Spam Filtering

In Chapter 9, we illustrate how to configure client-side spam filtering, which is provided as part of Microsoft Outlook, Outlook Express, Mozilla Mail, and Eudora. Mozilla Mail has junk mail filtering capabilities using integrated tools, and it even supports a plug-in architecture for such packages as SpamAssassin. Outlook and Outlook Express have limited spam-fighting resources, but they have strong ties to other tools using their plug-in architecture.

In Chapter 10, we delve deep into the specific client-side anti-spam packages available for the Windows operating system. Table 4-2 compares and contrasts their major features.

Spam Fighting Features: Windows Package	Rules/ Patterns/ Signatures	Act as a Proxy	Sorts to Folders	Statistical or Other Bayesian Classifier	Black/ Whitelists	Real-time Blacklist Lookups	Automation for Updates to Rules, Software, Signatures (P2P)
SpamBayes		√*	√				√
SpamPal	(√)**	√		(√)	√	√	√
SpamCatcher	√				√		√
MailShield	√	√		√	√		

Table 4-2.   Windows Spam-Filtering Client Comparison

Chapter 4: Anti-Spam Implementation Strategies

Spam Fighting Features: Windows Package	Rules/ Patterns/ Signatures	Act as a Proxy	Sorts to Folders	Statistical or Other Bayesian Classifier	Black/ Whitelists	Real-time Blacklist Lookups	Automation for Updates to Rules, Software, Signatures (P2P)
SpamFighter	√				√		√
SpamButcher	√				√		√
iHateSpam	√			√	√		√
SpamNet		√					√
KnockKnock					√		(√)
POPfile	√	√	√	√	√		

* √—Integrated feature
** (√)—Feature available through additional steps

Table 4-2. Windows Spam-Filtering Client Comparison *(continued)*

Macintosh Client Spam Solutions

In Chapter 12 we review some Macintosh client solutions along the same lines that we measured the Windows solutions. Table 4-3 compares and contrasts their major features.

Server-Based Spam Systems

In Chapter 11, we cover the server-based spam filtering solutions available for the Windows operating system. All of the same features and functions that you have grown to

Spam Fighting Features: Mac Package	Rules/ Patterns/ Signatures	Act as a Proxy	Sorts to Folders	Statistical or Other Bayesian Classifier	Black/ Whitelists	Real-time Blacklist Lookups	Automation for Updates to Rules, Software, Signatures (P2P)
Post Armor	√	√			√	√	
POPMonitorX	√				√		
SpamFire	√	√			√		√
MailGoGoGo	√	√			√		

Table 4-3. Macintosh Spam-Filtering Client Comparison

Anti-Spam Tool Kit

Spam Fighting Features: Packages	Rules/ Patterns/ Signatures	Act as a Proxy	Sorts to Folders	Statistical or Other Bayesian Classifier	Black/ Whitelists	Real-time Blacklist Lookups	Automation for Updates to Rules, Software, Signatures (P2P)
iHateSpam Server Edition	√		√	(√)	√		√
GFI Mail Essentials	√		√	√	√	√	√
Trend Spam Prevention	√	√			√		√

Table 4-4. Windows Server–Based Filtering Comparison

expect from a robust filtering solution all are provided, including black/whitelisting, Bayesian analysis, proxy setup, and automated rule updates. Table 4-4 summarizes the similarities and differences between a few of the major Window's-based server offerings covered later in the book.

Linux/UNIX Server-Based Filtering

In Chapter 13, we cover the basics of what spam-fighting software is available for the UNIX/Linux Operating System. As with most things UNIX, all of the expected functions are present, but some of the configuration necessities are time-consuming and esoteric. In addition, other bleeding-edge features are often available, which could be both good and bad, depending on your tolerance for advanced code. Table 4-5 compares and contrasts the softwares' features.

Gateway-Based Spam Systems

Gateway-based spam solutions are growing in popularity and as of this writing, almost two dozen vendors, some as established as five years old, are already dominating the scene. Generally, these gateway products operate as a mail exchanger replacement and typically reside on the company's network edge, often behind the company's external firewall. These vendors target medium to large enterprises, with many employees in several geographic locations for their gateway products. Some of the better-known names in the group include Symantec, Trend Micro, Surf Control, Borderware, Brightmail, and CipherTrust. The style of offering varies from hardware-only appliances to software-only solutions, or varied combinations of each.

Most of these vendors also support ties to other enterprise servers, such as backend mail servers like sendmail or Microsoft Exchange. This simplifies the ultimate filtering of mail, but it does add overhead for the dual transmission of acceptable content. Further,

Spam Fighting Features: Packages	Rules/ Patterns/ Signatures	Distribute Checksum Network	Sorts to Folders	Statistical or Other Bayesian Classifier	Challenge/Response System
Vipul's Razor		√			
DCC		√			
Bogofilter			√	√	
SpamBayes			√	√	
Quick Spam Filter			√	√	
Active Spam Killer					√
The Spam Bouncer	√		√		

Table 4-5. Linux/UNIX Server Filtering Comparison

some vendors even support interfacing with firewalls and other security-filtering equipment such as intrusion prevention and quality of service monitors. A few are anti-virus mail gateway vendors that have added anti-spam functionality.

Brightmail has one of the stronger offerings in the space and supports what's most critical with spam-control: automated rule and signature updates. We've harped a lot on this as being the key to longevity with stout spam-fighting, and we believe Brightmail's solution is a good example. Brightmail was one of the first vendors to incorporate a rule-updating philosophy into its core solution, and over the past few years it has built quite a significant network around that approach. Architecturally, Brightmail's method consists of the following:

- **Content Filtering** The Brightmail Server is installed as a gateway appliance on a DMZ network, acting as an inline gateway before the organization's main mail servers.

- **Rule Extraction** The BLOC (Brightmail Logistics and Operations Center) builds and utilizes real-time rules/signatures for filtering spam.

- **Distribution and Reporting** As part of a large distributed network that Brightmail maintains, the Brightmail server can set up dummy accounts for testing possible spam as well as exchanging the rule base with other Brightmail servers.

What makes Brightmail's solution especially enticing (which is also true for the entire group of gateway providers that sport some kind of dynamic rule network) is that it operates all day, every day, and grows even as spammers invent more and more clever workarounds. Also, to ensure the quality of the signatures provided by the Brightmail network, human operators provide one last look at the filtering rules that are automatically created by the participants in the network, just to provide a sanity check.

Provider-Based Spam Systems

Provider-based solutions appear technologically similar to the gateway-based ones covered in the preceding section, and, in fact, many of the offerings rely on the same technology incorporated into those gateway platforms. The biggest difference is that provider-based solutions are pure outsourced offerings, which takes all of the administrative, operational, and capital expenditure headaches off of the customer, while giving the provider opportunities of scale.

The following three most popular implementations are available today:

- Web-mail content-filtering
- External exchanger filtering
- ISP filtering

Quite a few of the offerings that we reviewed use third-party gateways to handle the actual process of spam-filtering, with Brightmail being one of the largest and most entrenched of the group. Brightmail has oriented itself as a "provider to providers," accounting some of the largest ISPs as its clientele: EarthLink, BellSouth, and AT&T, just to name a few.

Others use home-grown solutions, which are likely just recombinations of several of the many filtering software packages out there. Yahoo! and MSN both have internal resources that they have devoted to building spam-control, and each offers a full-featured hosted service to its customer base.

Gaining a foothold on the space, more than a dozen new companies have sprung up in the last few years, offering a rich set of provider-based content control, the bulk of which center around spam filtering. Numbering among these are Bind Networks, Mail Circuit, Big Fish, MessageLabs, and Extreme Programming.

Bind Networks

BindMail, a managed content service provided from Bind Networks, offers mail content filtering for viruses and spam control. Using pattern matching reduces spam. BindMail also uses keyword filters, blacklisted domains, and a rules-based interface allowing the end user to apply forwarding and quarantining where necessary. BindMail operates as a mail exchanger intermediary, and Bind Networks provides several days' worth of mail spooling should the client's mail delivery system go offline. We found the service to be fairly easy to use and reasonably priced. One of the nicer features is a periodic report, generated by Bind Networks regarding the frequency and performance of the mail filtering that's been deployed. For more information, check out the company's web site at *http://www.bindnetworks.com/*.

MailCircuit

MailCircuit (*http://www.mailcircuit.com*) offers enterprises an outsourced web-mail service using POP3 as a transport mechanism. MailCircuit, like many of the gateway and provider-based solutions, provides spam as well as virus filtering as its primary service. MailCircuit operates most like a filtering proxy, as it retrieves mail, filters it for content abuses, and then forwards it back to an enterprise mail system for the ultimate delivery. Also included is an authentication service, whereby the user is challenged with an authentication token delivered in a web page. Consistent with our speculations, authentication schemes are becoming more and more prevalent, and we are sure that during the next few years lots of different offerings will at least include some measure of them.

Big Fish

Another prominent web-mail vendor is FrontBridge Technologies, offering both anti-spam and anti-virus filtering through its hosted mail solution, SpamShark. Much like the other offerings we covered, FrontBridge has marketed its service to the enterprise market, where the many, many accounts it can secure with one large client gives it a robust set of users to build strong filtering rules. Much like the MailCircuit service, FrontBridge provides its services as a POP3 forwarding proxy. FrontBridge has developed its own spam scoring system that it uses to filter out unwanted mail content. FrontBridge quarantines questionable mail for offline review and has several rule modifications that are user controllable. A pleasant feature for administrators of large e-mail systems, FrontBridge offers a "system wide" filter that applies to all accounts, prior to being processed by the user's specific setup. The web address to get more information on the offering and the company is *http://www.frontbridge.com/services/spamfilter.php*.

MessageLabs

SkyScan, a hosted service provided by MessageLabs, has all the basic features of any outsourced filtering service: spam and virus filtering, most notably. As an added benefit, the SkyScan service also does filtering for pornographic material and other unwanted content. SkyScan uses the latest spam filtering as provided by the SpamAssassin package, but it applies continuous tweaking to the hundreds of rules provided using some advanced artificial intelligence techniques. According to the company, the tuning of its system happens quite frequently during the day and is one of the most automated systems on the market today. Check out MessageLabs at *http://www.mailability.com/products/antivirus/skyscan.htm*.

Extreme Programming

Our last hosted solution, a service called E-Mail Bouncer provided by Extreme Programming, has a somewhat different approach to spam-fighting. Most of the services that we've covered so far typically blend some form of keyword/pattern filtering, sprinkled with Bayesian analysis and blacklisting, to achieve a nice blend for cutting down spam. The E-Mail Bouncer service uses an aggressive authentication system to rid the user's inbox of spam.

As we briefly covered in Chapter 3 with the other "futuristic" challenge-response models for fighting spam, Extreme Programming has taken the necessary step of making a usable service out of the concept. Its service keeps all inbound e-mail in quarantine while the sender's authenticity is verified. Senders that have already been authenticated by the system are allowed access to transmit mail without holdup, but unknown senders are challenged by a response mail with an embedded web link back to the Extreme Programming server. Spam-bots, automated senders, advertising bots, and other unwanted bulk e-mail are all dumped once it is clear they don't respond to the challenge. More information can be found at *http://www.email-bouncer.com/*.

SUMMARY

In this chapter we covered where to implement the many different methods for spam control, as well the systems necessary for getting the job done. We also looked forward at the rest of the book, giving you an outline of the packages that we cover in depth and how they compare and contrast with each other. Lastly, we explored some of the newer offerings for outsourced enterprise shoppers and investigated a few of the gateway vendors, some of which have pure software offering and some of which sell spam-killing network appliances.

PART II
BUILDING YOUR ANTI-SPAM ARSENAL

CHAPTER 5
BLOCKING SPAMMERS WITH DNS BLACKLISTS

In Chapter 4 we introduced you to DNS Blacklists as one of several means for fighting spam. In this chapter, we will look at popular individual DNS Blacklists, explain how to implement them on a mail server, and help you decide which list is the best one to use. When referring to DNS Blacklists, the shorthand DNSBL is often used, and that's how we'll refer to them throughout this chapter.

Before we talk about specific blacklists and how to implement them, we'll delve into what DNSBLs are and how they work.

UNDERSTANDING DNS BLACKLISTS

DNSBLs are an integral part of any spam-fighting toolkit. The fact that many, many users on the Internet are updating them means you get the benefit of blocking a spammer before the first piece of spam even hits you. To understand how DNSBLs help, you need to know the types of DNSBLs available and how they work.

Types of DNSBLs

Currently, two different types of DNS Blacklists are used:

- IP-based blacklists
- Domain-based blacklists

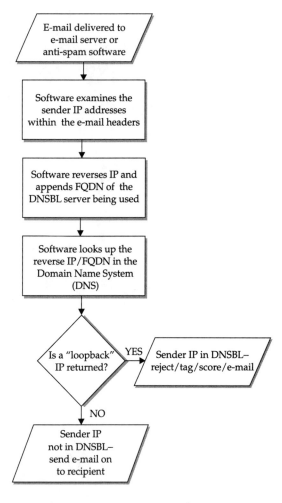

The majority of DNSBLs are IP-based, which look at the Internet Protocol (IP) address of the server sending the mail. Every host, including e-mail servers, connected to the Internet has its own unique IP address. This IP address is checked against a database to see whether or not it's for a known spammer, known open relay, or known open proxy. As a rule, IP-based DNSBLs work like this:

1. An attempted e-mail delivery to your mail server or anti-spam software occurs.
2. Your mail server or anti-spam software examines the IP addresses of the mail servers the e-mail passed through to get to you.

3. Your e-mail server or anti-spam software then reverses the order of the IP address and appends the fully qualified domain name (FQDN) of the DNSBL server being used. A FQDN is the Internet domain in which the server resides (such as ordb.org), plus the hostname of the server (such as relays.ordb.org). So, for instance, if the IP address of the sending server is 192.168.42.6, and the FQDN of the DNSBL server is relays.greatdnsbl.tld, the appended name is 6.42.168.192.relays.greatdnsbl.tld (note that a fictitious private IP address is used in this example).

4. Your server or anti-spam software then looks up the appended name in the Domain Name System (DNS). If an actual IP address is returned, the server exists in the blacklist. Otherwise, it doesn't exist or the blacklist is down. The IP address that gets returned should always be in the special-use "loopback" network (127.0.0.0/8, per RFC 3330). The IP address that gets returned may have some special meaning for an individual DNSBL.

5. Your mail server or anti-spam software uses the response from the DNSBL to decide what to do with the mail. If it determines that the mail has come from a system in the DNSBL, it may reject it, tag it, or score it, depending upon the software and its configuration.

Domain-based DNSBLs are also called *right-hand side blacklists* (RHSBLs). These lists look only at the second-level and top-level domains (for instance, the *.com* and the *yahoo* that comes before it—*yahoo.com*) of a given e-mail address or FQDN. Here's how they work:

1. An attempted e-mail delivery to your mail server or anti-spam software occurs.

2. Your mail server or anti-spam software looks at the domain on the right-hand side of the @ sign. For instance, spammer.tld would be parsed from spam4you@spammer.tld. Or, in the case of the server spamserver.spammer.tld, it would look only at spammer.tld.

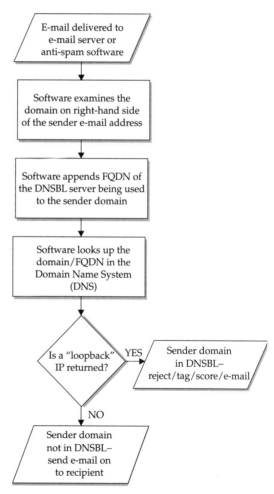

3. This domain name is then appended to the front of the FQDN of the DNSBL server. For instance, if the parsed domain is spammer.tld, and the name of the DNSBL server is relays.greatdnsbl.tld, the appended name is spammer.tld.relays.greatdnsbl.tld.

4. Your server or anti-spam software then looks up the appended name in the DNS. If an actual IP address is returned (again, from the loopback network range), the server exists in the blacklist. Otherwise, it doesn't exist or the blacklist is down.

5. Again, your mail server or anti-spam software takes the response from the RHSBL and then uses it to decide what to do with the mail.

So why have both IP-based and domain-based DNSBLs? IP-based lists typically consist of systems that have sent spam in the past or that are capable of sending spam (such as open relays). They sometimes also consist of entire networks that are capable of sending spam (such as dial-up lists). They are more specific, because they include only IP addresses or networks that actually performed the behavior that got them onto the list (that is, sending spam), rather than just being part of that domain.

Criteria for DNS Blacklists

Currently, most DNSBLs use one or more of the following criteria to determine whether or not an Internet host belongs in the list. Sometimes a DNSBL organization has a separate blacklist for each criterion, or it might have one or two lists that employ a mix of these.

- Open-relay list
- Open-proxy list
- Known spammer lists
- Dial-up user list

We will briefly discuss each of these.

Open-Relay List

Open-relay lists are extremely popular forms of DNSBLs. A machine is considered an open relay if it allows unauthorized users to e-mail to a third party—that is, neither the person sending the mail nor the person receiving the mail are within domains for which the e-mail system is a mail server. In the early days of the Internet, when spam wasn't such a problem, many systems were configured as open relays. Nowadays, it's no longer necessary to run mail servers as open relays, so systems that remain as such are generally run by administrators who simply lack the time, effort, or knowledge to configure them otherwise. Open relays are attractive to spammers because they allow spammers to use someone else's resources for sending bulk e-mail, and these systems remove spammers one step from the sender—thus making them more difficult to track.

Open Proxy Lists

Open proxy servers are even worse than open relays. A proxy in the networking world is similar to a proxy in the real world—that is, it's someone, or something, who stands in or acts as a substitute for someone, or something, else. In this case, the proxy is a network device or server that makes a connection to a network resource for an end user, rather than the end user making the connection directly to the resource. For instance, if a user wants to go to the web page *http://www.mcgraw-hill.com*, she types that URL into her browser. If her browser is configured to use an HTTP proxy server, the proxy server gets the request, goes out to *http://www.mcgraw-hill.com*, pulls down the web page, and sends it on to the browser. The user never connects directly to *http://www.mcgraw-hill.com*.

Using a proxy provides a certain level of inherent anonymity. The user's IP address never appears in the McGraw-Hill web server's logs—the proxy's IP address does. Typically, proxies limit what networks can connect to them. Open proxies, however, allow *any* user to connect to them from anywhere, and use them to go anywhere. An open proxy, therefore, allows a spammer to make a Simple Mail Transport Protocol (SMTP) connection to a mail server, but it hides where the mail is coming from. To the system to which they're connecting, it looks like the sender is the proxy—nothing behind that is seen by the mail server. It's yet another powerful tool in the spammers' toolkit.

Known Spammer Lists

Known spammer lists are domains, systems, or networks that are known spammer dens. Unlike open-relay and open-proxy servers, these are in the list not for technological reasons, but because they've actually sent spam.

Dial-Up User Lists

The idea behind dial-up user lists is to prevent what the Mail Abuse Prevention System organization (MAPS, which we'll talk about a little later) calls "spam trespassing," whereby a spammer dials into an ISP (possibly using a forged "trial" account) with a system running a mail server or "ratware" and sends out bulk e-mail. By doing so, the spammer gets around traditional spam detection measures. The spammer uses the ISP's network resources but not its server resources. These lists often also include other ISP accounts with dynamic IP addresses, such as cable modems and DSLs.

Adding or Removing Entries from a DNS Blacklist

Each DNSBL has a method for adding or removing entries from a blacklist. This is most often performed through the DNSBL's web page, although it can also be done through e-mail. Sometimes you have to be a "member" of a DNSBL to add entries to its blacklist, which sometimes means you have to be a paying customer (or donator).

Anyone who wants to remove a server, network, or domain from a DNSBL can generally do this, too. This is done at the DNSBL's web site. The listed item is retested before it is removed. If the listed server, network, or domain is under the control of a known spammer, or if it has multiple strikes against it, it may not be removed at all.

CHOOSING A DNS BLACKLIST

Many DNSBLs are out there—more than 100 public ones, and who knows how many private ones. Organizationally, they typically fall into three categories:

- Nonprofit organizations that are dedicated to spam-fighting. These organizations generally have employees and a semicorporate structure.
- A loose-knit group of administrators who have banded together to fight spam. These groups usually do not have full-time employees, and they resemble open-source projects more than anything else. (For example, though there may be a recognized leader, they follow democratic principles in decision-making.)
- Individuals who have set up their own DNSBLs for their own private use, but who allow others to use them if they like.

In addition to their organizational structure, DNSBLs differ greatly in the way they operate. Areas in which there might be differences include the following:

- Criteria on what constitutes a spammer (or potential spammer)
- The method they use to obtain candidates for their black hole lists
- Their rules for getting removed from their list
- The type of lists they run (open-relay, known spammer, dial-up, and so on)
- Whether or not you have to pay to use the service

All of these influence the effectiveness and ease-of-use of a particular DNSBL.

Because the lists are dynamic in nature and structured around the particular philosophies of their organizers, none can be considered the be-all and end-all authority on who is and who is not a spammer. All have the potential to give false positives and false negatives.

In general, nonprofit organizations have stricter rules as to which systems or domains end up in their blacklists, followed by the loose-knit groups, and then individuals. Therefore, if you're concerned about false positives, an organization is the better way to go.

The DNSBL that is right for you fits in well with your personal or organizational policy on spam. How tolerant are you of a little spam getting through? How tolerant are you of legitimate mail being rejected? Are you willing to pay (or donate) to use a blacklist?

An extensive list of blacklists can be found at the Declude web site: *http://www.declude.com/junkmail/support/ip4r.htm*. However, we'll overview several of the most popular and effective ones in the following sections.

MAIL ABUSE PREVENTION SYSTEM (MAPS)

Mail Abuse Prevention System, LLC (MAPS for short), is one of the biggest, oldest, most controversial, and most well-known DNSBLs around. Formed in 1997 by a small group that included Internet developer Paul Vixie (author of the BIND software found on the majority of Internet DNS servers), MAPS is a nonprofit corporation based in California. MAPS main web site can be found at *http://www.mail-abuse.org*.

Vixie's reputation and knowledge has given MAPS a lot of respect among system administrators and a lot of profiling in the press. Unfortunately, MAPS's methods (which really aren't all that different from many other blacklists), its high profile, and its ubiquity have made it the legal target for numerous bulk e-mail senders who feel that MAPS is unfairly persecuting them. MAPS even collects money online for its legal defense fund!

How MAPS Works

MAPS has one of the widest assortments of DNSBLs available. A different group within the MAPS organization operates each one, and each has its own documentation, policies, FAQ, and tools. Following is a brief rundown of the available lists.

Nonconfirming Mailing List (NML)

List type:	IP-based
DNSBL server:	nonconfirm.mail-abuse.org

The Nonconfirming Mailing List is MAPS newest offering. The NML contains a list of reported IP addresses that send e-mail to mailing lists without fully verifying that the recipient actually requested the information they're sending out. In other words, the senders didn't verify that the e-mail was solicited. Other things that could get someone on the list:

- Not fully disclosing the terms and conditions of the list
- Not using lists for their original intended purpose
- Not obtaining a separate verification for each list to which they add a subscriber

Opt-out clauses, by the way, do not count.

Dial-Up User List (DUL)

List type:	IP-based
DNSBL server:	dialups.mail-abuse.org

The DUL contains a list of reported IP address ranges that are part of an ISP's dial-up network or some other dynamically assigned range. Some ISPs work with MAPS to have their own dial-up networks added to the lists, so they won't be the unwitting accomplices of spammers.

Of course, some legitimate computer hobbyists and end users run SMTP servers on their dial-up accounts. To them, MAPS suggests that they do not send mail directly from their SMTP server, but instead send it through their ISP's SMTP server.

Relay Spam Stopper (RSS)

List type:	IP-based
DNSBL server:	relays.mail-abuse.org

The RSS contains a list of IP addresses reported to have sent bulk e-mails, most of which are open relays. Just because a system is an open relay, however, doesn't mean that it will be in the RSS—it actually has to have sent spam. In this way, this list differs from the ORDB's list, which we'll discuss later in this chapter in the section "Open Relay Database (ORDB)."

Realtime Blackhole List (RBL)

List type:	IP-based
DNSBL server:	blackholes.mail-abuse.org

This is the granddad of all MAPS lists. It includes networks or hosts that fall under the following criteria:

- They have been reported to send spam.
- They are an open relay.
- They are an open proxy.
- They provide support services to spammers, such as web hosting, software, e-mail drop boxes, and more.

Because they include the support-services aspect, the chance of wanted e-mails being blocked is higher than it might be with other, more singular lists.

Realtime Blackhole List+ (RBL+)

List type:	IP-based
DNSBL server:	blackholes.mail-abuse.org

The RBL+ is MAPS's premier subscription service and combines most of its lists, including the RBL, DUL, and RSS. It also includes a list that's available only to RBL+ subscribers, called the Open Proxy Monitor (OPM). The OPM is similar to the RSS, but it contains IPs of systems that are open-proxy servers and have been known to send spam. The RBL+ provides a robust blacklisting method, but you also have a higher chance of blocking wanted e-mails when you use it.

Subscribing to MAPS

After years of being free, MAPS converted to a fee-based service in July 2001. The service is still free for individuals and hobbyists, but all others must pay a yearly subscription fee. Payment levels depend on the type and size of your organization:

- Nonprofit/Educational
- Small Business (less than 100 users)
- Standard (everyone else)

Each list has its own price, with the RBL+ being the most expensive and the DUL being the cheapest. Each list also has different prices for a DNS query versus a DNS zone transfer. The Standard pricing level also has a per-user cost.

The RBL+ also has the capability for a Border Gateway Protocol (BGP) routing feed. BGP is the standard routing protocol on the Internet "backbone." Put another way, it's how Internet traffic knows how to get from point A to point B. If you're an ISP, MAPS can insert routes into your BGP routing table that will prevent spammers from reaching your network. This is a relatively extreme measure, as it blocks *all* Internet traffic from the spammer, not just mail traffic. BGP implementation is beyond the scope of this book.

No matter which level you are, even if you're a hobbyist or individual, you must mail MAPS a signed agreement for the list to which you're interested in subscribing. These agreements are available on the MAPS web site and are, on average, a dozen pages long. In this agreement, you agree that (among other things) you'll hold any information MAPS gives you confidential, and that you understand that just because you're a subscriber doesn't mean you're exempted from getting listed in a MAPS blacklist yourself.

In the agreement, you also put the IP address of the DNS or mail server you intend to use for querying or zone transferring with MAPS (or the address of your router if doing BGP). MAPS uses filters that prevent anyone who hasn't signed an agreement from accessing their lists.

If you're not a hobbyist or individual, pricing for MAPS's services is across the map (pun intended). They can range from $50 per year for a zone transfer of the DUL list for nonprofit pricing, to $1500 (or more) per year for a query against the RBL+ under standard pricing. For MAPS's latest Schedule of Annual Fees, visit its web site (*http://mail-abuse.org/feestructure.html*).

SPAMCOP

SpamCop is a popular DNSBL that has been around since 1998. SpamCop itself is based in Seattle and is run by Julian Haight (who wrote the code) and many contributors. SpamCop has a unique method of keeping its list fresh and removing sites that are no longer spamming in a timely manner, and that appears to make it one of the "fairest" DNSBLs around.

Apart from being a DNSBL, SpamCop also offers filtered POP/IMAP/web-mail accounts. In this chapter, we're not going to go into this service in-depth, but we'll briefly describe it since it's a major component of their business. The SpamCop service currently costs $30 per year per e-mail account. You can either forward your existing e-mail account to the service or use it as a new account under the domain spamcop.net (that is, your e-mail address would be *your_account*@spamcop.net). The service checks incoming mail for viruses, and then it uses SpamCop's DNSBL to decide whether or not the message is spam. If it decides it is spam, it drops the mail into a Hold folder for you to peruse (or not) later. You can check your mail using your existing mail client via either POP or IMAP, or you can use SpamCop's web-mail page.

How SpamCop Works

List type:	IP-based
DNSBLserver:	bl.spamcop.net

Unlike MAPS, SpamCop is a single list. SpamCop doesn't care whether you're running an open relay, open proxy, or mailing from a dial-up IP—it makes no checks of the site's configuration. The only way a site gets on the list is by having someone report it to SpamCop as being a spam sender. Anyone can sign up for SpamCop's free reporting service (though it does require a verifiable e-mail address).

SpamCop uses a ratio-based scoring system to decide how long to keep a site on the blacklist. The score is based on several factors, including how fresh the spam is, how long it has been on the blacklist, and how SpamCop was notified of the spam. We'll go into details on individual scores in the list that follows.

What follows is a breakdown of the submission process and how mail hosts are automatically added or removed from the blacklist:

1. A registered SpamCop user forwards suspected spam (with full headers!) to SpamCop as an attachment. SpamCop's site has a good list of criteria for what it considers spam and what therefore should be forwarded (viruses, hoaxes, and chain letters don't count, for instance).

2. If this is the first spam from that server to hit SpamCop's database, the server won't be immediately listed. If it's the second, it will be listed for 24 hours, unless more suspected spam messages arrive.

3. Suspected spam sites are weighted by freshness. The more recently a spam was received, the higher the score the site that sent it gets. Fresh spam gives the site a premodified score of 4:1, with it sliding down until it reaches a score of 1:1 after 48 hours. Reports older than one week are ignored when calculating weights.

4. SpamCop has a number of addresses called "spamtraps," which are e-mail addresses created for the sole purpose of collecting spam. Because these spamtraps aren't real people, they've never subscribed to any legitimate lists

and do not receive legitimate mail. Reports coming from these spamtraps have their scores multiplied by 5. For instance, if a site has two reports against it from spamtrap sites, it receives a total score of 2×5, or 10:1.

5. To avoid blocking legitimate mail from large sites that might also squeeze out some spam every once in a while (such as AOL), the spam reports are balanced against the total number of legitimate messages sent. This is done by monitoring selected third-party sites. Whenever one of these third-party sites checks against the SpamCop blacklist for an IP address that isn't in there, that host is given a nonspam point. After 1000 points, each subsequent point that a host receives counts for only half of its full value. For instance, a host that gets 3000 nonspam reports will only have 2000 total points.

6. If no spam reports have come in for a listed site within 48 hours, that site is removed from the list.

It's important to note that SpamCop does not block sites that support spammers, such as web sites or e-mail drop boxes; only those that actually sent the spam are blocked.

Subscribing to SpamCop

Unlike using their POP/IMAP/web-mail service, using SpamCop as a DNSBL is free. The company does, however, request a donation to help it keep the service running. If your site has 1 to 10 users, it requests $50 per year; for 11 to 100 users, it requests $150 per year; for sites with more than 100 users, it requests $1 per user per year. The suggested minimum donation for a site larger than 100 is $150; the minimum for a site of 10,000 users is $1000 per year.

SpamCop doesn't allow DNS zone transfers because its list is too dynamic to make zone transfers efficient. Instead, it allows you to mirror the list to your own DNS server using the rsync and SSH utilities. This service, however, costs $1000 per year.

You can make a donation (or pay for the mirroring) using PayPal on SpamCop's web site, or you can mail the company a check at its physical address.

OPEN RELAY DATABASE (ORDB)

The Open Relay Database (ORDB) lists open relays on the Internet and has done so since 2001. ISPs and organizations large and small use ORDB. It's a nonprofit headquartered in Denmark, but it has contributors and users the world over.

ORDB is simply a listing of reported and tested open relays. It's different than MAPS's RSS, in that ORDB doesn't care whether or not the site has actually been used to send spam before, only that it's *technically* an open relay. Therefore, if you use it, there's a chance of blocking mail from legitimate mail servers, even if those servers aren't currently being used by a spammer. The thought is that it's only a matter of time before a spammer finds the open relay and *does* use it, so it's better to go ahead and block the site. This also encourages systems administrators to close their open relays if they know their servers might get blocked. The company's web site is at *http://www.ordb.org*.

How ORDB Works

List type:	IP-based
DNSBL server:	relays.ordb.org

Open-relay candidates are tested when someone enters the IP address of the servers they wish tested on the ORDB web site. The person requesting the test must put in a valid e-mail address, because a reply is required before testing commences. This adds at least some accountability and reduces abuse of the system. Testing can take up to 72 hours, depending on the size of the queue. If a site fails the test and is found to be an open relay, that site will be added to the ORDB blacklist.

Removal of a site occurs in the same way. The IP addresses are entered into the web form, and e-mail is sent to which the submitter must reply; then the site is rechecked. If it passes and isn't found to be an open relay, the site is removed within 72 hours. It the test still detects an open relay, the site stays on the list.

Subscribing to ORDB

ORDB does not require payment, nor do you sign an agreement. Anyone is free to use it, and the organizers believe that use is the best way to support ORDB. It does, however, accept donations of any size on its web site via PayPal, or you can mail a check or money order to the postal address on the site.

DISTRIBUTED SERVER BOYCOTT LIST (DSBL)

The Distributed Server Boycott List (DSBL) is a group of administrators and users who have banded together to fight spam. They are primarily concerned with spam sources that are open relays or open proxies. The DSBL web site is at *http://www.dsbl.org*.

How DSBL Works

The DSBL does not test sites itself. Anybody can submit a site to the DSBL, but two types of users actually do so: *untrusted* and *trusted*. An untrusted user is anyone who reports spam to the DSBL. A trusted user is someone who has requested an account with the DSBL and provides a rationale as to why they should be a trusted user. The DSBL then gives the user a provisional account that can be revoked if the user violates reporting standards the DSBL sets forth.

List

List Type:	IP-based
DNSBLServer:	list.dsbl.org

This list contains only spam sources verified by users trusted to the DSBL staff. Because of this, it has a lower incidence of false positives than the other DSBL lists.

Multihop

List Type:	*IP-based*
DNSBL Server:	*multihop.dsbl.org*

This list contains only multihop relayed spam sources that are verified by users trusted to the DSBL staff. Even though the users are trusted, this list still may cause false positives because it catches all the hops in a spam's path.

Unconfirmed

List Type:	*IP-based*
DNSBL Server:	*unconfirmed.dsbl.org*

Additions to this list are made by untrusted users, so there's a high likelihood of false positives. It's best to use this list sparingly or with some other program, such as SpamAssassin, that just scores or tags likely spam rather than rejecting it outright.

Subscribing to DSBL

No subscription or form is required for any of the DSBL lists. Simply start using them.
In addition to regular query lookups, you can also download the entire zone file using the rsync utility or via HTTP at DSBL's web site.

SPAMHAUS

The operators of Spamhaus believe that 90 percent of all spam in Europe and North America is sent by less than 200 known spammers, which they keep up with in their Registry of Known Spam Operators (ROKSO). By knowing their enemy and tracking their movements from one ISP to another, the Spamhaus Blacklist (SBL) has become a popular and effective DNSBL. Its web site is at *http://www.spamhaus.org*.

How Spamhaus Works

List type:	*IP-based*
DNSBL Server:	*sbl.spamhaus.org*

Spamhaus is updated around the clock by an international team of administrators who are on the watch for known spammers and spamming in progress. Updates are made to the SBL once per hour.
The SBL contains a list of known spammers. It does not contain a list of open proxies or open relays, so Spamhaus suggests using its list in combination with a good open relay/open

proxy list. It uses the following criteria to decide whether a given IP address will be listed in the SBL:

- **Spam Sources**   Spammers sending bulk e-mail from an IP address directly under the spammer's control
- **Spam Gangs**   Netblocks of known spammers listed in the ROKSO
- **Spam Services**   Web servers, mail servers, DNS servers, and other services used by spammers
- **Spam Support Services**   IP addresses that knowingly provide hosting, spamware, or other support services for spammers

IP addresses that end up in the SBL remain there until the spamming source has been removed and Spamhaus has been notified. Spamhaus itself does no further checks on the IP addresses. However, to keep entries from getting old, Spamhaus expires records from the SBL. The timeouts are two, seven, or fourteen days for unidentified spam sources; six months for persistent spammers; or a year or more for well-known spammers such as those in the ROKSO.

Subscribing to Spamhaus

Spamhaus doesn't cost anything to use, and you don't have to fill out any forms to use it. You simply set it up as you would any other DNSBL. It even allows DNS zone transfers for free if you're from a large enough organization (such as an ISP, university, or large company). To request this service, you must contact Spamhaus directly.

NOT JUST ANOTHER BOGUS LIST (NJABL)

Not Just Another Bogus List (NJABL) is run by a group of e-mail administrators who are frustrated with the policies and uptime of existing DNSBLs. They decided to take matters into their own hands and created a blacklist that is almost entirely supported by the e-mail administrators who use it.

How NJABL Works

List type:	IP-based
DNSBL server:	dnsbl.njabl.org

The NJABL has only one list. The NJABL includes any IP address in its list that meets the following criteria:

- The system is an open relay, open proxy, or is running an open web-to-mail gateway.

- The IP address belongs to a dial-up or dynamic range. This information is received through American Registry for Internet Numbers (ARIN) records or by ISPs reporting such ranges to them directly.
- The system has been used to send out spam directly.

NJABL tests for open proxies by scanning individual servers for them. It then does an open-relay test by scanning the SMTP port. It takes about four weeks to remove a system from the list.

Subscribing to NJABL

NJABL is basically run by the administrators who use it. You don't need to pay anything to subscribe, nor do you have to sign up anywhere. You can simply start using it whenever you like. The only thing they ask is that you subscribe to *list@njabl.org* to receive the latest announcements.

You can also contribute to NJABL by feeding IP addresses that connect to your mail server. You change your connection method so that anyone connecting to your server consents to be scanned as an open relay. Later, NJABL tests each of those servers for open relays.

NJABL is normally used in query mode, but you can also get an rsync zone transfer by e-mailing *help@njabl.org*.

RFC IGNORANT (RFCI)

RFCI sets itself apart from the rest of the DNSBLs because it is not concerned whether or not a site is, or could be, a spammer. In fact, instead of worrying about spam, RFCI is more concerned about whether or not a domain or IP network block's administrator is a good "Netizen" (that is, citizen of the Internet). The domain and network blocks in the RFCI have been placed there because their owners are deemed "RFC ignorant."

You may have heard the term *RFC* before and are vaguely aware of it being related to Internet standards (numerous companies tout their products as being "RFC compliant"). *RFC* stands for *Request for Comments*, which is the common name for the rules and best practices ratified and published by the Internet Engineering Task Force (IETF). Many RFCs are like technical blueprints, but some RFCs are human protocols—best practices for configuring and running networks and servers on the Internet. Domains are listed in the RFCI because their owners have refused or ignored these policies and procedures.

How is this related to spamming? Spammers try to hide as much information about themselves as possible. Most of the RFC practices that RFCI checks for relate to actually getting into contact with a human being. If a spammer has registered a domain, he's likely to provide bogus contact information so that you can't track him down and complain (or, possibly, litigate). Hence, a good portion of RFCI's denizens are likely to be spammers.

RFCI can be found at *http://www.rfc-ignorant.org*. The online RFC papers can be found at *http://www.ietf.org* under "RFC Pages."

What Makes Someone RFC Ignorant?

RFCs aren't laws, so no criminal penalty is enforced for breaking them. Since the beginnings of the Internet, however, administrators have chosen to shun unrepentant violators (some software programmatically does this). For inclusion in the RFCI, a site has to demonstrate that its owners failed to implement one or more of the RFC guidelines listed in the following sections.

Delivery Status Notification (DSN)-Related

List type:	Domain-based
DNSBL server:	dsn.rfc-ignorant.org
Relevant RFCs:	821, 2821, 2505, 1123

Inclusion in this list occurs if the mail exchanger (MX) record for the sender's domain does not accept mail with the originating address given as <> (blank). For instance, if we send mail to the MX server exampledomain.tld using these SMTP commands,

```
MAIL FROM <>
RCPT TO <postmaster@exampledomain.tld>
```

and the server doesn't accept the message, exampledomain.tld is added to the list. All MX records for a domain are checked, and having one that doesn't accept mail with a blank sender address is cause for inclusion. Domains with MX records that contain private or reserved IP addresses (for instance, a loopback address or networks in RFC 1918, such as 10.0.0.0/8) are also listed.

Postmaster-Related

List type:	Domain-based
DNSBL server:	postmaster.rfc-ignorant.org
Relevant RFC:	2821

The postmaster address is designated for reporting problems with mail servers. Inclusion in this list occurs if the sender's domain (with an MX record) does not have a valid postmaster e-mail address. An example is postmaster@exampledomain.tld. And, yes, e-mails to the postmaster must ultimately go to a human being, even if an auto-response is sent first.

Abuse-Related

List type:	Domain-based
DNSBL server:	abuse.rfc-ignorant.org
Relevant RFC:	2142

The abuse address is designated to report spamming, fraud, and other mail-related incidents by a given domain's users. Inclusion in this list occurs if the sender's domain (with an MX record) does not have a valid abuse e-mail address—for example, abuse@exampledomain.net. As with the postmaster, the abuse address must ultimately go to a human being.

WHOIS-Related

List type:	Domain-based
DNSBL server:	postmaster.rfc-ignorant.org
Relevant RFC:	954

The WHOIS database contains contact information for owners of a domain, including e-mail addresses. This applies to both the generic Top Level Domains (or gTLDs, such as .com, .org., or .net), as well as the country-coded Top Level Domains (ccTLDs, such as .us, .uk, or .de). The registrars for these domains run their own WHOIS servers to provide this information.

Many domain registrars, however, don't check up on the information their customers provide, so it's possible to include bogus points of contact, leave some information blank, or let information get stale.

A domain is included in this list if it meets the following criteria:

- Information is obviously bogus or wrong (such as a U.S. phone number of 555-1212 or address of 1600 Pennsylvania Ave., Washington, D.C.—for any user other than the White House).

- Information is provably wrong, such as phone lines that are out of service, e-mail addresses that bounce, or returned snail mail.

- The TLD for that domain does not have an operating WHOIS server, referred to by the root WHOIS server at whois.iana.org.

- The domains in the e-mail contact addresses do not have valid MX records, or have records that are obviously bogus (such as a loopback address or an RFC 1918 reserved address such as 10.10.10.10).

A domain's record does not need to have a valid fax number, as not everyone has a fax. However, the domain site is expected to have valid voice phone numbers, e-mail accounts, and postal addresses that someone actually checks and responds to.

IPWHOIS-Related

List type:	IP-based
DNSBL server:	postmaster.rfc-ignorant.org
Relevant RFC:	954

IPWHOIS is much like WHOIS except it relates to the registry contact information for IP address network blocks, rather than domains. The policy for inclusion in this list is practically the same as for the WHOIS databases. If any bogus information is included in the IPWHOIS record in that netblock's Regional Internet Registry (RIR), the netblock will be included. If a large netblock is included in the list, such as 192.168.0.0/16, all subnets under that network are also included (for instance, 192.168.5.0/24). Thus, a problem with the parent network causes problems with the child. In other words, if your ISP turns out to be noncompliant, your network isn't compliant either.

It's important to note that IPWHOIS is the only RFCI service that is IP-based (that is, the criteria is based on the IP address of the e-mail's sender, rather than the domain).

Subscribing to RFCI

Use of RFCI is completely free, and you don't need to sign an agreement to use its services. Just put the listing servers you want to use in your DNSBL-capable mail server or client, and that's it. RFCI provides a web interface to report RFC ignorance and e-mail address to have a domain or IP netblock removed. You can also subscribe to a mailing list for community-based support.

Now that you've been introduced to some of the blacklists, we'll show you how to implement them. We focus on three mail server packages: Sendmail and Postfix for Linux and Unix, and Exchange for Microsoft Windows.

IMPLEMENTING DNSBLS WITHIN SENDMAIL

Sendmail is the most venerable mail transfer agent on the Internet and runs on most Unix and Unix-like operating systems. (In fact, almost every major distribution of Linux comes with Sendmail.) Sendmail added direct DNSBL support with version 8.9, and changed the syntax slightly in 8.10. Support was also possible in version 8.8, but you had to hack your sendmail.cf configuration file to do it. However, due to security vulnerabilities in earlier versions of Sendmail, including major buffer overflows discovered in the spring and fall of 2003 (see CERT Advisories CA-2003-12 and CA-2003-25), we highly recommend that you run the latest stable version. You can find Sendmail at http://www.sendmail.org.

Configuring Sendmail for IP-Based DNSBLs

By Sendmail standards, configuring Sendmail to use IP-based DNSBLs post version 8.10 is quite straightforward. Edit the sendmail.mc file, or equivalent .mc file, that you're using. If you are unfamiliar with .mc files, they are macro definitions compiled with the *m4* application to create sendmail.cf configuration files. Check Sendmail's documentation or web site for more information. DSNBL support is configured as an m4 Feature.

The easiest DNSBL to use is the MAPS RBL, as support is preconfigured. All you have to do is edit your sendmail.mc file and add the following line *before* the MAILER section:

```
FEATURE(`dnsbl')
```

Note that the first single quote is actually the *grave accent* (a backward apostrophe that's typically on the upper-left side of your keyboard).

Then, back up your current sendmail.cf file and compile your mc file to create the .cf file:

```
# m4 sendmail.mc > sendmail.cf
```

If it's successful, you won't get any messages. Then restart Sendmail using the new .cf file.

To use other DNSBLs, you have to specify the server within the FEATURE command. Here's the basic syntax:

```
FEATURE(`dnsbl',<zone server>, <rejection message for remote server and logs>)
```

Here's the ORDB's DNSBL for an example:

```
FEATURE(`dnsbl',`relays.ordb.org',`"550 Email rejected due to sending server ¬
misconfiguration - see http://www.ordb.org/faq/\#why_rejected"')dnl
```

For multiple entries, add a FEATURE line for each relay you wish to use.

Configuring Sendmail for Domain-Based RHSBLs

Using RHSBLs under Sendmail requires that you add a different FEATURE command to your sendmail.mc file. This feature is not part of the standard Sendmail distribution. You can download Derek J. Balling's rhbl.m4 file from *http://www.megacity.org/software_downloads/ rhsbl.m4*. Put this file in the ./cf/feature directory of your Sendmail source tree, or wherever you have stored your .cf configuration files. Then add the RHSBL to your .mc file using this syntax:

```
FEATURE(rhsbl, <zone server>, <rejection message for remote server and logs>)
```

For example, here's how to use the RFCI's DSN domain-based blacklist:

```
FEATURE(rhsbl,`dsn.rfc-ignorant.org',`"550 Mail from domain " $`'&{RHS} "
refused. ¬
MX of domain do not accept bounces. This violates RFC 821/2505/2821 - see ¬
http://www.rfc-ignorant.org/"')
```

As with the DNSBLs, add a FEATURE statement for each RHSBL you want to use.

IMPLEMENTING DNSBLS WITH POSTFIX

Postfix is another popular Sendmail replacement for Unix and Unix-like operating systems, designed by Wietse Venema while he worked at IBM. IBM released it to the public in 1998 and Postfix is credited with instigating Big Blue's open-source strategy. Postfix was designed with security and speed in mind. We're going to cover only Postfix 2.*x* here. Postfix can be had at *http://www.postfix.org*.

Configuring Postfix for IP-Based DNSBLs

Postfix is probably one of the simplest mail servers to configure for DNSBLs. All you have to do is edit your main.cf file (usually in /etc/postfix) and modify (or add) the `smtpd_client_restrictions` line. This line controls many spam-related functions, including anti-relaying provisions.

To configure Postfix 2.x to reject mail included in a DNSBL, make the following modifications:

```
smtpd_client_restrictions =
      reject_rbl_client <zone server>
```

where `<zone server>` is the DNSBL you want to use. For instance:

```
smtpd_clients_restrictions =
      reject_rbl_client sbl.spamhaus.org
```

To add multiple listings, separate each `reject_rbl_client` line with a comma:

```
smtpd_client_restrictions =
      reject_rbl_client sbl.spamhaus.org,
      reject_rbl_client relays.ordb.org,
      reject_rbl_client lists.dsbl.org
```

Restart Postfix to implement the changes. Rejected e-mails show up in your log file.

Configuring Postfix for Domain-Based RHSBLs

Postfix 2.*x* has built-in RHSBL support. You configure it much the same way as you do DNSBLs, except that you use the `reject_rhsbl_sender` command. Configure it like this:

```
smtpd_client_restrictions =
      reject_rhsbl_sender <zone server>
```

Here is an example with an RFC Ignorant list:

```
smtpd_client_restrictions =
     reject_rhsbl_sender dsn.rfc-ignorant.org
```

To add multiple RHSBLs (or combine them with DNSBLs) simply separate them by commas:

```
smtpd_client_restrictions =
     reject_rbl_client sbl.spamhaus.org,
     reject_rbl_client relays.ordb.org,
     reject_rbl_client list.dsbl.org,
     reject_rhsbl_sender dsn.rfc-ignorant.org,
     reject_rhsbl_sender postmaster.rfc-ignorant.org,
     reject_rhsbl_sender whois.rfc-ignorant.org
```

Restart Postfix after making changes. Rejected e-mails will show up in your log file.

IMPLEMENTING DNSBLS WITH MICROSOFT EXCHANGE

While Sendmail and Postfix are still the darlings of many ISPs, data centers, and Unix-based shops, Microsoft's Exchange Server is the most popular corporate e-mail system. While many companies no doubt front-end their Exchange Server with a server running one of the three implementations mentioned earlier, without a doubt many Exchange servers also process mail on the front-end.

Exchange 2000 (assuming most of you have upgraded from Exchange 5 and 5.5 by now) had little in the way of anti-spam features. Exchange 2000 required third-party plug-ins or front-end servers to deal with spam. Exchange 2003 has rectified the situation by introducing its own spam-fighting features. We'll discuss this progression as it pertains to DNSBLs.

Exchange 2000

Exchange 2000 requires that you use a third-party application to implement DNSBLs. Almost any anti-spam package for Exchange supports DNSBLs, including those we cover in Chapter 11. You can also use two freeware (but not open-source) programs with Exchange 2000.

The first is a freeware version of GFI Mail Essentials, which can be found at http://www.gfi.com. The freeware version lacks a few of the anti-spam features of its full version, but for DNSBLs it should work just fine. If an e-mail is identified as coming from a spammer, GFI lets you tag it and optionally shunt it off into a public folder. Note that GFI also requires that you run Internet Information Services 5 (IIS 5) SMTP service.

Another piece of free DNSBL software for Exchange is ORFilter, available at *http://www.martijnjongen.com/eng/orfilter/*. You can configure ORFilter to block spam or to tag it. ORFilter runs on Exchange 2000 or the Microsoft SMTP service.

Exchange 2003

Microsoft Exchange 2003 has the built-in ability to use IP-based DNSBLs. RHSBL support may come in the future, but it is not currently available. As might be expected in a Windows environment, a nice graphical user interface (GUI) is available for managing DNSBLs, blacklists, and whitelists.

To add DNSBLs to Exchange 2003, open the Exchange System Manager by selecting Start | Programs | Microsoft Exchange (if you've installed it elsewhere, go to the appropriate menu item). The Exchange System Manager should appear. Under the Tree tab on the left-hand side of the window, open the Global Settings folder, as shown in Figure 5-1.

Right-click the Message Delivery item underneath the Global Settings folder and select Properties. Then click the Connection Filtering tab at the top. You will see a Message Deliver Properties window like that shown in Figure 5-2. The Block List Service Configuration box includes two columns: Rule and Enabled. If you've never configured a DNSBL on your server before, these areas will be empty.

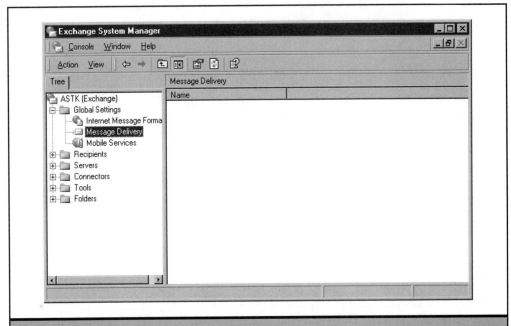

Figure 5-1. The Exchange System Manager for Exchange 2003

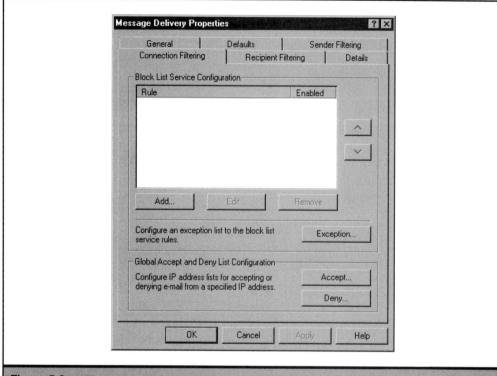

Figure 5-2. The Message Delivery Properties window, where you manage DNSBLs on Exchange 2003

To add a DNSBL, click the Add button. A Connection Filtering Rule dialog box pops up. This is where you'll add your DNSBL information. The first field is Display Name, where you can type in any description you want to give this particular rule. Our first DNSBL will be the Spamhaus SBL; therefore, we'll call our first rule, SpamHaus Black List. The second field, DNS Suffix Of Provider, is equivalent to what we've been referring to as the DNSBL Server in this chapter. Spamhaus' zone server is *sbl.spamhaus.org*, so we'll add that in. This is really all you need to get started, and it will look like Figure 5-3.

At this point, you can go back and add other IP-based DNSBLs in addition to Spamhaus.

Another option in this window is to add a custom error message by entering it into the Custom Error Message To Return field. This is an optional field and is not required for the DNSBL to work. It is useful, however, if you want the mail to be rejected with some specific error message (no taunting, please!).

Finally, you can also modify what return status code from the DNSBL the Exchange server uses by clicking the Return Status Code From Provider Service button. You will then see the Return Status Code dialog box, as shown in Figure 5-4. Remember that most DNSBLs respond with "codes" (actually IP addresses) within the loopback range of

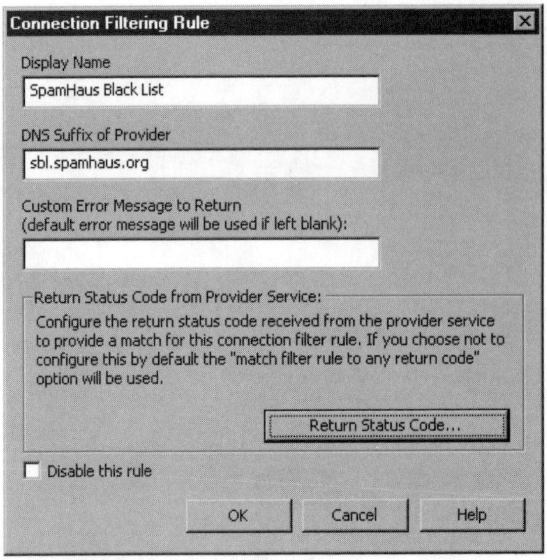

Figure 5-3. The Connection Filtering Rule dialog box for adding DNSBLs in Exchange 2003

127.0.0.0/8. The default (and first radio button) option is to use any response from the DNSBL as a positive response. The second radio button option lets you use a specific mask for the loopback range. The third option lets you select a specific value for the response. The last two options are useful for DNSBLs that have one Zone Server but specific "lists" underneath that server. For instance, a DNSBL's open relay list might return a 127.0.0.5, their open proxy list 127.0.0.6, and their dial-up list 127.0.0.7. This lets you create separate rules for each one of those lists.

Returning to the Message Delivery Properties window (Figure 5-2), you will see a button labeled Exception. Clicking this will bring up the Block List Service Configuration Settings dialog box, as shown in Figure 5-5. Here you can add local e-mail addresses to which you do not want the blacklists to apply. This is especially useful for addresses that must accept mail delivery, such as postmaster or abuse, and for addresses that concern you because they might lose mail—a sales address, for example.

Other options on the Message Delivery Properties window include the ability to allow and deny certain IP addresses or IP subnets from sending you mail. These are equivalent to local whitelists and blacklists and are configured in dialog boxes that open by clicking the Accept and Deny buttons, respectively. Note that these settings override the DNSBL settings, and that addresses or networks under the Accept list will override those under the Deny list.

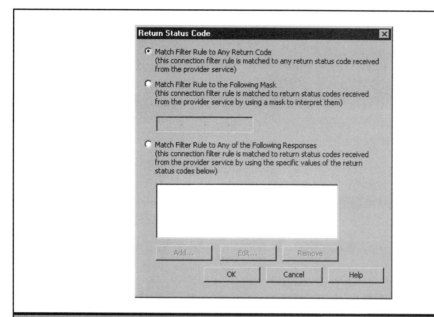

Figure 5-4. The Return Status Code dialog box lets you modify expected responses from DNSBLs under Exchange 2003.

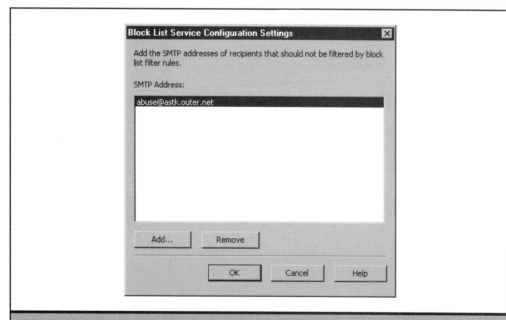

Figure 5-5. The Block List Service Configuration Settings dialog box lets you exclude local users from having their inbound mail checked against the blacklists in Exchange 2003.

Anti-Spam Tool Kit

Once you configured your rules and have clicked OK, you're not quite done yet. You still need to apply the filters to your virtual SMTP servers. Back under the Tree tab of the Exchange System Manager, open the Servers folder and go to Servers | <Your System Name> | SMTP | Default SMTP Virtual Server, as shown in Figure 5-6.

Right-click Default SMTP Virtual Server and select Properties. You will then see the Default SMTP Virtual Server Properties window, as shown in Figure 5-7. Click the Advanced button.

The Advanced button will take you to the Advanced window, which lists the IP identities for the virtual server and tells you whether or not it's filtered. This is shown in Figure 5-8. Select the identity of the server to which you want to apply the filter and click the Edit button.

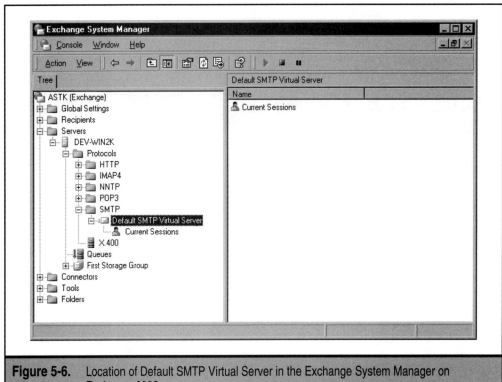

Figure 5-6. Location of Default SMTP Virtual Server in the Exchange System Manager on Exchange 2003

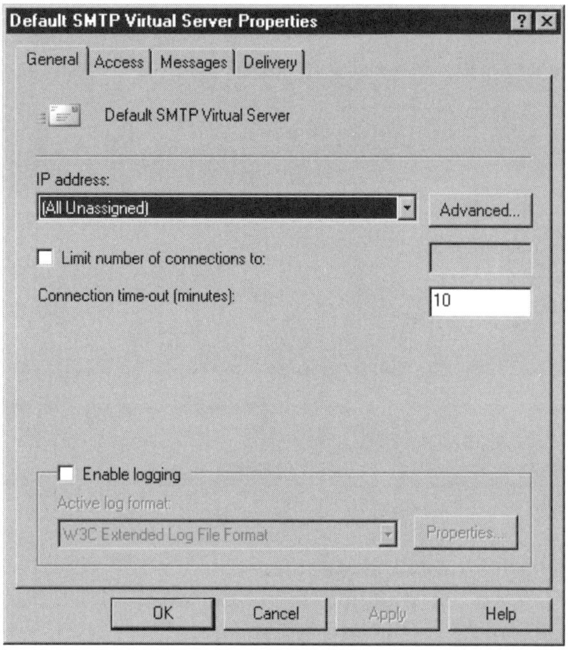

Chapter 5: Blocking Spammers with DNS Blacklists

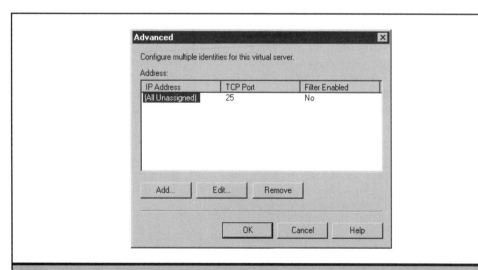

Figure 5-7. The Default SMTP Virtual Server Properties window in Exchange 2003

Figure 5-8. The Advanced properties window tells you the filtering status of your virtual server identities in Exchange 2003.

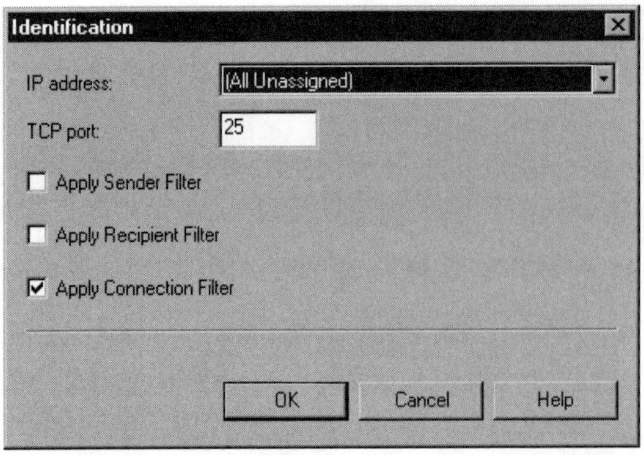

Figure 5-9. The Identification dialog box is where you apply DNSBL filters to a virtual server in Exchange 2003.

After clicking the Edit button, the Identification dialog box will appear. The only item that concerns the filters on this dialog is the bottommost check box, Apply Connection Filters, as shown in Figure 5-9. Check this box, and then click OK to apply this setting. Verify it is enabled in the Advanced properties window. You must follow these steps for each virtual server to which you want to apply your DNSBL filters.

SUMMARY

DNS Blacklists help you reduce spam by allowing you to reject, tag, or score e-mail that comes from known or potential spam sources. It gives you the benefit of the experience and resources of others. The primary pitfall of a DNSBL is the relatively high chance of gross false positives—more than most other anti-spam solutions. Entire networks of e-mail could potentially be lost should a major mail server or service reach a DNSBL. Likewise, you're placing a high degree of trust in the people running and contributing to the DNSBLs.

By understanding the technology and philosophy behind individual blacklists, you'll be able to choose those that suit your needs. Most e-mail servers and anti-spam software support DNSBLs either natively or through third-party add-ons, so there's no reason why DNSBLs shouldn't be a part of your anti-spam strategy. Just don't rely on them as your primary means to thwart spam.

CHAPTER 6
FILTERING SPAM WITH SPAMASSASSIN

Now that you understand the theoretical, philosophical, and practical basics of spamming and spam fighting, and you have a thorough understanding of DNS Blacklists and their place in your arsenal, we'll look at one of the most popular anti-spam programs to hit the Internet in recent years: SpamAssassin. SpamAssassin uses a number of techniques to identify spam, including blacklists, pattern matching, and Bayesian learning. In this chapter, we'll introduce you to SpamAssassin, help you understand how it works, and show you how to install and configure it on your system. Chapter 7 will delve deeper into SpamAssassin Bayesian learning capabilities, and Chapter 8 will cover advanced SpamAssassin topics, including integration with other mail-filtering programs.

DOSSIER OF A SPAM ASSASSIN

SpamAssassin is a spam filtering utility written in the Perl scripting language (*http://www.perl.org*), with a few extra utilities written in the C programming language. SpamAssassin made its appearance in April 2001. Since that time, it has steadily grown in popularity and attained wide support in the open-source community. The SpamAssassin project's web site is at *http://www.spamassassin.org/*.

SpamAssassin = Spam Detective

SpamAssassin analyzes the headers and body of incoming e-mail against its rather large (nearing 900) and often-updated set of rules. It uses these rules to assign the e-mail a score that is used to decide whether or not it is spam. The rules go beyond simple pattern-matching and employ heuristics to determine whether a rule is appropriate. The analysis strategies of SpamAssassin include these:

- **Header analysis** SpamAssassin looks at the source of the mail, whether or not it was sent from a valid e-mail client (or if it's from known spamware), invalid time zones, and other signs of erroneous or forged information.

- **Body analysis** A lot of spam "looks" the same. For instance, it may have a number of lines beckoning you to "click here," a lot of YELLING!, bad HTML, disclaimers, and key phrases such as "don't miss out" and "absolutely free." SpamAssassin pores over the body of each message looking for such indicators.

- **Bayesian analysis** Since version 2.5, SpamAssassin has included a Bayesian spam classifier. This allows SpamAssassin to "learn" what is and what is not spam from a user's input. It can also auto-learn whether a piece of e-mail is spam or ham (a piece of mail the user wants) based on its score. We will look at SpamAssassin Bayesian functionality in depth in Chapter 7.

- **DNS Blacklists** SpamAssassin includes ready support for most of the major DNSBLs. As discussed in Chapter 5, one downside of DNSBLs is their propensity for false positives. If your mail server is configured to reject mail outright based on DNSBLs, the chance of losing legitimate mail is high. The advantage of using SpamAssassin is that instead of outright rejecting mail, it simply adds to the e-mail's overall spam score—thus mitigating the false positive effect. The scores can also be tweaked based on your own experiences with individual DNSBLs.

- **Checksum databases**   SpamAssassin can also use collaborative checksum databases such as Vipul's Razor (discussed in Chapter 13) and the Distributed Checksum Clearinghouse (DCC). As with blacklists, being listed in one of these databases merely adds to an e-mail's overall spam score.

Because SpamAssassin is a "hybrid" anti-spam tool that uses a variety of analysis techniques to identify spam, it is more effective than any one of these techniques used singly. This makes it more difficult for spammers to defeat. Even if a spammer manages to stay out of the DNSBLs or the checksum databases, for instance, there is still a good chance that the header and body analysis features will catch them.

SpamAssassin Rules!

The key to how SpamAssassin works is in its *rules*—tests against the header and body of messages to determine the likelihood of the message being spam. Many of these rules are regular expression (regex) checks against headers and bodies. Regular expressions are ways you can search and match full or partial text, and they're often used in shell and Perl scripts. In fact, Perl excels at this sort of text parsing. Other rules call specific SpamAssassin functions that are too complex for mere pattern matching.

SpamAssassin's rules are stored within a series of configuration files, each file categorized based on its test (for example, headers, body, DNSBL, porn, HTML, and so on). You can also create your own regex-based rules, which we'll talk about in Chapter 8.

Here's an example of a regex header check on the subject of a message:

```
header SUBJ_GUARANTEED        Subject =~ /^guaranteed|(?-i:GUARANTEE)/i
describe SUBJ_GUARANTEED      Subject GUARANTEED
```

The `header` directive tells SpamAssassin that it's a header check. `SUBJ_GUARANTEED` is a unique identifier for this particular rule. The `Subject=` line lets it know that it's a subject check. The rest is a regular expression looking for the words *guaranteed* or *guarantee*. The `i` switch tells it to ignore the case of the word (which is good, because otherwise the spammer could just randomize the case). The line after that, the `describe` line, just gives a description of the rule.

SpamAssassin Scores!

Each SpamAssassin rule is assigned a specific score. The SpamAssassin team derives this score from probability statistics (using a genetic algorithm) based on a corpus of spam and ham (nonspam). For instance, for our `SUBJ_GUARANTEED` rule, we have this:

```
score SUBJ_GUARANTEED 2.895 2.407 2.696 2.504
```

All those numbers after the rule identifier are scores. Why do four different scores appear? SpamAssassin will use a different score based on your particular configuration. They are, in order, as follows:

1. Both Bayesian analysis and network tests (for example, DNSBLs) are disabled.
2. Bayes is disabled, but network tests are enabled.
3. Bayes is enabled, but network tests are disabled.
4. Both Bayes and network tests are enabled.

For each test on which the message hits, that score is then added to the message's total score. By default, a total score of 5 or above will classify a message as spam. This can be changed, however, on a per-user or site-wide basis, as we'll see later in this chapter in the sections "The local.cf Configuration File" and "The user_prefs Configuration File."

For an illustration of SpamAssassin's data flow, see Figure 6-1.

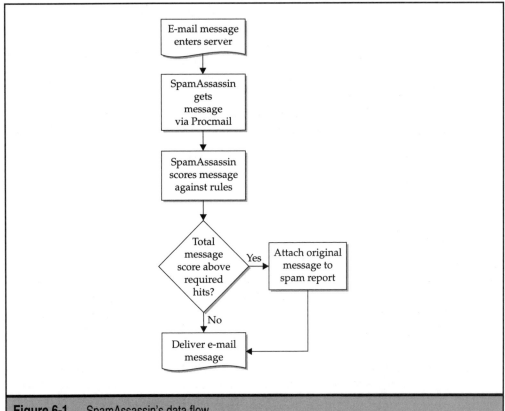

Figure 6-1. SpamAssassin's data flow

Killer Features

While its robust spam-detection measures are great features, SpamAssassin provides a number of other practical reasons for its widespread use, which also explains why we're giving it so many pages in Part II of this book.

- *It's user-modifiable.* Most of SpamAssassin's configuration is done through text-based configuration files. The majority of the rules, and the scores associated with those rules, are in text-based configuration files. This means that it's easy for a user or an administrator to make his or her own modifications to how SpamAssassin identifies and deals with spam.
- *It's free.* SpamAssassin is distributed under the same artistic license as Perl, which makes sense given how much it relies on the Perl scripting language. This means you can use it in as many installations as you want, without regard to licensing fees.
- *It's an application programming interface.* SpamAssassin isn't just a program. Most of its functions are part of a Perl application programming interface (API) module called Mail::SpamAssassin. This means that SpamAssassin classes can be used in a variety of other programs on a number of platforms.

SpamAssassin's licensing and its API means that it's also easy for commercial software developers to incorporate it into their products. We'll discuss some of them in the section that follows.

SpamAssassin Gone Commercial

The SpamAssassin trademark is owned by Network Associates, Inc., and the company allows the open-source project to use it. The SpamAssassin code, as we've said, is under the same artistic license as Perl. The artistic license states—among other things—that SpamAssassin can be included as part of a larger commercial package if it is embedded in that package. Therefore, the SpamAssassin engine has found its way into a number of commercial products, including the following:

- **Spamnix**   A Eudora plug-in for both Windows and Mac platforms. Web site: *http://www.spamnix.com/*
- **SpamKiller for Microsoft Exchange Small Business**   This product was formerly known as Deersoft's SpamAssassin for Exchange until Network Associates bought that company. Now it's part of the SpamKiller line. Web site: *http://www.nai.com/*
- **PureMessage**   This product, from Active State, acts as a mail gateway and also filters viruses. Many universities and large organizations use Active State, and it runs on nearly all Unix-based platforms. Web site: *http://www.activestate.com/*

In this chapter, we don't cover the commercial variants of SpamAssassin, only the main distribution (for Linux) from the SpamAssassin web site. See Part III for commercial versions and versions for other platforms.

INSTALLING SPAMASSASSIN

In this section we walk you through the installation of SpamAssassin on Linux-based systems. (This also applies to most Unix-based systems.) Typically, when you talk about installing software, you list hardware requirements and any prerequisite software you might need. Here, we also recommend that you have experience installing software on a Linux or Unix system. Although SpamAssassin's installation and configuration process is simple relative to some tools, we don't recommend that you cut your Unix teeth on it, either. A good working knowledge of how your system processes mail and its message transfer agent (MTA) is also recommended. MTAs can include the previously discussed Sendmail and Postfix.

In this section we'll discuss installing SpamAssassin in depth—the requirements for using it and how to install it. You can install SpamAssassin via three main methods:

- **The Comprehensive Perl Archive Network (CPAN)**   An automated means of downloading and installing Perl programs and modules. Web site: *http://www.cpan.org/*.
- **Tarball**   A *tarball* is Unix lingo for a file and directory archive created by the *tar* utility. In this case, it contains the entire build directory of SpamAssassin.
- **CVS**   The Concurrent Versioning System is the file tree that developers use to write code and make changes to SpamAssassin. This allows the check-in and check-out of modified code. As an anonymous user, you'll only be able to check it out.

We'll cover all of these methods in depth and give you the pros and cons of each. Now, let's get ready to install SpamAssassin.

Software and Hardware Requirements

SpamAssassin won't run as-is on most systems. First you must install a number of software prerequisites. To run all this software and process e-mail, your computer system will need to match certain basic minimum requirements.

Required Software

You must install the following tools before installing SpamAssassin:

- **A Linux, BSD, or Unix OS**   The main SpamAssassin distribution runs only on Unix and Unix-like operating systems. We're going to concentrate on running it on Linux, since it's the most widely used of any of these operating systems.

- **Perl**   SpamAssassin itself is a Perl API, and it relies heavily on Perl. Any modern version of Perl should do the trick, but you'll probably at least want version 5.6.0. For this installation, we're using version 5.8.0. Perl is included with all major Linux distributions and can be found at *http://www.perl.org/*.

- **An MTA**   This can be any mail server for Unix, the three most popular being Sendmail, postfix, and qmail. Because these are external-facing services that accept remote connections, we highly recommend you use the latest version of each. For this installation, we're using Sendmail 8.12.10, so if you want to follow along, you should also use Sendmail. Sendmail is probably the oldest and most widely available MTA. If your Linux distribution doesn't already include Sendmail (which is highly unlikely), you can find it at *http://www.sendmail.org/*.

- **Procmail**   You must have some way for your MTA to send mail to SpamAssassin for analysis and tagging. The easiest way to do this is through Procmail. Other options are available, however, and we'll cover them in Chapter 8. Any modern version of Procmail should work fine. For this installation, we're running version 3.22. You can find Procmail in most Linux distributions or at *http://www.procmail.org/*.

- **GCC and GNU Make**   These are required to build the C portion of SpamAssassin. They come standard with most Linux distributions, or they can be found at *http://www.gnu.org/*.

In addition to Perl, MTA, Procmail, and the GNU tools, make sure you have any other utilities you might need, such as syslog (or equivalent) for logging and sshd for secure remote access to your server, both of which come by default on nearly every Linux distribution.

The Perl Modules

In addition to the aforementioned programs, SpamAssassin works with a number of Perl modules. We'll go through these and assign each a "status" for inclusion based on the following list:

- **Required**   "Must-have" modules necessary for SpamAssassin to run on your system

- **Recommended**   Modules that greatly increase SpamAssassin's performance or functionality

- **Optional**   Modules that usually add features but that are not required for SpamAssassin to run or perform at its peak

Those features that are required for SpamAssassin to work will be labeled as such. We'll use the label *Recommended* for those modules that we believe greatly increase SpamAssassin's functionality. Others are labeled *Optional*.

ExtUtils::MakeMaker

Status: Required

ExtUtils::MakeMaker is actually required for SpamAssassin to *build*, so there's no getting around it. You'll need version 5.45 or later. It's included in Perl 5.6, or it is available in the Comprehensive Perl Archive Network (CPAN), available at *http://www.cpan.org/*.

File::Spec

Status: Required

File::Spec is required for certain file operations SpamAssassin performs. You must have version 0.8 or later. It is also included with Perl 5.6 or available at CPAN.

Pod::Usage

Status: Required

This module deals with documentation operations within SpamAssassin. You need version 1.10 or later. Pod::Usage is included in Perl 5.6 or is available at CPAN.

HTML::Parser

Status: Required

As you might expect, this module parses HTML. With all the e-mail clients (and spammers!) using HTML these days, version 3.0 or later of HTML::Parser is required. You might as well get the latest version. It comes with Perl 5.6 or is available at CPAN.

Sys::Syslog

Status: Required

Sys::Syslog allows one of the SpamAssassin utilities (spamd, which we'll talk about in the section "Understanding SpamAssassin's Components") to log to the Syslog logging facility. If you're running Perl 5.6, it's already there (actually, it's included in earlier 5.*x* versions as well, but you might as well be up to date if possible and run at least Perl 5.6). It's also available at CPAN.

DB_File

Status: Required/Recommended

DB_File is a database package that SpamAssassin needs for its Bayes data. So if Bayesian analysis is a requirement for you, so is this file. It will also speed up access to the automatic whitelist (autowhitelist) database. If you don't care about doing Bayesian analysis, it's not required, but we still recommend it. It's available on CPAN.

Net::DNS

Status: Recommended

This module gives SpamAssassin the DNS functionality to check DNS Blacklists (DNSBLs), including those discussed in Chapter 5. You'll probably want this. It's available from CPAN.

Razor, DCC, and Pyzor

Status: Recommended

These are actually three separate modules, but all perform the same basic function: They allow SpamAssassin to check messages against three different collaborative filtering networks. The first, Razor, will check against Vipul's Razor; DCC against the Distributed Checksum Clearinghouse; and Pyzor against the Razor-like Pyzor database. Because we cover these in Chapter 13, we won't go in depth here. Suffice to say that you'll need them if you want to use SpamAssassin in conjunction with these filtering networks. You can find them at *http://razor.sourceforge.net*, *http://www.rhyolite.com/anti-spam/dcc/*, and *http://pyzor.sourceforge.net/*, respectively.

Mail::Audit

Status: Optional

Mail::Audit adds some useful mail functionality, such as auto-responses and whatnot. Basically, you need this only if some other program you're using requires it (such as MIMEDefang, discussed in Chapter 8). In most cases, you won't need to use it if you're just running SpamAssassin. If you do need it, you can get it from CPAN.

Digest::SHA1

> Status: Optional

Again, this module is not required, but it may be required by other modules or programs (such as MIMEDefang, discussed in Chapter 8). If you use it, however, it may increase the performance of some hash tests. It is available at CPAN as well.

Required Hardware

The short answer for what kind of hardware you should use is that it should be as fast as possible, have as much RAM as possible, and have enough hard drive space to spool the amount of mail you get. The long answer is going to depend greatly on the following factors:

- The amount of e-mail received by your server
- The rate at which you receive e-mail (for example, messages per hour)
- How much processing SpamAssassin performs on the mail
- What else the SpamAssassin server is doing

Perhaps the best thing to do is show you some of the installations we've set up or seen. A breakdown of these is shown in Table 6-1. All of these installations handle the amount of messages they are processing per day reasonably well. Your mileage may vary!

Before You Start

Before you begin your SpamAssassin installation, make sure that the system is passing e-mail normally without SpamAssassin installed. This applies if you're going to create a SpamAssassin server as a gateway, rather than the final destination for e-mail. Don't set

System Specifications	Average Messages Processed Per Day
CPU: 500 MHz K6-3D RAM: 256MB Hard Drive: 4GB	2300
CPU: Dual 600 MHz PIII RAM: 1GB Hard Drive: 17GB	28,200
CPU: Dual 850 MHz PIII RAM: 1GB Hard Drive: 30GB	58,000

Table 6-1.   Hardware Specifications for Sample SpamAssassin Installations

up the system, put SpamAssassin on it, and then insert it into your mail stream. First, follow these steps:

1. Get your system installed and prepped.
2. Ensure that you have network connectivity.
3. Check your address (A) and mail exchanger (MX) records for the server in DNS.
4. Put your MTA on it (in this case, Sendmail), and configure it appropriately to accept or pass mail.
5. Test your system by sending mail to it. It should either accept it or pass it along. If it doesn't, you know you have a configuration problem on your MTA before SpamAssassin is even installed. This kind of preemptive troubleshooting will save you a lot of time and headaches later on.

We also recommend that if you've turned on any type of DNSBL lookups in your MTA configuration (as we showed you how to do in Chapter 5), you now turn them *off*. Completely remove DNSBLs from your configuration. We're going to let SpamAssassin handle that from now on, to take advantage of its heuristics and scoring system.

Installing the Easy Way: From CPAN

Installing from CPAN is by far the simplest way to install SpamAssassin on your system. What makes it so simple is that all the prerequisites and dependencies are taken care of for you. Remember those required Perl modules we talked about earlier? By using the CPAN method of installation, you don't have to install those individually. Note that you *must have Perl* already installed on your system for CPAN to work. Since Perl comes standard with most Linux distributions, though, this shouldn't be a problem. Just make sure you also install Perl when you install your system, or get and install the appropriate packages (such as a RPM Package Manager [RPM] in the case of Red Hat Linux)—they will be on your distribution CDs or the distribution's web site. You will also need the CPAN.pm interactive Perl module to use the automated features. This isn't a chicken/egg problem. Most Perl implementations already have CPAN.pm as part of their distribution. To determine whether you have it installed, use the *find* utility to locate it:

```
root # find / -name CPAN.pm
```

You should see something like this:

```
/usr/lib/perl5/5.8.0/CPAN.pm
```

If the `find` command comes up blank, you'll need to install CPAN.pm. You can get it from *http://search.cpan.org/dist/CPAN/*.

The only downside of CPAN is that it may take an extra day or two for new releases of SpamAssassin to be published on the site. If you're not the type of person who likes to wait, you may want to go with the tarball installation instead. Also, CPAN contains only major and minor releases and release candidates, so if you're looking for bleeding-edge code, you'll be better off getting it from the nightly CVS builds. Finally, if you're a Unix guru who likes to have your fingers on every bit of code that gets installed on your system, and you don't like the idea of an automated utility checking dependencies and installing software for you, CPAN may not be a good fit for you.

For nearly everyone else, however, CPAN should be perfect, and it's the way we recommend that you install it—especially if you're a beginner to Unix or Perl.

Using CPAN

Installing via CPAN takes a few steps. As long as you already have Perl and CPAN.pm installed on your system, you won't need to download anything. You will, however, need to make sure you're logged in as root, or that you can *su* to root.

The first step is to run the CPAN interactive module:

```
perl -MCPAN -e shell
```

If this is your first time to run the CPAN interactive module, you will be asked several things about configuration. First it will give you the option of auto or manual configuration. Auto-configuration may work fine for you. If you choose manual, many of the defaults will work. If it has trouble finding certain programs, you can input their locations. It will also ask you for proxy server information and what mirror you want to use (based on your geographical location).

After it's done, you will see a `cpan>` prompt. First, configure CPAN to ask if you want it to install prerequisites:

```
cpan> o conf prerequisites_policy ask
Next, install SpamAssassin.
install Mail::SpamAssassin
```

CPAN.pm will first install any prerequisites that are required for Mail::SpamAssassin. If the installation is successful, you should see this:

```
  /usr/bin/make install  -- OK
```

You'll then be back at the `cpan>` prompt. To exit, type this:

```
cpan> quit
```

SpamAssassin is now installed.

If the installation was not successful, CPAN bails wherever it failed. The most common failures are due to the installation script being unable to find required compilation components or SpamAssassin failing one test or another. Generally, this can be remedied by finding the missing component, installing it, and then relaunching your CPAN install.

Installing the Less Easy Way: From Tarball

As we said, a *tarball* is just Unix jargon for an archive file created with the tar utility. A tarball is a common means for distributing ready-to-build source code for Unix systems, especially in the open-source community. A tarball filename ends with the .tar extension and is often compressed with either gzip or bzip2, thus giving the filename the extension .tar.gz or .tar.bz2, respectively.

In SpamAssassin's case, its tarball is further compressed with gzip and will usually look something like this:

```
Mail-SpamAssassin-<version>.tar.gz
```

Where *<version>* is whatever version of SpamAssassin you downloaded. Obtain the tarball from SpamAssassin's main web site at *http://www.spamassassin.org/*.

On its download site, notice that SpamAssassin is distributed in both .tar.gz and .zip formats. Since we're installing on Linux, go ahead and download the .tar.gz version into a temporary directory.

Once it's downloaded, unzip and untar it into that directory. This can be done with a command like this:

```
tar -zxvf Mail-SpamAssassin-<version>.tar.gz
```

So, for example, if your version is 2.60, it'll look like this:

```
tar -zxvf Mail-SpamAssassin-2.60.tar.gz
```

If you're running Linux, this empties the contents of the tarball into your temporary directory, creating any subdirectories that it needs. If you're not running Linux, you *might* have to unzip the .tar.gz file with *gunzip* before untaring it. In that case, you'll drop the z option from the tar switches, as shown here:

```
gunzip Mail-SpamAssassin-2.6.0.tar.gz
tar -xvf Mail-SpamAssassin-2.6.0.tar
```

We're not quite ready to build yet. The downside of the tarball versus using CPAN is that the tarball doesn't take care of the prerequisites for you, so you'll have to install them yourself. Have a look at the section entitled "The Perl Modules," earlier in the chapter, to decide what you need. Download these files directly from CPAN or use the CPAN.pm interactive module to install them (with the exception of those that can't be installed through CPAN, such as Razor, Pyzor, and DCC).

Change to the directory created by untaring the tarball:

```
cd Mail-SpamAssassin-2.60
```

You now have to decide whether this is going to be a *site-wide* or *personal* installation. A site-wide installation allows all users of the system to take advantage of SpamAssassin. A personal installation is for a single user only. A site-wide installation requires that you have root access to the system on which you're installing, whereas a personal installation installs and runs as your user. If you don't have root access to the system on which you want to install SpamAssassin, a personal installation is your only choice. Otherwise, go ahead and choose site-wide. We'll cover both in the following sections.

Site-Wide Installation

First, run the Perl makefile for SpamAssassin using the Perl interpreter from a shell. From the top of the SpamAssassin source directory (where you should be after the cd earlier), run the following:

```
perl Makefile.PL
```

The makefile first asks you for an e-mail address or URL to include in the suspected spam report. The suspected spam report is sent to a user when an e-mail destined for him or her has been classified as possibly being spam (that is, it attained a score higher than the threshold set to determine whether something is or isn't spam). If you're running a site with other users (for instance, if you're an ISP or the mail administrator for an organization), users may become confused as to why their spam was tagged or what SpamAssassin is. By filling in this field, you give your users a resource to visit (either a web page or administrator's e-mail address) to find out more about your spam-fighting efforts.

In our case, we're going to enter a URL for a web page with information about our spam filter, so it will look like this:

```
What email address or URL should be used in the suspected-spam report text for
users who want more information on your filter installation? (In particular,
ISPs should change this to a local Postmaster contact) default text:
the administrator of that system] http://yourhost.yourdomain.tld/spamfilter.txt
```

If everything works out, you should see this:

```
Checking if your kit is complete...
Looks good
Writing Makefile for Mail::SpamAssassin
```

If an error occurs, it will most likely be a missing required Perl module, so go back and install the appropriate one, if need be. Otherwise, you now have a makefile and are ready to proceed. Next, type the following and press ENTER:

```
make
```

SpamAssassin builds and finishes by building the man pages (the Unix manual pages for SpamAssassin). If you get that far, you're good to go. Finally, install it by running this:

```
make install
```

SpamAssassin finishes by changing permissions (chmoding) the /usr/share/spamassassin directory. If you see that and get no other errors, the installation was successful. Any errors you get are likely due to one of two things:

- You do not have the appropriate prerequisites installed. Go back and see what you're missing, install those modules, and then try again.
- You do not have permission to modify the directories in which you're installing SpamAssassin. Make sure you're running as root.

Next we will instruct you on how to install SpamAssassin for personal use.

Personal Use Installation

Personal use installation is similar to site-wide. The only real difference is that you need to specify where to install your usr and etc directories, which cannot be the system /usr and /etc directories, as typically only root can write to those. Instead, use the PREFIX and SYSCONFDIR settings. For instance, if you want to install SpamAssassin within your home directory, have it install in directories such as sausr and saetc. These settings are used when you build the makefile using Perl. For example, from the SpamAssassin source tree in your temporary directory, run the following:

```
perl Makefile.PL PREFIX=~/sausr SYSCONFDIR=~/saetc
```

The tilde (~) is Unix command shell shorthand for the user's home directory.

As with the site-wide installation, you're asked for an e-mail address or URL to direct those getting the reports to answers. Since you're installing for personal use, you get the report, so it will hardly matter what you add here. You might as well leave it as default or add your own e-mail address:

```
$ perl Makefile.PL PREFIX=~sausr SYSCONFDIR=~/saetc

What email address or URL should be used in the suspected-spam report
text for users who want more information on your filter installation?
(In particular, ISPs should change this to a local Postmaster contact)
default text: [the administrator of that system] elvis@outer.net

Checking if your kit is complete...
Looks good
Writing Makefile for Mail::SpamAssassin
```

As you can see from the preceding listing, everything looks good so far for our build, and the makefile was created.

Finally, run make and make install, just as you did for the site-wide installation. If everything goes okay, you should have a nice new SpamAssassin installation in your ~sausr directory and configuration files in ~saetc.

Installing from the Edge: CVS

As we said, CVS is a common system developers employ to manage files used in a programming project. Many open-source projects grant the general public anonymous read-only access to their CVS development trees so that their users can test the latest and greatest code. SpamAssassin is no exception, making its CVS available as a nightly build.

NOTE Installing from CVS is always a risk. Because you're getting a "snapshot" of the development process, some components may not function correctly yet, or they may be downright buggy, making the program unstable. It's therefore recommended that you not install from CVS unless you're doing so specifically to test new features, and are in a test—rather than production—environment. The exception to this is that you may sometimes need to "check out" certain files that contain bug fixes and copy them into your build tree.

Installing SpamAssassin's CVS is fairly straightforward. You don't need to know any CVS commands because the company makes the tree available nightly as a tarball. Simply go to the download page, download the nightly CVS build, and work with it just like we wrote about in the section "Installing the Less Easy Way: From Tarball."

Other Ways to Install

In addition to CPAN, tarball, and CVS, SpamAssassin has a few other ways to install that are specific to Linux distributions. They include Red Hat RPMs, Debian packages, and Gentoo portage.

Red Hat RPMs

Newer versions of Red Hat, including Red Hat 9, include SpamAssassin as an optional part of the distribution. These usually include whatever version was current whenever the distribution was released. If you want the latest version, however, the best place to go is the SpamAssassin main web site at *http://spamassassin.kluge.net/RPMS/*.

Look for the RPMs for your particular version of Red Hat. The RPMs are given the naming convention of *package-name-release.RedHatVersion.type.rpm. Type* is either *i386* for an i386 binary or *src* for source code. Note that RPMs for the version you are running may not exist.

Even if you do find a binary version that suits you, it may not work due to differences in environments and the Perl installations. It may be better just to install the source RPM and build SpamAssassin from there. Toy with it to see whether it's possible, but don't count on the RPMs.

Debian Packages

You can install SpamAssassin on Debian GNU/Linux by using the apt-get application.

```
apt-get install spamassassin
```

Using apt-get will also take care of any prerequisites you may need—note that this means only the required modules, not the recommended or optional ones.

Gentoo Portage

Gentoo Linux has a simple installation process due to its portage tree. One nice thing about Gentoo is that it downloads the source and compiles the program on your system, so you're not downloading a binary built somewhere else for the lowest common denominator. The other nice thing about it is that it figures out all the dependencies and prerequisites for you. As with apt-get, it downloads only the required prerequisite, not recommended or optional prerequisites. If you want those, you'll have to install them separately.

To install SpamAssassin on Gentoo, first make sure your portage tree is up to date:

```
emerge rsync
```

Then "emerge" (Gentoo's parlance for downloading and building) SpamAssassin with the following command:

```
emerge Mail-SpamAssassin
```

That's all there is to it!

UNDERSTANDING SPAMASSASSIN'S COMPONENTS

SpamAssassin isn't just one application; rather it's a collection of tools and an API that can be used in a multitude of ways. In this section we talk about SpamAssassin's major components. You need to know what it installed before you can begin configuration.

The spamassassin Utility

The spamassassin utility is a Perl script that calls on the Mail::SpamAssassin Perl module. In many cases, it's the major workhorse of a SpamAssassin installation. Since it's just a script, spamassassin has to be called from Procmail or from a mail filter-type utility, such as MIMEDefang or amavisd-new, both of which we discuss in Chapter 8.

By default, spamassassin is installed in /usr/bin (or ~/sausr/bin if it's a personal installation). Essentially, Procmail pipes e-mail through spamassassin and compares the messages against its rules. Spamassassin also has a host of other command-line options, such as adding and removing addresses (inside an e-mail) from your blacklist or whitelist. You can get the complete usage listing with the following command:

```
spamassassin -h
```

The Spamd Daemon

The spamd daemon is a Perl script that runs (you guessed it) as a daemon on your system. You can run it either on the host that gets the mail or on a secondary processing server (we cover advanced installations such as this in Chapter 8). Spamd sits and listens on the localhost address (127.0.0.1) and TCP port 783 by default, but this can be changed if you have it installed on a secondary processing server or if you simply want to change the port. Changing the port might be a good idea if you want to run several incidents of spamd on your system, you have something else running on TCP port 783, or you want to hide the fact that spamd is running. The following command provides you with a list of command-line options for spamd:

```
spamd -h
```

We go over many of spamd's tantalizing options later in this chapter, and in Chapters 7 and 8. The spamd daemon waits for a connection and input from the spamc client, which we talk about in the next section.

The Spamc Client

Unlike most of the rest of SpamAssassin, the spamc client is written in C, not Perl. It is designed to be a replacement for spamassassin (that is, you would call spamc in place of spamassassin in your Procmail recipes and mail scripts). Whenever spamc detects mail coming it, it connects and sends it to spamd, which then checks the mail; spamd then sends its results back to spamc, which gives the output. See Figure 6-2 for how this works.

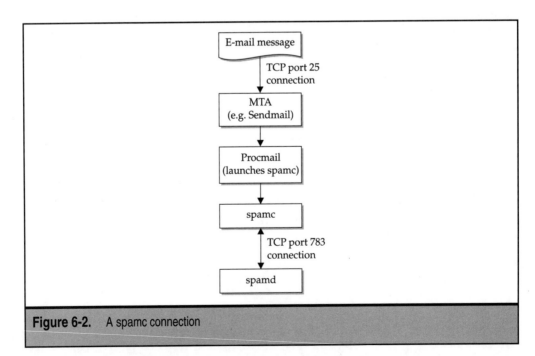

Figure 6-2.   A spamc connection

The fact that spamc is a compiled program and that spamd is running all the time means that this method has less overhead than running a separate instance of spamassassin for each piece of mail. As with the other utilities, spamc has many options, which you can see with the following command:

```
spamc -h
```

Again, we go over spamc's features in Chapters 7 and 8. Now, we familiarize you with SpamAssassin's configuration files.

The local.cf Configuration File

The local.cf file is in stored in /etc/mail/spamassassin by default or in ~/saetc/mail/spamassassin if you did a personal installation. This is the master configuration file for SpamAssassin, where you put custom configuration options and rules that you want to apply to the entire installation, including modified scores, blacklisted and whitelisted addresses, and message handling. Here's what it looks like:

```
# This is the right place to customize your installation of SpamAssassin.
# See 'perldoc Mail::SpamAssassin::Conf' for details of what can be
# tweaked.
#
###########################################################################
#
#rewrite_subject 0
#report_safe 1
```

When you first look at this file, it seems quite sparse; that's because the default SpamAssassin configuration options and rules are actually stored in a number of files in the /usr/share/spamassassin. Rules and configuration options placed in the local.cf file override or add to those already in /usr/share/spamassassin.

The two options shown as examples, `rewrite_subject` and `report_safe`, help us illustrate what you can do. As an option, SpamAssassin has the ability to rewrite the subject of a suspected spam message—essentially prefacing it with ***SPAM*** or some other customizable string. Normally this option is set to 0, which means that it's "off" and won't rewrite the subject. If you change the `rewrite_subject` configuration option to 1, it overrides this default behavior and tags the subject.

Also by default, SpamAssassin does not modify the original message of any e-mail detected as spam. In other words, it won't make any changes to the body or headers. Instead, it attaches the entire message as a MIME-part message/rfc822 (RFC 822 covers e-mail standards) to a spam report message and sends that message to you. The entire contents of the message are preserved, no matter what format it's in and what attachments it has. In Outlook, you see these attachments as envelope icons within a message. As long as your e-mail client doesn't open attachments by default, this should be relatively safe: it hides the spam or other potentially damaging message from you, but if it's a false positive, it allows you to retrieve the entire message in full. This is what happens when `report_safe` is set to 1.

If you set `report_safe` to 2, SpamAssassin still attaches the suspected spam e-mail to the report, but it does so as a MIME-part of text/plain instead of message/rfc822. Depending on the original message format (for instance, a graphic or HTML), this may make the message more difficult to view. However, it does make the message safer because any HTML "bugs" (to track whether or not the message was opened) and other possibly unsafe code or attachments are broken by this process.

You can also set `report_safe` to 0, which changes only the headers of the message but doesn't modify the body at all (even by putting it in an attachment).

These two are just a taste of the multitude of options you can tweak. We cover more of them in detail in Chapters 7 and 8.

The user_prefs Configuration File

The user_prefs configuration file is very similar to local.cf; however it applies only to individual users. A user puts this file in his ~/.spamassassin directory in his home directory. Note that this directory may not exist until a user gets his first piece of mail after SpamAssassin has been installed. The same is true for the user_prefs file itself: A template from /usr/share /spamassassin is copied into the user's home directory the first time SpamAssassin runs. The user can then modify it. Here's what the default user_prefs looks like:

```
# SpamAssassin user preferences file.  See 'perldoc Mail::SpamAssassin::Conf'
# for details of what can be tweaked.
#*
#* Note: this file is not read by SpamAssassin until copied into the user
#* directory. At runtime, if a user has no preferences in their home directory
#* already, it will be copied for them, allowing them to perform personalized
#* customisation.  If you want to make changes to the site-wide defaults,
#* create a file in /etc/spamassassin or /etc/mail/spamassassin instead.
########################################################################

# How many hits before a mail is considered spam.
# required_hits          5

# Whitelist and blacklist addresses are now file-glob-style patterns, so
# "friend@somewhere.com", "*@isp.com", or "*.domain.net" will all work.
# whitelist_from         someone@somewhere.com

# Add your own customised scores for some tests below.  The default scores are
# read from the installed spamassassin rules files, but you can override them
# here.  To see the list of tests and their default scores, go to
# http://spamassassin.org/tests.html .
#
# score SYMBOLIC_TEST_NAME n.nn

# Speakers of Asian languages, like Chinese, Japanese and Korean, will almost
# definitely want to uncomment the following lines.  They will switch off some
# rules that detect 8-bit characters, which commonly trigger on mails using CJK
```

```
# character sets, or that assume a western-style charset is in use.
#
# score HTML_COMMENT_8BITS     0
# score UPPERCASE_25_50        0
# score UPPERCASE_50_75        0
# score UPPERCASE_75_100       0
```

Essentially, anything that you can modify in local.cf can also be applied to `user_prefs`. This gives users a lot of flexibility in the way SpamAssassin works for *them*. It is especially useful because users can create their own blacklisted and whitelisted addresses or turn off particular rules that they don't want to use.

Giving individual users this much flexibility may not be practical for every site. In some cases, users do not have access to their home directories (or there may not be home directories at all, if you're simply passing mail to another "smart host"). In other cases, mail administrators want full control over how spam is dealt with on their systems.

Now that you've installed SpamAssassin and have a basic understanding of its components, get ready to configure it to run on the system.

CONFIGURING SPAMASSASSIN

You can run SpamAssassin in two ways: One is to use Procmail to run the spamassassin utility. The other is to run the spamd daemon and use it in conjunction with the spamc client (also run by Procmail).

In this section, we cover configuring SpamAssassin for both per-user and site-wide installations. The primary difference is that site-wide installations can use spamassassin or spamd/spamc, while per-user installations can only use spamassassin. We used Procmail for this installation, but we also cover other mail filters in Chapter 8.

Per-User Configuration

A per-user configuration should be implemented when an individual user wants to run SpamAssassin. This is required for a personal use installation, but it can also be used if a particular site offers SpamAssassin but doesn't "turn it on" by default for all users.

The first thing you need to do is set yourself up to use Procmail, if you're not using it already. To do this, first locate Procmail on the system by using a program such as whereis, locate, or find. Then edit or create a .forward file in your home directory (this file is typically used to forward e-mail to another account), and add the following line to it:

```
"| exec /usr/bin/procmail -f- || exit 75 #user"
```

Note that if you're running the Sendmail restricted shell (smrsh), you must put Procmail in smrsh's /usr/adm/sm.bin directory, and change this line to look like this:

```
"| exec /usr/adm/sm.bin/procmail -f- || exit 75 #user"
```

Here, *user* is your username.

Next, edit or create a .procmailrc file in your home directory. This is what's called a *recipe file* in Procmail parlance. The .procmailrc file needs to contain the following line:

```
:0fw: spamassassin.lock
| ~/sausr/bin/spamassassin
```

Or, if you did a site installation, it should look like this:

```
:0fw: spamassassin.lock
| /usr/bin/spamassassin
```

This forwards all your mail through the spamassassin Perl script for analysis and tagging (if required).

That's it for per-user configuration!

Site-Wide Configuration

The main difference between site-wide and per-user configuration is that you must configure Procmail to run directly from Sendmail, Postfix, or another MTA. Configuring your MTA to do so is beyond the scope of this chapter, but instructions can be found at *http://www.procmail.org/*.

This setup is similar to the site installation for per-user configuration. Instead of editing a .procmailrc file in a home directory, create or edit a file called /etc/procmailrc. Add the following lines to it:

```
:0fw
| /usr/bin/spamassassin
```

Now, all mail for your site gets processed by spamassassin.

Spamd Configuration

When you built SpamAssassin, spamc and spamd were built as well. By default, spamd won't run—it needs you to launch it. The easiest way to do this is to grab the appropriate rc startup script that came with your SpamAssassin source code. These rc startup files are used on Unix systems to launch daemons and programs at boot time.

The spamd rc files are located in your SpamAssassin source tree. Go to this directory:

```
cd ./Mail- SpamAssassin-*/spamd
```

Here the rc startup scripts reside, which all end in *.sh*. Included are scripts for Debian GNU Linux (debian-rc-script.sh), Red Hat Linux (redhat-rc-script.sh), NetBSD (netbsd-rc-script.sh), Solaris (solaris-rc-script.sh), and others. The one called pld-rc-script.sh works with many Linux distributions with a little tweaking.

Choose the appropriate script for your operating system and copy it to the location of your other rc files. Typically, these are somewhere in the /etc directory. Red Hat's rc files, for instance, are in /etc/rc.d/init.d. Gentoo's are in /etc/init.d. Once there, you can run this script to launch spamd (you may need to modify permissions to allow execution of the script). You can also simply launch spamd by hand with the following command:

```
/usr/bin/spamd
```

After spamd is running, you now have to configure Procmail to send your mail through spamc. This is similar to how we configured Procmail for spamassassin. You can have each individual user run spamc in her .procmailrc file, or you can put it in the site-wide /etc/procmailrc file. Either way, the configuration of that file looks like this:

```
:0fw:
| /usr/bin/spamc
```

As we said earlier, many configuration switches exist for both spamd and spamc, but we cover those in Chapter 8.

AN INTRODUCTION TO SPAMASSSASSIN'S OUTPUT

Now your users should receive spam messages attached to spam reports, letting them make the decision as to whether the messages are legitimate or spam. Either way, SpamAssassin's process protects users by keeping them from viewing spam messages.

Looking at a Message

A sample spam report is shown in Figure 6-3. By default, the report preserves the Subject line and the From address, so users can quickly decide whether the mail came from a legitimate user.

If you open the mail, the spam report appears. It states that the attached e-mail is probably spam and gives you a resource to visit if you need more information (this is the e-mail address or URL we filled in earlier). It goes on to provide a text-only preview of the content, if it can (some messages are simply a few HTML tags and GIF images or otherwise cannot be displayed in the preview). Finally, it offers its analysis of the content, breaking it down on a per-rule basis, giving you the score it got for each rule, plus the total score.

Is This the Only Option?

So is the only option to allow users to get the spam and have them delete it? The answer is an unequivocal "No!" In many cases, you might not want the users to get the spam in the first place. Why burden them with having to delete it? What's the difference between that and what they're currently doing?

The good news is that by using Procmail or mail filters, you specify what will be done with suspected spam before a user even sees it. You can have spam with a score of 10 or higher get shunted off into a different folder, for instance, while those with scores less than 10 get sent to the user for inspection (scores between 5 and 10 are more likely to be false positives). The possibilities are limitless, but we discuss a few of the best and most popular things you can do in Chapter 8.

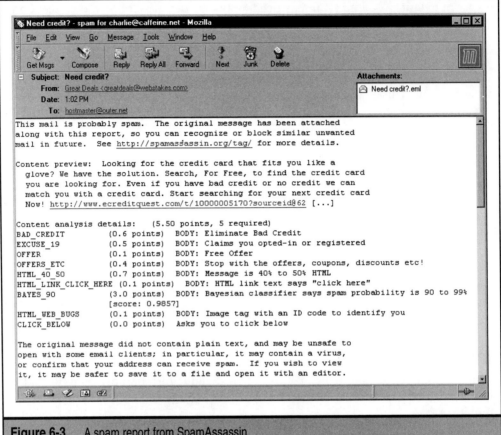

Figure 6-3. A spam report from SpamAssassin

SUMMARY

SpamAssassin is one of the most popular anti-spam tools available on Linux today. It's free, extensible, and packed with features, such as Bayesian analysis, DNSBLs, and an extremely large number of header and body tests. You can install and run SpamAssassin on your system in several ways, as a user or an administrator, and you'll have to pick the method that best fits your plan against spam.

Now that you understand the basics of how to install and configure SpamAssassin, in Chapters 7 and 8 we cover its Bayesian analysis features and advanced configuration examples.

CHAPTER 7

CATCHING SPAM WITH SPAMASSASSIN'S BAYESIAN CLASSIFIER

Version 2.50 of SpamAssassin was the first version of the software to include a *Bayesian classifier*. Prior to that version's release, if you wanted to use Bayesian analysis you had to run a separate program, such as SpamBayes or Bogofilter, in conjunction with SpamAssassin. While both of those are fine programs, including Bayesian analysis in SpamAssassin makes your anti-spam implementation much simpler and cleaner. SpamAssassin allows you to use Bayesian analysis with either site-wide or user-specific Bayes databases.

Like many other Bayes implementations, SpamAssassin based its algorithms on those described in Paul Graham's forward-thinking paper, "A Plan for Spam," found at *http://www.paulgraham.com/spam.html*. (Note that this chapter does not explain how Bayesian classification works. For a detailed explanation, see Chapter 4.)

IMPLEMENTING SPAMASSASSIN'S BAYESIAN CLASSIFIER

Bayesian analysis is turned on by default in SpamAssassin. However, if you need to turn it on (or turn it off) manually, you can modify the following in your local.cf or user_prefs files:

```
use_bayes (0|1)
```

Setting `use_bayes` to 1 turns it on, and setting it to 0 turns it off.

Important to note is that although Bayes is turned on by default, SpamAssassin won't actually use Bayesian analysis until it has been "trained" with at least 200 spam and 200 ham (nonspam) e-mails.

By default, SpamAssassin is configured so that each user has his or her own Bayes database. Site-wide sharing of databases is also possible (and in some cases preferable), and we cover this later in the chapter in the section entitled "Implementing Bayes System-Wide."

LOOKING AT SPAMASSASSIN'S BAYES-RELATED FILES

The SpamAssassin Bayesian classifier uses a number of files to track and analyze tokens. *Tokens* are *words* that, through "learning," are found to have a certain probability of being in spam or ham. By default, SpamAssassin builds separate Bayes databases for each user and stores each database in the user's home directory in ~/spamassassin. Each Bayes database–related SpamAssassin file begins with *bayes_*, and each is described here:

- **bayes_toks** This is the database of tokens (words) that are taken from analyzed messages. Each token is given a count of its frequency in spam and ham messages, along with the message count of the last message in which it was seen. This file is a binary file, but you can use the Unix `strings` command to see the various tokens. It makes for amusing reading. You can also get a dump of the file using the sa-learn utility, which we talk about later in this chapter in the section "Teaching SpamAssassin's Bayesian Classifier."

- **bayes_seen**   This database contains the message ID for each message learned, along with whether it was learned as ham or spam. SpamAssassin uses this to ensure that it's not relearning from a message that it has already processed. The file is also used to retrain SpamAssassin if a message was previously learned incorrectly.

- **bayes_journal**   The journal is used by SpamAssassin to keep track of tokens while scanning a message, so that it doesn't have to write to the database directly.

 If you must manipulate these files, use only the sa-learn utility to do so. If you modify their contents or permissions using some other means, erratic behavior could result.

SPAMASSASSIN'S BAYES RULES

SpamAssassin's Bayes rules are stored in a file called 23_bayes.cf in /usr/share/spamassassin. You won't learn much by looking at the rules themselves, however, since an internal Bayesian engine performs all Bayesian calculations, but it does give you an idea of how SpamAssassin ranks its Bayesian scores. As you can see in the following list (taken directly from 23_bayes.cf), SpamAssassin groups percentages of probability together, rather than create a separate rule for each percentage. So, for example, any message that Bayes gives a 66 percent chance of being spam is assigned to the BAYES_60 rule.

```
describe BAYES_00      Bayesian spam probability is 0 to 1%
describe BAYES_01      Bayesian spam probability is 1 to 10%
describe BAYES_10      Bayesian spam probability is 10 to 20%
describe BAYES_20      Bayesian spam probability is 20 to 30%
describe BAYES_30      Bayesian spam probability is 30 to 40%
describe BAYES_40      Bayesian spam probability is 40 to 44%
describe BAYES_44      Bayesian spam probability is 44 to 50%
describe BAYES_50      Bayesian spam probability is 50 to 56%
describe BAYES_56      Bayesian spam probability is 56 to 60%
describe BAYES_60      Bayesian spam probability is 60 to 70%
describe BAYES_70      Bayesian spam probability is 70 to 80%
describe BAYES_80      Bayesian spam probability is 80 to 90%
describe BAYES_90      Bayesian spam probability is 90 to 99%
describe BAYES_99      Bayesian spam probability is 99 to 100%
```

Each of these levels of "spamness" has a specific score assigned to it, as shown in the following list:

```
score BAYES_00 0 0 -4.901 -4.900
score BAYES_01 0 0 -0.600 -1.524
```

```
score BAYES_10 0 0 -0.734 -0.908
score BAYES_20 0 0 -0.127 -1.428
score BAYES_30 0 0 -0.349 -0.904
score BAYES_40 0 0 -0.001 -0.001
score BAYES_44 0 0 -0.001 -0.001
score BAYES_50 0 0 0.001 0.001
score BAYES_56 0 0 0.001 0.001
score BAYES_60 0 0 1.789 1.592
score BAYES_70 0 0 2.142 2.255
score BAYES_80 0 0 2.442 1.657
score BAYES_90 0 0 2.454 2.101
score BAYES_99 0 0 5.400 5.400
```

Let's have a look at the numbers. As we learned in Chapter 6, the first two scores are used only when Bayesian analysis is turned off, so it makes sense that they're zeros. The third score is used when Bayesian analysis is on, but network tests (such as DNS Blacklist, or DNSBL, tests) are turned off. The fourth score is used when both Bayes and network tests are turned on. It's interesting to look at the discrepancies between the third and fourth scores: The third score column is lower on the BAYES_70 rule but higher on all the others. Remember that SpamAssassin's scores are algorithmically generated at development time by running a large volume of messages through it, so BAYES_70 may be a "middle ground," where Bayes proved equally effective with or without network tests.

Like any SpamAssassin rule, these scores can be modified in your local.cf or user_prefs file. For instance, if you get few false positives with BAYES_90, you may want to bump up the score to 3.0 or even 4.0 to give it a higher chance of hitting your required_hits score for spam tagging.

AUTOMATED LEARNING

SpamAssassin has the option of allowing the Bayesian classifier to auto-learn what is spam and what is ham based on the score SpamAssassin assigns to a message using its various other rules and pattern-matching. Bayesian auto-learning is turned on by default. However, you can turn it on or off using the following line in your local.cf or user_prefs file:

```
bayes_auto_learn (0|1)
```

You don't necessarily want SpamAssassin to learn from *any* message tagged as spam—especially if your required hits are set to 5—because doing so will mean a large number of false positives will get analyzed for spam keywords. Likewise, you don't want just any message that doesn't get tagged as spam to be auto-learned as ham, because a few spams will get through (as false negatives) for scores between 0 and 5.

Fortunately, SpamAssassin has a way around this conundrum. It allows you to set minimum and maximum score thresholds for when to auto-learn. By default, SpamAssassin auto-learns as spam messages that have a score of at least 12.0, and it auto-learns as ham messages that have a score of 0.1 or less. You can set these to different scores by modifying the following options. First, for ham:

`bayes_auto_learn_threshold_nonspam` *n.nn*

And then for spam:

`bayes_auto_learn_threshold_spam` *n.nn*

(In both cases, *n* is the score in a floating decimal format.)

Note also that SpamAssassin requires at least 3 points from the header and 3 points from the body. Because of this, for example, `bayes_auto_learn_threshold_spam` has a minimum value of 6.

TRAINING SPAMASSASSIN'S BAYESIAN CLASSIFIER

To train SpamAssassin's Bayesian classifier, you use an included command-line utility called sa-learn. In fact, this powerful tool is used to control much of the Bayesian classifier. To run the tool, you'll need access to the system on which SpamAssassin resides. On a Unix system, this means shell access, unless your system administrator has set up a way for you to run sa-learn through a web-based system such as Webmin, Usermin, or some other utility.

Giving sa-learn Input

The sa-learn utility can take input from three different sources: text-based files, directories, or the Unix mbox (that is, mailbox) format. A *file* is just what you'd expect: An individual e-mail is saved off as a file and then given to sa-learn as input. A *directory* is a place where a collection of such files is stored. By default, sa-learn treats any input source as a file or directory, so no special command-line switches are required. If you're using a mail transfer agent (MTA) that's configured to use maildir format, where individual messages are saved off as individual files, or if you simply save off your messages from your client as individual files, this is what you need to use.

You can also give sa-learn a listing of files or directories by creating a file containing the path and name of those files and directories. You use this with the `-f` or `--folders` command-line option.

The Unix mbox format is a special kind of file. It's not a single e-mail, but several messages all concatenated in the same file (which makes it a sort of virtual folder, but not in the same sense as a directory). This is the older, more traditional mail format type on Unix systems, where all the user's incoming messages are stored in single files in /var/spool/mail or in the home directory. You tell sa-learn to read from this format using the command-line switch `--mbox`.

Training with Ham

To give sa-learn a ham message for training, use the following command line:

```
sa-learn --ham <file or directory>
```

If it's in mbox format, use the following line:

```
sa-learn --ham --mbox <mbox file>
```

So, for instance, if you have an mbox-formatted file named Ham in your ~/mail/ directory, you can scan it using the following line:

```
elvis@astk ~ $ sa-learn --ham --mbox ./mail/Ham
Learned from 3 message(s) (3 message(s) examined).
```

The last line tells you how many messages it learned from. If you've learned from this mbox file before, the number of messages learned from will be less than the number of messages examined.

Training with Spam

Spam training is similar to ham training. The command-line to train for spam is shown here:

```
sa-learn --spam <file or directory>
```

Here's the command for an mbox formatted file:

```
sa-learn --spam --mbox <mbox file>
```

So, to train off of an mbox formatted file called Spam in your ~/mail/ directory, you can use the following:

```
elvis@astk ~ $ sa-learn --spam --mbox ./mail/Spam
Learned from 4 message(s) (4 message(s) examined).
```

Once again, SpamAssassin won't relearn from messages already learned as spam, so if older messages are included, the number of messages examined will be higher than the number of messages from which it learned.

Correcting Mistakes

On occasion, you may incorrectly teach SpamAssassin that a nonspam message is spam, or vice versa. SpamAssassin's own automated learning may also teach the system incorrectly because a spam message got a peculiarly low score (likely for cases in which spammers figure out ways to "defeat" SpamAssassin's rules or use the negative scoring ones for their own purposes), or a ham message got a peculiarly high score (likely if the sender is in a lot of DNSBLs or uses a particularly "spammy" method of communicating).

Forgiving and Forgetting

sa-learn allows you to retrain the system in a couple of ways. The first way is to use the `--forget` switch, which "unlearns" any previously learned message. Use it in this way:

```
sa-learn --forget <file or directory>
```

Here's the mbox format:

```
sa-learn --forget --mbox <mbox file>
```

So, for instance, if we wanted to forget all those spam messages we learned earlier, we could use this:

```
elvis@astk ~ $ sa-learn --forget --mbox ./mail/Spam
Learned from 4 message(s) (4 message(s) examined).
```

Now it's as if those messages were never added to the database at all, and we can do with them what we see fit—including relearning them as something else.

Reclassifying Learned Messages

The second way to retrain the system is simply to run sa-learn with the switch opposite of whatever it was learned as previously. So if the message was accidentally learned as ham, you'd simply run sa-learn with the `--spam` switch, as discussed in the "Training with Ham" section earlier in the chapter. Here's an example:

```
elvis@astk ~ $ sa-learn --spam --mbox ./mail/HAM
Learned from 3 message(s) (3 message(s) examined).
```

NOTE Retraining with this method automatically runs the "forget" the way it previously learned the message, so you don't have to run sa-learn with the `--forget` switch first.

Bayes Database Expiration

To keep its Bayes databases from eventually filling up the disk, SpamAssassin can expire database entries either manually or automatically. Two components are used in the process: the first is syncing the Bayes journal with the database, and the second is expiring token entries from the database itself.

Some important configuration settings deal directly with syncing and expiration. These settings can go either in SpamAssassin's local.cf file or in an individual user_prefs file.

- **bayes_auto_expire** Tells SpamAssassin whether or not you want it to expire tokens from the database automatically when certain criteria are met. 1 means yes, 0 means no. The default is 1.

- **bayes_expiry_max_db_size**   Sets the maximum size—in tokens—of the database. The default is 150000 for 150,000 tokens. An expiry will keep 75 percent of the set value, or 100,000 tokens, whichever is larger. So a maximum size of 200000 will retain 150,000 tokens after an expiry.

- **bayes_journal_max_size**   Sets the maximum size of the journal before it is automatically synced with the database. The default is 102400. It also syncs once per day, even if this size is not reached. If you set bayes_journal_max_size, it performs its sync only once per day.

Automatic journal syncing with the database occurs when *both* of the following conditions are met,

- `bayes_journal_max_size` is not set to 0.
- The journal file (bayes_journal) exists.

and at least one of the following conditions are met,

- The bayes_journal file is larger than `bayes_journal_max_size`.
- The last journal sync happened one or more days ago.

You can also manually sync the journal with the following command:

```
elvis@astk ~ $ sa-learn --rebuild
synced Bayes databases from journal in 0 seconds: 768 unique entries
(1013 total entries)
```

Database entries are automatically expired when *all* of the following conditions are met:

- The `bayes_auto_expire` option is *not* set to 0.
- The number of tokens in the database is greater than 100,000.
- The number of tokens in the database is greater than the `bayes_expiry_max_db_size` setting.
- The last expire attempt was at least 12 hours ago.
- At least a 12-hour difference exists between the oldest and newest token access times (`atimes`).

You can manually expire the database using the `--force-expire` switch with sa-learn, as in the following:

```
elvis@astk ~ $ sa-learn --force-expire
synced Bayes databases from journal in 0 seconds: 88 unique entries

(88 total entries) .......................................................
............................................................................
```

```
...........expired old Bayes database entries in 63 seconds
157015 entries kept, 7120 deleted
token frequency: 1-occurence tokens: 63.38%
token frequency: less than 8 occurrences: 15.52%
```

Getting Bayes Statistics

Sa-learn provides you with the ability to get information on the database by using the --dump switch. Here is the command syntax:

```
sa-learn --dump [all | magic | data]
```

If you select `magic`, only the magic tokens are dumped. Magic tokens include the number of ham and spam messages learned (nspam and nham), the total number of tokens in the database (ntokens), the message count of the last expiry run (last expire reduction count), the message-count of the oldest token in the database (oldest atime), and the message count of the current message (newest atime). Here is some example output:

```
elvis@astk ~ $ sa-learn --dump magic
0.000          0             2    0  non-token data: bayes db version
0.000          0         10723    0  non-token data: nspam
0.000          0          4282    0  non-token data: nham
0.000          0        158727    0  non-token data: ntokens
0.000          0    1067051067    0  non-token data: oldest atime
0.000          0    1067754083    0  non-token data: newest atime
0.000          0    1067742856    0  non-token data: last journal sync atime
0.000          0    1067742833    0  non-token data: last expiry atime
0.000          0        691200    0  non-token data: last expire atime delta
0.000          0          7120    0  non-token data: last expire
                                                     reduction count
```

If you choose `data`, only the data tokens (actual words) are dumped. Here's a truncated sample:

```
elvis@astk ~ $ sa-learn --dump data
0.818        191       17 1067683472   largest
0.005          0       10 1067235302   17682
0.004          0       12 1067300101   19495
0.002          0       33 1067681701   04.15
0.003          0       16 1067696102   14715
0.003          0       16 1067177701   27533
0.004          0       12 1067152501   448
0.004          0       14 1067688902   6154
0.012          3      105 1067743083   H*r:66.218.67
0.582          7        2 1067534224   anticipate
```

The first column is the probability that the token appears in a spam message. The second is the number of occurrences of that token in spam. Third is the number of occurrences in spam. The fourth column is the message count of the last message in which the token was detected. The final column is the token itself.

IMPLEMENTING BAYES SYSTEM-WIDE

Thus far we have discussed implementing SpamAssassin's Bayesian classifier on a per-user basis, with each user having his or her own database and journal. In some instances, it may be desirable to run SpamAssassin on a system-wide basis instead. One such instance is when you're running SpamAssassin system-wide and do not allow users to train the Bayesian system themselves. When your SpamAssassin server isn't the final destination for the mail, but it simply forwards processed mail onto a "smart host" that contains the user accounts, it's not possible or practical for users to have individual Bayes databases (we explore an example of this in Chapter 8) or for users to train the database.

For an entire system to share the Bayes databases among users, you must set the `bayes_path` configuration option in local.cf, using the following syntax:

```
bayes_path /path/to/file
```

The default path is ~/spamassassin. For sharing the databases system-wide, you may want to create another directory. A good one might be called /var/spool/spamassassin, so that your configuration option would look like this:

```
bayes_path /var/spool/spamassassin
```

If you're not using a system-wide install (for example, individual users launch spamassassin or spamc themselves out of their .procmailrc files), but you still want users to share the Bayesian database (to save disk space, for instance), you'll need to make sure all users can read and write to the database files. To do this, set the `bayes_file_mode` setting in local.cf. The default file mode is 0700, which gives the file owner read, write, and execute permissions. Execute permissions are granted because a directory may be created. However, if a file is created instead, that file has only read and write permissions. In a system-wide setup where you're using a shared database, ensure that all users can read and write to the file and directory. First, grant all users access to read/write/execute in the bayes_path directory by setting permissions on that directory to 0777. Second, set the `bayes_file_mode` setting in local.cf to 0777:

```
bayes_file_mode 0777
```

BAYESIAN LEARNING CAVEATS

While Bayesian learning is a vast improvement over many of the older methods of spam detection, it still has its downsides, weak points, and "gotchas." When using Bayesian learning with SpamAssassin, keep the following in mind:

- The database needs to learn from at least 200 ham and 200 spam messages before message analysis (and thus SpamAssassin's Bayes scoring rules) kicks in.
- It may take at least 1000 spam and 1000 ham messages before Bayesian analysis becomes most effective.
- If you're running SpamAssassin in a site-wide configuration where it forwards mail on to a smart host after processing, it may not be possible for users to teach the system easily. This is because when the mail reaches the smart host, it's no longer in the same place (server) as the Bayes database. The trick is to get it *back* to that server for processing, which, depending on the smart host MTA and end-user client, may not be possible (we discuss options that address this in Chapter 8).
- To teach the system, users must run sa-learn. This may be through shell access, a web interface such as Usermin, or a cron (automated task) job set up by the system administrator.
- Using common site-wide Bayes databases for all your users might not be as effective as having individual Bayes databases. Unless all your users have the same tastes and requirements for what is spam and what is ham, this will definitely be the case. For instance, an insurance company may have a medical group that gets mail on drugs and a housing insurance group that gets mail on mortgages. If the housing group gets a lot of spam that contains drug names and housing users teach the system that it's spam, this could detrimentally affect the mail the medical group receives. If the medical group teaches the system that its drug mail is ham, this could negate much of what the housing group had taught it.

When implementing SpamAssassin's Bayesian classifier, keep in mind that it's there to bolster SpamAssassin's existing capabilities, not replace them. In some situations, you may want to turn off the classifier completely and rely just on SpamAssassin's own rules. In situations for which individual users can train the Bayesian classifier, however, the classifier will only increase SpamAssassin's effectiveness.

SUMMARY

Bayesian classification is an excellent addition to SpamAssassin, even if its sole purpose is to eliminate the need to have a separate program running to perform this task. It's implemented by default in SpamAssassin and can be tailored to your needs using SpamAssassin's straightforward text configuration files. Teaching the system is accomplished through the sa-learn command-line tool.

Although the Bayesian classifier uses per-user databases by default, it can also be configured to run on a site-wide basis—though this may reduce its effectiveness. In Chapter 8, we address Bayesian classification again, and we cover some of the more advanced capabilities included within SpamAssassin.

CHAPTER 8

ENHANCING AND MAINTAINING SPAMASSASSIN

Anti-Spam Tool Kit

SpamAssassin runs well without any kind of tuning, but if you want to get the most out of your system, you need to know when and where to make modifications. After a couple months of running SpamAssassin, you will inevitably start to see more spam sneak through. This is a sign that spammers have adapted to your defenses, so you must adapt as well.

In this chapter, we cover ways in which you can fine-tune and improve your SpamAssassin installation. We go in-depth with some specific configuration options and touch upon helper programs.

CREATING YOUR OWN RULES

One of SpamAssassin's most powerful features is that it lets you create your own rules. While the SpamAssassin developers put out a new version every few months, you're likely to get a crafty spam that doesn't match any of your current rules or—worse—uses SpamAssassin's own rules against you. In such cases, the ability to create and modify rules is invaluable.

SpamAssassin's Double-Edged Sword

That SpamAssassin's source code is freely available is one of the things that makes it so powerful and easy to update. Unfortunately, this freedom means spammers can also download the code and reverse engineer it for ways to defeat its defenses. This happened with SpamAssassin 2.53, when spammers used SpamAssassin's own "nice" rules against it. These rules look at the headers to see which mail user agent (MUA) a sender is using (USER_AGENT rules). At the time, SpamAssassin gave certain MUAs, such as Pine or Mozilla, a very low score (–4.0 for instance) because spammers rarely use them. Unfortunately, it also aggregated scores for multiple MUA headers, so spammers would spoof multiple MUA headers in their messages (put one for Pine, one for Mozilla, and so on) and get, say, 8.0 points subtracted from the total hits on their message. This would often counteract any positive hits they would get for the rest of the spam content, bring the total score below the spam threshold, and allow the message to get through.

To correct these problems, the SpamAssassin developers released 2.54 about a month later, which raised the scores for those nonspammer MUAs and added a TOO_MANY_MUAS meta rule. In the meantime, however, SpamAssassin users were quickly and easily able to modify rules and scores on their own, once the spammer's ploy was discovered. If SpamAssassin weren't open source and spammers had managed, through trial and error, to defeat it, users would not have been able to make their own modifications to correct the problem. In SpamAssassin 2.60, the USER_AGENT rules were removed completely, at least for the time being, because of the chance for forgeries.

Where to Create and Modify Rules

SpamAssassin's rules are stored in /usr/share/spamassassin (or ~/sausr/share/spamassassin) in *.cf* files. All English rule files are prefaced with *20_*. So, for instance, body tests are stored in the file *20_body_test.cf*. Scores are kept separately in a file called *50_scores.cf*.

Whenever you create and modify your own rules or scores, however, do so in your /etc/mail/local.cf or ~/spamassassin/user_prefs file. *Do not modify SpamAssassin's default configuration files!* If you do, you'll write over any additions or changes you've made the next time you upgrade SpamAssassin.

Components of a Rule

In Chapter 6 we briefly discussed SpamAssassin rules. In this section, we take a more in-depth look and create some rules of our own.

Any SpamAssassin rule is comprised of three components: the rule type, the description, and the score.

- **Rule Type** This tag gives SpamAssassin a pointer to where to apply the rule in a message. Rules types include header, body, uri, rawbody, and meta.
- **Description** This tag gives a brief description of the rule. The description also appears in the spam report generated by SpamAssassin.
- **Score** This tag is used to assign the score to the rule. It can be a positive or negative real number or integer.

In looking at the rule GUARANTEED_100_PERCENT, you see each of these pieces. We extracted this rule from the file 20_phrases.cf, which contains rules for common spam phrases:

```
body GUARANTEED_100_PERCENT      /100% GUARANTEED/i
describe GUARANTEED_100_PERCENT One hundred percent guaranteed
```

In this case, the rule type is `body` and the line `describe` includes the description. Both are followed by the rule name (GUARANTEED_100_PERCENT) and the variable piece. In the 50_scores.cf file, the following score for that rule exists. Here is the score line. It includes the tag `score`, followed by the rule name, followed by the scores themselves.

```
score GUARANTEED_100_PERCENT 1.101 1.101 1.001 1.000
```

Rule Types

This line is the meat of the rule. It not only says what kind of rule it is (header, body, rawbody, uri, meta), but also what the rule is doing (pattern matching, running a program, and so on). By directing the rule at a specific part of the message, processing is faster than it would be if the whole message were scanned. Here we discuss each of the specific rule types and give examples of each.

header   As the name implies, the header rule type looks at the message headers. This includes To, From, Reply-to, Message-ID, Date, and Subject. An example from SpamAssassin's 20_head_tests.cf file is shown here:

```
header TO_HAS_SPACES           To:addr =~ /\s/
```

This rule checks for spaces in the To address.

body   The body is the textual part of the message. All MIME parts are stripped. Any base64 or quoted-printable encoded messages are decoded.

rawbody   This is a search of all parts of a message, including MIME parts. Any base64 or quoted-printable encoded messages are decided.

uri   This looks for URIs within the mail. (Uniform Resource Identifiers are pretty much the same as URLs.)

meta   A meta rule performs operations on a Boolean expression of several rules to return a Boolean value (true or false, 1 or 0).

```
meta SYMBOLIC_TEST_NAME <Boolean expression>
```

The meta rule is especially useful if you notice that certain spam messages trigger multiple rules, but not quite enough to push the message's score past the required hits. So, for example, this meta rule creates a new rule called BOSS_AND_MONEY_BANGS containing the rules BANG_BOSS and BANG_MONEY (where the body text contains *boss!* and *money!*):

```
meta BOSS_AND_MONEY_BANGS BANG_BOSS && BANG_MONEY
```

Together, these rules generate a total score of between 1.1 and 2.5 (depending on how SpamAssassin is configured). But by adding a score to the meta rule, you can jack up their total score even higher.

```
score BOSS_AND_MONEY_BANGS 3.0
```

This adds another three points to the score the two rules already received separately, bringing the total to between 4.1 and 5.5—much more likely to trigger the spam threshold with just a little nudge.

tflags   Tflags rules set extra flags on a rule that's used by the back-end SpamAssassin system for rules processing. In most cases, you do not have to add or modify a tflags rule unless you are adding to or modifying the SpamAssassin code itself. Here's a description of the various tflags that can be utilized:

- **learn**   Indicates that the rule requires learning before it can be used. The BAYES_ rules all have this flag set.

- **net**   Indicates a network test, such as a DNS Blacklist (DNSBL) test.
- **nice**   Indicates that the test is used to counteract false positives, and therefore must have a negative score.
- **userconf**   This test requires user configuration before it can be used. That is, it must appear in the user_prefs file, such as the language tests ok_languages and ok_locales.

Several flags can appear in a tflags line. For instance, the low-percentage BAYES_ rules (BAYES_00 through BAYES_44) have both the `nice` and `learn` flags set.

The Description

The `describe` tag is exactly what it sounds like. You can give a rule any description you desire. The description appears in the spam report to which the original message is attached (if you configure your connection to do this). It's also a handy way for you to remember what a rule does, since the symbolic rule names can sometimes be cryptic.

```
describe SYMBOLIC_TEST_NAME <description>
```

The conventional maximum length of the description is no more than 50 characters, including spaces. The description does not have to be enclosed in quotation marks or any other delimiter for that matter.

Scoring

The `score` tag sets the score(s) for a particular test. The score range can be between –100.0 and 100.0. A rule with a score of 0 will be ignored completely. (You use a score of 0 to essentially "turn off" one of SpamAssassin's preconfigured rules.) If no score is specified, it will have a default of 1.0 (or 0.01 if the rule is a test rule beginning with $T\_$). The syntax is shown here:

```
score SYMBOLIC_TEST_NAME n.nn [n.nn n.nn n.nn]
```

where *n.nn* is the numeric score assigned. The score can either be an integer or a real number. If you simply add one number, it will apply in all cases. If you choose also to include the optional scores in brackets, each number applies in a different SpamAssassin configuration. As we mentioned in Chapter 6, the first score is used when both Bayes and network tests are disabled; the second when Bayes is enabled but network tests are disabled; the third when Bayes is disabled but network tests are enabled; and the fourth when both Bayes and network tests are enabled.

Building a Rule

Let's say that you're regularly getting e-mails that purport to shrink the size of your feet using a newly discovered herbal combination. The mails exclaim: "Reduce your shoe size by one or two sizes!!! New FDA approved foot-shrinking formula gives guaranteed results!!!"

You're rather happy with your foot size and are not interested in receiving these e-mails. They come so frequently and from such questionable sources that you believe unsubscribing to them all is impossible. So you decide to create a SpamAssassin rule to deal with them.

The first step is to decide what factors of the message you want to trigger the rule. The trick is that it needs to be something relatively specific to the message you're trying to tag so as to prevent false positives, but generic enough that it will tag similar spams once spammers begin modifying the message (and they will!). In this case, two different rules may be in order: one for "FDA approved" and another for "foot-shrinking." We'll start with the first.

These new rules can be stored either in the /etc/mail/local.cf file for site-wide usage (the only way if you're using *spamd*) or in an individual's ~/.spamassassin/user_prefs file if you're using SpamAssassin with procmail.

The first part of the rule should tell SpamAssassin to search the message body for what you're looking for. Here's an example:

```
body FDA_APPROVED1 /fda[\s-]approved/i
```

This tells SpamAssassin to search the body only. You can make the tag anything you like as long as it's unique (no other rules are using it). It's usually a good idea to make it somewhat descriptive. The number *1* we added to the end of the tag will just help ensure its uniqueness if we ever add any other rules that deal with "FDA Approved." In our search, we want it to trigger whether the message says "FDA approved" or "FDA-approved," so we have it look for either a space (\s) or a dash (-) in between *fda* and *approved*. The i tells SpamAssassin to ignore case for the match.

```
describe FDA_APPROVED1 Claims that it is FDA approved.
```

The description line is the simplest part of the message. Basically, we just say what the rule looks for. This will appear in the SpamAssassin report that appears as part of the tagged message.

```
score FDA_APPROVED1 2.5
```

Picking a score can also be difficult. We chose 2.5 because it will not be enough to send a message over the spam threshold on its own, but enough that it will make an impact when combined with other rules. Since we have only one score listed, the score will be the same no matter what we have for our SpamAssassin configuration (with or without Bayes, with or without network tests).

To bolster our spam-fighting attempt, we'll also add this rule:

```
body FOOT_SHRINKING1 /(foot|feet)[\s-]shrinking/i
describe FOOT_SHRINKING1 Talks about foot or feet shrinking.
score FOOT_SHRINKING1 2.5
```

This is very similar to the other rule and adds another 2.5 points when triggered. This will ensure that a message that includes both "FDA approved" and "foot-shrinking" will hit the threshold of 5 (unless spammers find a way to use SpamAssassin's "nice" rules to their advantage, the message gets a low Bayes score, or the sender is whitelisted).

Testing the Rule

After the new rule is created, it is important that you test both its syntax and efficacy. Fortunately, SpamAssassin makes syntax checking easy. Those of you who program in C might be familiar with the *lint* utility, which checks C source code for syntax errors and potential security issues (lints are also available for a number of other programming languages). SpamAssassin has similar lint functionality for its configuration files and rules. It is invoked this way:

```
spamassassin --lint
```

This checks the syntax of configuration files in /etc/mail/spamassassin, as well as the user_prefs file of the user you're running `spamassassin --lint` as.

If no errors occur, SpamAssassin returns a *0* (useful if you're running it within a script) and produces no output. If any syntax errors are found, it returns a *1* and outputs the line it's having trouble with.

It's important to realize that "linting" the configuration files tells you only whether a syntax error is causing SpamAssassin to ignore the rule. The lint function does not tell you whether your rule is actually working the way you intend it to. A rule's syntax can be perfectly legal, but it may not match the text you're looking for. Any number of typos can creep in—such as misspelling *approved* as *approvd*. Or you may neglect the *i* so that the rule is case-sensitive. Therefore, if possible, send multiple iterations of sample messages through that trigger your rules.

WHITELISTING AND BLACKLISTING

SpamAssassin has many, many whitelisting and blacklisting features. We've already covered the most obvious ones in Chapter 6: whitelist_from and blacklist_from. A few other rules let you customize what networks you trust and how much spam individual users receive.

trusted_networks

The trusted_networks setting (in local.cf or user_prefs) is a way of whitelisting e-mail coming from specific IP networks. Hosts in listed networks are never checked against DNSBLs. It's important to include only networks that you are sure do not contain open proxies or open relays, or those that are used by spammers.

Networks with netmasks are entered in classless interdomain routing (CIDR) notation (/24, /16, and so on). So, for example, if you want e-mail from the entire (fictional) class C address 192.168.100.0, you enter this:

```
trusted_networks 192.168.100.0/24
```

If you do not specify the last octet but leave a trailing dot, the maximum number of hosts for that network is used. So, the above example is equivalent to this:

```
trusted_networks 192.168.100.
```

If you bring the IP out to the last octet, specifying an individual host, the mask /32 is assumed:

```
trusted_networks 192.168.100.25
```

whitelist_to

Users listed in whitelist_to receive more spam than they would otherwise. This is very useful on system-wide installations. The syntax is shown here:

```
whitelist_to <e-mail address>
```

It takes one user per line. So, for example, this ensures that Elvis gets extra spam:

```
whitelist_to elvis@someisp.tld
```

This setting triggers the USER_IN_WHITELIST_TO rule, which simply subtracts six points (–6.0) from the total score of the message, letting more spam leak through. This rule's score can be modified.

This setting is useful on an account that gets more false positives but still needs most spam tagged or blocked.

more_spam_to

The more_spam_to whitelist allows through more spam than whitelist_to. The syntax is basically the same:

```
more_spam_to <e-mail address>
```

E-mail addresses in this setting trigger the USER_IN_MORE_SPAM_TO rule, which subtracts 20 points (–20.0) from the overall score of the message. This means that the majority of spam is allowed through to the user, unless it has an extremely high score (typically greater than 25). This is useful for "sales@" addresses, where false positives could potentially cost a company customers and revenue.

all_spam_to

If you have users who want to get all e-mail, regardless of whether or not it's spam (believe it or not, there are such animals), you can include their e-mail address in this setting. This is useful for an "abuse@" address, where you're likely to receive forwarded spam. The syntax is similar to the whitelist_to setting:

```
all_spam_to <e-mail address>
```

E-mail addresses in this setting trigger the USER_IN_ALL_SPAM_TO rule, which subtracts 100 points (–100.0) from the total score of the message. With this setting, practically all spam hits the listed account—the only exception might be messages that trigger the USER_IN_BLACKLIST rule (which adds 100 points) in addition to others (which add another 5 points).

LOCALIZING

An easy way to tweak SpamAssassin to reduce spam from foreign sources is to localize it to your particular user base. That is, if all of the users on your mail system are English-only speakers, they are unlikely to get messages they want in a Chinese character set. SpamAssassin gives you the ability to score such messages higher.

You can test message localization in two ways in SpamAssassin, and both can be configured either in the local.cf or user_prefs files. The first is the ok_locales setting and the second is the ok_languages setting.

ok_locales

This ok_locales setting checks the character set of the received e-mail. It activates the rules CHARSET_FARAWAY, CHARSET_FARAWAY_BODY, and CHARSET_FARAWAY_HEADERS. It supports only the settings shown in Table 8-1.

Setting	Description
all	All character sets (default)
en	English (and other western) character sets
ja	Japanese character sets
ko	Korean character sets
ru	Cyrillic character sets
th	Thai character sets
zh	Chinese (simplified and traditional) character sets

Table 8-1.   Settings for ok_locales

For example, the following setting allows English and Korean mails to pass through without triggering the CHARSET_ rules:

```
ok_locales en ja
```

Note that all character sets are added on one line, separated by a space, rather than appearing on separate lines. Also keep in mind that ISO-8859-* and Windows code page character sets are always permitted by default.

ok_languages

SpamAssassin can go beyond merely checking the character sets and can attempt to determine the language that the e-mail is written in. While this takes more processing power (and time) per message, you get more granularity in the languages you're willing to accept, and it gets around problems with spoofed character sets. If you get a message in a language that's not set in ok_languages, the UNWANTED_LANGUAGE_BODY rule triggers. Table 8-2 shows a list of acceptable languages and their two or three letter code.

Code	Language	Code	Language
all	All languages	ka	Georgian
af	Afrikaans	ko	Korean
am	Amharic	la	Latin
ar	Arabic	lt	Lithuanian
be	Byelorussian	lv	Latvian
bg	Bulgarian	mr	Marathi
bs	Bosnian	ms	Malay
ca	Catalan	ne	Nepali
cs	Czech	nl	Dutch
cy	Welsh	no	Norwegian
da	Danish	pl	Polish
de	German	pt	Portuguese
el	Greek	qu	Quechua
en	English	rm	Rhaeto-Romance
eo	Esperanto	ro	Romanian
es	Spanish	ru	Russian
et	Estonian	sa	Sanskrit
eu	Basque	sco	Scots

Table 8-2. Settings for ok_languages

Code	Language	Code	Language
fa	Persian	sk	Slovak
fi	Finnish	sl	Slovenian
fr	French	sq	Albanian
fy	Frisian	sr	Serbian
ga	Irish Gaelic	sv	Swedish
gd	Scottish Gaelic	sw	Swahili
he	Hebrew	ta	Tamil
hi	Hindi	th	Thai
hr	Croatian	tl	Tagalog
hu	Hungarian	tr	Turkish
hy	Armenian	uk	Ukrainian
id	Indonesian	vi	Vietnamese
is	Icelandic	yi	Yiddish
it	Italian	zh	Chinese
ja	Japanese		

Table 8-2. Settings for ok_languages *(continued)*

The following example allows e-mails in English, Spanish, and Chinese without triggering the UNWANTED_LANGUAGE_BODY rule:

```
ok_languages en es zh
```

Language codes are separated by spaces and appear all on one line.

USING MIMEDEFANG WITH SPAMASSASSIN

MIMEDefang is a mail filtering processor for UNIX systems that was originally created as a way to thwart viruses by deleting attachments likely to contain them (such as .exe and .com executables). It still has that functionality, along with the ability to convert Microsoft Word .doc files into HTML, and it can "defang" MIME attachments in other ways. It can also be used in conjunction with a number of anti-virus programs to detect and remove viruses based on signatures. Its focus has shifted to anti-spam activities, and it can now work with SpamAssassin to tag or reject spam. It is written primarily in Perl (with some C components for quick processing) and is therefore highly configurable by system administrators.

Like many thriving open-source projects, MIMEDefang is available both as a freely available package and a fully-supported commercial product. Its free, community-supported version is available at *http://www.mimedefang.org/*. The commercial version is available from Roaring Penguin Software Inc. at *http://www.roaringpenguin.com/*. Roaring Penguin was founded by MIMEDefang author David Skoll. There isn't much difference between the free and commercial versions other than the support. Roaring Penguin also offers CanIt, which is a proprietary anti-spam/anti-virus product based around MIMEDefang. Not only do you get support, but you also get a web-based user interface for management and monitoring.

MIMEDefang requires sendmail 8.12 or later, and it runs under sendmail's "milter" (mail filter) functionality. This puts MIMEDefang directly in the SMTP stream, rather than after the mail has already passed through the MTA (as in the case of procmail). MIMEDefang runs on each message, rather than each user, so this reduces overhead for processing on messages to multiple recipients. Figure 8-1 gives a visual roadmap of where MIMEDefang sits in your mail flow.

MIMEDefang and SpamAssassin

Rather than simply running the spamassassin program, or spamc, MIMEDefang uses the SpamAssassin Perl module (Mail::SpamAssassin) to detect and tag spam. Although much of SpamAssassin's functionality is the same when run through MIMEDefang, some critical differences are worth noting.

Instead of using /etc/mail/local.cf to configure SpamAssassin with MIMEDefang, make all changes to /etc/mail/sa-mimedefang.cf. Syntax and commands available are the same as you might find in your users_prefs or local.cf file, with the addition of a few more.

MIMEDefang Requirements

MIMEDefang 2.39 (current at the time of this writing) requires Perl 5.001 or later. It can run on almost any UNIX or Linux-based platform, yet it is developed and tested on Linux, and that's what we'll continue to use in our examples. The order in which you install things is

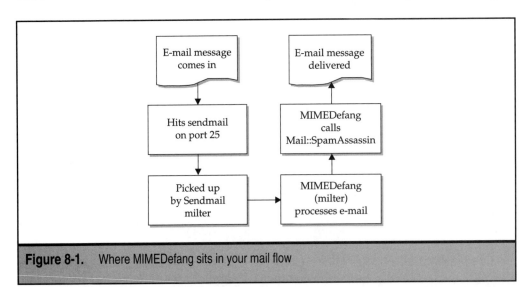

Figure 8-1. Where MIMEDefang sits in your mail flow

important with MIMEDefang. So that you'll know what you're getting into, here's a simplified list of the things that must be done to get MIMEDefang to work:

1. Obtain and compile (or recompile) sendmail with mail filter (milter) support.
2. Build a sendmail.cf file with milter support.
3. Copy sendmail's headers and library files into a shared directory where MIMEDefang can get to them.
4. Obtain and install Perl modules required for SpamAssassin (see Chapter 6).
5. Obtain and install SpamAssassin. (Mail::SpamAssassin in Perl module parlance. Again, see Chapter 6.)
6. Obtain and install Perl modules required for MIMEDefang (see Table 8-3).
7. Obtain and install MIMEDefang.
8. Add MIMEDefang to your startup scripts.

As you can see, it's not a simple process, and it requires that you spend some time compiling and debugging.

A complete guide to installing and using MIMEDefang is well beyond the scope of this chapter. However, an excellent installation How To is available at *http://www.rudolphtire.com/mimedefang-howto/* (there's also a link to it at *http://www.mimedefang.org* under "HOWTO"). This gives you step-by-step instructions on setting up a complete MIMEDefang installation.

Unfortunately, information on editing and writing your own "mimedefang-filter" script is somewhat lacking. You'll find some good information on the various functions in the MIMEDefang How To, but it may be daunting to someone with little or no Perl programming experience. That's where subscribing to the MIMEDefang mailing list comes in handy (at *http://lists.roaringpenguin.com/mailman/listinfo/mimedefang*). Note that you shouldn't post MIMEDefang-related questions to the SpamAssassin mailing list. Though there are probably many people with the experience to help you, you should post to the MIMEDefang

Module	Version	Location
MIME::tools	>= 5.411a	*http://www.mimedefang.org*
IO:stringy	>= 1.212	CPAN
MIME::Base64	>= 2.11	CPAN
MailTools	>= 1.1401	CPAN
Digest::SHA1	>= 2.00	CPAN

* Note that the MIMEDefang authors recommend using their patched version of MIME::tools.

Table 8-3. Perl Modules Required for MIMEDefang 2.39*

list first—especially if SpamAssassin works fine when it's not run using MIMEDefang. Of course, you can also purchase MIMEDefang support from Roaring Penguin Software.

USING AMAVISD-NEW WITH SPAMASSASSIN

amavisd-new is to postfix what MIMEDefang is to sendmail—or at least that's the simplest way to put it. Actually, you can run amavisd-new with a number of MTAs, including sendmail and qmail, but it seems to be the mail filter of choice for postfix users.

amavisd-new sprang out of the AMaViS project (which stands for A Mail Virus Scanner). Whereas AMaViS focused mostly on integrating virus scanning with MTAs, amavisd-new also added SpamAssassin integration and other features. Like SpamAssassin itself, amavisd-new is written in Perl with some helper components written in C.

amavisd-new works by running as a daemon on a specified port on the mail host. Incoming mail is sent to your MTA as usual, then back out the MTA and through amavisd-new (where scanning and modifications are made), and then back to your MTA for delivery. amavisd-new does not run as a plug-in to your MTA, but it runs as a separate ESMTP mailer on a specified port. Your MTA also listens on two ports. Figure 8-2 shows a diagram of this process.

Newer versions of amavisd-new can also run as sendmail milters (much like MIMEDefang), but this limits some of the functionality (such as adding spam or virus headers to a message).

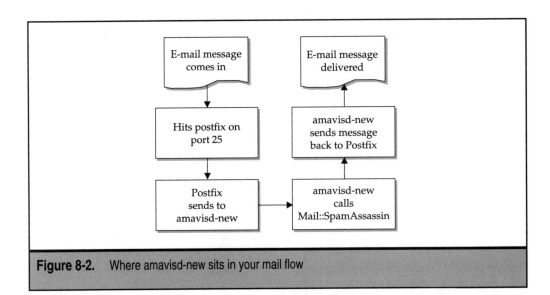

Figure 8-2. Where amavisd-new sits in your mail flow

amavisd-new and SpamAssassin

As with MIMEDefang, amavisd-new uses the Mail::SpamAssassin Perl module rather than invoking spamassassin or spamc. SpamAssassin configuration is performed using the standard SpamAssassin local.cf and user_prefs files. Because amavisd-new is running SpamAssassin system-wide, however, Bayesian filtering and other user-based configuration options may not work.

amavisd-new Requirements

The release of amavisd-new, current as of this writing, is 20030616-p6. amavisd-new uses a "snapshot" method of versioning rather than a major and minor release number. amavisd-new requires Perl 5.005 or later and a number of Perl modules to help it along (Table 8-4). Version 4.06 or later of the UNIX *file* utility is also required.

Steps for installing and configuring amavisd-new to interoperate with various mailers is beyond the scope of this chapter. A number of links to How To documents can be found on the amavisd-new web site at *http://www.ijs.si/software/amavisd/*. The source code distribution also contains a directory called README_FILES that has instructions for postfix, sendmail (both as a milter and not), and Exim.

Module	Version	Location
Archive::Tar	Any	CPAN
Archive::Zip	Any	CPAN
Compress::Zlib	Any	CPAN
Convert::TNEF	Any	CPAN
Convert::UUlib	Any	CPAN
MIME::Base64	Any	CPAN
MIME::Tools	MIMEDefang version or >= 6.2	http://www.mimedefang.org/ or CPAN
MailTools	>= 1.58	CPAN
Net::Server	Any	CPAN
libnet	>= 1.16	CPAN
Digest::MD5	Any	CPAN
IO::stringy	Any	CPAN
Time::HiRes	>= 1.49	CPAN
Unix::Syslog	Any	CPAN

Table 8-4. Perl Module Requirements for amavisd-new

USING SPAMASSASSIN AS A GATEWAY TO ANOTHER MAIL SERVER

You don't need to run SpamAssassin on the server that is the ultimate destination of the mail. In fact, in many cases this may not be possible. In such a case, the MTA running SpamAssassin can simply act as a gateway to another "smart host" after scanning. One situation where this makes sense is when you have a public-facing mail server on your DMZ (semitrusted network) where you scan mail for spam and viruses before it hits the interior mail server. Another is when you aren't running a UNIX or Linux system as your final-destination mail server (you're running Microsoft Exchange or Lotus Notes, for instance), but still want to run SpamAssassin. Figure 8-3 shows a configuration example.

The best way to configure a SpamAssassin server as a mail gateway is to use either MIMEDefang or amavisd-new. If you simply use Procmail in conjunction with the *spamassassin* program, you filter mail after it has already been processed by the MTA (so it can't use the MTA's "smart host" capabilities, and it won't be possible to send it on to a smart host unless you forward each individual user's accounts to separate accounts on the final destination server.

To filter the mail and send it on to a smart host, use either MIMEDefang as a milter or amavisd-new as a mailer daemon. With MIMEDefang, configure the milter in sendmail, and then make the destination server that gateway's smart host by adding the following to the server's sendmail.mc file and rebuilding the sendmail.cf file:

```
define(`SMART_HOST', `smart-host.yourdomain.tld')
```

With amavisd-new, either run it as a milter with sendmail, or modify the `$forward_method` variable in amavisd-new.conf to send mail on to your "smart host":

```
$forward_method = 'smtp:smart-host.yourdomain.tld:25';
```

That's it. We're confident that this is the best way to configure SpamAssassin on large installations, as it separates the sometimes expensive (resource-wise) task of scanning spam from the server where users check their mail.

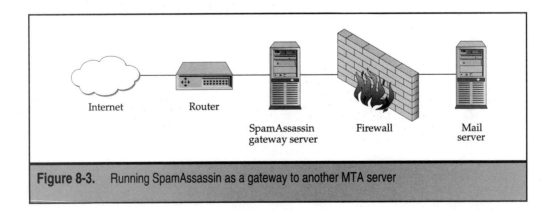

Figure 8-3. Running SpamAssassin as a gateway to another MTA server

SUMMARY

In this chapter we learned how to tweak SpamAssassin to make it more effective. One way to do this is to add and modify your own SpamAssassin rules, which can be challenging to get right, but of great benefit. Modifying whitelists and blacklists is another powerful way to fine-tune how much spam is allowed to get through and avoid false positives and false negatives. Localizing SpamAssassin for the languages in which you normally get e-mail reduces foreign spam. Finally, using filtering programs such as MIMEDefang and amavisd-new gives you the ability to filter for viruses, manipulate headers, and use smart hosts.

CHAPTER 9

CONFIGURING POPULAR E-MAIL CLIENTS FOR SPAM FILTERING

In Chapters 6, 7, and 8 we installed and configured SpamAssassin. In most cases, however, this takes care of only half the job that needs to be done. SpamAssassin is now tagging messages it thinks are spam, but the messages are still coming through, and a manual process for dealing with them is still necessary. Fortunately, most e-mail clients allow you to filter e-mail based on certain criteria—such as specific text in a header. By doing this, we can filter out and eliminate messages that are tagged by SpamAssassin.

In this chapter, we'll configure the anti-spam and filtering features on four popular e-mail clients: Eudora, Mozilla Mail, Outlook Express, and Outlook.

CONFIGURING SPAM FILTERS ON EUDORA

Eudora is a popular e-mail client that has been around since the early 1990s, with versions for both Windows and Macintosh (OS 9 and OS X) platforms. In this chapter we cover only the Windows version, but the features are the same for the Mac. Eudora is developed and distributed by QUALCOMM, Inc., as part of its Eudora product line (which also includes a mail server). It can be found at *http://www.eudora.com/*.

One of the most interesting aspects about Eudora is its licensing. Eudora is "shipped" (actually downloaded) as a single program, but it can run in three different modes:

- **Paid mode**   The full-featured version that includes SpamWatch and technical support. This costs $40 to $50, depending on whether or not you're upgrading.

- **Sponsored mode**   This version includes all the features of Paid mode, except for SpamWatch and technical support. You will see an ad window while running Eudora in this mode, as well as up to three sponsored toolbar links. Note that it does *not* insert ads or sponsor links into your outbound e-mails.

- **Light mode**   This version has only a subset of the features found in Paid or Sponsored mode. Does not include SpamWatch or technical support, but you don't have to put up with the ads.

Since spam is our primary concern, we're going to focus mostly on Paid mode and SpamWatch. Filtering for SpamAssassin tags, however, also works in Sponsored and Light modes.

Watching for Spam with Eudora's SpamWatch

Starting with version 6.0, the Paid version of Eudora includes SpamWatch, which currently includes two anti-spam plug-ins:

- **Bayesian plug-in**   Matches against keyword frequencies in much the same way SpamAssassin, SpamBayes, and other Bayesian filters work.

- **Header plug-in**   Automatically scans for headers inserted by other anti-spam programs, such as SpamAssassin or ActiveState's PureMessage (formerly PerlMX).

Chapter 9: Configuring Popular E-mail Clients for Spam Filtering

You read correctly: Eudora's SpamWatch will automatically look for SpamAssassin's headers. That makes Eudora the easiest client to use with SpamAssassin. SpamWatch also includes whitelisting so you can keep certain legitimate senders from being tagged as spam.

Turning On Eudora's SpamWatch

You can turn on SpamWatch in a couple of ways. The first can occur when you install Eudora. One of the questions you're asked during the installation process is whether or not you want to put garbage e-mail in the Junk mailbox automatically. The Junk mailbox is created automatically by Eudora.

The other way to turn on SpamWatch is within the Junk Mail options. Choose Tools | Options, and you'll see the Options window, shown in Figure 9-1. Scroll down the icons on the left-hand side until you come across the Junk Mail icon, which looks like a can of sardines. Make sure that, under the Junk Mail section, the item Automatically Place Junk In Junk Mailbox is checked.

Tweaking Eudora's SpamWatch

Take another look at Figure 9-1, and you'll see several other options regarding Eudora's junk mail processing. The first is the Junk Threshold slider at the top of the window that allows you to set the minimum score threshold at which mail is considered junk. By default, it's set to 50. If you want to catch more potential spam, you can lower this to 30 or 40, but you risk catching some legitimate mail. If you raise the threshold, more spam might get through but you'll avoid false positives. This score is based on the Bayesian probability that

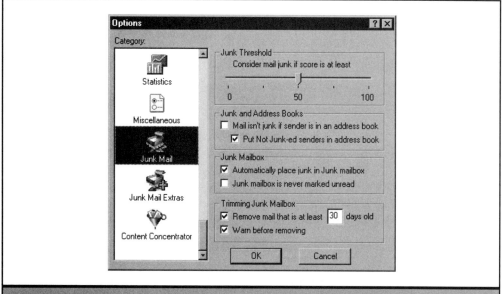

Figure 9-1. SpamWatch's Junk Mail Options window in Eudora

a message is spam. Think of it as a percentage chance that a given message is spam. Therefore, a score of 50 means that it's a coin toss as to whether or not a message is spam (a 50 percent chance), but SpamWatch doesn't give it the benefit of the doubt with its default setting.

The Junk And Address Books section gives you options for whitelisting addresses in your address book. To do this, simply check Mail Isn't Junk If Sender Is In An Address Book. Checking the Put Not Junk-ed Senders In Address Book checkbox will whitelist the sender of any message that you deem "Not Junk" (as we'll show later in the section "Training Eudora's SpamWatch").

Under the Junk Mailbox section, along with the Automatically Place Junk In Junk Mailbox option, is the option Junk Mailbox Is Never Marked As Unread. Normally, folders with unread messages appear in boldface type in Eudora. If this option is checked, messages in the Junk mailbox will never appear in boldface.

The options in the Trimming Junk Mailbox section let you decide what to do with old spam. The first checkbox configures the auto-removal of junk mail after a specified number of days. Generally, 30 days is more than sufficient if you want to look for false positives, such as when you're expecting e-mail and you haven't seen it yet. If you get hundreds of junk mail messages per day, however, you may want to shorten this to a week or so to conserve disk space. The Warn Before Removing option simply tells SpamWatch whether or not you want to be warned before it removes the mail.

Training Eudora's SpamWatch

Even though it comes with a database of common spam keywords, as with other Bayesian filters, Eudora's SpamWatch must be trained before it's effective. Training it is simple. If a message hits your inbox and you decide it is spam, follow these steps:

1. Select the message.
2. Either right-click the message and choose Junk, choose Message | Junk, as shown here, or press CTRL-J.

The message is then moved into the Junk folder and is run through Bayesian analysis.

A similar process is used to teach SpamWatch that a message isn't spam. Go to your Junk mail folder, look for a message that isn't spam, and follow these steps:

1. Select the message.
2. Either right-click the message and choose Not Junk, choose Message | Not Junk, or press CTRL-SHIFT-J.

That's all there is to it. After 100 or so messages, Eudora should have a pretty good idea what is and is not spam.

CONFIGURING SPAM FILTERS ON MOZILLA MAIL

Mozilla Mail is included as an optional part of the Mozilla browser suite installation. (It's actually Mozilla Mail & Newsgroups, but since we're not concerned about reading news in this chapter, we'll drop the Newsgroups part.) Mozilla spawned when Netscape, experiencing intense competition with its Communicator browser suite from Microsoft's Internet Explorer, released its source code to the open-source community in 1998. Since then, Mozilla has become a popular cross-platform browser (it's the default browser in Red Hat and many other Linux distributions), but it still barely made a dent in Microsoft's market share. The Mozilla Foundation releases binaries of Mozilla and Mozilla Mail for Windows, Linux, and Mac OS X, though you can also typically find binaries for Solaris and HP-UX, to name a couple. If a binary doesn't exist for your platform, there's always the option of compiling it yourself from source code, which Mozilla makes readily available.

NOTE Mozilla can be downloaded from *http://www.mozilla.org/*. For this chapter, we're using Mozilla 1.5.

Mozilla's Junk Mail Controls

Junk mail controls were added to Mozilla in version 1.3. The Mozilla developers designed it to include a variety of plug-ins to deal with spam, but initially they chose to use a Bayesian classifier similar to what you might find in SpamAssassin, SpamBayes, and other tools. Like other projects, developers chose to use a Bayesian system as outlined in Paul Graham's "A Plan for Spam" paper (*http://www.paulgraham.com/spam.html*), where words within a message are given a statistical probability of being a common word in a spam message. This means, as with other Bayesian classifiers, that you need to teach the system what spam looks like versus what legitimate mail looks like. It also means it may take dozens of spam and legitimate messages to fine tune the filter.

The Fox and the Bird: Two New Mozilla Projects

The Mozilla Foundation has begun an initiative to develop and distribute individual Mozilla components. The idea is that separating the components removes some of the bloat and crud that slow down the full-blown Mozilla. The initial fruits of this effort are the Firefox browser and the Thunderbird mail and news client. You can download and install one or both at *http://www.mozilla.org/*. As of this writing, both are in pre-1.0 releases, but initial reviews of Firefox (and our own tests) have shown that it delivers the speed it promises. Thunderbird is lagging behind Firefox in development, but it also appears solid (and has a Bayesian classifier for junk mail). While we're not going to cover Thunderbird in this chapter, we are keeping an eye on these projects, and we encourage you to do the same.

Turning It On

Do the following to turn on junk mail controls in Mozilla:

1. Choose Tools | Junk Mail Controls. The Junk Mail Controls window will open, as shown in Figure 9-2.

2. In the Account pull-down field, make sure the account to which you want to apply junk mail controls is selected.

3. Make sure that Enable Junk Mail Controls is checked.

4. Choose whether or not you want to mark messages as junk if the sender is in your address book. This is a handy whitelisting function and we suggest you enable it, unless your friends and coworkers tend to get their addresses spoofed by spammers.

5. Check the checkbox next to Move Incoming Messages Determined To Be Junk Mail To, and under that option choose what you want done with incoming junk mail. In our case, we'll have it moved to our account's Junk folder. You can also have junk mail go directly to your Trash folder. Uncheck the Move Incoming Messages checkbox if you don't want Mozilla to do anything with those messages. The risk of sending them directly to the Trash, of course, is that you might miss catching a false positive message.

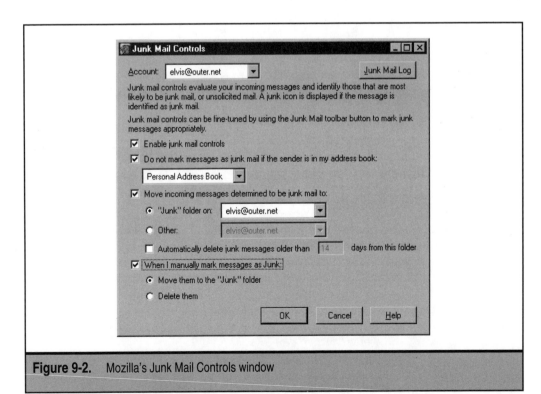

Figure 9-2. Mozilla's Junk Mail Controls window

6. You can choose whether or not to delete junk mail messages automatically after a certain number of days. We're going to leave this option unchecked so that we can deal with those messages ourselves.

7. Finally, if you want something to be done with messages that you manually mark as Junk, check that box. You can have these messages deleted or moved to the Junk folder. We're going to have such messages moved to our Junk folder.

8. Click OK when you are done.

Providing Training

Now that junk mail control is enabled, we have to train the system to identify spam. Select a spam message that wasn't already classified as junk, and then do one of the following in the Eudora window:

- Click the Junk icon on the top icon bar that looks like a recycling bin.
- Click in the column headed by the smaller recycling bin next to the message you want to classify as junk.

Once you've done this, the message is tagged as junk and moved into your Junk folder (or wherever you told it to go). If you look in that folder, you'll see the junk mail there (see Figure 9-3). Notice the recycling bin icon appears in the junk column in the upper pane, and the words "Mozilla thinks this message is junk mail" appears in the message in the lower pane.

Dealing with False Positives

If a message gets tagged as junk but it really isn't, simply select the message and either click the Not Junk button, which appears in the lower pane in Figure 9-3, or click the recycling bin icon next to the message. Another option is to click the Junk icon that appears in the toolbar. You'll then have to move the message back into the correct folder.

Finally, to run a scan manually against a folder for junk mail, choose Tools | Run Junk Mail Controls On Folder. If you want to delete junk-tagged messages within a folder, choose Tools | Delete Mail Marked As Junk In Folder.

Using Mozilla Message Filters with SpamAssassin

Like many other mail clients, Mozilla mail lets you filter messages based on what appears in the subject, body, or header of a message. We can use this to our benefit when filtering mail that has been tagged with SpamAssassin. As we saw in Chapter 8, SpamAssassin tags messages with a hidden header called X-Spam-Flag. This flag is set to either YES or NO, depending on whether or not a message is spam. It also tags messages with an X-Spam-Level header that adds an asterisk (*) for each point the message scored. We can set up Mozilla to look for one or both of these.

Anti-Spam Tool Kit

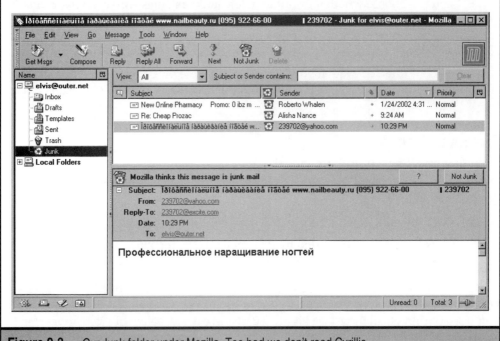

Figure 9-3. Our Junk folder under Mozilla. Too bad we don't read Cyrillic.

To configure Mozilla Mail to filter on the X-Spam-Flag header, do the following:

1. Choose Tools | Message Filters. The Message Filters window appears, as shown here.

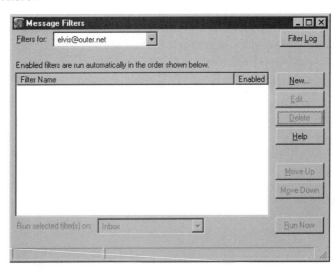

2. Click the New button to add a new filter. A Filter Rules window appears, as shown here.

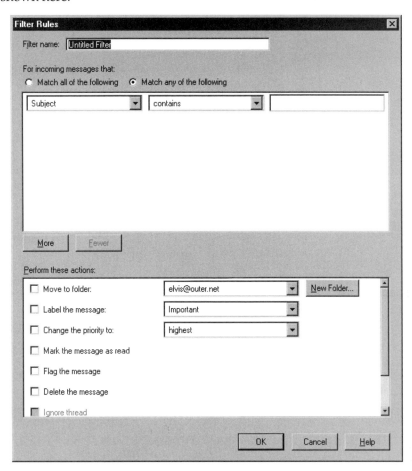

3. In the Filter Name field, name the filter **SpamAssassin Flag**.
4. In the top pane is a pull-down selection menu called Subject. Pull down the menu and choose the bottom-most option, Customize. A Customize Headers window appears.
5. In the New Message Header field, type **X-Spam-Flag**, as shown next. Click Add, and then click OK.

6. Back at the Filter Rules window, pull down the menu that says Subject and select your new X-Spam-Flag header. The second pull-down menu reads Contains; leave it as is. In the third field, furthest to the right, type the word **YES**.

7. Now let's indicate what we want to do with our tagged spam. In the Perform These Actions area, check the first checkbox that says Move To Folder, and in the first field select your spam folder—in our case, Junk.

8. Click OK to save the changes, and this puts you back at the Message Filters window. You should see your new filter, along with a check mark next to it to say that it's enabled.

9. Select your new filter and click Run Now to run it against your inbox (you can also use the pull-down menu to select other folders).

Now let's say you want to send any spam messages that have a SpamAssassin score of 20 or greater directly to your deleted items folder. To do this, follow the same steps above, but instead of the New Message Header being set to X-Spam-Flag (in step 5), make it X-Spam-Level. Also, in the field to the right of Contains, type in 20 asterisks (********************). Run the filter, and any message with a score of 20 or higher will be moved directly into your deleted items folder.

CONFIGURING SPAM FILTERS IN OUTLOOK EXPRESS

Microsoft Outlook Express (OE) for Windows is distributed for free as part of Internet Explorer. It's designed primarily to be an Internet mail and news client for home users, as it lacks the corporate features of Outlook (such as a Microsoft Exchange connector, scheduling, and so on). It supports the Post Office Protocol (POP), Internet Message Access Protocol (IMAP), and Hypertext Transfer Protocol (HTTP) for reading mail, as well as the Secure Socket Layer (SSL) versions of POP and IMAP. For sending mail, OE supports Simple Mail Transport Protocol (SMTP), and for Internet News, Network News Transfer Protocol (NNTP). For many Windows users, OE is their first and only e-mail client.

As of this writing, Outlook Express 6 (a component of Internet Explorer 6) is the latest version. Even though OE has been around for many years, it lacks solid anti-spam features and requires third-party applications and plug-ins—such as those we cover in Chapter 10—to provide any real spam filtering functionality. Nonetheless, a few OE features come in handy for thwarting spam.

Blocking Senders in Outlook Express

Outlook Express provides a convenient method for blacklisting senders from whom you don't want to get mail. OE refers to this as "Blocking Senders." Basically, it's a blacklist that you update and maintain. If a sender's address is in your blocked senders list, their messages automatically go to your deleted items folder. Note that this function works only if you're using POP—*not* IMAP or HTTP.

You can blacklist e-mail in two ways:

- Block a sender after you receive e-mail from them.
- Manually add an address from which you know you don't want to get mail.

The first method is the easiest. If you get a spam message (or any other offensive message) and you no longer want to receive e-mail from that sender, simply follow these steps:

1. Open the message.
2. Right-click the sender's name.
3. In the pop-up menu, choose Block Sender (as shown in the "Debt Elimination" e-mail shown next).

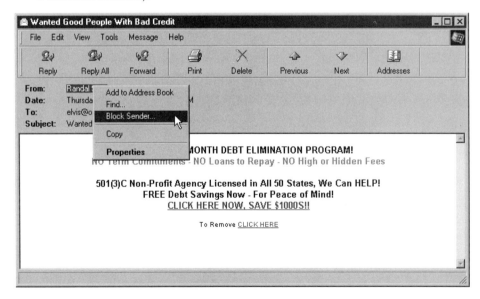

Anti-Spam Tool Kit

4. If the address is successfully blocked, you'll see this pop-up dialog:

NOTE Another method, similar to this, is to simply highlight the message and choose Message | Block Sender from the toolbar. This is useful if you're concerned about opening the message because it might contain a virus or offensive content.

The second method is to add an entry manually to your blocked senders list. This is useful if you already know that you want to blacklist certain addresses or domains. To use the blocked senders list, follow these instructions:

1. Choose Tools | Message Rules | Blocked Senders List, as shown here:

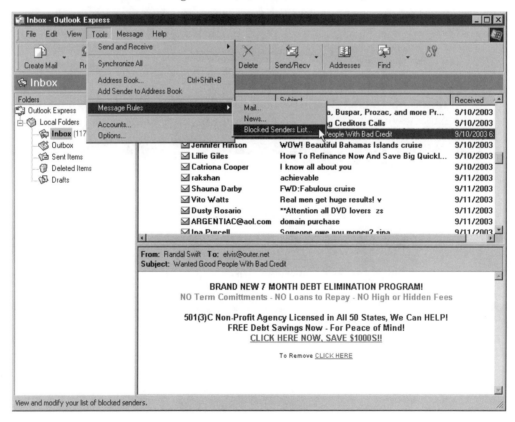

Chapter 9: Configuring Popular E-mail Clients for Spam Filtering

2. The Message Rules window appears next. Make sure the Blocked Senders tab is selected. You see a list of senders that have already been blocked (if any). On the right are buttons to Add, Modify, or Remove blocked senders.

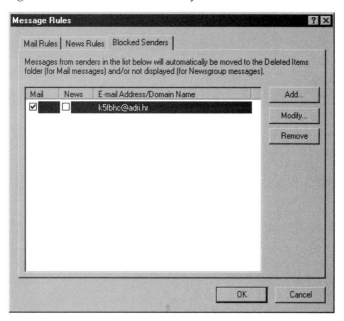

3. For our example, we'll modify our sole existing entry. Suppose we get messages from several e-mail addresses within that domain (adri.hr) and not just the message we're currently blocking. Click the Modify button, and you'll see an Edit Sender dialog box, like the one shown next. Remove the username and "at sign" (@) from the e-mail address so that only the domain remains. This blocks anyone who tries to send you e-mail from that domain. Click OK to save your changes.

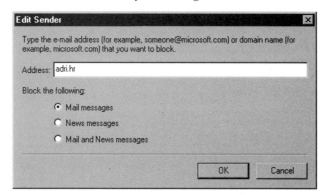

The advantage of the blocked senders list is that it provides a quick and easy way for you to block specific addresses or domains. Unfortunately, it also carries with it all the negative aspects of such lists. As you know, spammers often randomize and spoof the sender's address, meaning that you may see spam only from that particular address once in your e-mail-reading life. So, for example, you might get spam from 3t63wer@spammer.tld the first time, but the next spam you get from the same company might be from wrw3432f@spammy.tld. This limits the practical use of blocking individual addresses to being effective only against bulk e-mailers that are trying to remain legit by using their real addresses and domain names. The other negative aspect of blocked senders is that if you block an entire domain, such as msn.com, you end up blocking e-mail from every user in that domain—some of it legitimate.

Using OE Message Rules with SpamAssassin

You can also set up Message Rules in OE to filter incoming mail based on specifics about the message content. This is useful if you want OE to look for messages that have been tagged as spam by SpamAssassin. Like Blocked Senders, this works only with POP e-mail accounts—not IMAP or HTTP accounts.

Another limitation of OE's Message Rules is its inability to filter on hidden message header information. It can filter only on the From, To, CC, and Subject lines; the body; and a few other options such as whether or not the message has an attachment, its size, and its priority level. Unfortunately, this means you can't filter messages based on the hidden X-Spam-Flag or X-Spam-Status headers.

Your options are twofold:

- Set the `rewrite_subject` option in SpamAssassin's system-wide local.cf file (or `user_prefs` for an individual user) to 1. This appends *****SPAM***** to the beginning of the message's subject. It's messy, but it works—and it allows you to filter spam in OE based on the message having this tag in the subject line. Remember that you can also change the subject to something less obnoxious using the `subject_tag` option in local.cf or `user_prefs`.

- Filter based on the contents of the body. The "intro" body text to a SpamAssassin-caught message always looks the same on your server. For example, unless you've changed the intro text, it begins with, "Spam detection software, running on the system." This is a good phrase to filter on.

Rather than modify the subject line, we'll configure OE to filter on the second option. Follow these procedures:

1. Choose Tools | Message Rules | Mail, as shown next.

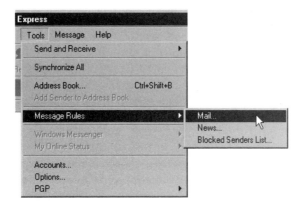

2. The Message Rules window appears next. Make sure the Mail Rules tab is selected. Click the New button to add a new rule.

3. The New Mail Rule window appears. In the first grouping of checkboxes, Select The Conditions For Your Rule, check the box that says Where The Subject Line Contains Specific Words.

4. In the second grouping of checkboxes, Select The Actions For Your Rule, check the box that says Move It To The Specified Folder. (Make sure you check to Move the message, rather than Copy it—or else you'll just end up with two copies of the same spam!)

5. Under the third box, Rule Description, click the hyperlinked phrase, *Contains Specific Words*. A Type Specific Words window opens. In the first field, type in the intro phrase **Spam detection software, running on the system**. Click the Add button, and then click OK.

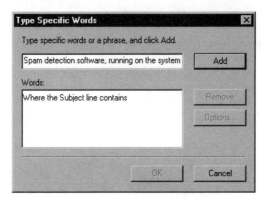

6. Back in the New Mail Rule window, click the hyperlinked word *Specified*. A Move window appears. Now you can select a folder or create a new one. We'll create one and call it **Junk**. Click OK.
7. Finally, in the fourth field on the New Mail Rule window, name the rule you just created. Type in **Junk Mail**. Now, your New Mail Rule window should look like the one in Figure 9-4. Click OK to save it.

You end up back at the Message Rules window. On the right side, next to your new rule, is an Apply Now button. Click this to open the Apply Now window, where you select the rules you want to apply, and then click Apply Now again. This applies the new rule (and any old ones) to the messages currently in your Inbox. When finished, click OK and then Close to go back to the Message Rules window. Finally, click OK to exit.

CONFIGURING SPAM FILTERS ON OUTLOOK

Microsoft Outlook comes with the Microsoft Office suite of programs. Microsoft's corporate-class e-mail client has many more features than Outlook Express. In fact, the primary similarity between Outlook and Outlook Express is the name—almost everything else is different. Like OE, though, Outlook can connect to mail servers using POP, IMAP, and HTTP (for web accounts). But it can also connect directly to Microsoft Exchange servers for e-mail, calendaring, and public folders.

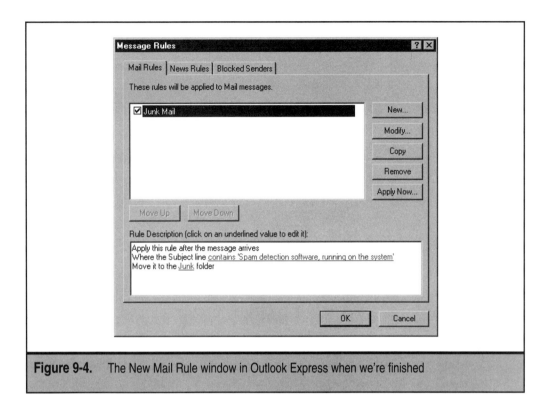

Figure 9-4. The New Mail Rule window in Outlook Express when we're finished

We are covering Outlook 2002 (part of Office XP) in this chapter. The version you have installed depends on the version of Office you are using (Outlook 97 came with Office 97, Outlook 2000 came with Office 2000, and so on).

Configuring Outlook's Junk and Adult Content E-mail Filters

Outlook 2002 has built-in Adult and Junk e-mail filters. These filters operate by comparing the messages headers and body against a list of keywords and also by comparing user-defined lists of known Junk and Adult content senders. They are configured by setting up Outlook Rules.

To turn on the Junk e-mail filter, do the following:

1. Choose Tools | Rules Wizard. The Rules Wizard window, shown next, will appear.

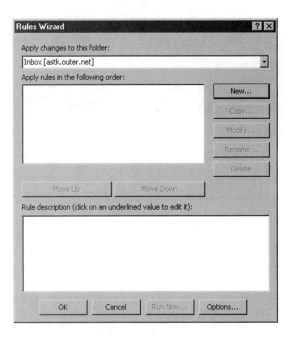

2. Click the New button on the right-hand side. A second Rules Wizard window appears. Click the radio button at the top that says Start From A Blank Rule, as shown next. Check Messages When They Arrive should be highlighted in the top window pane, because that's what we want this rule to do.

3. Click the Next button. Scroll down the list of conditions in the Which Condition(s) Do You Want To Check? window pane until you get to the bottom. The rule we

Chapter 9: Configuring Popular E-mail Clients for Spam Filtering

want is Suspected To Be Junk E-Mail Or From Junk Senders, which is fourth from the bottom. Select this rule, as shown next, and then click Next.

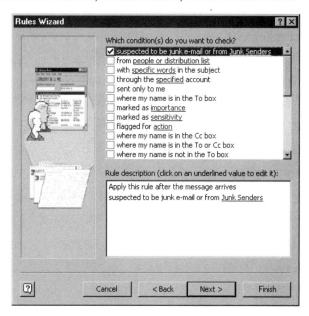

4. Check the topmost item in the next window, Move It To A Specified Folder, as shown next. Then select the word specified in the bottommost pane and create a new folder called Junk (if you don't already have one). Select the new folder and click Next.

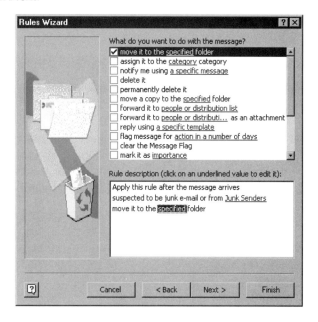

Anti-Spam Tool Kit

5. You then have the option of adding any exceptions to the rule. One good exception might be to exclude people listed in your Address Book. We're not going to do that here, so we'll just click Next and move on.

6. On the final window, shown next, you can specify a name for your rule. We'll use the default name Junk Senders. The checkbox Run This Rule Now On Messages Already In "Inbox" will tell Outlook to go ahead and run this rule against your Inbox. This is handy if your Inbox is already brimming with spam. The checkbox Turn On This Rule should already be checked. If it isn't, check it now.

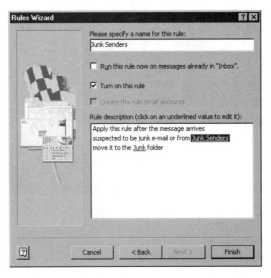

7. Click Finish and you're done. You should see your new rule, as shown in Figure 9-5. Click OK to apply the rule.

Outlook considers Junk and Adult mail as two separate issues and doesn't lump the two types together. So, to add an Adult Content mail rule, follow the same steps just covered, but instead of selecting Suspected To Be Junk Mail in step 3, select Containing Adult Content For From Adult Content Senders.

Adding Junk and Adult Content Senders

If you receive an e-mail containing junk or adult content, you can add the sender of that e-mail to your Junk or Adult Content Senders lists. This is similar to Outlook Express's Blocked Senders list. To add someone to either list, do the following:

1. First, turn on the Junk and Adult Content Senders organizing feature, if it isn't already on. Do this by choosing Tools | Organize. Then select the Junk E-Mail tab from the list of ways to organize your Inbox. It should look like Figure 9-6. Click both buttons that say Turn On.

2. Select the junk or adult e-mail message in your Inbox.

Chapter 9: Configuring Popular E-mail Clients for Spam Filtering

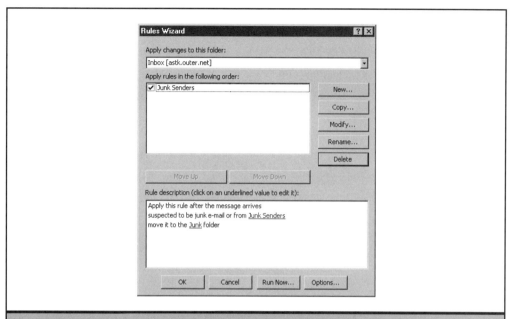

Figure 9-5. Your new Junk Senders Outlook rule

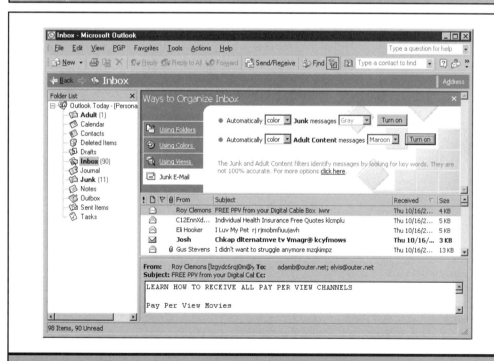

Figure 9-6. Turning on Adult and Junk senders organizing in Outlook

3. Right-click the message and choose Junk E-mail, or choose Actions | Junk E-Mail | Add To Junk Senders List or Add To Adult Content Senders List, as shown in Figure 9-7.

As with OE's blocked senders list, the adult content and junk senders lists should be used with caution and with the knowledge that spammers can easily forward the From address to bypass such lists.

What Outlook's Junk E-mail Filter Looks For

As we've said, Outlook's Junk and Adult e-mail filters work by looking for specific keywords or phrases. Here's a list of the exact keywords and phrases that Outlook 2000 looks for (note that Outlook 2002's list isn't published). We put it here for educational purposes only.

Junk E-mail Filter
First eight characters of From are digits
Subject contains "advertisement"
Body contains "money back "
Body contains "cards accepted"
Body contains "removal instructions"
Body contains "extra income"
Subject contains "!" AND Subject contains "$"
Subject contains "!" AND Subject contains "free"
Body contains ",000" AND Body contains "!!" AND Body contains "$"
Body contains "Dear friend"
Body contains "for free?"
Body contains "for free!"
Body contains "Guarantee" AND (Body contains "satisfaction" OR Body contains "absolute")
Body contains "more info " AND Body contains "visit " AND Body contains "$"
Body contains "SPECIAL PROMOTION"
Body contains "one-time mail"
Subject contains "$$"
Body contains "order today"
Body contains "order now!"
Body contains "money-back guarantee"
Body contains "100% satisfied"
To contains "friend@"
To contains "public@"
To contains "success@"
From contains "sales@"
From contains "success."

What Outlook's Junk E-mail Filter Looks For *(continued)*

From contains "success@"
From contains "mail@"
From contains "@public"
From contains "@savvy"
From contains "profits@"
From contains "hello@"
Body contains " mlm"
Body contains "@mlm"
Body contains "///////////////"
Body contains "check or money order"

Adult Content Filter
Subject contains " xxx"
Subject contains "over 18"
Subject contains "over 21"
Subject contains "adult s"
Subject contains "adults only"
Subject contains "be 18"
Subject contains "18+"
Body contains "over 18"
Body contains "over 21"
Body contains "must be 18"
Body contains "adults only"
Body contains "adult web"
Body contains "must be 21"
Body contains "adult en"
Body contains "18+"
Subject contains "erotic"
Subject contains "adult en"
Subject contains " sex"
Body contains " xxx "
Body contains " xxx!"
Subject contains "free" AND Subject contains "adult"
Subject contains "free" AND Subject contains "sex"

Source: Microsoft Junk Mail Filter Readme at http://office.microsoft.com/ under Assistance | Office 2000 | Outlook 2000.

This is not an extremely thorough list, so a crafty spammer can easily bypass these filters. We found that these filters catch about 10 percent of spam, but they can also cause a lot of false positives. This is compared to the 90 to 95 percent catch rate on Bayesian filters.

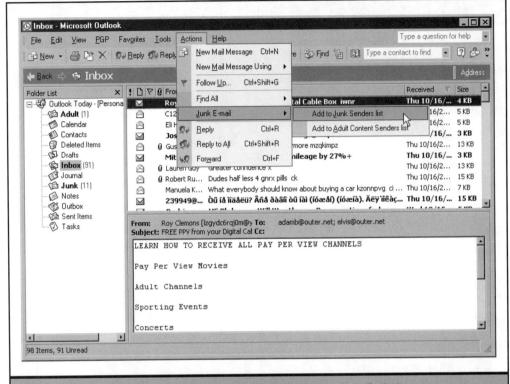

Figure 9-7. Adding a sender to the adult content or junk senders list in Outlook

Using Outlook Message Rules with SpamAssassin

Unlike Outlook Express, Outlook does allow you to filter messages based on any message header, including hidden ones. This makes the job of filtering for messages tagged by SpamAssassin much easier. To set up the Rules, do the following:

1. Choose Tools | Rules Wizard.
2. Click New, and chose Start From A Blank Rule. Click Next.
3. In the Which Condition(s) Do You Want To Check? area, scroll down until you find With Specific Words In The Message Header. Check the box next to it, as shown next.

Chapter 9: Configuring Popular E-mail Clients for Spam Filtering

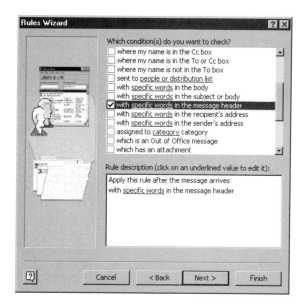

4. In the bottom pane, click Specific Words to enter the words you want to look for. Enter **X-Spam Flag: YES** in the Search Text window, as shown next. Click Add and then OK. When you're back in the Rules Wizard, click Next.

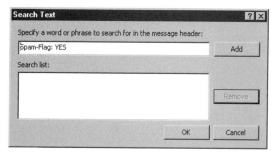

5. Click the Move It To The Specified Folder checkbox.
6. Select the word *Specified* in the bottom pane. Select the folder to which you want to send SpamAssassin tagged mail (such as the Junk folder). Click Next.
7. Add any exceptions you want to make. Then click Next.
8. If you want to, change the name of the rule (we're going to leave ours as X-Spam Flag: YES). Then click Finish.

Now, any messages that contain the hidden X-Spam-Flag header set to YES will be moved into your Junk folder. You can get even more granular by, instead of using X-Spam-Flag, use X-Spam-Level and a number of asterisks for the spam score. For instance, to move any messages with a spam score of 10 to your Junk folder, you can have the header look for *X-Spam-Level: ***********.

SUMMARY

In this chapter we've looked at four popular e-mail clients: Eudora, Mozilla Mail, Outlook Express, and Outlook. Each has its own set of anti-spam features. Some, such as Eudora's SpamWatch, are quite robust and full-featured. Others, such as Outlook Express, offer little more than manual blacklists. All of them will allow you to filter messages based on certain criteria, which makes them extremely useful when filtering SpamAssassin-tagged messages. Configuring your e-mail clients in this way is helpful in keeping spam out of sight.

PART III

IMPLEMENTING OTHER POPULAR ANTI-SPAM TOOLS

CHAPTER 10

ANTI-SPAM CLIENTS FOR WINDOWS

By now you've learned about powerful tools that can stop an unwanted e-mail message before it reaches your inbox. But what if these tools don't provide enough protection? Your mail system might block 99 percent of the spam that hits the mail exchanger, but if you get 10,000 pieces of spam a day, you still end up with 100 pieces of unwanted e-mail every day. And what do you do if your ISP doesn't filter mail at the mail server? That's where anti-spam clients come in.

As the last line of defense (other than the Delete button) in the war on spam, client-side mail filters use a variety of standard and advanced methods for detecting, matching, filtering, and tweaking spam. In this chapter, we cover spam-client solutions for the Microsoft Windows operating systems (for the most part tested on Windows 2000 or XP systems). The clients covered are organized by method of detection (POP proxy, Outlook plug-in, and Other) and method of filtering (blacklist, Bayesian/fuzzy filters, and combination). Several, such as KnockKnock, have unique methods and features that either are on the cutting edge of spam fighting or are extremely effective (such as SpamNet—for now) at stopping spam.

By far, we found the Bayesian-based filters to be the most effective over the long haul, with the least amount of time and learning investment. However, SpamNet, a peer-to-peer (P2P) client, outperformed every anti-spam tool we discuss in this chapter—with the caveat that this could be a temporary condition until the spammers exploit P2P network spam solutions.

SPAMBAYES

SpamBayes is an open-source anti-spam tool. The development group released a version of SpamBayes, first developed as a platform-independent spam filter for UNIX, as a plug-in for Microsoft Outlook 2000 and Outlook XP. This plug-in uses Bayesian statistical analysis to quantify incoming e-mail messages as spam, ham (good e-mail), or unknown. SpamBayes then sorts the classified mail according to your configuration and the mail folders you have set up.

How It Works

SpamBayes is a powerful Outlook plug-in that relies heavily on user interaction (on the front-end) and machine learning to classify incoming mail as spam or ham. First, the user presents examples of spam to SpamBayes—the more examples the better. The program analyzes the e-mail's headers, including To and From e-mail addresses, Subject, and the text of the message itself, building a statistical model definition of spam for that user. Next, the user presents examples of legitimate e-mail, and SpamBayes repeats the process, building a model of what you want to see in your Inbox.

The user sets up a filter to segregate the spam and unknown e-mail (that is, SpamBayes cannot determine the status of a message) into their respective folders, and SpamBayes is ready to go. As e-mail comes in to the Outlook client, SpamBayes measures the incoming message against its statistical models. If it matches spam, off the message goes to the user-designated spam folder. If the e-mail is considered legitimate, it arrives in the user's

Inbox (subject to whatever other user-defined filters are in place). If SpamBayes cannot determine the status of an incoming e-mail, the mail is tagged as "unknown" and is filtered into a user-defined unknown folder for further dispensation.

The user continues to train SpamBayes by designating each unknown or misfiltered message as spam or ham. SpamBayes then factors this information into the applicable statistical model and continues its operation.

Installing SpamBayes

The SpamBayes Outlook 2000 or Outlook XP plug-in is available via Internet download from the Sourceforge web site at *http://spambayes.sourceforge.net*. Several versions of SpamBayes are available. Be sure to download the current plug-in for Outlook. (We talk about the UNIX version of SpamBayes in Chapter 13.)

Preinstall Checklist

Before you install the SpamBayes plug-in, perform these preinstall steps to ensure that SpamBayes can operate as desired:

1. Make folders for incoming spam, e-mails that SpamBayes classifies as unknown, and a training folder. (The training folder is discussed in the "User Knowledge and Machine Learning" section a bit later in the chapter.)
2. Allow as much spam and legitimate mail as you can to pile up in your Inbox. For our testing purposes, we started with 500 of each.
3. Sort all spam into the training folder and leave all legitimate mail in your Inbox.

Installing SpamBayes

To install SpamBayes, first exit Microsoft Outlook, and then follow these steps:

1. Double-click the file you downloaded from the Internet. The Welcome screen appears.
2. Click the Next button. The Select Destination Directory screen appears.
3. Browse to and click the appropriate folder into which you will install SpamBayes.
4. Click the Next button. The Ready To Install window appears.
5. Confirm that the information provided is correct, and click the Install button.
6. SpamBayes installs, and a completion screen appears.
7. The final screen gives you the option to view the about.html file (which includes SpamBayes information and configuration guides). Check the checkbox if you want to view the file, or leave it blank if you don't, and then click the Finish button, as shown in Figure 10-1.

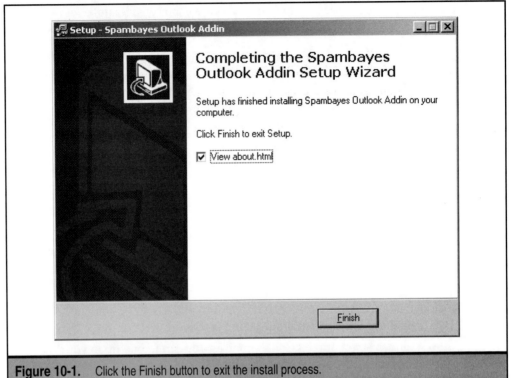

Figure 10-1. Click the Finish button to exit the install process.

User Knowledge and Machine Learning

Once the plug-in is installed, you're ready to teach SpamBayes the ins and outs of spam fighting. SpamBayes learns what spam is by being trained, and you're the trainer. The human operator can spot spam faster and more accurately than any anti-spam software ever created, so there's no better teacher for your anti-spam plug-in. The plug-in's initial training is very important, but even if you lack bulk quantities of spam and legitimate mail, the program does quite a good job at picking up the basics with just a few messages. We performed a "low-threshold" test on SpamBayes, with only 10 legitimate e-mails and 30 spam e-mails. Once trained, SpamBayes classified only 1 spam e-mail in 100 as legitimate and never pushed a legitimate e-mail to the unknown or spam folder.

Now it's time for SpamBayes training. If you followed the steps in the "Preinstall Checklist," you should have one Outlook folder full of spam and your Inbox folder full of legitimate e-mail. You should also notice that SpamBayes has added two new buttons to your Outlook toolbar, as shown in Figure 10-2. The first button, Delete As Spam, does not function until SpamBayes is ready to filter. The second button, labeled SpamBayes, is actually a drop-down menu.

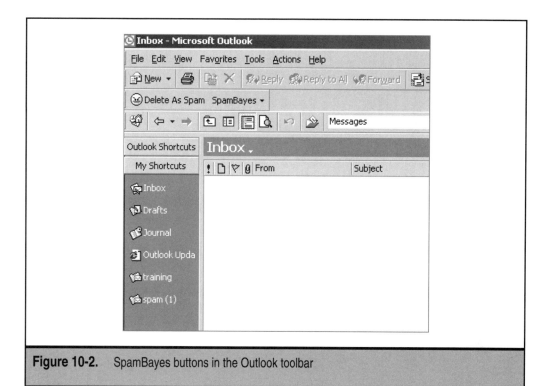

Figure 10-2. SpamBayes buttons in the Outlook toolbar

Training

To train SpamBayes, you must launch the SpamBayes Manager. Click the SpamBayes button located in your Outlook toolbar and a drop-down menu appears, as shown here.

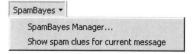

The Show Spam Clues For Current Message option does not work until SpamBayes is trained and its filters are operational. So at this point, choose the SpamBayes Manager menu option, and the SpamBayes Manager window appears, as shown in Figure 10-3.

This window is divided into two sections, called Training and Filtering. For now, we'll concern ourselves with training. Notice the two training checkboxes; these are used for day-to-day training of SpamBayes. If both checkboxes are checked, SpamBayes updates its filters database every time you recover a legitimate e-mail from the spam folder or delete a spam from a legitimate folder (such as the Inbox). The text box to the left of the Train Now button displays how many legitimate and spam messages SpamBayes has trained on to date.

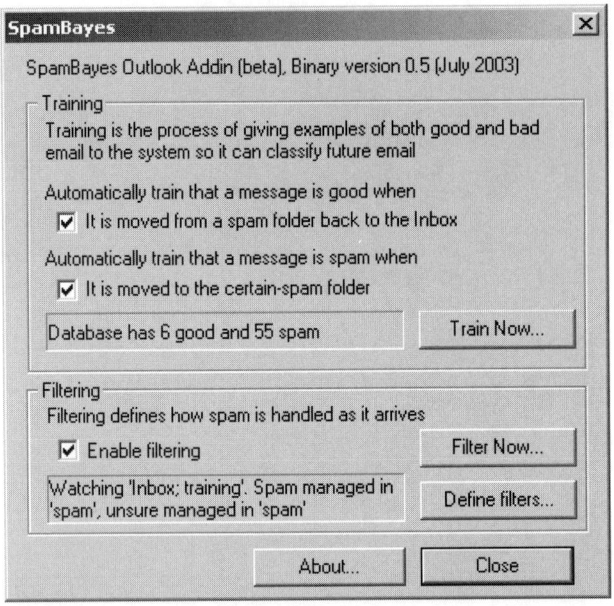

Figure 10-3. The SpamBayes Manager window

Click the Train Now button. The Training dialog box appears, as shown in Figure 10-4, and requires that you indicate several configuration points.

In the preinstall checklist, you set up two folders with a bulk of spam and legitimate e-mail. Now we'll use those folders. We put all of our current spam into a training folder and keep legitimate e-mails in the Inbox. So to configure the training folder, click the Browse button in the Folders With Known Good Messages area and the Select Folders window should appear, as shown in Figure 10-5.

In this case, only the Inbox is selected, but you can select as many folders as you wish that contain legitimate e-mails. As mentioned earlier in this chapter, the more messages of each type you can include, the more accurate your SpamBayes filters will be. So click the Inbox and any other folders you wish to include, and then click OK.

The names of the folders you selected should appear in the top text box of the Training dialog box. Now do the same with folders that contain *only* spam. (Make sure that you *don't* point SpamBayes at a folder containing legitimate e-mail, claiming it's spam. This will decrease the filters' effectiveness considerably.) Click the Browse button for the second dialog box and select your training folder or folders. Once selected, click OK.

Now the folder name or names you selected should appear in the Folders With Known Spam Or Other Junk Messages text box in the Training dialog box. At this point, you want the messages scored as well, though on future messages, you may not care what their "spam scores" are. SpamBayes is ready for its first training session.

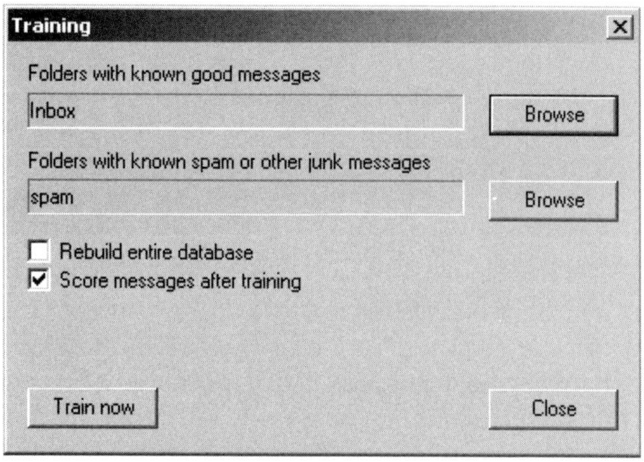

Figure 10-4. The Training dialog box provides functions for enhancing SpamBayes spam-fighting knowledge.

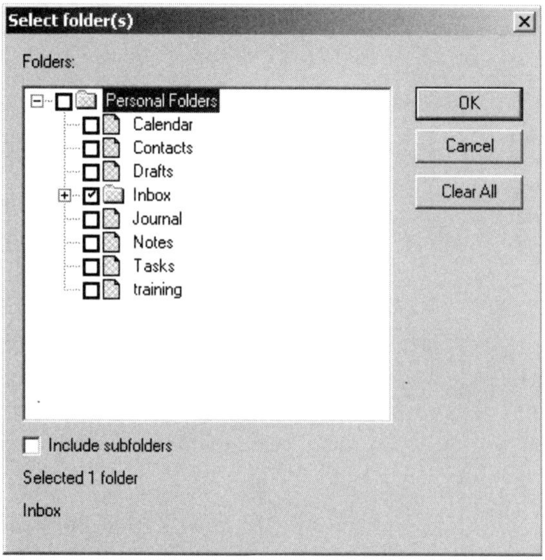

Figure 10-5. Browse to and select the appropriate ham folders.

Click the Train Now button. Depending on how many messages are in each folder, SpamBayes should take from seconds to a few minutes to complete its training operation. Once it's done, the Training dialog box should display a message just above the Train Now button stating "Scoring: Completed Training With *XX* Spam And *YY* Good Messages" (where *XX* and *YY* are the number of messages processed by the training function). With this complete, you're ready to set up filtering. Click the Close button on the Training dialog box.

Filtering

Now that we're back in the SpamBayes Manager window, refer to the Filtering section at the bottom of the window. The Filter Now button does not function until you have defined your filters, so that's the next thing we'll do. A filter tells SpamBayes what Outlook folders to watch as mail arrives and on what folders to filter spam messages and those messages SpamBayes considers "uncertain." Filtering is enabled or disabled in the Manager window by checking or unchecking the Enable Filtering checkbox.

Defining Filters   Okay. Ready to set up some spam filters?

1. Click the Define Filters button on the SpamBayes Manager window and the Filter Rules dialog box appears, as shown in Figure 10-6.

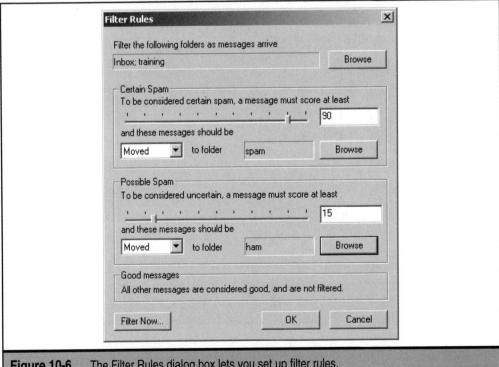

Figure 10-6.   The Filter Rules dialog box lets you set up filter rules.

2. Watch at least one folder that receives new mail. Obviously, this includes the Inbox and any other folders where new messages are automatically filtered by Outlook or some other process.

3. Click the Browse button next to the Filter The Following Folders As Messages Arrive text box and you'll see a window similar to the one shown previously in Figure 10-5.

4. Our test e-mail client uses the Inbox folder for all incoming mail, but your configuration may vary. Select all appropriate folders that you wish to cover, and click OK. Now, the folder names you selected should appear in the Filter Rules dialog box.

Next we delve into the filters themselves. SpamBayes does not expect you to be an e-mail architect with programming experience to configure filtering. All you really have to do is select a threshold score that you consider to be spam. The SpamBayes default is 90 for the Certain Spam setting, but you can move the slider to a more restrictive (down to 1 percent) or less restrictive (up to 100 percent) filter. A medium restrictive filter (about 50 percent) says that if SpamBayes assigns a score of 50 or more to an e-mail, it's considered spam and should go into the folder specified. Thus, a less restrictive filter (say 99 percent), will filter a mail only if it scores 99 or 100. (More on scoring and what this means in the sections that follow.) For now, just leave the Certain Spam filter set at 90.

The real configuration decisions here are the actual actions you wish the filter to take. You have three options: you can have the filter move the offending messages into a separate folder, copy them into a separate folder, or do nothing. To select a specific folder to contain spam or copies of spam, you need only click the Browse button and select the folder or folders. The folder(s) you select appears in the text box next to the Browse button. We configured ours to move all messages that scored 90 or higher to a folder called *spam*.

Next, SpamBayes wants to know what to do with messages that may or may not be legitimate. The setup for this filter is similar to the spam filter; however, you want a less restrictive filter in this case. The SpamBayes default is 15, and in most cases this seems to be almost perfect, but you may have different needs. Move the slider to the desired setting (or type it into the box provided to the right of the slider) and then select your filter action and destination. For our "might be spam" filter, we left the score setting at the default and decided to move messages that scored 15 or higher into a folder called *ham*.

NOTE You can create folders from within the Browse selection window.

At the bottom of the Filter Rules dialog box is a self-explanatory statement labeled "Good Messages. All Other Messages Are Considered Good, And Are Not Filtered." Now you're ready to filter those messages. When you're filtering for the first time, you want to move all the spam messages from the training folder that you created during the training phase, back to a folder that you just configured your filters to watch. Thus, we moved all our spam from the training folder back to the Inbox.

Filtering for Fun and Profit   On this initial configuration, just click the Filter Now button. This displays the Filter Now dialog box, as shown in Figure 10-7.

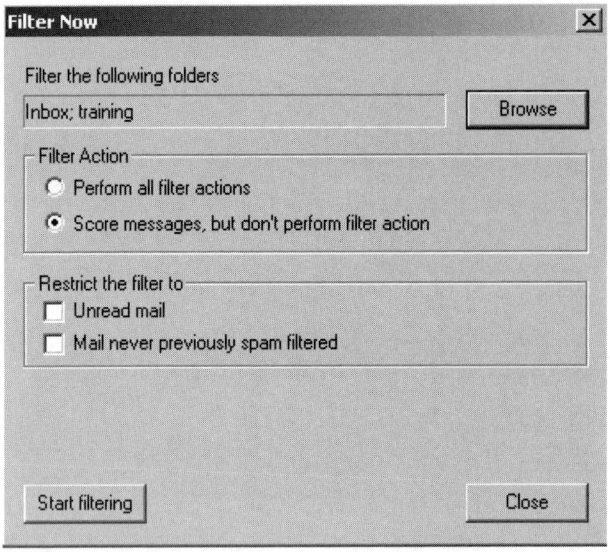

Figure 10-7. Filter now or filter later.

Here you can select which folders to filter. For initial setup purposes, we've selected only the Inbox, but you may select as many folders as you wish. The Filter Action section allows you to ask SpamBayes to score the messages in the selected folders but not filter them. Selecting the Perform All Filter Actions radio button configures the filter process to do just that: filter messages as configured. You can likewise restrict your filtering to unread messages and mail that has never previously been filtered by clicking the appropriate boxes in the Restrict The Filter To section of the dialog box. When you're ready, click the Start Filtering button and SpamBayes does just that—unless, of course, you selected the Score Messages, But Don't Perform Filter Actions radio button; then SpamBayes does that instead.

Once the filtering (or scoring) operation completes, SpamBayes reports how many spam messages were found, how many were unknown, and how many were classified as ham and displays the information above the Start Filtering button.

Your filter is complete. Now, as e-mail arrives to the appropriate folders, SpamBayes evaluates, scores, and filters the messages as you specified. Reconfiguration and training are possible any time you desire, but as stated earlier, be sure to train SpamBayes with the appropriate messages to get the best results (that is, if it's spam, don't tell SpamBayes it's not spam).

SpamBayes Operation and Spam Management

With all your rules and filters built and your first filter operation out of the way, we can revisit some of the functions that now provide management and functionality. SpamBayes is a fairly low-maintenance program. Filters do not have to be manually updated or downloaded from a central server, and no P2P ties need to be monitored or reported to. Everything that SpamBayes does and knows is in your hands.

Troubleshooting False Negatives   Occasionally, SpamBayes identifies a spam e-mail as a legitimate message and leaves it in your Inbox or filters it to whatever folder you've specified for good mail. As earlier reported in our tests, SpamBayes misidentified a spam message as legitimate about 1 percent of the time, but our configuration used the program defaults, with little added differences other than the training itself.

When a misidentification happens, your actions are simple. Select the spam message in your Inbox or good e-mail folder and click the Delete As Spam button. The message immediately moves the e-mail to your designated spam folder and SpamBayes uses the information to retrain itself and, hopefully, make its spam identification better on future messages.

Troubleshooting False Positives   On the flip side, a legitimate e-mail message can somehow score enough "spam points" to get filtered into your designated spam folder. Again, the remedy is simple. While the spam folder is open, the Delete As Spam button changes to the Recover From Spam button. Select the misidentified message, click the Recover button, and voilà! The message moves to the Inbox, and SpamBayes' database is updated appropriately.

Try as we might, we could not construct a legitimate e-mail that both seemed legitimate and managed to score high enough for SpamBayes to filter it to spam by mistake. Even messages from most list servers (mailing lists) were immediately recognized and left alone—although a couple had their messages tagged as "unknown," as described next.

Troubleshooting Possible Spam   Finally, SpamBayes' "unknown" feature provides extra training functionality. If a message trips the Possible Spam threshold on your filter rules, it ends up in the folder you designated for questionable messages. Occasionally, you'll have to sort through this folder to determine whether a message is wanted or unwanted.

To do this, open the folder you've designated to hold unknown mails. You'll notice that a third button appears on the SpamBayes toolbar. Now, you can Delete As Spam or Recover From Spam (see Figure 10-8).

Select the message, verify whether or not it's spam, and click the appropriate button. The message moves to the folder you designated, and SpamBayes updates its database.

We found that just after signing up for a mailing list or commercial offer, our ham folder had to be perused. We usually sorted the messages, and then went back and retrained SpamBayes using the procedures discussed earlier in the "Training" section, if the mailing list e-mail seemed to be inordinately likely to be designated as unknown. Once retrained, SpamBayes correctly identified every message from the new mailing list.

Anti-Spam Tool Kit

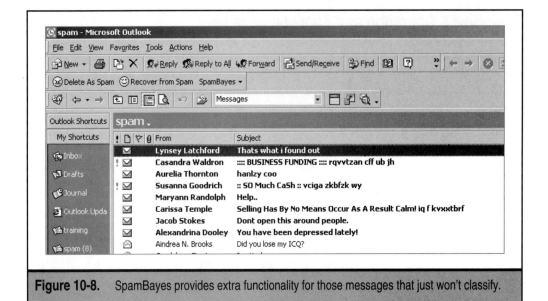

Figure 10-8. SpamBayes provides extra functionality for those messages that just won't classify.

How Spammy or Hammy Is It? Finally, SpamBayes provides information on the criteria it uses to reach its conclusions about a given mail. This information is most useful when a message has been misdirected as either legit or spam.

If you wish to see only the percentage chance that a message is spam, you can use a built-in function of Outlook to display the score in a columnar format. From a folder's main window, follow these steps:

1. Right-click the column headers for the folder and select Field Chooser. A Field Chooser window appears.

2. Click the New button and the New Field dialog box appears, as shown here.

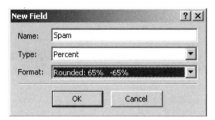

3. Name the column, and set the type to Percent and the format to Rounded: 65% –65%.
4. Click OK, and the User-Defined field appears in the Field Chooser window.
5. Drag-and-drop the field to the folder header to add the column to the folder view, as shown in the following illustration. The Spam column now displays the message's "spam factor."

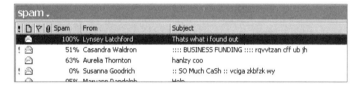

Finally, SpamBayes has a function under the SpamBayes button in the Outlook toolbar called Show Spam Clues For Current Message. Select any message, legit or spam, and click this button. A file pops up showing the message's score, the factors that added to (or subtracted from) that score, the message headers, and the message itself, as shown in Figure 10-9. This function is useful if you're trying to determine why a spam message got through the filter or why a legitimate e-mail ended up in the unknown folder.

SPAMPAL

SpamPal is an anti-spam proxy program that relies on DNS blacklist/banlist information to tag and sort suspected spam. SpamPal is available for Windows $9x$/2000/XP and is compatible with any standard Post Office Protocol 3 (POP3) e-mail client, such as Eudora, Outlook/Outlook Express, and Pegasus Mail.

How It Works

SpamPal monitors POP3 messages as they pass to the user's mail client, acting as a type of proxy between the mail server and mail client. SpamPal compares the From header field to DNS blacklists (DNSBLs). If the message has passed through any host on these blacklists to reach your mailbox, SpamPal flags the message as spam with a special message header. The user configures the mail client to sort messages containing this special spam header into a specific folder for further review.

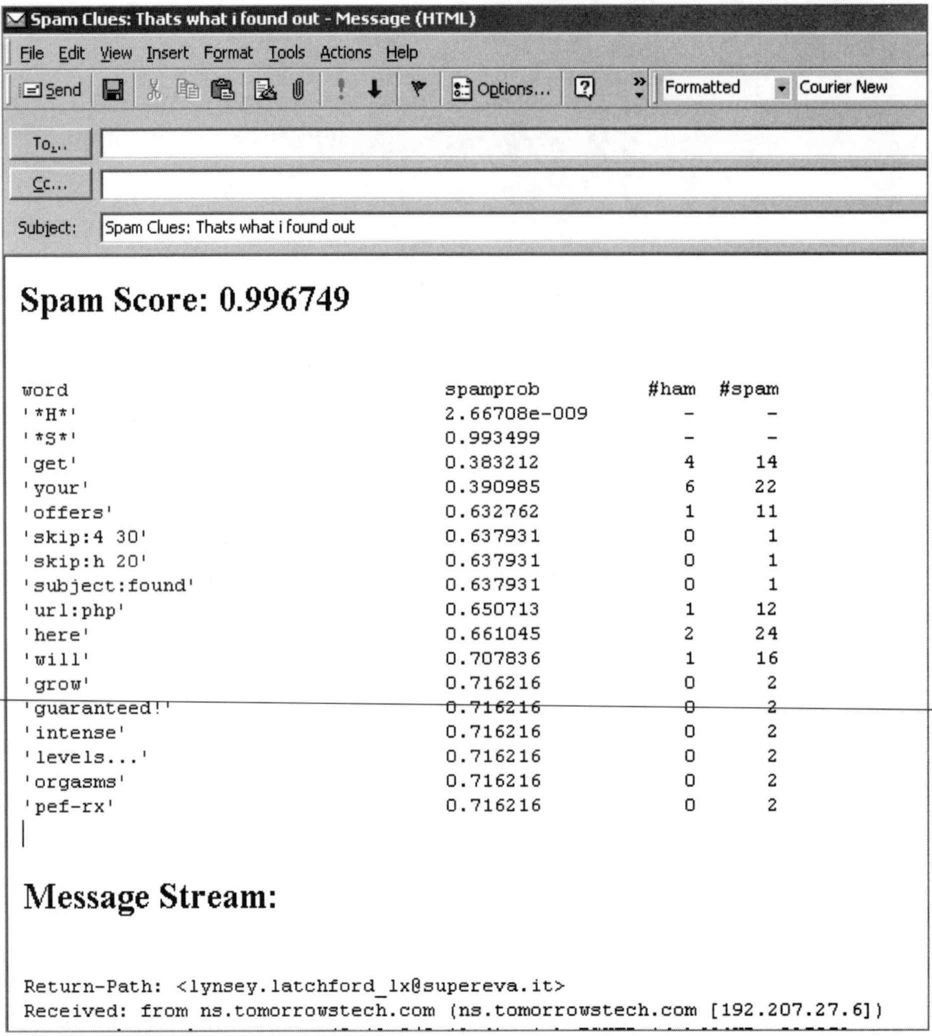

Figure 10-9. Showing spam clues for current message

Of course, as with any blacklist-based spam filter, many legitimate messages pass through blacklist hosts to reach your Inbox. Thus, these legitimate messages must be hand sorted back to the user's regular mail folders and SpamPal's whitelist must be updated with the legitimate sender or host information, essentially configuring SpamPal to allow specific messages from specific senders or messages from senders on designated networks without tagging.

Installing SpamPal

SpamPal takes about ten minutes to download, install, and configure. SpamPal is available via Internet download from the SpamPal site at *http://www.spampal.org*.

 NOTE The SpamPal version covered in this chapter is the Beta release 1.2912. This version differs slightly in functionality and interface from older versions, such as 1.14.

Once the setup file is downloaded, you're ready to install.

Preinstall Checklist

Before SpamPal installs, you'll want to prepare your system and mail program.

1. *Set up a mail filter for your POP3 client.* We explain how to do this with Outlook Express later in this chapter, but you should configure your POP3 client to filter all mail with the string **SPAM** in the Subject line to a folder you create and specify for incoming spam.

2. Ensure that your virus-protection program is not currently acting as a proxy for your POP3 client. If it is, you'll have to configure the virus program to check mail through SpamPal, and leave your e-mail client checking mail through the spam filter.

3. Check your other security programs, such as ZoneAlarm or other personal firewalls, to ensure that the POP3 port is available and unrestricted.

NOTE While the installation instructions that follow cover installation for Outlook Express, SpamPal maintains detailed instructions for installation and configuration of its product in conjunction with 20 e-mail clients and other Internet applications, such as virus scanners and workstation firewall products.

Preparing Outlook Express   We've chosen Outlook Express 6 for our SpamPal testing and setup. Before you install SpamPal, you need only set up a Mail Message Rule to filter tagged messages to a quarantine folder. Follow these steps to do that:

1. Open Outlook Express and choose Tools | Message Rules | Mail. A Message Rules window appears.

2. Click the New button, and the New Mail Rule dialog box appears.

3. In the Select The Conditions For Your Rule area, check the box beside Where The Subject Line Contains Specific Words.

4. In the Select Actions For Your Rule section, check the box next to Move It To The Specified Folder.

5. In the Rule Description section, click the "contains specific words" link. The Type Specific Words dialog box appears.

6. In the dialog box, type ****SPAM**** and click the Add button. The Words box should now read "Where the Subject line contains '**SPAM**'".

7. Click OK.

8. In the Rule Description section, click the "specified" link. The Move box appears.

9. Click the New Folder button, and add a specific folder for the collection of suspected spam. (Ours is called spammity.)

10. Click OK. Section 3: Rule Description, should read "Apply this rule after the message arrives Where the Subject line contains '**SPAM**' Move it to the spammity folder."

11. In Section 4, type an appropriate name for the rule, and then click OK.

Outlook Express is now ready to filter incoming messages tagged by SpamPal to the folder you selected. Once in the folder, it's up to you to ensure that the messages are, in fact, spam.

Installing SpamPal

Once downloaded, follow these steps to install SpamPal and integrate it into Outlook Express:

1. Double-click the setup package and the Welcome screen should appear.

2. Select the appropriate language and click Next.

3. In the Copyright And Information screen, click Next.

4. Check the checkbox to agree to the SpamPal license agreement, and then click Next.

5. In the Destination Folder window, type a destination path or leave the default set in the text box, and then click Next (see Figure 10-10).

6. In the Program Group window, specify a program group shortcut name and location. Click Next.

7. In the Setup Type window, select Standard or Custom. The Standard option installs the SpamPal Program Files and the Programs Menu Group shortcuts, and sets SpamPal to run at startup (see Figure 10-11). If you select Custom in the Setup Type window, you can click to remove the Startup and Programs Menu options.

8. At the Ready screen, click Next to install SpamPal with the options you've selected. SpamPal installs and, when complete, displays an Installation Complete window with the option to start SpamPal now.

9. Select what's appropriate and click the OK button.

Chapter 10: Anti-Spam Clients for Windows 187

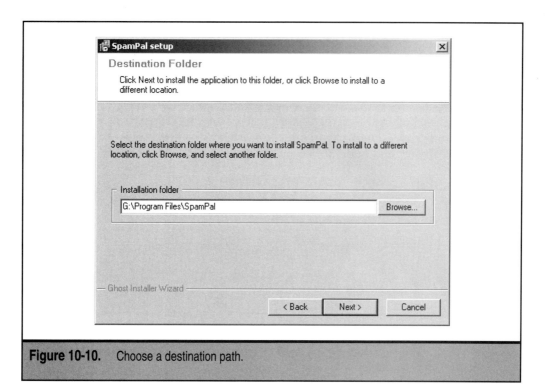

Figure 10-10. Choose a destination path.

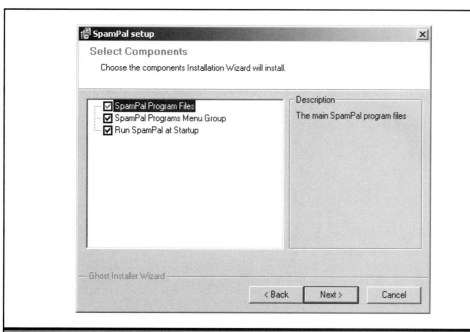

Figure 10-11. The Setup Type window

Controlling the World Through Lists

SpamPal is a list-based e-mail filter, thus configuring and maintaining blacklists and whitelists are important aspects of the filter. For the most part, this is an automated process. SpamPal checks public DNSBLs for mail relays that allow anonymous exchange of e-mail and flags messages that use these relays for transit. If the mail hitting your Inbox passed through any of these mail relays, the message is tagged as spam, and, according to your client filter, dropped into a quarantine folder. Other configuration options allow for better spam detection, and, more important, they reduce the rate of false positives.

Spam Detection

In support of the initial setup, several configuration options allow you to tweak SpamPal's detection capabilities. Through the use of custom whitelists, blacklists, and ignore lists, as well as custom configurations and plug-ins, you can really drill down into the heart of the spam problem from the SpamPal developers' take. These configuration options are available by right-clicking the SpamPal umbrella icon in the lower-right system tray and selecting Options from the system tray menu.

Whitelists Whitelists are essentially mail from individuals and networks that are "known good." Your grandparents, Mom, colleagues, and anyone on a particular mailing list to which you belong are all examples of e-mail addresses you should put in a whitelist. That way, no matter where Mom logs in from and sends mail through, her message always reaches your Inbox. SpamPal provides three configuration options for custom whitelists: E-mail Addresses, Automatic, and Exclusions, as shown in the Category pane of Figure 10-12.

The e-mail address whitelist option allows you to enter individual e-mail accounts to allow them to pass through SpamPal's spam filters, regardless of the path they took through the Internet to get to you. You just type in the e-mail addresses you want in the actual white-space in the right pane and SpamPal does the rest. These addresses should probably mirror your POP client's address book of common correspondents. SpamPal, unfortunately, does not have an import feature you can use to copy address book entries to this whitelist, but the SpamPal web site offers independently developed plug-ins that you can use for specific e-mail clients (see the "Plug-ins" section, a little later in the chapter).

SpamPal has an automatic whitelisting feature that you can configure to add an e-mail address to your whitelist for a certain number of days after you've received e-mail from that address. Click Automatic in the Category pane, and you'll see that the default is seven days, as shown in Figure 10-13. You may set this value to anything you want. You may also enable or disable the automatic feature, as well as manage and log the automatic whitelist addresses in this screen.

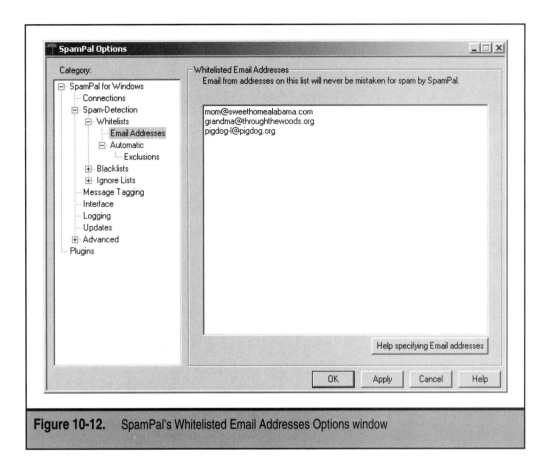

Figure 10-12. SpamPal's Whitelisted Email Addresses Options window

Select the Exclusions option in the Category pane and you'll see the exclusions screen (Email Addresses To Never Automatically Whitelist), as shown in Figure 10-14. As a subset to the Automatic Whitelist feature, you can add addresses here that should never be whitelisted by the automated process. You should include your own e-mail address in this list, as many spammers may spoof your e-mail address to the From field to fool older spam filters.

Blacklists Blacklists are the heart of SpamPal's functionality. Using a combination of public and user-specific e-mail and network lists, SpamPal blocks e-mail from known spammers and their resources. Select Blacklists in the Category pane and the Blacklists configuration screen opens, where you can configure Public Blacklists (DNSBLs), modify countries, and manage your personal e-mail address and IP address blacklists.

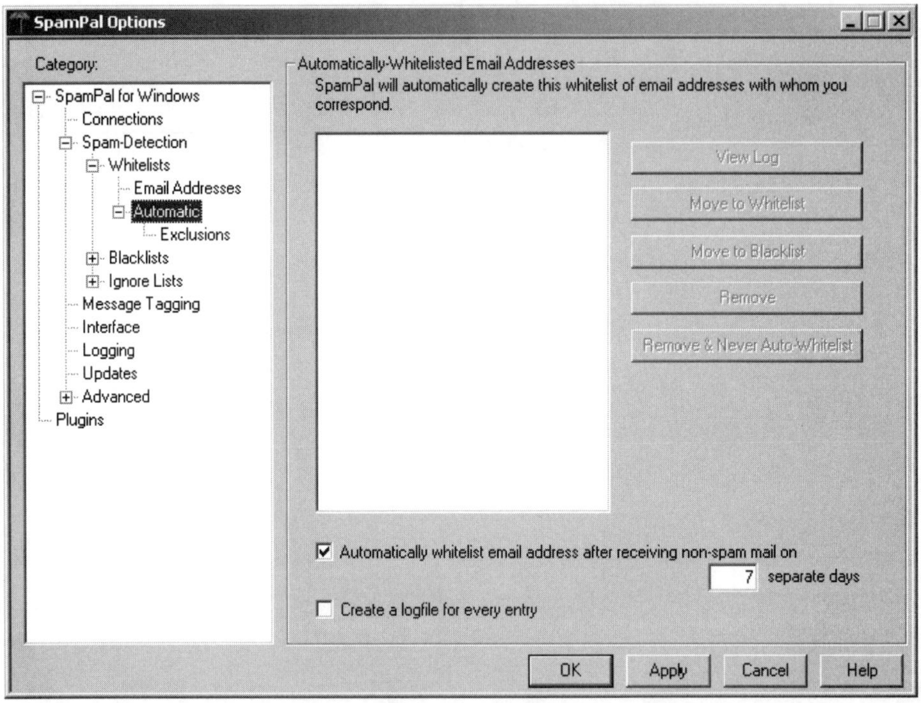

Figure 10-13. SpamPal can automatically add an address to your whitelist according to your configuration.

The Public Blacklists configuration screen allows you to select specific public blacklists of e-mail addresses, gateways, and networks that either produce a large percentage of spam traffic or are insecure enough to allow spammers to use their resources. (Refer to Chapter 5 for specific information on public blacklists.) The configuration option Precreated Filtering Strategies provides a default level of filtering on three levels: Safe, Medium, and Aggressive. A fourth option, Custom, allows you to select which blacklists to include.

The Countries configuration option allows for the blacklisting of e-mail originating in 14 countries known either for lots of spam or the use of their domain names and networks for spammers' purposes. Simply select the countries you wish to block, but be sure you don't have legitimate contacts in those countries, since they will be unable to send you e-mail.

The Email Addresses configuration option allows you to add specific e-mail addresses to a personal blacklist. While this area can contain any address, most often it's used for known spammers and others from which you wish to block e-mail contact. You can add a wildcard asterisk character (*) with a domain, essentially blocking all e-mail from that domain, by typing *@*spammersparadise.com* (replacing *spammersparadise.com* with the domain you wish to block). To block individual e-mail, simply type the e-mail

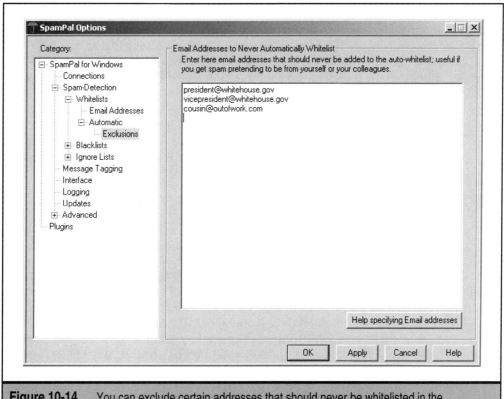

Figure 10-14. You can exclude certain addresses that should never be whitelisted in the exclusions screen.

address of the spammer in the field provided. Adding a pound sign (#) in front of text prevents the blacklist engine from processing it, so you can add notes to yourself about the blocked address by preceding the notes with the pound sign.

Finally, you can blacklist a single IP address, a block of addresses, or an entire network of addresses using the IP Addresses configuration window. Like the previous whitelist and blacklist configuration options, you simply add the IP address of a specific spammer, a range of addresses, or an entire network. Once updated, any mail originating on or passing through these addresses is tagged as spam and filtered to your spam folder. As with the other configuration screens, preceding a line with the pound sign (#) allows you to add comments that will be ignored by SpamPal's filtering process.

Ignore Lists Selecting the Ignore Lists configuration option provides a kind of backdoor allow feature, in case other filters want to block e-mail originating on or passing through specific providers' domains and user configurable IP address ranges. Additionally, an automatic feature, similar to the feature used on whitelists, adds some functionality to the mix.

The Providers configuration screen allows you to select from a list of eight providers to exclude from SpamPal's typical blacklist lookup feature. Thus, if you select Yahoo! to be excluded, for example, SpamPal allows all mail that originates from and passes through hosts on the yahoo.com domain to pass through without being tagged as spam. This is useful if, somehow, one of these providers ends up blacklisted somewhere, and you still want to receive mail from users on those domains.

You'll notice that the IP Addresses configuration screen looks similar to the whitelist and blacklist configuration screens in other areas. This feature allows you to add IP addresses, blocks of addresses, or whole networks to the exclude function. Thus, if you have contacts that happen to send mail through known spammer-friendly resources, you only need to add their specific IP addresses, address ranges, or networks to allow them through SpamPal's filter. Again, adding a pound sign in front of a line of text prevents SpamPal from processing that line, allowing you to add comments.

NOTE Adding the address range 127.0.0.0/*XX* (where *XX* is the size of your network) prevents SpamPal from attempting to look up hosts and addresses on your own network. This significantly speeds up e-mail from sources internal to your network (such as mail from a coworker).

The Automatic configuration screen operates similar to the automatic feature covered in the "Whitelists" section earlier. When SpamPal frequently processes e-mail from a specific IP address for a set amount of time (the default is 12 days, but you can set it to whatever you want), the program automatically adds that IP address to the Ignore list, thus always allowing e-mail from that IP address to pass through its filter. This is most useful if some of these automatic IPs are eventually found on one of the public blacklists that SpamPal uses to identify spam. Additionally, you can disable this feature, allow SpamPal to log instances of automatic addition of an IP address, and manage IPs that SpamPal adds.

Advanced Options Selecting Advanced opens the Advanced Configuration Options screen, which provides additional tweaking of SpamPal's operations. Here you can configure the DNSBL query timeout, in case these queries are taking too long to process incoming e-mail, and you can set the maximum simultaneous DNSBL queries. You may also turn off filtering and specific auto-whitelist and auto-ignorelist functions. DNSBL results may be retained (significantly speeding up the query process) for both suspected spam and legitimate mail for hours or days, depending on the user configuration. The SpamPal default is two days for spam and three days for negative query results. Finally, the path to SpamPal's configuration files is listed at the bottom of the window.

SpamPal allows for other hosts to connect to their e-mail accounts through a single SpamPal installation. This is useful if you plan to run SpamPal in a small office as a single anti-spam proxy point for several e-mail users. Through these options, you can configure SpamPal to listen on a different IP address, add IP addresses that are allowed to connect through this instance of SpamPal, and add additional DNSBL entries displayed on the Public Blacklists configuration screen under the Blacklists configuration options. Since SpamPal suggests that its product not be used as a single e-mail proxy, we will not cover these features here, although the SpamPal web site lists plug-ins and instructions for using the program in this way.

Other Configuration Options Other configuration screens accessed via the SpamPal Options window allow for specific configuration options related to e-mail retrieval, message tagging, the SpamPal program interface, logging, and automatic updates. Access these options by right-clicking the SpamPal umbrella icon in the taskbar in the lower right-hand corner of your desktop, and then select the Options menu.

The Connections, Ports, and Protocols screen allows you to configure e-mail retrieval options specific to your situation. These options are user specific, and typically the default settings are fine. These settings are used if your e-mail server (POP or IMAP) does not use the standard port number for communication, uses other authentication methods, or otherwise requires specific configuration options. Since variations exist, it's best to consult your ISP or configuration information within your e-mail client for more information on these settings. Note that while SpamPal does not support e-mail over Secure Sockets Layer (SSL) encrypted protocol, it does support Authenticated Post Office Protocol (APOP) and the Simple Authentication and Security Layer (SASL) protocol for encrypting the connection between the mail client and the mail server. Both of these protocols are configurable from within the Connections screen.

Select Message Tagging, and the Message Tagging screen allows you to mark spam messages in a variety of ways. The default SpamPal configuration marks suspected spam messages with **SPAM** in the Subject line so that your e-mail program can then filter the offending message to an appropriate folder for further review, but you can set this to be whatever you want. Additionally, you can add X-SpamPal, X-Wlist-Pattern, and X-Blist-Pattern header information to the message for more precise filtering options.

> **NOTE** Adding these filters over an IMAP connection to your e-mail significantly increases the amount of time it takes to check your mail.

The Interface and Logging category functions of SpamPal are pretty self-explanatory. The Interface screen controls how you interact with the SpamPal program. You can add or remove it from the system tray, control how to launch SpamPal's interface, and display various status windows while SpamPal performs its operations. The Logging configuration screen allows for specific or general logging of SpamPal's operations. This logging can be as minimal or verbose as you desire. This screen also shows the file path to the program's log files.

Finally, select Updates to have SpamPal send you automatic updates. The Updates configuration window allows you to automatically check for new SpamPal, related plug-in, and beta releases, and update the list of known DNS Blacklist services. You may also configure SpamPal to alert you while checking for these updates. Simply check the appropriate boxes in the Updates window and click the Apply button when you're finished.

Plug-ins While we will not cover SpamPal plug-ins in-depth, we mention some of the additional functionality they provide to an already feature-rich program. Following is a sample list of plug-ins available on SpamPal's web site and the functionality those plug-ins add to the program's operation. A Plugins configuration screen in the SpamPal

Options window allows you to find and download additional functionality for the SpamPal program.

- **Bayesian** This plug-in adds basic Bayesian filter logic.
- **Export Email** Though technically not a plug-in, this Outlook macro exports the Outlook Address book to SpamPal's whitelist.
- **URL-Body** This plug-in parses URL data from the body of a message and compares that information for filtering purposes through a DNSBL query.
- **HTML-Tagger** This plug-in tags any message that contains HTML code with **HTML** in the Subject line and comments out the code so that it won't be rendered by your e-mail client.
- **Bad Words** This plug-in filters e-mail messages based on a list of offensive words common in advertising for pornographic web sites.

SPAMCATCHER

Mailshell SpamCatcher is a complex e-mail filtering plug-in for Microsoft Outlook 2000/2002/XP as well as for POP3 clients, such as Eudora, Netscape Messenger, and the like. Thwarting spam utilizing both approve and block lists and a remote algorithmic rules engine, SpamCatcher identifies, tags, and filters incoming spam. In addition to the POP client version, a SpamCatcher service is also available for web-based e-mail sites, such as Yahoo!, Hotmail, and America Online.

How It Works

SpamCatcher Universal installs as a proxy to the mail client. Once installed, the user can stay with SpamCatcher network's default configuration or set custom filter strengths and further customize the proxy with approve/block e-mail lists. E-mail accounts already in the user's address book automatically update to the default Approved Senders list. SpamCatcher scans each e-mail, assigning it a "fingerprint" ID (essentially an algorithmic hash), and compares it to IDs on the SpamCatcher network. If the hashes match, the e-mail is flagged and dumped into the local SpamCatcher folder within the mail client. SpamCatcher also updates its network with any blocked or approved e-mails the user identifies. What emerges from this process is a *% of being spam* value. SpamCatcher's default setting is the esoteric Lenient, but the user can set this value all the way up to Exclusive, meaning that only mail from a user or domain on the Approved list makes it through the filter.

Installing SpamCatcher

Mailshell SpamCatcher is available in two client versions: SpamCatcher Outlook and Universal. For the purposes of our evaluation, we've used the Universal version with the Eudora POP client. Both client versions are available for download from the Mailshell web site and both have 30-day full-featured evaluations. You can download the products at *http://www.mailshell.com/spamcatcher/download.html*.

Preinstall Checklist

Before installing SpamCatcher, you'll want to prepare your POP client to check mail through its proxy and set up a filter for the incoming spam. The following instructions are specific to Eudora, but Mailshell maintains individualized instructions for each major POP program.

To configure Eudora to check mail through SpamCatcher, follow these steps:

1. Choose Tools | Options. The Options window appears.
2. Click the Getting Started icon.
3. Change the MailServer field to **localhost**.
4. Change the login name to **emailname#mailserver** (where *emailname* is your normal login name and *mailserver* is the POP e-mail server from which you normally retrieve your mail). See Figure 10-15.

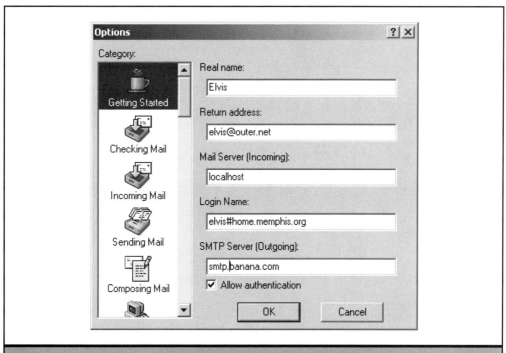

Figure 10-15.   Configure your mail client to check mail through SpamCatcher.

Next, you'll set up a filter for the incoming spam. Follow these steps to complete this on Eudora:

1. Choose Tools | Filters. The Filters window appears.
2. Click the New button to create a new filter.
3. Check the Incoming checkbox.
4. Select the <AnyHeader> entry in the Header field, and then type the following over <AnyHeader>: **X-SpamCatcher-Flag**.
5. Type **yes** in the field next to the Contains drop-down box.
6. Finally, in the Action section, click the drop-down box and select Transfer To. Then click the In button and select New.
7. Name the new folder something relevant. See Figure 10-16 for the completed filter.

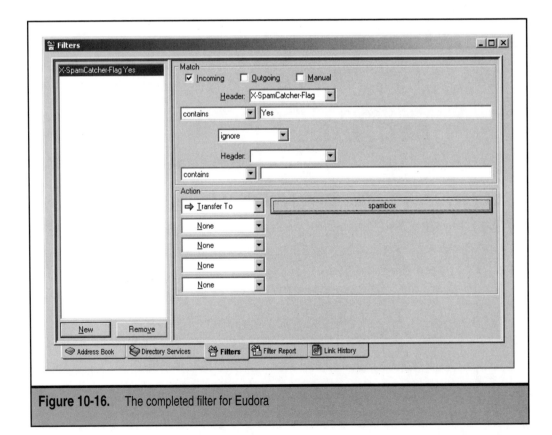

Figure 10-16. The completed filter for Eudora

Installing SpamCatcher

To install SpamCatcher, first exit all other programs and follow these steps:

1. Double-click the installation file. The Welcome screen appears.
2. Click Next. Read and accept the license agreement, and then click Next. The Select Installation Folder window appears, as shown in Figure 10-17.
3. Select an appropriate volume and directory, and click Next.
4. SpamCatcher installs and updates the Windows registry. The Installation Complete window appears. Click Close.
5. A registration key entry box appears. Enter the registration key as issued by Mailshell.

Once installed, the configuration window will appear, as shown in Figure 10-18.

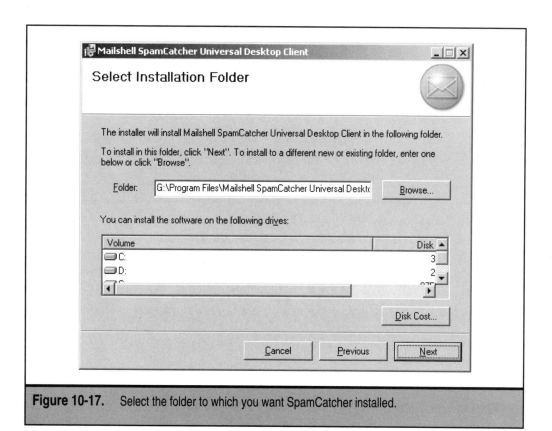

Figure 10-17. Select the folder to which you want SpamCatcher installed.

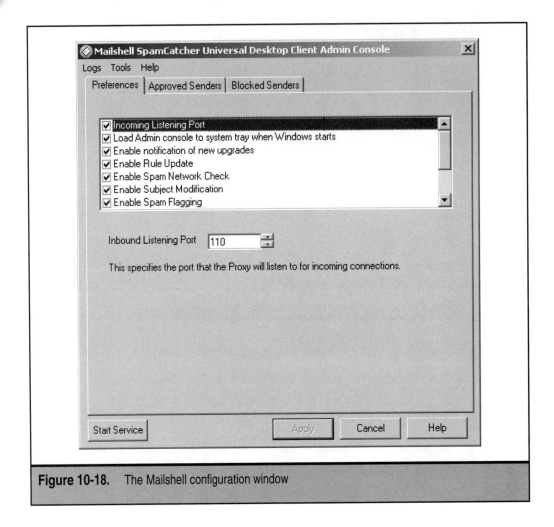

Figure 10-18. The Mailshell configuration window

Making Contact with the SpamCatcher Network

Of the Windows client tools we reviewed for this book, SpamCatcher was the quickest and easiest to install and configure, comprising a total of about eight minutes. After installation and registration, you must configure preferences and any allowed or blocked senders, and then start the SpamCatcher service. (SpamCatcher runs as a service on Windows 2000 and XP.)

Ports and Updates

The first configuration selections are fairly basic. The Incoming Listening Port setting should be changed only if you specifically know that you check POP e-mail on a port other than 110. (For more information on your POP port, contact your ISP.) The next few settings are a matter of personal preference. SpamCatcher can display its Admin console icon in the Windows system tray or not, depending on whether you check the box or not, as shown in Figure 10-19.

SpamCatcher can also automatically update its program files at your whim. The rules by which SpamCatcher works its spam-catching magic can be updated automatically. Checking the Enable Rule Update box enables automatic updates of spam rules. In that configuration window's Preferences tab, you have the option of setting the automatic updates to every 15 minutes, every hour, or every day, week, or month, depending on your specific needs and network resources. The configuration window is shown in Figure 10-19.

Finally, to enable the Spam Network Check feature, click that checkbox.

NOTE You must be connected to the Internet to update program files and spam rules and to participate in the Spam Network in this way.

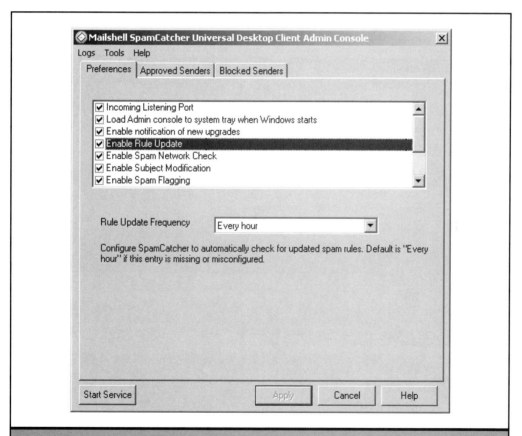

Figure 10-19. Set your automatic rules updates depending on your needs and network resources.

Flagging and Modification

Both SpamCatcher's Flagging and Modification functions allow for Lenient to Exclusive settings, as shown in Figure 10-20. These settings configure thresholds by which SpamCatcher flags an e-mail message with the X-SpamCatcher-*XXX* mail headers and spam designator in the Subject line of the e-mail message (the default designator is *[spamcatcher]*). These headers and the Subject designator allow your e-mail client to recognize and filter incoming spam to the spam folder you've designated.

The Lenient setting applies a header or subject designator (a.k.a. modifier) if the spam score is 90 or above. The score scales down to 1 on the Exclusive setting, meaning that every e-mail, except those from Approved Senders, is designated as spam. Settings for the Header and Subject designators are in separate configuration windows and both or either may be forgone by unchecking their respective checkboxes in the Console.

Timeouts and Custom Settings

The remainder of SpamCatcher's settings supports further tweaking and custom configurations. The Enable Spam Score Timeout setting allows you to set the amount of time

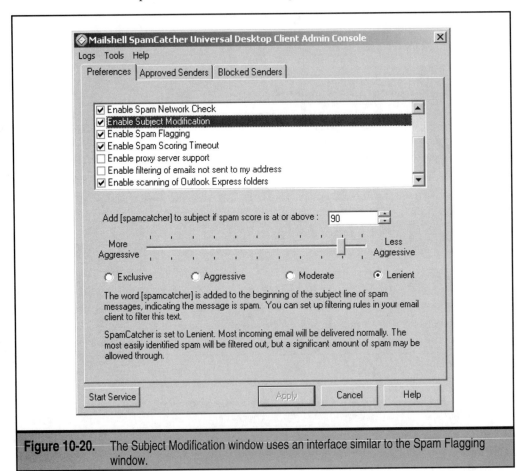

Figure 10-20. The Subject Modification window uses an interface similar to the Spam Flagging window.

you want SpamCatcher to wait for a spam score from the SpamCatcher network, before moving on to the next e-mail. The default for this setting is 5 seconds, and during our trials, we never encountered a need to change this.

If you go through a network proxy for Internet access, SpamCatcher has a configuration window you can use to set up proxy settings, as well. If you have questions about your proxy settings, consult your ISP or IT department for information. This option is unchecked by default, but when enabled, it requires a proxy server address (IP or full hostname) and the communication port for the proxy, both of which are standard information. Further, you can configure SpamCatcher to filter or not filter e-mails that arrive with a different recipient (in the To field). This tactic is used mostly to expedite e-mail that's actually addressed to your e-mail address, but also to allow messages through from mailing lists and the like that may be addressed to the list, rather than you, personally.

Finally, SpamCatcher provides a feature in the Universal package that's helpful to users of Outlook Express. By enabling scanning (see Figure 10-21), SpamCatcher can periodically scan your Outlook folders for spam. This feature enables SpamCatcher to refilter messages that may not have been designated spam when downloaded but later receive that designation through the SpamCatcher Network.

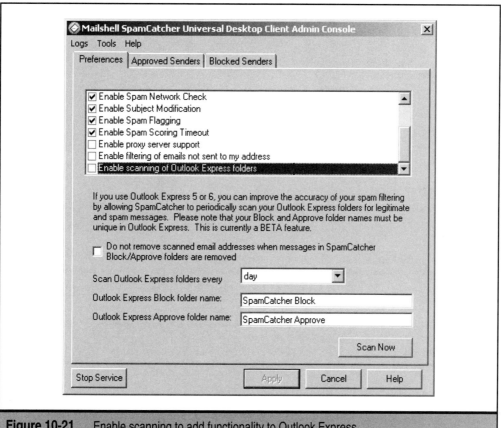

Figure 10-21. Enable scanning to add functionality to Outlook Express.

Approved and Blocked Senders

SpamCatcher's final configuration options consist of standard whitelists and blacklists of e-mail addresses. In each tab, Approved Senders and Blocked Senders, as depicted in Figures 10-22 and 10-23, respectively, click the Add button and type the e-mail address into the dialog box that pops up. You can also import and export blocked and allowed e-mail addresses from flat text files.

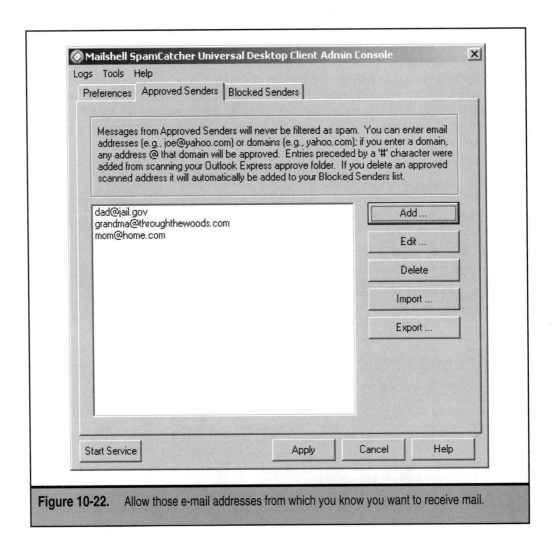

Figure 10-22. Allow those e-mail addresses from which you know you want to receive mail.

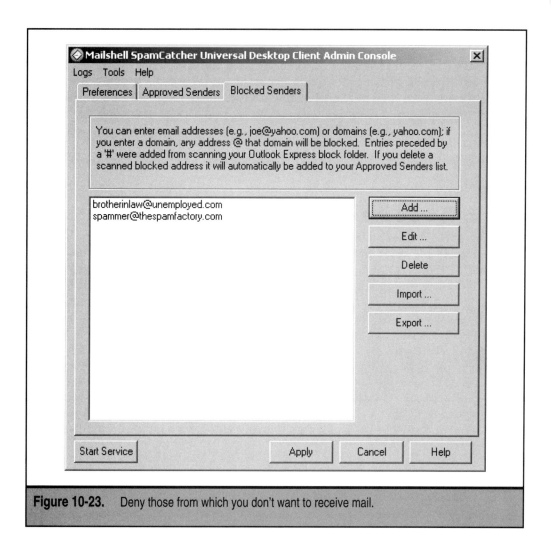

Figure 10-23. Deny those from which you don't want to receive mail.

LYRIS MAILSHIELD DESKTOP

Lyris MailShield Desktop is an e-mail proxy application that uses filtering rules, "fuzzy logic," and e-mail lists to filter incoming spam before it reaches your Inbox. Supporting POP, IMAP, and MAPI protocols as well as msn.com and Hotmail's HTML interfaces, Lyris MailShield Desktop also integrates a spam reporting system with numerous configuration options. MailShield Desktop runs on Windows 98, Me, 2000, and XP and supports any POP3, IMAP, or MAPI e-mail client.

How It Works

MailShield uses a combination of tactics to detect, score, and filter both legitimate and spam e-mail. First, MailShield uses a complex set of token-based rulesets that scan every word in an e-mail and weight the appearance of certain words. Words are weighted for *where* they appear in the message as well, and these word lists are user-configurable. Additionally, MailShield employs standard e-mail whitelists and blacklists, sender/domain verification, and other more personalized settings to do its dirty work. The sheer level of customization ensures that most of the spam you receive never sees the light outside the recycle bin.

Installing MailShield Desktop

Lyris distributes MailShield Desktop as a single compressed installation file from its web site. This install file accommodates any POP3, IMAP, MAPI, or web-based mail client MailShield supports. In this section, we cover installation of MailShield Desktop for use with Hotmail web-based e-mail. Other installation options may vary from client-to-client. A fully functional trial version and support information can be obtained at the Lyris web site at *http://www.mailshield.com/products/mailshield/desktop/index.html*.

Preinstall Checklist

Before installing Lyris MailShield Desktop, consider the following:

- Have your e-mail address and password handy. For Hotmail, MailShield automatically fills in the proper domain names for checking and sending e-mail (though it launches a browser to Hotmail to send e-mail from the MailShield interface).

That's IT! Though for other types of installs, you'll need standard e-mail information, such as POP and SMTP servers, MailShield requires no other preinstall configurations of clients or other applications.

Installing MailShield Desktop

After you've downloaded the MailShield install file, double-click that file and follow these steps:

1. At the MailShield Installation window, click the Next button. The Welcome window appears.
2. Select the type of installation by clicking the appropriate radio button, and then click the Next button.
3. Click to accept the license agreement, and then click the Next button.
4. Choose an installation directory for the program. The default creates a directory in Program Files called, oddly enough, MailSheildDesktop. Once you've made this momentous decision, click the Next button.

5. The Program Group window allows you the standard installation options of placing shortcut icons in various convenient places. Click the Next button, if you're confused.

6. You're finished with the install—after you click the Done button, that is.

Initial Configuration

As part of the installation process, MailShield Desktop walks you through several configuration options to set up communications with your mailbox, note any oddities with your mail (such as mailing lists), and make network configuration settings.

1. Enter your e-mail address in the appropriate area and click the Next button.

2. Select your network configuration and the e-mail client that you use. Then click Next.

3. Enter your typical e-mail configuration information, such as mail server, username, and password, and then configure MailShield to check mail at an appropriate interval. When you're finished, click Next. (Note that if you select MSN/HotMail, server information appears automatically and you need to supply only your username and password.)

4. Enter your name and e-mail address for verification purposes. If you use more than one e-mail address to the same mailbox, or some other similar configuration, enter all e-mail addresses separated by a semicolon (;), or enter a domain name if you receive mail from several accounts on the same domain. Once you're done, click the Next button.

5. On the Details About Accepted E-Mail screen, follow the directions. This screen sets MailShield settings concerning mass e-mailings, such as those from mailing lists or "friend" lists where your e-mail address might appear with many others in the message headers. Once done, click the Next button. (See Figure 10-24.)

6. If you selected the I Am Subscribed To Mailing Lists checkbox in the Details screen, MailShield asks you for details about the mailing lists to which you belong. Enter keywords unique to the mailing list, such as regular subject lines (for example, Subject: The Swinehound List: Weekly Ramblings), or enter words and phrases used in list message signatures, such as the list's web site or the like. This configuration allows MailShield to separate mail that you want to see from mail that you don't want to see. Click Next when you're done.

7. The three remaining configuration screens are actually informational; they let you know a little bit about how MailShield interacts with your mail client and how it detects spam, and it shows its tip-of-the-day feature.

8. Once done, the program window appears (Figure 10-25) and you're ready to start spam-fighting.

Anti-Spam Tool Kit

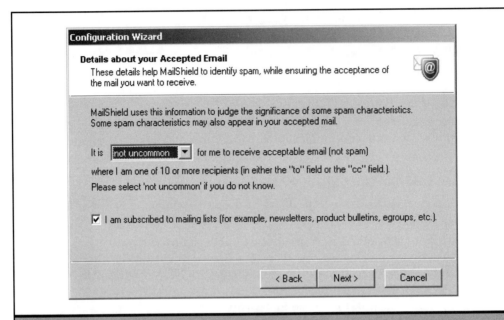

Figure 10-24. Answer the questions and click the Next button.

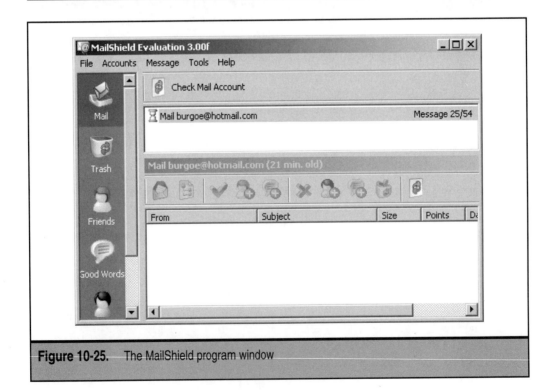

Figure 10-25. The MailShield program window

Manipulating MailShield to Suit Your Needs

MailShield has several configuration and analysis options that allow you to tweak its mail filters, whitelists and blacklists, and other spam triggers. Most of this tuning can be accomplished from the main interface. These tuning options are duplicated in the menu options, with the added functionality of being able to edit the configuration and filtering files directly, set mail and spam handling options, and add an extra layer of spam defense with domain-name and mail-server lookups.

The MailShield Interface

MailShield's main interface is easy to use and understand on first glance. The main interface window is divided into three panes. The pane at the far left lists important functions: Mail, Trash, Friends, Good Words, Spammers, and Bad Words. The largest pane displays your mail with further functions located on the toolbar above it to preview and view analysis of a given message, add the sender or words in the mail to the good or bad lists, and tag or untag the message as spam or legitimate. The thin upper pane lists all the accounts you have MailShield checking and the status of those accounts, as shown in Figure 10-26.

Spam and Filters Configuration By clicking the Spammers icon in the left pane on the main interface, you initiate MailShield's blacklist configuration window, shown in Figure 10-27. From here, you may Add, Edit, or Delete a name, domain name, e-mail address, or user name from your blacklist. Thus, if you always receive spam from someone named Ryder T. Moses with an e-mail address of ryder@moses.com, you could add the name *Ryder T. Moses* (if it shows up as the real name of the sender in the headers), or you could add *ryder@*, or *moses.com*. All three options would block the sender from ever seeing your Inbox again, unless he changes the variable you are filtering against, of course.

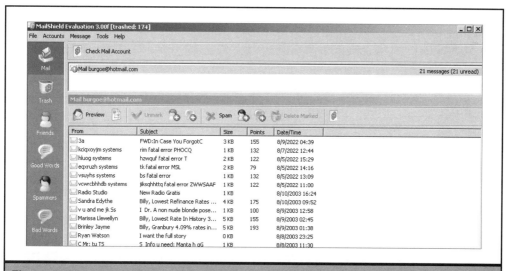

Figure 10-26. The MailShield interface is easy to use and understand.

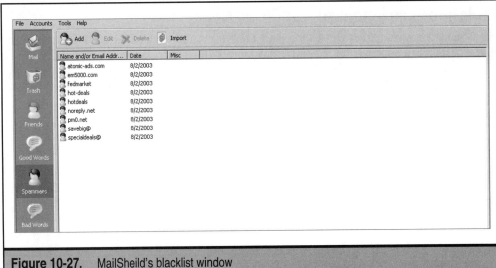

Figure 10-27. MailSheild's blacklist window

Also from the main interface, you can manage Bad Words—words and phrases that might appear in the header, subject, or body of the message that you want MailShield's filters to recognize, score, and possibly designate as spam. To manage the filter settings, click Bad Words in the left pane. You are presented with four options—Spam Indicators, Spam Subjects, Spam Word (body), and Spam Words (header)—as shown in Figure 10-28. These are the standard filter settings, although you can remove them and add as many as you want.

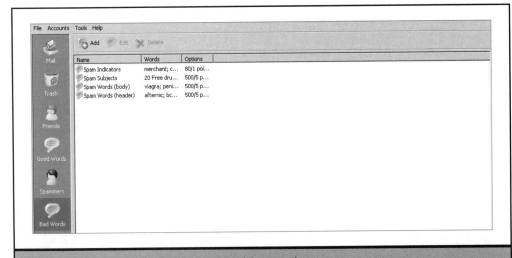

Figure 10-28. Managing filter triggers is a tricky operation.

Double-click the filter setting to manage it (Spam Indicators was chosen in Figure 10-29). For Spam Indicators, type in the words you see regularly in spam but don't necessarily see in regular mail. The Relevance drop-down menu gives you options such as Custom Setting, Suspicious, Highly Suspicious, and Kill Word (definitely spam). These settings change the Spam Value setting below the drop-down menu and change the significance (the number of "trips" on the spam filter counter). MailShield uses the overall Spam Value and Significance indicators to determine whether or not the message is spam, so you should take care not to value too high words and phrases you might commonly see in your e-mail. Finally, the Occurrence area allows you to check where MailShield should look for and score these words: mail body, subject, header, and only uppercase. You can add as many of these filter settings as you wish, tweaking MailShield down to an efficient spam-killing machine.

Let the Good Guys Pass MailShield's Friends and Good Words features allow you to alert the filter that certain senders are friendly and that certain words should score a message away from spam indications. MailShield imports contacts from Outlook Express and you can add as many friends as you want. From the main interface, simply click the Friends icon, and you are presented with your contacts/whitelist. From here, you may add, edit, or delete known good domains, users, or names, as in the preceding section on Spammers.

The Good Words function operates similarly to the Bad Words function. You may add as many entries as you wish to ensure that your legitimate mail comes through the filter. Clicking the Good Words icon brings up the list, as shown in Figure 10-30.

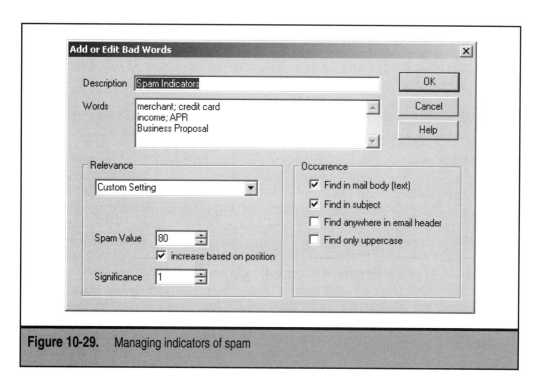

Figure 10-29. Managing indicators of spam

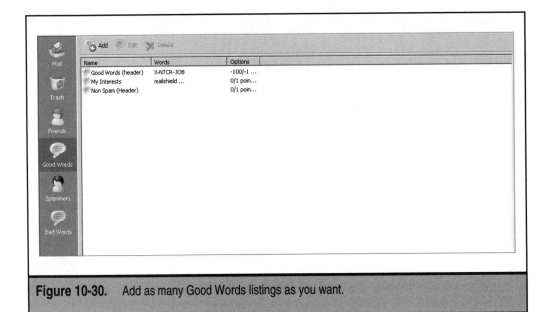

Figure 10-30. Add as many Good Words listings as you want.

Double-clicking a filter or clicking the Add button brings up an interface similar to the Bad Words filters. Here you may add words that indicate that a particular mail is not spam. Examples of words you might want to add are the name of a mailing list to which you belong and that always appears in the subject, a signature line or word that appears in an friend's e-mail, and names of certain services or businesses you frequent on the Web, such as eBay, PayPal, and so on. You then set the relevance: Preferred Word, Custom, or Exception (never spam). These settings change the Bonus Points applied to a message, to offset any spam points it might accumulate. Again, in the Occurrence area of the Add or Edit Good Words dialog box, you may target where you wish MailShield to look for and score these Good Words by clicking the appropriate checkboxes.

Advanced Spam Wrangling From the program menu, additional tweaking and configuration options are available by choosing Tools | Spam Handling And Detection. You'll see the Spam Handling And Detection window shown in Figure 10-31. This set of configuration menus allows you to set the number of significant indicators, tweak the filter configuration files directly, and set up DNS and mail server checks on incoming mail. Configuration options available when the product first installed are accessible from here as well.

The Spam Management tab of the Handling And Detection window allows you to manage what MailShield actually does with messages that score a certain amount of points. The options, as shown in Figure 10-31, allow you to ignore messages, mark messages for deletion, delete them, and keep them in the Trash Mail folder, to mention a few. Beside each option, you can set the amount of spam points required for these rules to trigger. These settings are fully configurable and do not endanger your legitimate e-mail;

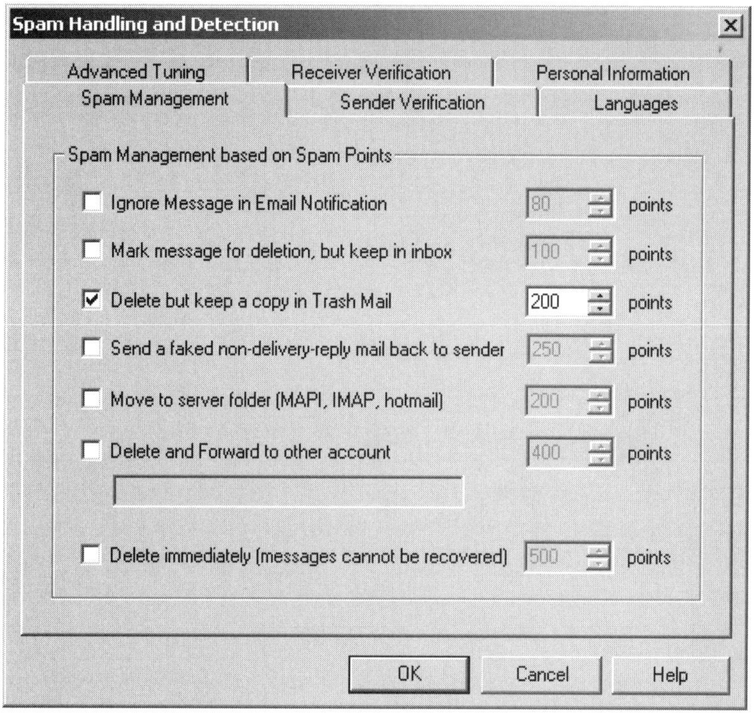

Figure 10-31. Spam Management tab of the Handling And Detection window

however, the last option, Delete Immediately, should be used only if you are very sure of your settings. With this option, messages detected as spam are lost and cannot be recovered. We suggest enabling this setting only once you have a feel for how MailShield scores mail, if you use it at all. During the course of our testing, we crafted targeted innocent mails with the intention of tripping MailShield's filters. Some of these legitimate mails scored in the 800s–900s. Had this setting been enabled (its default is 500 points), those mails would have been lost.

Advanced users may find The Advanced Tuning tab (see Figure 10-32) fairly self-explanatory. Clicking the appropriate buttons allows you to edit the filter configuration files directly. While the text-based configuration files for the mail filters are well commented, modifying these files can lead to unexpected results. Such modifications are outside the scope of this book, but you should feel free to dig in and find out how these settings can fine-tune MailShield. Also on this tab, you can set the minimum number of significant indications before MailShield calls a message spam. The default is 3, but we found this a bit lenient. Additionally, you may set a URL for any spam-reporting service you use.

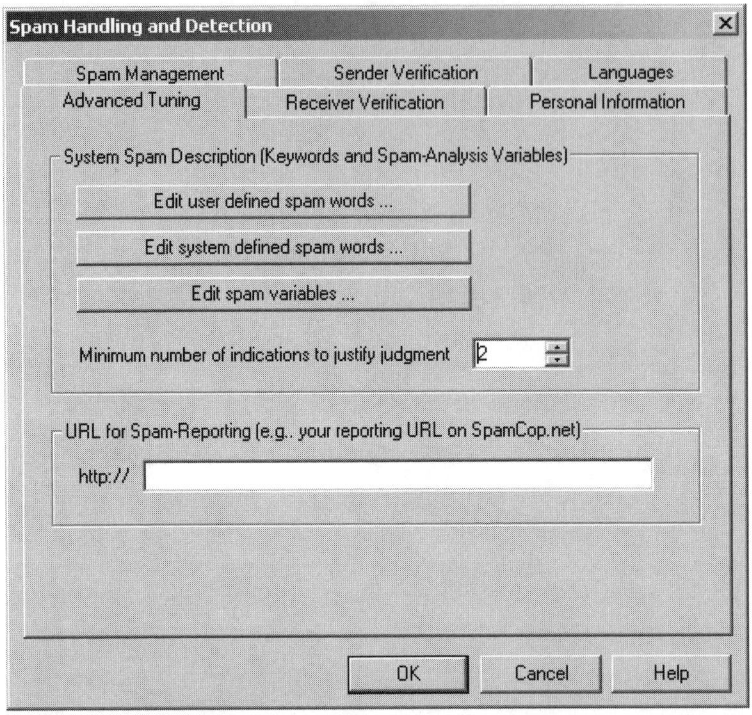

Figure 10-32. Fine-tune MailShield from the Advanced Tuning tab.

Finally, in addition to the installation configuration options discussed earlier, you may set specific languages and character sets as prime indications of spam. A number of checkboxes on the Languages tab allow for Chinese, Korean, German, French, and Spanish to be set as indications of spam. Likewise, you can set mail that contains special characters, such as 8-bit, Unicode, or other character sets as spam.

SPAMFIGHTER

SPAMfighter is a distributed anti-spam solution that relies on individual users of the client software to update a central server with known spam messages. SPAMfighter is available for Windows 98/Me/2000/XP and functions as a plug-in for Microsoft Outlook 2000/2002/2003 and with Outlook Express.

How It Works

Once installed, SPAMfighter compares incoming e-mail to known spam messages as communicated to the central SPAMfighter server. Messages matching those found on the server are automatically sent to the SPAMfighter folder within Outlook. Spam messages that manage to get through SPAMfighter's filter system can be flagged as spam. Flagging spam messages automatically updates SPAMfighter's central server, and if enough users report the same spam message, the message is flagged for all other SPAMfighter users.

Few details about the "gut-level" operation of SPAMfighter appear on the product web site. As SPAMfighter's designers put it, "the spammers might be reading our site as well."

Installing SPAMfighter

To obtain SPAMfighter, download it from *http://www.spamfighter.com*.

Currently the program is free, although the designers intend to charge for both the program and the continued service in the future. Quoting from the web site: "Our plan is to have two versions: one 'premium' with all the features for a small price, and one 'light' version for free. The light version could be limited in features."

Preinstall Checklist

Not much needs to happen before you install SPAMfighter. You should ensure that you have a folder set up to contain messages that SPAMfighter tags as spam, and then you're ready to go.

Installing SPAMfighter

To install SPAMfighter, first close Microsoft Outlook and then follow these steps:

1. Double-click the SPAMfighter Setup file. A Welcome window appears.
2. Click Next. A License Agreement window appears.
3. Select the I Agree radio button and click Next. An Installation Folder window appears.
4. Type in the appropriate installation folder or use the default, and then click the Next button. A Confirmation window appears.
5. Click Next, and wait while the installation process occurs. When an Installation Complete window appears, you're done.

After the installation is complete, the first of several registration windows pop up. Follow these steps to register SPAMfighter:

1. At the SPAMfighter Registration window, select the language (the default is English) and click the Next button.

2. With a new install, you'll need to make a new account with SPAMfighter. Click the radio button next to I Wish To Make A New Account, and then click the Next button.

3. At the Account Creation window, enter your e-mail address and a password to use on the SPAMfighter network. *Do not enter your e-mail account as your password!*

4. Click the Next button, and you're done.

Open Outlook and you should see three SPAMfighter buttons in the top-left corner: Block, Unblock, and More (see Figure 10-33). We discuss further configuration options in the next section.

Configuring SPAMfighter

SPAMfighter requires little user intervention. In fact, on a fresh install, it managed to identify 80 percent of incoming spam correctly using its default configuration options. For us, this was a considerable amount of false negatives, especially compared to the performance of other anti-spam tools covered in this and other chapters. The strength of both blacklist and P2P anti-spam tools, however, is user feedback. Additionally, a couple of settings increase SPAMfighter's effectiveness.

First, though, you'll need to give SPAMfighter the few settings it needs in order to operate:

1. Click the More button in the Outlook toolbar to access SPAMfighter's configuration interface.

2. Click the Choose button in the Spam Folder section of the window. You're presented with a standard Outlook folder tree.

3. Select the folder into which you want all your spam to dump, as shown in Figure 10-34, or create a new folder by clicking the New button, and then click OK.

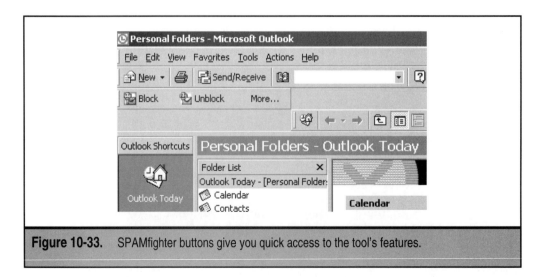

Figure 10-33. SPAMfighter buttons give you quick access to the tool's features.

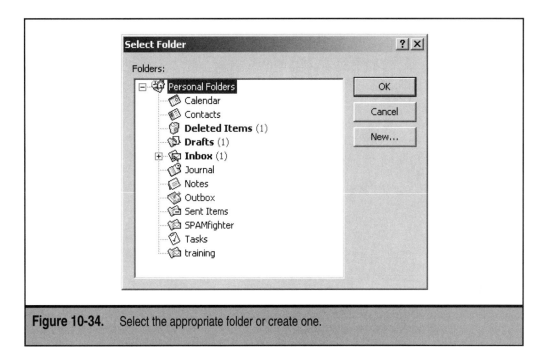

Figure 10-34. Select the appropriate folder or create one.

4. If this is your first use, all your mail has likely already been downloaded. No problem. From the main configuration window, click the Choose button under the Recheck folder section of the Options window (see Figure 10-35).

5. The standard Outlook folder tree appears. Simply click the folder you want SPAMfighter to scan (usually Inbox), and then click OK. SPAMfighter scans the folder and sorts any spam messages to your designated spam folder.

Becoming Part of the Solution

The first and most effective spam-fighting tool for any P2P anti-spam solution is the ability to communicate spam messages to the spam-fighting community. SPAMfighter gives you whitelists and blacklists to use in managing your own incoming mail.

Blocking and Tackling Spam SPAMfighter takes a simplistic approach to blocking and tackling spam. When you find a spam message in your Inbox, simply select the message and click the Block button in the Outlook toolbar. The message jumps to your designated spam folder, and SPAMfighter communicates the specifics of the message to the central servers. This effectively blocks that same message for everyone on the SPAMfighter network.

Should you inadvertently block a legitimate message, locate the message in your spam folder and click the Unblock button. This moves the e-mail back to your Inbox and removes the message from the SPAMfighter network.

Using the Whitelists and Blacklists While we've discussed the benefits and limitations of whitelists and blacklists in other parts of this book, with SPAMfighter, whitelists and

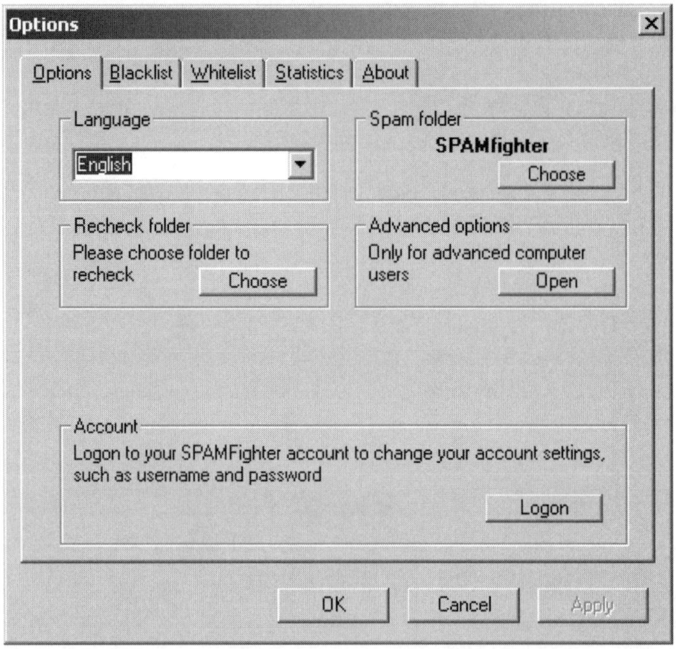

Figure 10-35. Recheck your folder for spam.

blacklists are practically unnecessary. In our testing, with bulk amounts of spam and legitimate mail (500 each), SPAMfighter designated only one legitimate e-mail as spam (and this mail was a forward of a spam mail from a legitimate account). Blacklists, as discussed, do little to increase the effectiveness of SPAMfighter, unless you happen to receive spam from the same user or domain name, which is rare.

To access the whitelist and blacklist, click the More button and then click the appropriate tab, as shown in Figure 10-36.

For each list, SPAMfighter gives you the option of adding individual e-mail addresses or domain names in separate panes of the window that should be considered as trusted sources. The Whitelist tab adds import functionality, allowing you to import your Outlook address book into the whitelist.

Advanced Options

As mentioned earlier in this section, SPAMfighter requires little user intervention; however, we found the need to tweak the settings to increase the program's effectiveness. SPAMfighter claims that its solution blocks 90 percent of spam e-mail with the standard configuration, but we found it closer to 80 percent. To tweak SPAMfighter's settings, click the More button in your Outlook toolbar and then click the Open button under Advanced Settings on the Options tab to open the Advanced Options window, as shown in Figure 10-37.

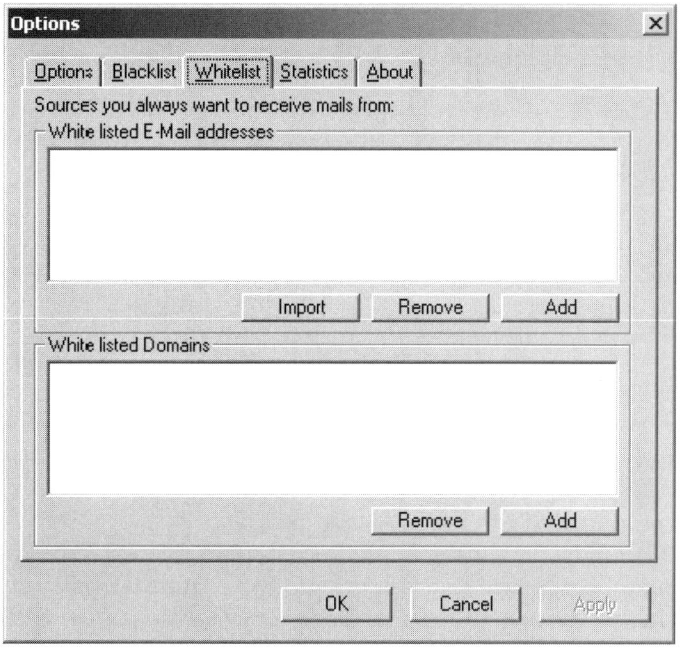

Chapter 10: Anti-Spam Clients for Windows

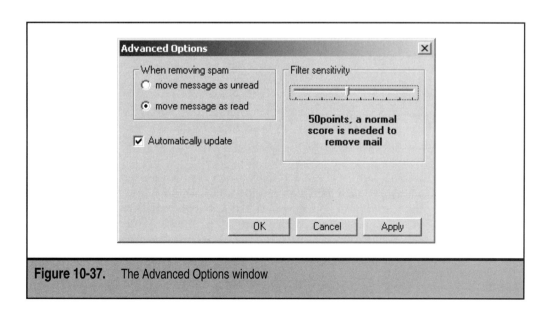

Figure 10-36. SPAMfighter's whitelist

Figure 10-37. The Advanced Options window

The Filter Sensitivity slider affects how granularly SPAMfighter applies its filter. The default setting is 50, and at that setting we never saw more than an 80 percent hit rate on spam, with no false positives (legitimate mail tagged as spam). Cranking the setting all the way down to 10 (the strictest setting) still produced only an 85 percent hit rate (that is, SPAMfighter missed 15 percent of the actual spam in our inbox). Missed spam that we blocked and sent up to SPAMfighter's network increased the hit rate to the advertised 90 percent when we reran the spam through the process.

Also in the Advanced Options window, two radio buttons allow you to mark spam either as Read or Unread. This is more of a personal preference setting and doesn't affect the operation of the program itself. If you don't like to see unread messages inside your spam folder, mark them as Read, and the incoming spam messages are automatically marked as such by the mail client.

Extras   Finally, SPAMfighter provides both Statistics and About tab features in the Options window. The Statistics tab displays the total number of e-mails processed, spam mails caught, and messages that you've blocked or unblocked. Additionally, communications statistics appear at the bottom of this window to give you information on the application's communication with the SPAMfighter network.

The About tab on the Options window provides information about the program, including version number, as well as support and FAQ information. Finally, clicking the Update button in the About tab allows you to update the application when new versions are released, as shown in Figure 10-38.

SPAMBUTCHER

SpamButcher is a POP3 proxy anti-spam tool that uses an unconfigurable "fuzzy logic" system to filter suspected spam. Available for Windows 95 and up, SpamButcher functions with any POP3 client application, including Outlook, Outlook Express, Eudora, Pegasus, and the like.

How It Works

SpamButcher runs as a proxy to a POP3 client, downloading e-mail messages, performing matching to blacklists and whitelists, and executing anti-spam filtering rules against the message headers, subject, and body. Messages detected as spam are flagged and deleted, while legitimate messages are passed on to the POP client. As suggested, e-mail addresses can be added to SpamButcher's whitelist for automatic passage to the mail client or added to the blacklist for automatic designation as spam. Additionally, SpamButcher issues a regular spam report that lists messages the application has deleted. These messages can be restored if SpamButcher has inadvertently deleted a legitimate message. The user can restore false-negative messages; however, these messages are sent back to the user's POP3 server with different From and To fields.

Chapter 10: Anti-Spam Clients for Windows

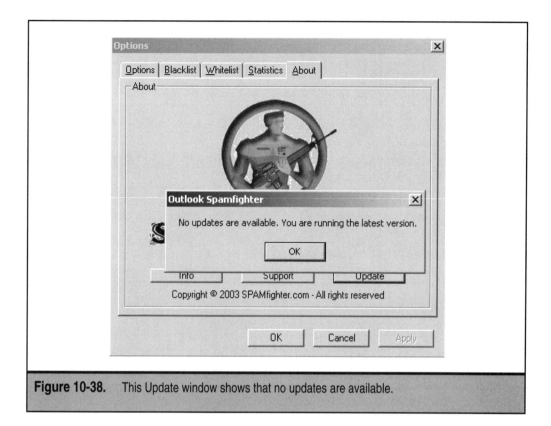

Figure 10-38. This Update window shows that no updates are available.

Installing SpamButcher

SpamButcher is available for download only from the group's web site at *http://www.spambutcher.com*.

The application works only with POP3 e-mail clients such as Pegasus, Eudora, and Outlook Express, and a SpamButcher version is available for Microsoft Windows–based operating systems only.

Preinstall Checklist

Before installing SpamButcher, do the following:

1. Record your e-mail settings, such as username/e-mail address and password.
2. Additionally, be sure to turn off the automatic checking feature for your e-mail client. Conflicts between SpamButcher and your e-mail client might either terminate both programs or allow spam to get through the filter.

Other than these steps, shut off your e-mail client and any other programs while installing SpamButcher, and you're ready to go.

Installing SpamButcher

To install SpamButcher on your PC, complete the following steps:

1. Download the install file from SpamButcher's web site and double-click the file. A standard Welcome screen appears.
2. Click the Next button and then click the Yes button to agree to the license agreement.
3. Type a path to a folder to which you'll install the program. (The default path is C:\Program Files\Spambutcher.) Then click the Next button. SpamButcher installs as directed.
4. Click the Finish button, and you're done.

SpamButcher moves directly to the initial configuration screens after installation completes.

Butchering Spam

SpamButcher launches after the installation completes and attempts to auto-detect your e-mail settings. Once it's done, you'll see a confirmation screen.

1. Click the OK button to proceed.
2. In the Account Configuration window that opens next, shown in Figure 10-39, confirm all of your e-mail settings, including username, e-mail address, password, SMTP and POP servers, as well as authentication methods, such as SSL or authenticated SMTP servers.
3. As shown in Figure 10-39, click the POP3 Test and SMTP Test buttons to test detection of POP and SMTP servers and ensure that your settings are correct. You can also have SpamButcher auto-detect an SMTP server (by clicking Detect SMTP Server), if you do not have this information handy.
4. If your ISP uses different network communication ports for POP and SMTP traffic, click the Advanced button in the respective section to change the port number.
5. Click the OK button, and SpamButcher asks whether you use a dial-up connection to the Internet. Click Yes or No.
6. Then it asks whether you want SpamButcher to send you daily e-mail summaries of intercepted spam. Again, click Yes or No. SpamButcher sends spam reports to the e-mail address of your choice, allowing you to review the spam caught by the program and to recover legitimate mails that may have been inadvertently butchered.

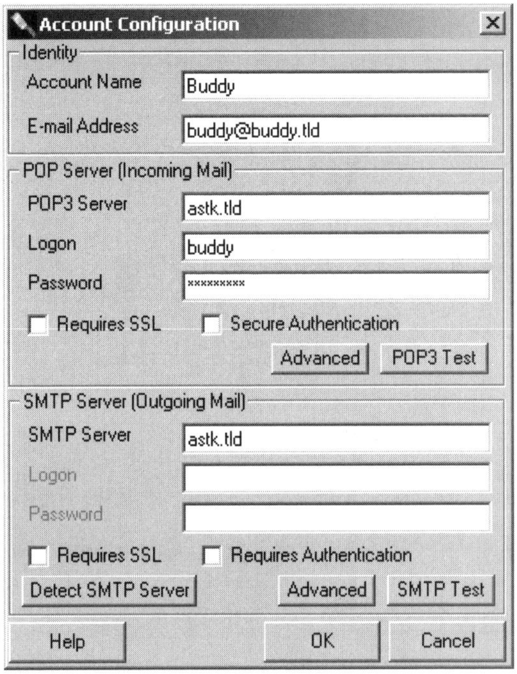

Figure 10-39. SpamButcher supports various authentication methods.

Once you've answered all the questions, SpamButcher is ready for use. From the main interface, shown in Figure 10-40, you have several options, as well as a view of the spam captured.

Click the Check Now button to have SpamButcher check your default POP mailbox immediately. The View Message and Recover Message buttons allow you to view the actual spam message and recover the selected message to your Inbox. The Recover Message feature sends the mail back to your POP mail address with different headers, stripping out all the "Received: from" information. Also, if you recover the message, SpamButcher prompts you to add the sender to your whitelist. Clicking the Purge Spam button permanently deletes all spam messages; no recovery of these e-mails is possible. The Configure button pulls up the configuration interface discussed in the next section.

On a fresh install with no additional tweaking, SpamButcher checks your POP mail box every 90 seconds, intercepts spam messages, and leaves everything else alone. It is configured to send spam reports every day at 10 A.M. local time, and its Filter setting is set to Normal.

Figure 10-40. SpamButcher's main program interface

Tweaks, Lists, and Words

As with other anti-spam tools discussed in this and other chapters, SpamButcher uses a combination of blacklists and whitelists, word filters, and other undisclosed methods for detecting and thwarting spam. Uniquely, SpamButcher adds a reporting component that serves both to inform you of the program's activities as well as allow you to recover any messages that might have been deleted in error. Additionally, you may add other accounts to the interface and configure the aggressiveness of its filters. All of these functions are available from the Configuration window shown in Figure 10-41, which is accessed by clicking the Configure button on the main interface.

Chapter 10: Anti-Spam Clients for Windows

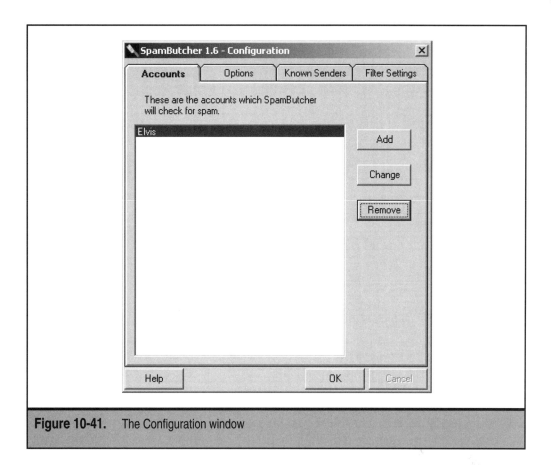

Figure 10-41. The Configuration window

Accounts and Configuration   The Accounts tab of the Configuration window allows you to add accounts for SpamButcher to check. Click the Add button to launch an Account Configuration window similar to the one shown previously in Figure 10-39. The Change and Remove buttons perform those actions for the selected account.

NOTE   You cannot change the account name once it's been set.

In the Options tab, you can set Checking and Reporting variables for the program. The Checking options are fairly self-explanatory, really a matter of personal preference. The Reporting section allows you to set the days of the week and the times you

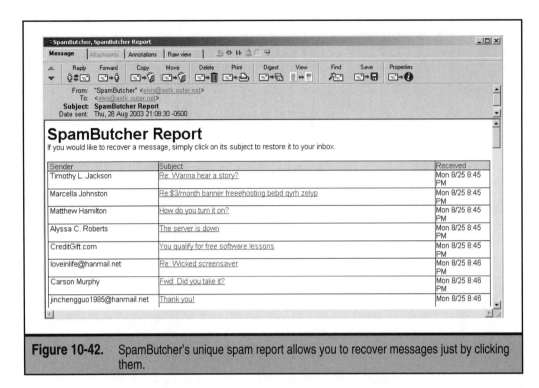

Figure 10-42. SpamButcher's unique spam report allows you to recover messages just by clicking them.

wish to receive SpamButcher's spam report, as shown in Figure 10-42. You may also set the receiving account for the report by selecting the account in the drop-down menu. The account *must* be listed in SpamButcher's Accounts tab or it won't appear in this menu. Finally, you may generate a spam report at any time by clicking the Report Now button.

Are They on the List? The Known Senders tab allows you to set Known Good Senders and Recipients as well as Known Bad Senders, as shown in Figure 10-43. Both lists function similarly. Simply click the Add button and type in the domain or e-mail address you wish to approve or block. SpamButcher imports the address book/contact list from your chosen POP client, though it accepts only comma-delimited text format. Of course, you can remove an address from both lists by clicking the respective address or domain and then clicking the Remove button.

The Butcher's Knives The business end of SpamButcher is contained in the Filter Settings tab. Here you may set the filter settings at Conservative, Normal, or Aggressive, as well as block potentially dangerous attachments, as shown in Figure 10-44.

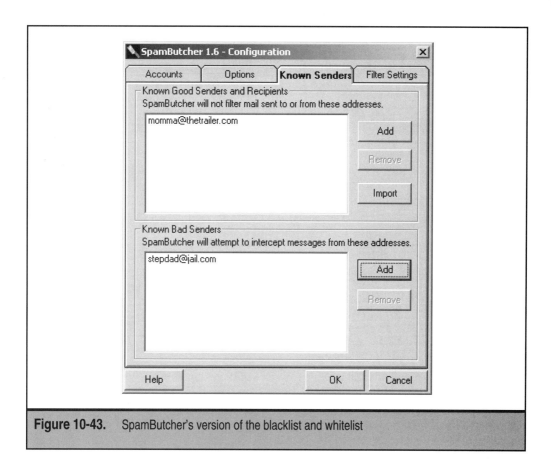

Figure 10-43. SpamButcher's version of the blacklist and whitelist

Additionally, you may add known good phrases and known bad phrases by clicking the Custom Filters button on the Filter Settings window. This brings up the Custom Filters window, shown in Figure 10-45.

Known good phrases include the names of mailing lists to which you belong, names or company names of contacts, and even a password you agree upon with your correspondents (though this is a clumsy method for challenge-password spam-fighting). The known bad phrases are anything you find in a spam message that identifies that message as unwanted. Be careful here, though. Some words in common usage trip word filters, especially if several of these words appear in one message. (You be the judge of what's common usage for your e-mail traffic.) SpamButcher advises that you define longer, more

Anti-Spam Tool Kit

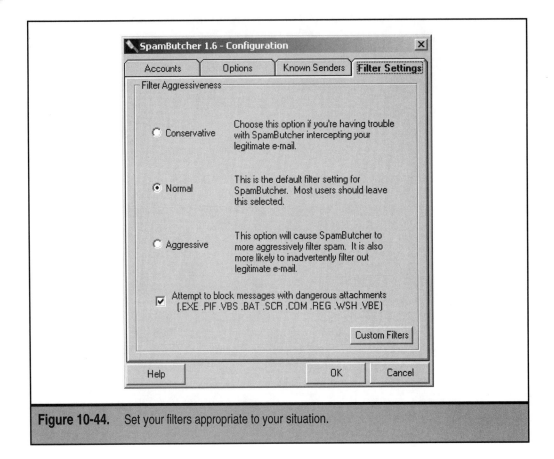

Figure 10-44. Set your filters appropriate to your situation.

complex phrases as both known good and known bad phrases, such as the full name of your mailing list or a whole sentence or company name from spam.

What's the Cut?

We found SpamButcher to be the least functional of all the spam-fighting client tools we evaluated for Windows. In addition to a lack of "gut-level" configuration functionality, the "black box" nature of the solution left much to be desired. With our standard 1000 test messages (500 legitimate and 500 spam), SpamButcher had an inordinate false-positive rate, and it still caught only 75 percent of the spam we shot at it in its Normal setting.

The Aggressive setting was not much better. We lost at least twice as much legitimate mail, and the Butcher snagged only 78 percent of the incoming spam. Without the ability to dig through configuration, word weight, and filter lists, pinpointing the problem was impossible.

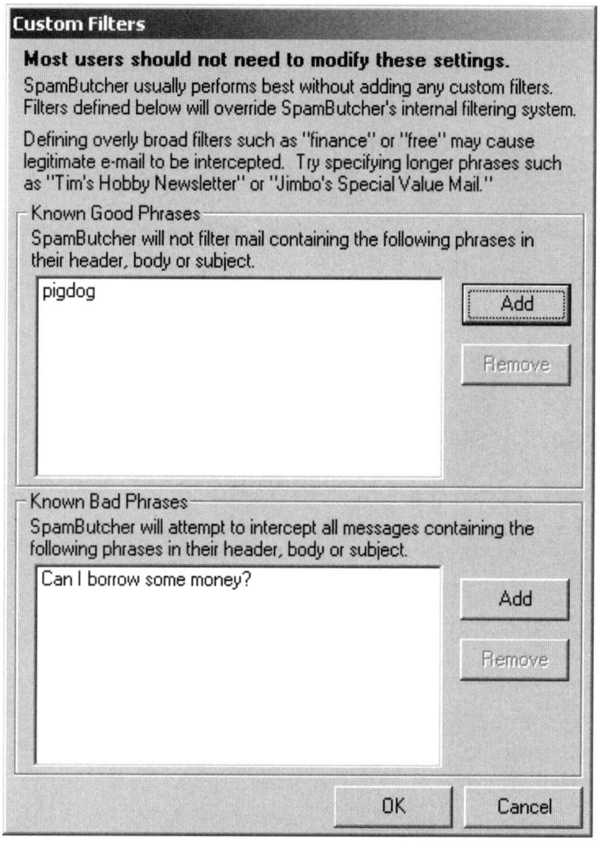

Figure 10-45. Custom Filters window

> **NOTE** Our test was conducted without using the Known Good/Known Bad Senders lists and was a fresh install test of spam detection.

IHATESPAM

iHateSpam from Sunbelt Software uses heuristic processing, rules-based engines, and block/unblock lists to identify incoming spam messages. Running as an Outlook or Outlook Express plug-in, iHateSpam processes e-mail and quarantines spam outside of the mail client for further review. iHateSpam runs on Windows 9x/Me/2000/XP and supports all versions of Outlook and Outlook Express. iHateSpam is also distributed as Postal Inspector by the Giant Company, though the configuration and operation of the program is essentially the same. Postal Inspector also works as a plug-in with AOL versions 6.0 and 7.0.

How It Works

The iHateSpam spam detection engine uses libraries of spam and nonspam semantic knowledge available on the Sunbelt Software central server and the user's incoming mail. Using a heuristic-determined probability based on the process as described, user-definable rules-based filtering, and blacklists, iHateSpam designates the message as spam or ham, catching spam in an offline management console and pushing ham to the user's inbox. Additionally, the user can provide feedback to iHateSpam's community and the spammer's ISP by reporting spammers and messages, as well as sending fake bounce messages to the spammers themselves.

Installing iHateSpam

iHateSpam can be purchased from Sunbelt Software's web site at *http://www.sunbelt-software.com/product.cfm?id=930*.

The program is distributed as a single compressed setup file (5.35MB), and separate downloads are available for Outlook and Outlook Express.

Preinstall Checklist

Before installing iHateSpam, shut down your e-mail client and any other programs you are running. iHateSpam creates a spam folder within your mail client's folder structure automatically, so there's really nothing else to do, other than launch the program. You must reboot after installing this program.

Installing iHateSpam

To install iHateSpam, first download the install file and follow these steps:

1. Double-click the install file and click the Next button at the Welcome window.
2. Read the license agreement and click the Yes button to proceed.
3. In the User Name field, type your name (not your e-mail or network username), and type the name of your company in the Company Name field, if applicable.
4. Choose the install path by clicking the Browse button, or leave it as the default (C:\Program Files\iHateSpam). Then click the Next button, and iHateSpam installs.
5. Click the OK button on the Installation Complete window, and you're ready to configure.

Initial Configuration

When you launch your mail client, iHateSpam presents the Registration window shown in Figure 10-46.

Chapter 10: Anti-Spam Clients for Windows

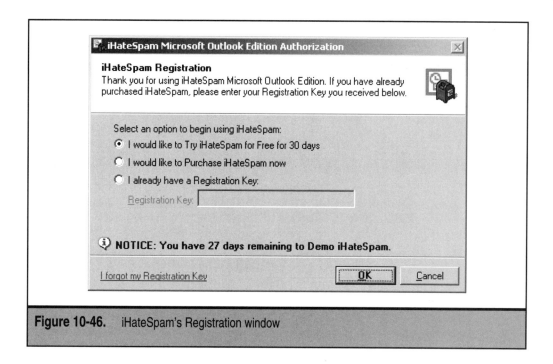

Figure 10-46. iHateSpam's Registration window

Make the appropriate selection and click the OK button. That's it! The iHateSpam plug-in runs as a background process, accessible from the system tray icon. The program also adds buttons, which will give you most of the functionality you'll need, to the Outlook toolbar, as shown here.

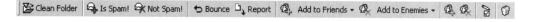

Turning iHate to Action

iHateSpam generally manages itself, although at times the plug-in will quarantine a legitimate mail or let a spam message through. The program updates its profile automatically, and when you add addresses and domains to your Friends or Enemies list, iHateSpam focuses its hatred even better.

As you receive mail, be sure to check your quarantine folder, or the Quarantine management interface, by right-clicking the iHateSpam icon in the system tray and selecting Show Quarantined Messages. The Quarantined Messages management interface appears, as shown in Figure 10-47.

From this list, you can read the quarantined message, tag it as Not Spam, add the sender to the Friends or Enemies list, or send the spammer a bounced e-mail message by clicking the appropriate button.

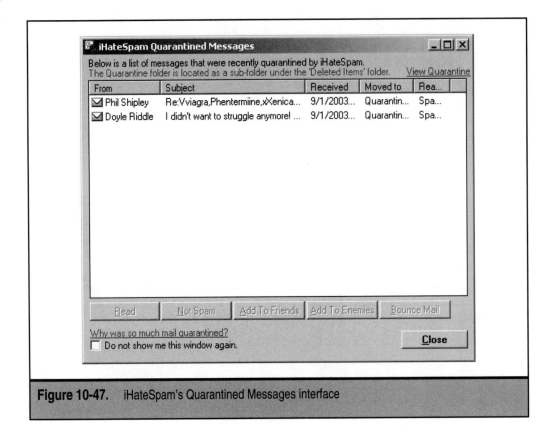

Figure 10-47. iHateSpam's Quarantined Messages interface

Access additional configuration options from the Outlook toolbar by clicking the iHateSpam Options button (the Options button's icon is a pencil hovering over a checkbox). You'll see the Options window shown in Figure 10-48.

From this Options window's Quarantine tab, you can modify the way iHateSpam alerts you to quarantined items, how messages are checked, and the setup of quarantine folders (if you use them). Options under the other tabs allow you to configure the program for operation with an Exchange server, send anonymous reports of iHateSpam's activities to a central server, and block mails with certain character sets (such as Cyrillic, Arabic, and Chinese).

Friends and Enemies

Finally, you can manage the wittily-named Friends and Enemies lists (basically whitelists and blacklists) by clicking the Add To Friends or Add To Enemies button in the Outlook toolbar. The Settings dialog box for adding friends is shown in Figure 10-49.

In both the Manage Your Friends and Manage Your Enemies dialogs, you add Friends or Enemies on the left side of the window by adding either a domain name or an

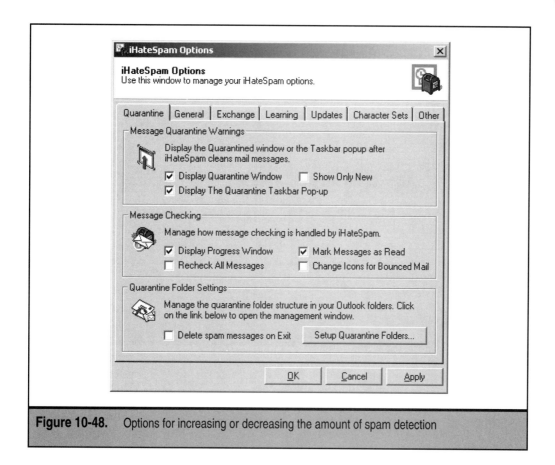

Figure 10-48. Options for increasing or decreasing the amount of spam detection

e-mail address to the list. Additionally, you can import e-mail addresses from contacts lists, distribution lists, the Windows Address Book, or an Outlook mailbox folder. To delete a friend or enemy, simply check the checkbox next to the name or domain name in the right pane of the window and click the Delete Checked button.

SPAMNET

Cloudmark bills SpamNet as "collaborative spamfighting." Operating as a P2P network application, users running SpamNet contribute to the anti-spam community just by deleting spam from their Inbox. Once deleted, other SpamNet users can tag these unwanted e-mails as spam. SpamNet operates on Windows 98/NT/2000/XP and works with Outlook 2000/2002/XP.

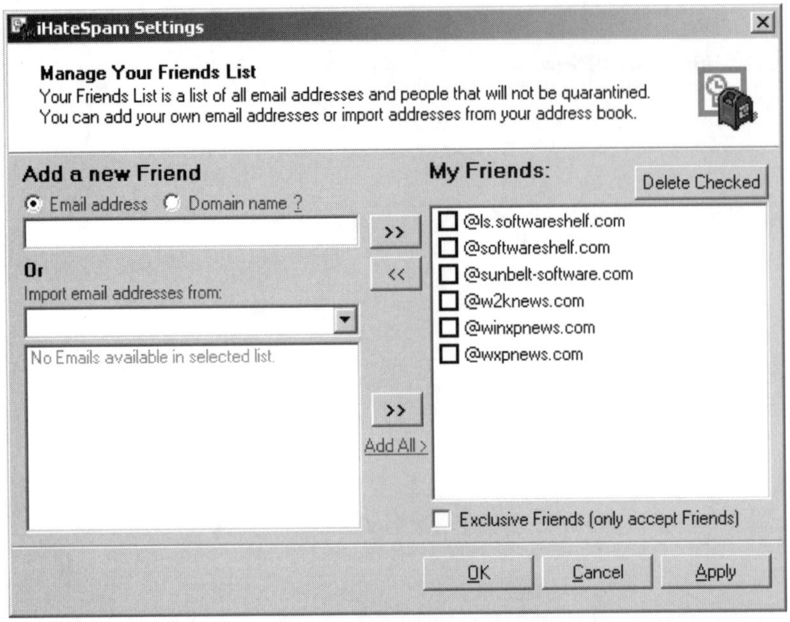

Anti-Spam Tool Kit

Figure 10-49. Manage Your Friends List dialog

How It Works

SpamNet functions as an Outlook plug-in. When anyone within the SpamNet community designates an e-mail as spam, this information is sent to Cloudmark's central repository. Here the report is evaluated. If it's a legitimate report of spam, the message is added to the SpamNet block list, and the message filters as spam for other SpamNet users. To prevent abuse, each SpamNet reporter is ranked according to the number of "good" reports they have made.

As the message arrives at the user's e-mail application, SpamNet generates a one-way hash that represents the e-mail. The SpamNet application transmits this message fingerprint to the central server and queries its database, comparing the fingerprint to those on the server. If the fingerprint matches, the message is designated as spam and is moved from the user's Inbox to a designated spam folder.

Installing SpamNet

SpamNet is distributed for purchase at the SpamNet web site at *http://www.cloudmark.com*. A 30-day evaluation version is available.

Preinstall Checklist

Download the installation file and exit out of all other programs, including Outlook. SpamNet handles all the Outlook folder and filter configurations.

Installing SpamNet

Once you've downloaded the installation file, follow these steps:

1. SpamNet checks your operating system and Outlook versions and then starts the Install Shield wizard. Click the Next button at Welcome window.
2. Read and accept the terms of the license agreement to continue. Click the Next button.
3. Click the Install button to finish the install.
4. At the Complete window, click the Finish button, and then launch Outlook.

Netting Spam with SpamNet

By far, SpamNet is the quickest to set up and the most impressive spam-fighting tool out of the box for Microsoft Outlook. Without so much as a filter update, SpamNet axed 97 percent of all spam we shot at it and did not mistag a single legitimate mail. Just to be sure, we ran SpamNet for a week on a mailbox we use specifically for spam, while shooting legitimate mails at random intervals. Not a single legitimate mail was tagged, and the 97 percent rate never changed.

Of course, as we discuss in Chapter 3, spammers can still thwart network-based spam-hash solutions by slightly altering each message so that it has a different hash and thus appears as a different message altogether. Not only does this allow messages through the filter, but also the exponential effect of thousands of "unique" messages could overload P2P spam network resources pretty quick.

As far as continued configuration and maintenance, little is required with SpamNet. It offers options for updating the program, and you can run the program's filters against any folder at any time. As with most anti-spam clients, SpamNet watches incoming mail and filters it automatically. Also at any time, you can select a message and either block or unblock it. In addition to moving the message either to or recovering from the spam folder, SpamNet sends a hash of the message to its P2P network for update. We discuss these options in the following sections.

Configuration and Tweaks

The configuration options are few, relative to other spam-fighting tools, and the tweaks are nonexistent. But this is a good thing. SpamNet seems to identify and filter spam just fine on its own. To access SpamNet's configuration interface, click the Cloudmark menu in the upper-left corner of your Outlook window and choose Options, as shown in Figure 10-50.

The Options window has four sections: Incoming Mail, Spam Detection Action, Statistics, and Options, as shown in Figure 10-51.

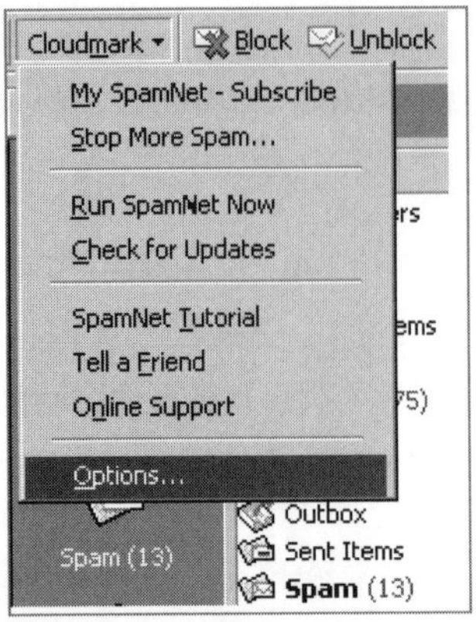

Anti-Spam Tool Kit

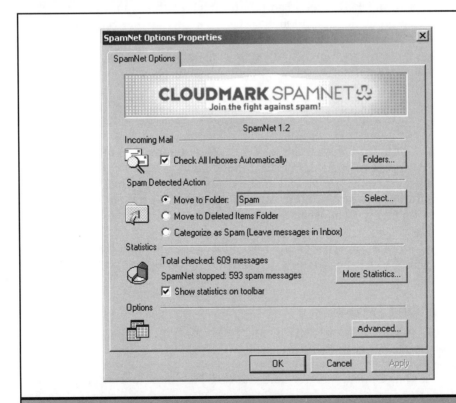

Figure 10-50. SpamNet's configuration menu

Figure 10-51. The SpamNet Options window

The Incoming Mail section offers a checkbox that allows you to indicate whether SpamNet should or should not check all Inboxes automatically.

To add folders to SpamNet's filtering, perform these steps:

1. Click the Cloudmark icon in the upper left-hand corner of your Outlook window and then select the Options menu. The SpamNet Options Properties window appears.
2. Click the Folders button to access the AutoScan Folders window.
3. From there, click the Add button. Your list of Outlook folders will appear.
4. Select the folder you wish SpamNet to filter and click the OK button. The folders list disappears, and your folder is added to the AutoScan Folders list.

You can set the order in which SpamNet scans these folders by selecting the appropriate folder and clicking the Move Up or Move Down button. You can also remove a folder from the automatic scan by selecting the folder and clicking the Remove button.

The Spam Detected Action section of the Options window allows you to designate SpamNet's actions when spam is detected in a folder. You can have spam moved to a folder (the default is the Spam folder), have it moved to a deleted items folder, or have the message tagged as spam and remain in the folder where SpamNet found it.

The Statistics section tells you how many messages SpamNet has checked and allows you to select whether you want those stats displayed in the toolbar. Clicking the More Statistics button brings up a Statistics window that displays the total number of messages stopped, how many spam messages you've blocked, and the total number of messages checked.

The Options section gives you advanced configuration actions, such as whitelists (both e-mail addresses and domains), firewall configurations (if your organization or ISP uses a SOCKS or HTTP proxy), and some general options, such as spam mail header reporting and marking spam messages as "read" in Outlook.

The SpamNet

SpamNet's spam-fighting options are easy and quick. The program automatically filters incoming spam without modification to configuration options. If a spam message remains in your Inbox or other folder, simply select the message and click the Block button on the toolbar, as shown here. The message moves to your spam folder and a hash of the message is reported to SpamNet's central servers. Conversely, if SpamNet tags a legitimate e-mail as spam, select the message and click the Unblock button. The message restores to your Inbox and SpamNet again updates its central servers.

As an additional spam-fighting feature, you may have SpamNet run its filters against all the mail messages in a selected folder. Click the Cloudmark drop-down menu and choose Run SpamNet Now. In the Select Folder window, select the folder you want to scan and click the OK button.

The program runs through all the mail in the folder and filters those messages it tags as spam.

KNOCKKNOCK

KnockKnock is a POP3 e-mail filter that manages spam using approved and denied lists with a twist. The program incorporates secret passwords and an interesting management system to prevent nonsolicited e-mail from reaching you at all. KnockKnock is available for Windows 9*x*/2000/XP and works with most POP3 clients, including Netscape, Outlook Express, and Eudora.

How It Works

With KnockKnock, you set up approved and blocked senders lists on the outset, and these lists function as other spam clients of this ilk. When you subsequently receive e-mail from a sender that's not on one of the lists, KnockKnock compiles the sender addresses and subjects of the questionable messages and mails them to you for review. From here, you accept or deny the messages (and thus the senders), allowing KnockKnock to learn, after a fashion, what spam is to you. Additionally, you can issue a secret word that senders not on your approved list can include in the subject of their e-mail to bypass KnockKnock's process completely.

Installing KnockKnock

KnockKnock is available for purchase as a full package or for free for a 30-day evaluation version from the Sinbad Networks web site at *http://www.knockmail.com*.

Knockmail distributes KnockKnock as an archive or a compressed setup file.

Preinstalling Checklist

KnockKnock requires little in the way of preparation. Exit out of all programs, including your e-mail client, as this spam-fighting tool requires a restart after installation. KnockKnock also requires Microsoft's .NET Framework, which installs as part of the setup process.

Installing KnockKnock

To install KnockKnock, follow these steps:

1. Double-click the setup file to start the install. KnockKnock checks your operating system version, as well as the presence of .NET.
2. If you do not have .NET installed, the setup process prompts you for install. Simply click the Yes button at this prompt to continue.
3. Click the I Agree radio button to agree to the .NET license agreement and then click the Install button.
4. At the Welcome window, click the Next button.
5. At the KnockKnock license agreement, click the Yes button.

6. On the Customer Information window, enter your name and company name (if applicable), and then click the Next button.

7. Select an install folder or stick with the default at the Destination window, and then click the Next button. The .NET Framework and KnockKnock installs. This can take up to 10 minutes on a slower machine.

8. Once completed, a Complete window appears. Click the Yes radio button to restart your computer, and then click the Finish button. Your computer restarts.

KnockKnock configures itself to start automatically when Windows starts. Once Windows restarts, a few initial configuration screens need to be set.

Initial Configuration

The first time you launch your e-mail client after KnockKnock installs, you should see the KnockKnock Registration window.

1. Type the Registration Name and Key Code in the fields provided, and click the Unlock KnockKnock button. If you are trying out KnockKnock, simply click the Free Trial button to continue. The Account Configuration Utility window appears, as shown in Figure 10-52.

2. KnockKnock can automatically fill in all the e-mail information it needs from Outlook Express. Type in your name and click the Configure Outlook Express button to start.

3. Select the correct e-mail account from the drop-down box (the pertinent information should appear in the table at the bottom of the window).

4. Click the checkbox next to the appropriate account, and click the Save button to save the configuration. Note that you can configure KnockKnock to protect more than one e-mail account.

5. When finished, click the Exit button to continue on to your e-mail.

KnockKnock's interface loads into the system tray in the lower-right side of your desktop. All other configuration is accomplished from this menu.

Knocking on a Spammer's Door

KnockKnock is unique among Windows-based spam-fighting clients in that it assumes that all messages are spam unless otherwise specified by you. After the initial install, you get no e-mail from any sender other than KnockKnock itself. The program scans your POP mailbox, assembles a report of all messages found there, and sends this report to you for evaluation, where you can accept or deny the messages. All senders receive a message that says their email account is protected by KnockKnock and that their address is being evaluated.

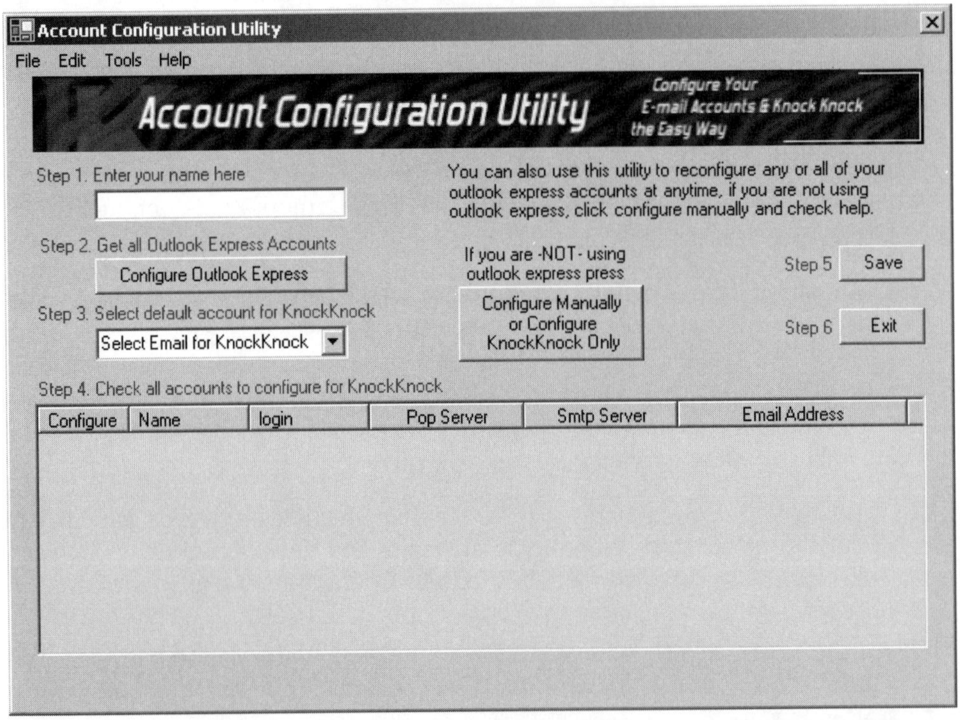

Figure 10-52. Account Configuration Utility window

KnockKnock has many configuration options and tweaks to make spam-fighting more precise, but most of them are outside the scope of this section. We do cover basic operation and some of the advanced options available.

Getting Mail, and Knocking Out Spam

The most important question for any new KnockKnock user is "How do I receive the mail I want and block the mail I don't with this tool?" Various KnockKnock interfaces allow for both acceptance and denial of pending messages. When KnockKnock sends you a report of pending messages, you may add a sender to your accepted list by either sending an e-mail to that person, enabling the user's information in the Manage Addresses database, or using Knock Preview to view and manage messages on the server. To deny a message and sender, use the Manage Addresses window or the KnockKnock Preview.

Manage Addresses To bring up the Manage Addresses window, right-click the KnockKnock icon in your system tray and choose Manage Addresses. You'll see the Address Management window shown in Figure 10-53.

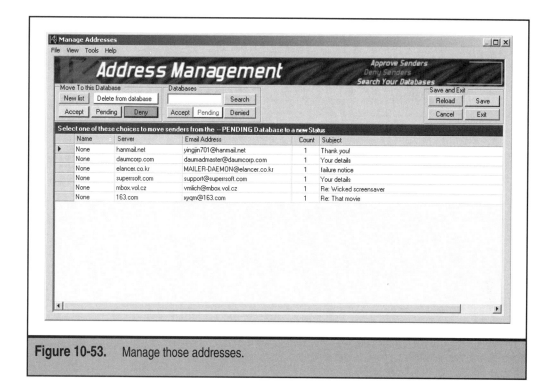

Figure 10-53. Manage those addresses.

Simply select each of the legitimate messages and click the Accept button. The sender is added to the approved list and the message is released to download to your Inbox the next time Outlook checks for mail.

To block senders and messages, select the spam message and click the Deny button. The sender is automatically blocked and the message is analyzed by KnockKnock's Auto Spam Killer logic for subsequent message blocking.

KnockKnock Preview To view messages in the KnockKnock Preview window, right-click the KnockKnock icon in the system tray and choose Preview Pending Emails. You'll see the Knock Preview window shown in Figure 10-54.

Again, simply select legitimate messages and click the Accept button. For spam, select the message and click the Deny button. Then click the Save button and the KnockKnock database is updated with the new information.

Advanced Configuration

KnockKnock has several tweaks and advanced management options to let you drill-down on pesky spam and to ensure that legitimate mail gets through. KnockKnock uses "secret codes" that, when included in the body of an incoming mail, automatically allows

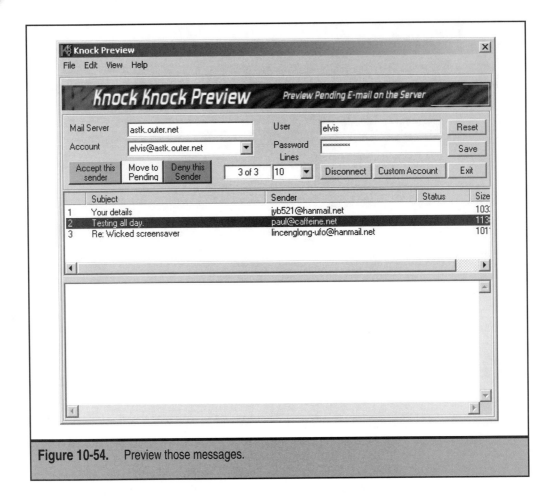

Figure 10-54. Preview those messages.

the message passage to your Inbox. Additionally, you can add words or phrases that, when detected in the subject of an e-mail, automatically block the message.

To configure your secret codes, right-click the KnockKnock icon in the system tray and choose KnockKnock Settings. When the KnockSettings window appears, click the Secrets tab, as shown in Figure 10-55.

To enable a secret word or phrase, click the Add New button and type in the desired text. Select an expiration date for the secret code and click the Save And Exit button. Share this secret word or phrase with your contacts and their e-mails breeze through the KnockKnock process without the intervening verification process.

To add blocked words, click the Subjects tab in the Settings window. Type a word or phrase in the field provided and click the Add button. Now any e-mail that arrives with this word or phrase in the Subject line is automatically blocked. Obviously, you want to be careful with this feature, since common words and phrases may appear in legitimate e-mail.

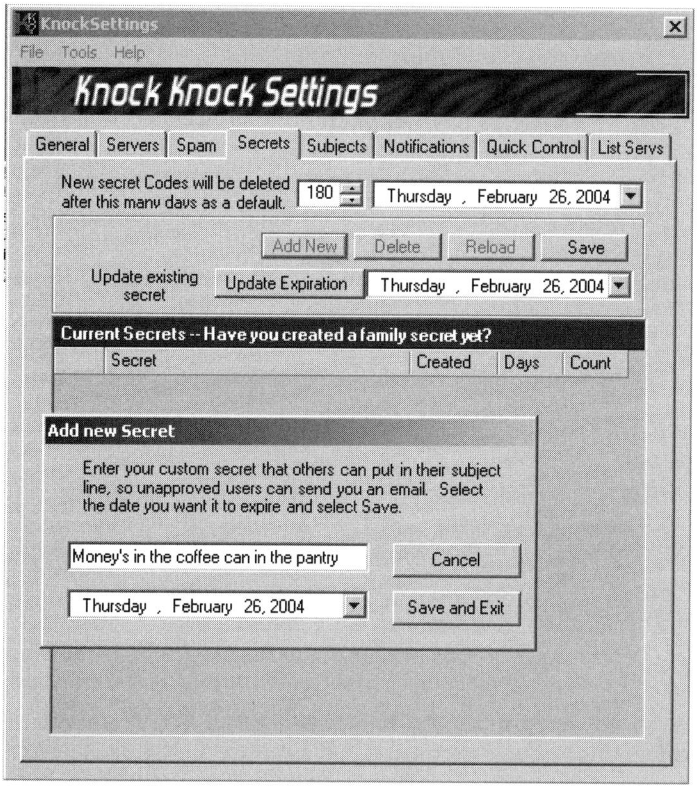

Figure 10-55. Secret passwords allow e-mail to bypass the KnockKnock net.

Knocking KnockKnock

While KnockKnock certainly uses an aggressive approach, we found the overall philosophy of its approach to be somewhat flawed. Training the program to recognize spam was tedious and time-consuming. With proper training, it did a great job of passing through legitimate mail, though initially our correspondents had questions about the "pending approval" messages they received.

In testing the Windows-based clients in this chapter, KnockKnock just seemed overly complicated. Receiving several messages a day from the program telling you that you have messages pending for approval is the equivalent of a denial-of-service attack on a host. You must stop what you are doing, sift through the messages, approve or deny them, and then get back to what you were doing. If we wanted to look at spam messages, we wouldn't have installed a spam-fighting tool in the first place. Overall, KnockKnock did a great job of keeping spam out of our Inbox, but we still had to see and deal with almost every one of our e-mail messages.

POPFILE

POPFile is a free, open-source anti-spam tool that uses word and logic filters to classify e-mail and sort it into buckets (folders) as directed by you. As POPFile is trained by your direction, it starts to sort mail on its own. Although it functions as a spam-fighting tool, POPFile can also sort your e-mail into any buckets you desire. Thus, if you have personal and business messages arriving at the same POP box, POPFile can sort these by the same logic it uses to fight spam. POPFile is distributed in both a Windows-based version and a cross-platform version.

POPFile is compatible with any POP e-mail client and the Windows version operates on Windows 9x/NT/2000/XP/2003. The cross-platform version operates with any operating system that runs the Perl programming environment. We cover the Windows version in this chapter; however, both versions run exactly the same.

How It Works

POPFile operates as a POP mail proxy, scanning incoming messages for keywords and performing Bayesian logic to tag the messages and filter them into the buckets that you designate. Like all Bayesian filters, POPFile goes through a learning period in which it builds its database of good and bad mail qualities as you tag messages as legitimate and illegitimate. As POPFile handles more mail, it gets better at what it does, enabling the program to sort even different types of legitimate mails to different designated buckets, such as personal and business-related messages. All of this is accomplished using Bayesian statistical models similar to those discussed in the SpamBayes section earlier, though the implementation is different. Additional mail designation capabilities allow you to add "magnets," essentially your own good/bad word lists and whitelists/blacklists, in a combined functionality.

Installing POPFile

POPFile is distributed from the SourceForge web site either as a Windows-specific compressed setup file or a cross-platform zip file at *http://POPFile.sourceforge.net/*.

The program installs in just a few minutes. All configuration is done during the install process.

Preinstall Checklist

Like most Bayesian filters and POP proxies, you must prepare your POP client before operating POPFile. For this chapter, we used Outlook Express. Instructions for other POP clients differ; however, POPFile's manual contains detailed instructions for integration with Pegasus Mail and Eudora, as well as Outlook and Outlook Express.

To set up Outlook Express to check mail through POPFile, follow these steps:

1. Open Outlook Express and choose Tools | Accounts.
2. In the Internet Accounts window, double-click the account you want to configure.

3. Click the Servers tab, and change the Incoming Mail (POP3) field to **127.0.0.1**.
4. In Incoming Mail Server area, change the Account Name field to read ***incomingmailserver:yourusername***, where *incomingmailserver* is the POP3 mail server you check mail on and *yourusername* is your e-mail username. Thus, if your incoming mail server were *pop.host.tld* and your username were *elvis*, you would change the Account Name field to read **pop.host.tld:elvis**.
5. Click the Apply button and then click OK.
6. Close the Accounts window.

NOTE POPFile must be running for you to check e-mail with this configuration.

Additionally, you'll want to add the appropriate folders to Outlook Express as well as the filter rules before installing and using POPFile. Follow these steps to set that up:

1. Choose Tools | Message Rules | Mail. The Message Rules window appears with the Mail Rules tab open.
2. Click the New button. The New Mail Rule window appears.
3. Check the Where The Subject Line Contains Specific Words checkbox.
4. Check the Move It To The Specified Folder checkbox.
5. In the Rule Description pane, click the "contains" link.
6. Type the name of the POPFile bucket on which you wish to filter (see the "Buckets and Magnets" section a little later) and click the Add button. Then click OK.
7. Click the "specified, in the Rule Description pane" link.
8. From the folder tree, select or create the Outlook Express folder to which you want to move the filtered message.
9. Click the OK buttons on the Folder, the New Mail Rule, and Message Rules windows.

POPFile requires two buckets, so be sure that you set up one filter for spam and one for legitimate mail. Before installing POPFile, exit out of all programs, including your e-mail client.

Installing POPFile

Once your initial setup is complete, download POPFile and extract the setup.exe file. Double-click the setup file and follow these steps:

1. A POPFile Setup window appears. Click the No button to continue.

2. At the Welcome window, click the Next button.
3. Accept the GNU General Public License and click the Next button.
4. Select the components to install and click the Next button.
5. Click the Next button to install POPFile in the default location.
6. At the Installation Options window, use the recommended POP and User Interface port connections unless you know your POP port to be different. Click the checkbox if you wish to run POPFile automatically when Windows starts. When done, click the Install button.

After POPFile installs, you'll need to go through a few initial configuration settings, and then POPFile is ready to start learning. Follow these steps to complete the initial configuration:

1. In the Classification Bucket Creation window of the Setup wizard, shown in Figure 10-56, check the buckets you want to remove from the list in the right pane. You can create new buckets either by selecting a name from the list in the drop-down box or by typing the name of the bucket in the field provided. Click the Continue button to proceed.
2. A Confirmation window appears. Click the Yes button to proceed or click the No button to change your bucket selections.
3. POPFile can configure itself from the Main Identity file for Outlook or Outlook Express. If you are using one of these mail clients, simply click the checkbox to reconfigure the account to work with POPFile. (Note that we showed you the manual configuration in the preceding section.) Once done, click the Next button.
4. Click the Finish button to complete the install, and you're done!

POP Goes the Spammers

POPFile is easy to train and use. Its management interface uses a light HTTPd server to serve up configuration web pages, giving you the ability to train POPFile, add buckets and magnets, view reports and logs, and change configuration settings. To access the management interface, right-click the POPFile icon (the octopus) in your system tray and select the appropriate function.

Training the Octopus

POPFile knows nothing when you first start it up—in fact, all mail that passes through on this first launch simply dumps into your Inbox and is classified as unknown by POPFile. To train POPFile, launch the management interface. By default, the History page appears, as shown in Figure 10-57.

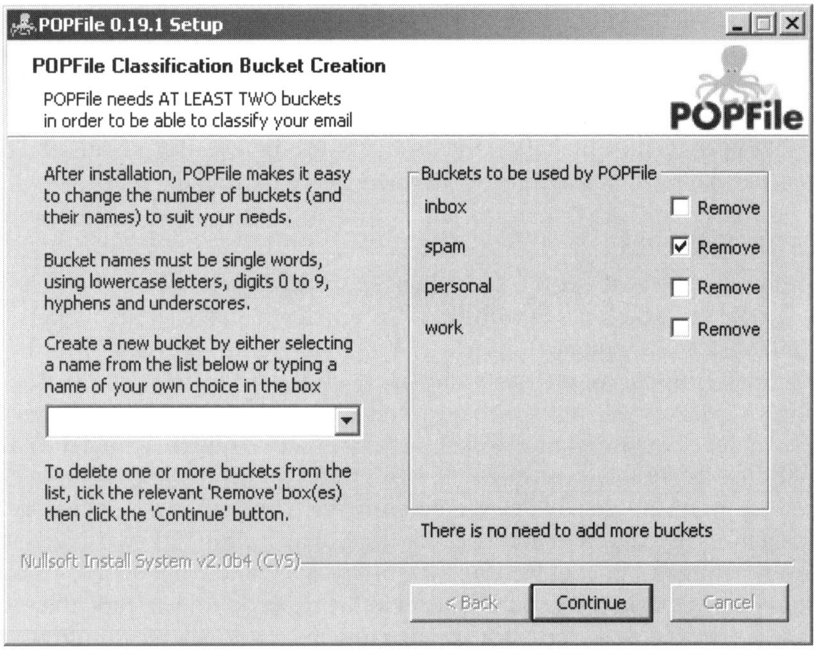

Chapter 10: Anti-Spam Clients for Windows

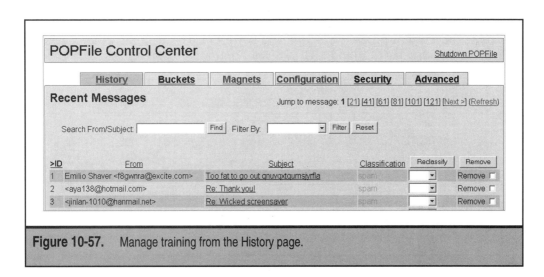

Figure 10-56. Fill up those buckets.

Figure 10-57. Manage training from the History page.

For each of the messages on the History page, click the Classification drop-down menu and select the bucket to which the message should have gone. Then click the Reclassify button. None of the mail in your Inbox moves, but POPFile updates its word lists and logic, making it a better spam-fighter in the future. Anytime POPFile misclassifies an e-mail, find the mail on the History page and reclassify it. We found that after about 20 e-mails, POPFile made few mistakes. By the end of testing with 500 spams and 500 legitimate mails, POPFile was running at about an 85 percent accuracy rate.

Buckets and Magnets

You shouldn't have to add additional buckets, unless you wish to use POPFile as a general mail-sorter as well as a spam-fighter. To add or manage your buckets, click the Buckets link on the management interface. You'll see some statistical information concerning accuracy, number of messages classified, and word counts. Bucket management options for the buckets you already have appear at the top of the page. From these options, you can turn the Subject modification feature off or on, which adds the name of the bucket to the subject of the incoming message.

At the bottom of the Buckets management page, you can add a bucket by typing a bucket name in the Create field and clicking the Create button. Likewise, you can delete buckets by selecting the bucket from the drop-down list and clicking the Delete button. Finally, to rename a bucket, select the bucket in the drop-down list, type the new bucket name in the field provided, and click the Rename button. Also, be sure to update your mail client's filters, since the client is parsing off of POPFile's subject addition and sorting the mail appropriately.

Magnets are user-customizable words or phrases that allow POPFile to classify an incoming mail immediately to a specific bucket. Magnets function as a blacklist or whitelist by matching e-mail addresses, names or domain names in the headers, or words in the subject. To add a magnet, click the Magnet link on the management interface, and then select the type of magnet you want from the drop-down list (To, CC, Subject, or From). Then type the word or phrase for POPFile to key off of. To finish, select the bucket to which you want the mail to go and click the Create button. The Magnet list should update and is shown in Figure 10-58.

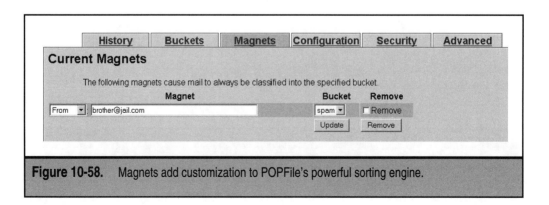

Figure 10-58. Magnets add customization to POPFile's powerful sorting engine.

Configuration, Security, and Word Management

Additional management options allow you to configure both mail checking and logging, and reporting and security, and they give you the ability to add words to bucket databases.

The Configuration page on the management interface offers several configuration options. You can change the POP3 listening port, connection timeouts, and user interface web port, as well as the appearance and operation of the management interface.

The Security page gives you the ability to set up Remote Authentication servers and set up remote access to the management interface. Additionally, POPFile can be configured to check the SourceForge site automatically for updates and patches. Finally, you can report anonymous usage statistics to POPFile's developer, which allows him to address issues in the future.

POPFile ignores certain common words, such as *and* and *the*. To view, add, and remove these ignored words, click the Advanced link. A list of ignored words appears, and you may add or delete them from the interface at the bottom of the page.

CHAPTER 11

ANTI-SPAM SERVERS FOR WINDOWS

In previous chapters, we've talked a lot about client anti-spam tools and how they are great for individual users. But what about tools for the organization? The logical chokepoint for spam is at the mail gateway, and since most organizations do not run UNIX-based e-mail solutions, we offer the following Windows-based server solutions.

IHATESPAM SERVER EDITION

Why not start with the tool whose name says how we all really feel about spam? If you think we already covered this product in Chapter 10, you're only half correct. In addition to a client tool, Sunbelt Software also distributes a server-based anti-spam tool. Like the client version, iHateSpam Server Edition is a multistrategy spam fighter using semantic and rules-based filtering and black/whitelists to block spam at the mail gateway. Out of the box, iHateSpam claims a 90 percent or better accuracy rate, although we had a considerably lower percentage on initial install.

iHateSpam runs on Windows 2000 Server with Service Pack 3 or later and MS Exchange 2000 with Service Pack 3 or later. iHateSpam Server Edition is a commercial program distributed either on CD or as a download from Sunbelt Software's web site at *http://www.sunbelt-software.com*. The base install allows for 25 mailboxes, with additional "packs" of mailboxes available for purchase separately.

How It Works

iHateSpam controls spam at the gateway by applying word-based and rules-based filters, blacklists, and whitelists either globally (to all e-mail accounts) or by policies (to one or groups of e-mail accounts). While both rules and e-mail lists are customizable, Sunbelt Software provides a regularly updated ruleset that covers most of the spam strategies out there. Mail that hits its spam rules are assigned a "spam probability," and if the administrator-definable threshold is reached, the mail is either deleted or pushed to a user-accessible quarantine folder for review. Additionally, iHateSpam has a powerful reporting engine that builds regular spam reports and stores them in an Access database file (included) or SQL file.

Installing iHateSpam

iHateSpam should be installed on the Windows server running Exchange. As stated previously, iHateSpam is distributed either as a single installation file from the Sunbelt Software web site or via CD. We installed the downloaded version on a Windows 2000 Server running Exchange 2000.

Preinstall Checklist

Other than the system requirements, you must have Administrator access to the machine where you wish to install iHateSpam. If you wish to install the Reporting facilities for MSSQL (either SQL 2000 or MSDE 2000), you must have SQL installed and running and mixed mode authentication turned on. Refer to SQL, Windows, and iHateSpam documentation for more information on using SQL with iHateSpam.

Installing

To install iHateSpam Server Edition on Windows, perform these steps:

1. Log in to your Windows server as Administrator or as user with Administrator rights.
2. Double-click the installation file, and the initial splash window appears.
3. Click Next. The Welcome screen appears.
4. Click Next. The User Information window appears, as shown in Figure 11-1.
5. Enter your name and your organization's name, and choose who will have access to the program. (We suggest you choose the Only For Me radio button for security reasons.) Then click the Next button.
6. At the License Agreement window, click the I Agree radio button and then click Next.
7. In the Destination Folder window, select an install directory. We suggest the default (*$Windowsroot*\SunbeltSoftware\iHateSpam Server Edition\), unless you have some other policy regarding program installation on your server. Click the Next button when you're ready.
8. The Select Features window allows you to install either the Server Components or Standalone Report Viewer (or both). For this install, leave it set at the default, which is both, and click Next.
9. The Ready window allows you to click Back if you want to change any of the settings or click Cancel to cancel the install. Click Next when you've pondered all that could go wrong and you decide to go ahead anyway.
10. After iHateSpam installs, the Installation Utility Object window appears, as shown in Figure 11-2. Here you can set up the database management system where iHateSpam stores its reports. The default is a Microsoft Access database called iHateSpamDB.MDB. You can configure iHateSpam to write to an SQL database (which it also creates) by clicking the Database Settings button. (See the "Preinstall Checklist" section for more information about enabling iHateSpam for SQL reporting.) Click Reporting Enabled to enable reporting, and then click the Done button.
11. The Exchange 2000 Event Sink Setup window opens. This window offers one checkbox for each instance of the Exchange SMTP service you're running on Exchange and two buttons: Install SMTP Sink and Cancel, as shown in Figure 11-3. Check each instance listed and click the Install SMTP Sink button to register iHateSpam with each service.
12. After you click the Install SMTP Sink button, a confirmation window appears, letting you know how many sinks have been registered successfully. Click OK, and the main Event Sink Setup window reappears, listing all instances of SMTP registered (the checkboxes should be grayed out now). Click OK to finish the initial configuration.

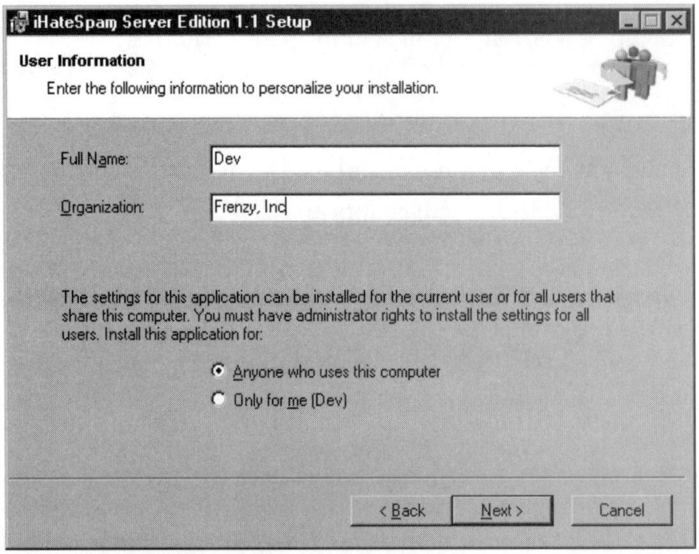

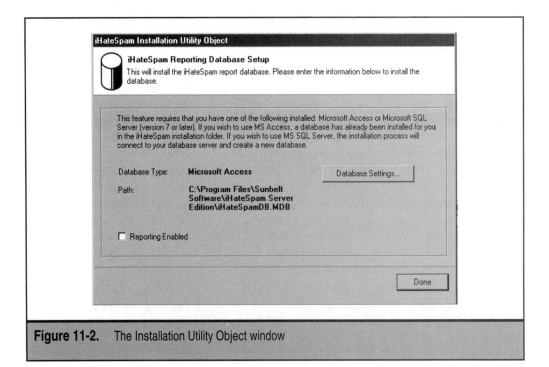

Figure 11-1. The User Information Window

Figure 11-2. The Installation Utility Object window

Chapter 11: Anti-Spam Servers for Windows   253

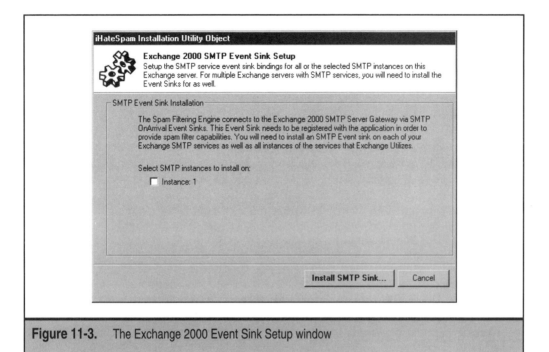

Figure 11-3. The Exchange 2000 Event Sink Setup window

13. A window proclaiming success appears. Click the Finish button, and iHateSpam prompts you to restart.

Exchange SMTP OnArrival Sink

iHateSpam uses the Exchange SMTP OnArrival Sink to scan incoming e-mail. This function communicates the incoming e-mail message, along with the transport envelope fields, to iHateSpam for rules processing. You don't really have to know how the SMTP sink works, since iHateSpam configures and registers itself for communication with Exchange, but be sure to check each Instance listed on the Exchange 2000 SMTP Sink Window (Figure 11-3). If you're curious, a very thorough description of SMTP/NNTP sinks and other Collaboration Data Objects (CDO) COM components appears on Microsoft's MSDN site at *http://msdn.microsoft.com/library/default.asp?url=/library/en-us/cdosys/html/_cdosys_smtp_nntp_transport_event_sinks_with_cdo.asp*.

Hating Spam in the Enterprise

Straight out of the box, iHateSpam does nothing for you. You have to configure it to get mail and apply its rules and policies. iHateSpam creates a shortcut on your desktop, but you can also access the management console by navigating to Start | Programs | iHateSpam Server Edition | iHateSpam Server Edition Manager. The iHateSpam management console appears, as shown in Figure 11-4.

To access the main management console window, click the iHateSpam Server Edition folder in the left pane. The right pane populates with big, friendly icons: Management, Spam Filtering, Reporting, About, Help, and Registration. Clicking any of these icons allows you to access the various functions described in the following sections. You may also navigate the management functions through the folder tree in the left pane, and you can always access the Help window by pressing the F1 key.

Management The Management group gives you access to both User and System Management configuration options.

User Management The User Management tool allows you to set policies for each individual user as well as disable filtering entirely per user. The User Management tool provides a search function, as well as a list of preconfigured searches, as shown in Figure 11-5.

To assign a policy to a user, enter the user's mailbox/username in the User Search field and click the Search button. The user appears in a table detailing his or her e-mail address,

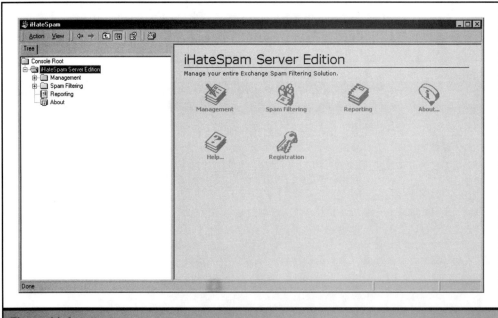

Figure 11-4. The iHateSpam management console

Chapter 11: Anti-Spam Servers for Windows 255

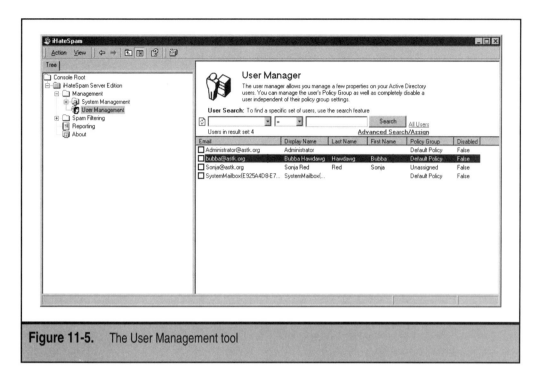

Figure 11-5. The User Management tool

display name, first and last name, Policy Group applied (default is Unassigned), and Disabled status (default is False). Double-click the username, and the Manage User window appears, as shown here. Select the policy you want to apply from the Policy Group drop-down and, if desired, disable filtering by clicking the Disabled Filtering checkbox (if desired). Click the OK button. Since only the Default Policy is available right now, we'll talk more about assigning user policies in the "Spam Filtering: Policies" section.

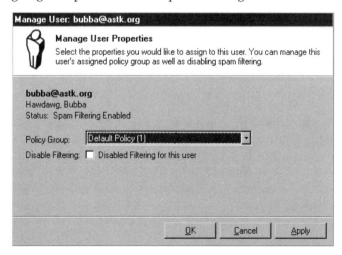

System Management If you click the System Management icon from the main management console, you'll see another console view with the following functionality: General Settings, Reporting, Registration, SMTP Event Bindings, Smart Caching, Replication, and Domain Configuration.

The General Settings window allows you to turn spam filtering on and off and also allows you to configure iHateSpam for Tracing Mode. Tracing Mode records all iHateSpam events to various trace or log files. This mode is used for troubleshooting problems, but click the Settings button now. A Trace Settings window appears, as shown next. Simply check the events you wish to log and click the OK button. Then, click the On radio button to enable Trace Mode.

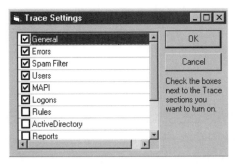

NOTE Trace Mode is used for tracking down problems, such as mail bottlenecks and other specific errors. iHateSpam in Trace Mode quickly generates very large log files. It's recommended, therefore, that you use this mode only if you need to troubleshoot a problem.

The Reporting icon (or the Reporting folder in the System Management tree) brings up the System Management: Reporting Settings window, as shown in Figure 11-6. This window should already be populated, as configured during the installation, with the Database Type (default: Microsoft Access), Path (default: $RootProgramFiles\Sunbelt Software\iHateSpam Server Edition\iHateSpamDB.MDB), and the Reporting Enabled checkbox checked. If this is not the case, click the Install/Configure Reporting button and the default settings should populate the fields. Check the Reporting Enabled checkbox, and then click the Done button. The settings should populate the fields in the Reporting Settings window.

Smart Caching is an iHateSpam feature that holds user, policy configuration, and filtering information in a cache to increase the performance of the filtering engine. The cache updates automatically on regular intervals. The Smart Caching window displays the Current Status (default: Smart Caching Enabled) and provides a button that you can click to clear/reset the cache. Normally, this isn't necessary, but if you make changes to user policies, filters, or other configuration information, you should clear the cache to apply the settings immediately.

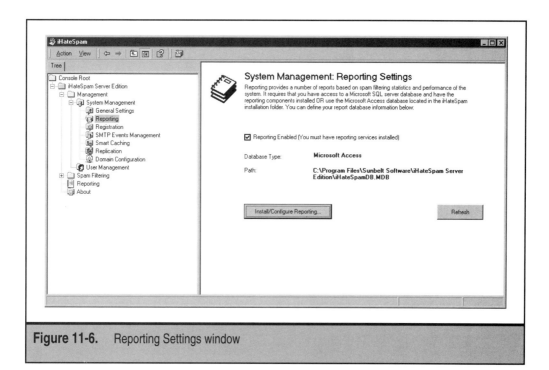

Figure 11-6. Reporting Settings window

TIP Are your rules not working? Receiving spam from a recently added blacklist domain? Go to the Smart Caching window, clear the cache, and test again.

The Replication management window, shown in Figure 11-7, allows you to add Exchange servers for centralized iHateSpam administration. To add an Exchange server, click the Add Server button. The Add Replication Server window appears (see Figure 11-8), where you can type the Server Name and the UNC Path to the iHateSpam installation folder in the appropriate fields. Click the OK button to save it. To remove a server, select the server in the Available Servers table of the Replication management window, and then click the Remove button.

NOTE You must add the proper SMTP sinks and domains (discussed in the section "Installing") for iHateSpam to work correctly on more than one server. This assumes that the access permissions between the various servers are properly configured as well.

Anti-Spam Tool Kit

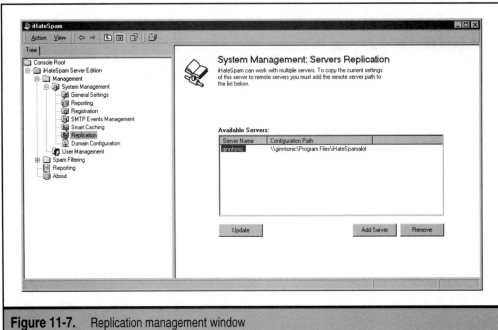

Figure 11-7. Replication management window

Figure 11-8. Add Replication Server window

The Domain Configuration window allows you to query user accounts (filter mail for them) on all the domains available to you. In most cases, you will not have to bother with this window. iHateSpam automatically populates this table with the appropriate domains (based on the SMTP sinks you configured during installation). However, if you manage many domains and you want iHateSpam to filter on only a few of them, pull up this window and uncheck those domains you don't wish to query for users. Again, this should not be necessary, since you probably didn't add the SMTP sink for those unwanted domains in the first place. Of course, if you happen to add a domain with an Exchange server to your wide-area network (WAN), you'll have to add the SMTP sink (discussed in the following paragraph). The domain itself will populate automatically in this case.

The SMTP Events Management window and the Registration window are rarely used. As discussed in the preceding paragraph, if you add another Exchange server, you will have to go to the SMTP Events management window and bind an SMTP sink to that server if you want to filter spam for its users. The Registration window allows you to register your software with iHateSpam. Simply enter your Registration Key and Number Of Seats in the appropriate fields and click the Register button. The registration function communicates with Sunbelt and your registration is processed. The information field at the bottom of the window details iHateSpam's registration status. The Number Of Seats is synonymous with the number of Exchange user mailboxes you pay for when you buy the software. Each "seat" equals an Exchange Mailbox. If you're running iHateSpam in Trial Mode and the trial period expires, mail passes through to the users normally—without filtering. Once you register, filtering kicks back in as previously configured.

Spam Filtering

Finally, we get to the business end of this spam fighter. iHateSpam blocks and filters spam globally and locally (to the user) with the following functions: whitelists/blacklists, blocked character sets, and weighted word filters. All of these functions are configurable for all users via the global filters or for individual users (or groups of users) with policies. These configuration options are available from the Spam Filtering management window. We discuss each option in the following sections.

General Settings The General Settings window allows you to enable/disable Bounce Message Filtering and enable/disable X-Header tags to nonspam. You may also update iHateSpam's global filtering definitions from this window.

iHateSpam Isn't Filtering!

Panic! The trial version expired, I registered it, and the software did not begin filtering! Relax! Go to the Smart Caching window under Systems Management, and click the Clear SmartCache Contents button. Everything should work as before.

The Bounce Message Filtering flag allows (or disallows) bounced messages through the filter without processing. Thus, if for some reason one of your users receives a bounce message from a mailer-daemon or postmaster (for example, if a message was sent to a nonexistent e-mail address), iHateMail would let this message through without attempting to filter it. The filter engine processes bounce messages normally if this feature is disabled.

> **NOTE** You'll probably want to filter bounce messages, since forging these messages is a well-known spammer tactic. The downside is that if a legitimate bounce gets filtered, it will make undelivered mail more difficult for you to troubleshoot.

The Spam Definitions tool allows you to update iHateSpam's global filtering definitions manually from Sunbelt Software's central server. Since these updates occur quite frequently, you'll want to configure automatic updates. (See the sidebar titled "Scheduling Automatic Updates with Windows Scheduled Tasks.") If you update the definitions, be sure to clear the Smart Cache for the settings to take effect immediately.

Scheduling Automatic Updates with Windows Scheduled Tasks

Although no tool is available for configuring automatic definition updates, the task is easy to do using the Windows Scheduled Tasks tool. To set up automatic updates, perform these steps:

1. Click the Start menu and navigate to Control Panel | Scheduled Tasks. Most Windows Server installations also launch the Scheduler automatically. The icon is located in the Windows system tray in the lower-right corner of the desktop.
2. Double-click the Add Scheduled Task icon. The Scheduled Task Wizard begins.
3. Click the Next button.
4. A list of available programs appears, but you'll probably have to browse to the file you want. The file you're looking for is GIANTSpamDefinitionsUpdater.exe located in the *$Programfilesroot*\Sunbelt Software\iHateSpam Server Edition\ folder. (*$Programfilesroot* is the directory where your program files are normally stored. Ours is C:\Program Files.)
5. Once located, double-click the filename. A Task window appears with the filename in the Program field and a series of radio buttons. Select Daily and click the Next button.
6. In the Time And Day window, select a start time (later the better, though it's not much of a resource hog), and select the Every radio button. Have the updater run every three days or so. Enter a desired start date (today is the default) and click the Next button.

> **Scheduling Automatic Updates with Windows Scheduled Tasks** *(continued)*
>
> 7. Enter the Administrator user (or a user with Administrator privileges), enter and confirm the user's password, and then click the Next button.
> 8. Click the Finish button and the GiantSpamDefinitionsUpdater icon should appear in the Scheduled Tasks window. You're done.

Global Filters As stated previously, global filters affect all e-mail users managed by iHateSpam. These filters include Whitelist Rules, Blacklist Rules, Custom Rules, Character Set Blocking, and Filter Plug-ins.

1. Click the Global Filters icon on the Spam Filtering management window to bring up an explanation of all the global filters.
2. First, we'll configure the Whitelist and Blacklist rules. Click the Whitelisted Senders folder in the left pane to open the Whitelist rules. You should see a Domain Address Type and sunbelt-software.com as a whitelisted E-mail Sender in the table in the right pane.
3. To add a whitelisted sender (either a full domain or an individual e-mail address), right-click anywhere on the table, and choose New | Whitelist Address. The Add An Allowed Sender window appears.
4. Select E-mail Address or Domain from the drop-down list and type the appropriate address into the field provided.
5. When you're done, click the OK button. The e-mail address or domain is added to the whitelist and allowed through the filter with almost no processing.

NOTE The Blacklisted Sender window works exactly the same way, except, of course, those domains and users are blocked.

CAUTION While the sample whitelist setting allowing any mail from sunbelt-software.com to pass your filtering process is fine for the sake of illustration here, you'll want to delete that whitelist entry, since any spammer can forge the From field of a spam message as coming from the whitelisted domain. It's never a good idea to stick with default settings such as these, since this information is freely available to anyone.

The Blocked Character Sets configuration automatically blocks any e-mail composed in whole or in part of the character sets designated. Thus, if you block all Arabic character sets, any e-mail iHateSpam processes composed in Arabic is automatically blocked. To add or remove character set blocks, right-click the Blocked Character Sets folder in the Global Settings tree, choose New | Blocked Character Sets. The Add A Blocked Character Set window appears, as shown here. Simply check the checkbox next to the character sets you wish to block (or uncheck those to unblock) and click the OK button. The blocked character sets should appear in the right pane.

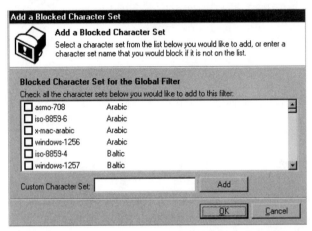

You may wish to create custom rules to apply to global definitions (as we did). To do this, simply click the Custom Filtering Rules folder in the Global Filters tree. The right pane of the management window displays current Custom Filtering Rules. By default, iHateSpam created its own custom filtering rule that fires on the word *ihatespam* and applies a –100 weight to that message (probably allowing it to pass through the filter). iHateSpam's rule "language" is simplistic compared to other tools, and we found it fairly constricting, although with several key rules applied in concert, we achieved a 92 percent accuracy rating during our limited testing.

First, let's look at iHateSpam's example rule. To view the rule, right-click it and choose Properties. The Properties window appears, as shown next. The Property drop-down menu allows you to select the area of the message you want iHateSpam to check, including the body, subject, sender, or receiver e-mail address, as well as Sender IP address and other header fields. The Operator drop-down menu has two options: Like and = (equals sign). The Like setting applies the word-matching function as a regular expression. The = operator matches the word exactly. The Value field holds the word you want iHateSpam to match on, and the Weight field applies the score entered (negative or positive) to any mail that matches the rule. Thus, this particular rule scans for *ihatespam* as a regular expression in the Subject field of incoming e-mails. If the value is found, iHateSpam applies a –100 weight to the mail. Depending on the other rules that fire on a particular message, the server either passes the message on or quarantines it.

Chapter 11: Anti-Spam Servers for Windows

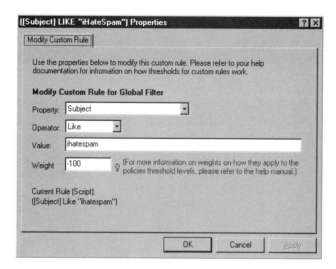

NOTE While this example rule is fine for illustration, you'll probably want to delete it from the Custom Filtering Rules window, since any spammer can figure out from the documentation, this book, or the iHateSpam program itself that a default rule applies a negative weight to the Value *ihatespam*, affording such a message a pretty good chance of getting through the filter.

To create a rule, right-click the Custom Filtering Rule folder and choose New | Custom Rule. The Properties window shown previously appears. Select the Properties you want iHateSpam to scan. To select multiple properties, hold down the CTRL key while you click. Select the Operator, input a value, and input a weight to apply to the mail. Click OK and the rule is added to the Filtering Rules table.

Policies Policies are used to apply Quarantine, Delete, and No Action Thresholds; set paths for quarantined mail; group whitelists or blacklists; and quarantine handling procedures. In addition, you can apply policy-specific Blocked Character Sets and Custom Filtering Rules. Policies are applied to individual users, although more than one user can utilize a given policy.

iHateSpam's Message Weighting System

The weighting system that iHateSpam uses is similar to those of other tools we've covered in this book. For each e-mail property that matches a given rule (global or policy), iHateSpam applies that value to the e-mail's "spam score." When all weights are applied, the numbers are added up and compared against the Quarantine and Delete Threshold (which is applied by Policies). If the mail is rated larger than one or both of these thresholds, iHateSpam handles it accordingly. If it's below the threshold, the mail goes on to the user's Inbox.

To access the Policies management window, click the Policies folder in the Spam Filtering tree. As with the Whitelist and Global Policy management windows, iHateSpam has a Default Policy, listed in the right pane of the management window. Right-click the Default Policy under the Policies tree and choose View | Customize. The right pane should populate with the Default Policy properties, as shown in Figure 11-9. The values in each field are modifiable and self-explanatory, though we'll cover Redirection and Policy Quarantine Actions next. No guidelines for threshold settings are available; these settings are a factor of what custom rules you're going to apply, what global custom rules are in effect, and the mix of spam to legitimate e-mail in your enterprise. The folder locations for Quarantine, Deleted, and Redirection are under the user's mailbox folder tree. The default policy places them in a root Spam folder and then a subfolder for each filter action.

NOTE Each folder name must end in a forward slash (/).

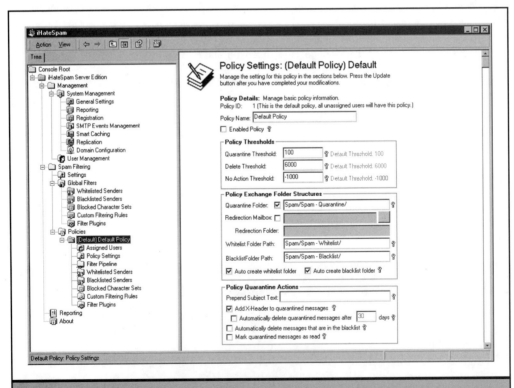

Figure 11-9. The Default Policy properties

Chapter 11: Anti-Spam Servers for Windows

The Redirection Mailbox function allows you to set up an e-mail box to direct all quarantined mail for a specific policy. This is useful if users do not want the bother of sifting through quarantined mail, or if the sheer volume of quarantined mail precludes downloading it to remote users. If you use this function, you'll definitely want to set the Automatically Delete Quarantined Messages After __ Days checkbox in the Policy Quarantine Actions section of the policy. This will prevent administrators from inadvertently forgetting to clear out this folder and causing a storage crisis.

The Policy Quarantine Actions section of the policy allows you to set custom Subject Text to prepend (add before) the actual subject of an incoming message, set an X-header (hidden header), and manage quarantined mail. This is useful if you are not using a Quarantine folder, but dumping all mail to the user's Inbox instead. If a message trips the quarantine threshold, your custom text is added to the Subject. The user can then set filters on the local mail client to sort these messages to local folders for later review. You can also add an X-header to the message that trips the quarantine threshold, also for the purposes of filtering at the client level. The X-header contains the weight applied to the message.

To add a new policy, right-click the Policies folder under the Spam Filtering tree in the management window and choose New | Create a Policy. The Create A New Policy Wizard window appears, as shown in Figure 11-10. Name the policy, set Policy Thresholds and Exchange Folder Structures as desired, and then click the OK button. The new Policy is added to the Policies tree.

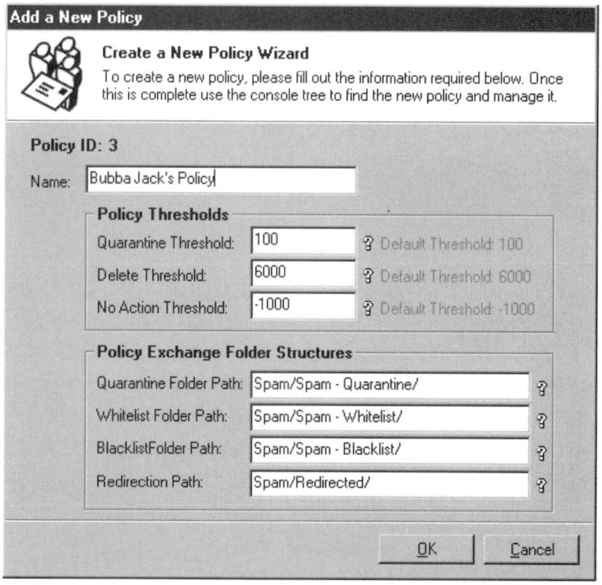

Figure 11-10. The Create A New Policy wizard

Anti-Spam Tool Kit

If you then click the + symbol next to your new policy folder in the management window, the tree expands with functions you'll recognize from previous sections. Here you can view, add to, or delete users from the policy (with the Assigned Users function), and view and change the Policy Settings, Whitelisted and Blacklisted Senders, Blocked Character Sets, and Custom Filtering Rules. All of these functions operate exactly as described earlier in this section. Remember that these settings are specific to this policy, only. After performing a major update, remember to reset the Smart Cache from the Smart Caching management window.

Reporting   The Reporting tool allows you to generate iHateSpam default reports on various criteria. To access the Reporting tool, click the Reporting icon in the Management tree. The Reporting management window appears in the right pane, as shown here. We found the reporting to be well done, although no function is available for generating custom reports. To generate a report, select a report type, Start Date, and End Date from the drop-down lists provided and click the Refresh button. The report appears in the box provided. Although you cannot output reports from the management console, iHateSpam includes a stand-alone report viewer that allows for printing.

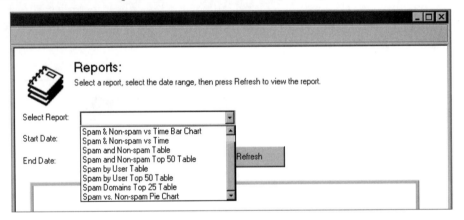

GFI MAILESSENTIALS

MailEssentials is a Bayesian filter-based anti-spam server solution available from GFI, Inc. In addition to spam filtering, MailEssentials adds server-based e-mail tools such as global disclaimer signatures, reporting, mail archiving, and auto-replies.

How It Works

MailEssentials controls spam at the gateway by applying Bayesian rulesets, blacklists and whitelists, and other functions to all incoming mail. Like most Bayesian filter-based tools, MailEssentials learns the difference between spam and legitimate e-mail over time within your specific enterprise. MailEssentials filters scan each message in its entirety, firing on keywords, checking for whitelisted/blacklisted domains and e-mail addresses, and verifying header information, such as domains, forged headers, mutation, and the like. Once the scan is done, it applies a weight to the message (its likely spam probability) and filters it according to thresholds that you set. In addition, MailEssentials checks third-party DNS blacklists, such as those discussed in Chapter 5 of this book. Messages tagged as spam can be deleted, forwarded to another address, or stored in customizable public or user folders. MailEssentials also provides features such as archiving all incoming and outgoing e-mail to a database, responding to spammers with a fake nondelivery report, and appending an organization-wide disclaimer to all outgoing e-mail. All of MailEssentials operations are logged and viewable from a reporting function.

Installing GFI MailEssentials

MailEssentials is available from the GFI web site at *http://www.gfi.com/mes/*. MailEssentials runs on a Windows 2000/2003 Server or Advanced Server with Microsoft Exchange 2000/2003. If you plan to use the MailEssentials reporter, Microsoft XML core services are also required (included with the install package). MailEssentials uses about 30MB of hard disk space and about 200MB of space for temporary files.

MailEssentials can be installed either on the Exchange server or on a separate machine. Though we cover only the first scenario here, the User Manual describes the installation and configuration procedures for running MailEssentials on a separate server.

Running MailEssentials on a separate server requires the following configuration:

- Windows 2000/2003 Professional or Advanced Server or Windows XP Professional
- Internet Information Server 5 SMTP service installed and running as an SMTP relay to your mail server
- Microsoft Exchange Server 2000, 2003, 4, 5, or 5.5; Lotus Notes 4.5 or higher; *or* an SMTP/POP3 mail server

Keep in mind that Windows 2000 and XP Professional accept only up to 10 incoming SMTP connections simultaneously; thus, if your organization uses e-mail more heavily than this, consider using Windows 2000 or 2003 Server or Advanced Server.

 NOTE For more information about running MailEssentials as a separate server, refer to the User's Manual on the GFI support web site.

Preinstall Checklist

You don't have much to do prior to installing MailEssentials. Ensure that you have Administrator access to the Exchange server and enough disk space, and download the installation archive. Double-click the archive to extract it to a temporary folder and perform the steps in the following section to install.

Installing

To install MailEssentials on your Exchange 2000/2003 server, perform the following steps:

1. Double-click the Setup.exe file in the temporary folder where you extracted the archive. The Welcome Screen appears.
2. Click the Next button and in the Check For Latest Build window, select the Do Not Check For A Newer Build radio button. Then click the Next button.
3. Agree to the license agreement and click the Next button.
4. Select a destination folder and click the Next button.
5. Enter your name (or just enter **Administrator**), your company name, and the software serial number, if applicable. (If you are installing the MailEssentials Evaluation Version, *Evaluation* appears in the Serial Number field. Click the Next button. The Administrator Email window appears.
6. Enter an administrator's e-mail address in the field provided. This does not necessarily have to be the Exchange or Windows Administrator account. This is the person (or group) to contact when MailEssentials issues a critical notification. Once you're done, click the Next button.
7. The Active Directory window provides configuration options depending on your current mail server setup. If your Exchange server has access to all the users in the Active Directory (that is, it's not a front-end server for another Exchange server behind the network DMZ), select the Yes radio button. If this Exchange server doesn't have access to all mail users in the Active Directory, select the No radio button. This runs MailEssentials in SMTP mode. In Active Directory mode, MailEssentials can apply user-based rules and configurations to users automatically, while in SMTP mode, you must manually enter the users before applying user-based rules.
8. In the Ready To Install window, verify the information you've entered and click the Next button.

NOTE The Ready To Install window lists your local domain. MailEssentials can filter only on your local domain; thus, if this information is incorrect, no mail will be filtered. It pulls this information from your IIS setup, so if the information is wrong, check here first.

9. The program installs. About halfway through the install process, MailEssentials asks whether you want to restart the SMTP service. Click the Yes button to restart it. You'll see the "Success" window, where you can click Finished.

Chapter 11: Anti-Spam Servers for Windows

Configuring the Essentials

MailEssentials uses a centralized management console for most of its functions, though the GFI Monitor, Reporting, Troubleshooter, and the Bayesian Analysis Wizard are separate programs. To access the management console, click the Start button, point to Programs | GFI MailEssentials | MailEssentials Configuration. The standard Windows management console appears with a tree of functions in the left pane and a table in the right pane. The Anti-Spam tree contains all of the functions covered in this section, including Blacklist/Whitelist, Bayesian Analysis, Header Checking, and Keyword Checking.

Blacklists/Whitelists

Click the Blacklists/Whitelists icon in the Anti-Spam tree to access these functions. Click the Properties icon in the right pane to pull up the Blacklist/Whitelist Properties window, as shown in Figure 11-11. The Properties window allows you to configure the Whitelists (and auto-whitelisting feature), Blacklists, and DNS Blacklists, as well as perform actions on e-mail that's blocked by the Blacklists.

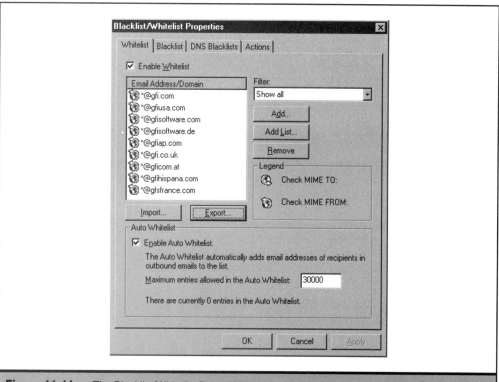

Figure 11-11. The Blacklist/Whitelist Properties window

Whitelists   The Whitelist configuration window is similar to other tools covered in this book. Here you may add an e-mail address, domain name, and mailing list MIME To fields, and you can import and export the whitelist. Additionally, you can enable (or disable) the auto-whitelisting feature that automatically adds recipient e-mail addresses for all outbound e-mail. Enabling this feature should be approached with caution, however, especially if users in your organization periodically respond to spam mail (even if only to remove themselves from the spammer's list) or if your organization is plagued by e-mail viruses originating from known e-mail addresses.

To add a whitelist entry, click the Add button, type in the e-mail address or domain name, and then click the OK button. To add a domain, be sure to put *@ before the domain name (thus, to add the domain astk.tld, you would enter ***@astk.tld**). To add multiple "extended" domains, such as support.astk.tld, finance.astk.tld, and so on, you would simply enter ***@*.astk.tld**. Note that GFI has included GFI-related domain names on the whitelist. These should be removed, unless you have a specific reason for adding them to your organization's whitelist. The Add List button allows you to add the newsletter/notice/mailing list e-mail addresses and domains found, not in the From field, but in the MIME To field of the message headers. Entry in the Add List window is the same as previously explained.

Blacklists   The Blacklists tab of the Properties window allows you to add domains and e-mail addresses you want to block automatically. Entering the information is similar to entering information in the Whitelist tab, although you can choose for MailEssentials to check the MIME To or MIME From field of the e-mail headers for the appropriate address or domain. You may also import from or export to an XML file containing e-mail addresses and domains.

DNS Blacklists   The DNS Blacklists tab of the Properties window allows you to configure MailEssentials to check up to two DNS Blacklist services. Simply check the appropriate checkboxes and select the services you wish to use from the drop-downs provided. Note that if you select two DNS Blacklists, they must select different services from each drop-down list. More information about DNS Blacklists can be found in Chapter 5 of this book.

Actions   The Actions tab of the Properties window allows you to configure what MailEssentials does with e-mail that triggers the local blacklist and the DNS Blacklist features. You may select one of the following actions:

- **Delete**   Deletes the mail automatically.
- **Forward To User's Spam Folder**   Puts the e-mail in the user's spam folder that you specify.
- **Forward To An Email Address**   Allows you to forward the blocked mail to any e-mail address.
- **Move To A Specified Folder**   Moves the mail to a folder on the server.

You can also tag the blocked e-mail with a definable word or phrase (prepended to the subject of the message) for handling after it reaches its destination. Logging of blacklist hits is configured from this window, as well as nondelivery reports generated to the spammers that find themselves on the blacklist.

Bayesian Analysis

To access the Bayesian Analysis Properties window (Figure 11-12), click the Bayesian Analysis icon in the Anti-Spam tree, and then click the Properties icon in the right pane of the management console. This window has only two tabs: General and Actions.

The General tab allows you to enable/disable Bayesian Analysis by clicking the respective checkbox. The Learning Updates Options section allows you to enable/disable Automatic Learning based on outgoing e-mails. This feature builds a stronger Bayesian filter, since MailEssentials learns keywords and phrases used in your organization's e-mail communications, likely good e-mail addresses and domains, and other information. You can also update your spam filter database from GFI's central servers by clicking the Download button. GFI updates these filters every few weeks.

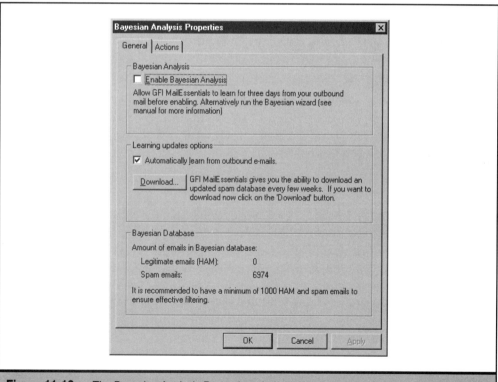

Figure 11-12. The Bayesian Analysis Properties window

The bottom section of this window gives you information on the Bayesian database. This information details the number of legitimate and spam e-mails the filter has processed and learned from. As stated in this window, MailEssentials needs about 1000 each of legitimate and spam mails to ensure effective filtering.

MailEssentials is essentially "dumb" out-of-the-box, so you have one of two options to start using the program immediately. Either use the outbound learning configuration option or download "spam knowledge" from GFI's web site. While either method works, the second is faster, since it may take a couple of days for enough outgoing mail to teach MailEssentials. Of course, learning what spam is to your organization is possible only by examining the e-mail received on your mail server.

The Actions tab is much like the Actions tab in the Whitelist/Blacklist Properties window. Here you can specify precisely what you want done with messages believed to be spam: delete, forward to a user's folder, forward to an e-mail address, or move to a local folder. You can also tag the message, enable the log file, and enable nondelivery messages, as described previously.

Header Checking

From the Header Checking configuration window, you can specify certain header checks that can assist MailEssentials spam profiling operations including MIME header fields scanning, DNS lookups, character set blocking, and handling actions. To access the Header Checking Properties window shown in Figure 11-13, click the Header Checking icon in the Anti-Spam tree, and then click the Properties icon in the right-hand pane of the management console.

General Settings   The General tab of the Header Checking Properties window allows you to configure specific checks on MIME and SMTP fields in an incoming e-mail message's headers. Using the General and General Contd. tabs' checkboxes, you can configure MailEssentials to check the following information:

- **MIME From:**   This checks to see whether the sender has configured an e-mail address in the mail client.

- **Malformed MIME From:**   This check verifies that the MIME From field matches the specifications of RFC 822.

- **Maximum number of recipients**   Though currently this is rarely an indication of spam, you can set the maximum number of recipients on a given e-mail. This is useful if you have internal or external "annoyance" spammers that send joke lists or chain e-mails, or that tend to reply to all recipients on a bandwidth-chewing e-mail thread that just won't die.

- **SMTP To: and MIME To: comparison**   This setting compares the two settings in a given message and kicks out those that don't match. Of course, e-mail list servers often fit this profile, so if your organization subscribes to e-mail discussion lists, newsletters, and the like, be sure to add the e-mail address or domain name to the whitelist if you enable this feature.

Chapter 11: Anti-Spam Servers for Windows

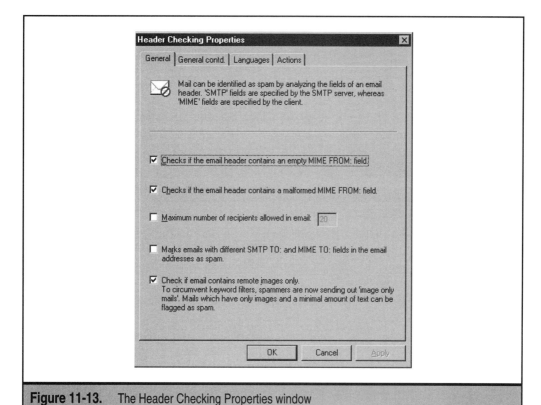

Figure 11-13. The Header Checking Properties window

- **Remote images** To combat a fairly new spammer tactic, this setting flags e-mails that contain only an image or an image with little text in the body of the e-mail. The drawback to this setting is that if your users often receive image files attached to e-mail messages, this could cause problems.
- **Domain validation** This setting is on the General Contd. tab. MailEssentials can look up the domain of an incoming message to verify that it's real and flag the message if it's not. The drawback is that the network overhead necessary to accomplish this may be excessive. Depending on e-mail volume, this could slow down both mail processing and spam filtering.
- **MIME from number limit**s A wily spammer tactic is to auto-generate a unique e-mail name (anything before the @ sign) to thwart blacklists. These generated names often contain numbers. Enable this feature and enter the threshold of numbers an e-mail name can contain before it's flagged.
- **Subject checking** This feature checks to see whether the Subject field of the message contains your name or e-mail name. Often spammers generate

"personalized" subjects from the recipient's e-mail address. Many e-mail administrators have received a message with the subject, "PostMaster, you're not going to believe this!" You can also add e-mail addresses to "Except" this rule, in cases where you often receive e-mails from legitimate sources that fit this profile.

Languages and Actions The Languages tab of the Header Checking Properties window allows you to specify lists of character sets (other languages) to block or not block automatically. To enable, click the Block Mails That Use These Languages checkbox and select either Block The List Below or Block All Except The List Below, and then select the character sets accordingly.

The Actions tab performs the same functions as the Actions tabs in the previous configuration windows: It blocks e-mails that fit the criteria set in this Properties window and either deletes, forwards to a user folder, forwards to an e-mail address, or moves the message to a local folder. You can also enable the Tag e-mail function, enable logging of events that meet this Properties' window configurations, and generate a fake non-delivery e-mail to the spammer.

Keyword Checking

In addition to the other header and list checks we've covered, MailEssentials also uses a complicated, yet easy-to-configure Keyword Checking function to identify spam. You can scan keywords or combinations of keywords in the message body or subject. To access the Keyword Checking Properties window shown in Figure 11-14, click the Keyword Checking icon in the Anti-Spam tree, and then click the Properties icon in the right pane of the management console.

The General tab contains the Scan Email Body table of keywords. It offers a sizable list of keyword and keyword combinations by default, but to add a keyword, click the Add Keyword button. In the text box, type the word or phrase you want MailEssentials to scan for, and then click OK.

MIME Fields in the Message Header

In a message header, MIME fields are generated by an e-mail sender's mail client, while SMTP fields are specified by the SMTP server through which the message passes. An example of a MIME field is the From field, designating the e-mail address of the sender, as configured by the sender's e-mail client. The Received field is an example of an SMTP generated e-mail header field. Note that MIME fields are not reliable sources of spam indication by themselves. For example, a misconfigured e-mail client (such as one without a name in the Name field), mail to multiple e-mail accounts (such as a legitimate mailing list), and the like could cause one of these rules to fire. Use them with care.

Chapter 11: Anti-Spam Servers for Windows 275

Figure 11-14. The Keyword Checking Properties window

You may also add a *condition*, which is a series of keywords linked by the operands *OR*, *AND*, *AND NOT*, and *OR NOT*. To access the Conditions window shown here, click the Add Condition button in the General tab. Type a keyword into the field provided, and then click the Add button. The keyword appears in the table with the operator *IF* beside it. Continue building the condition with the appropriate operators.

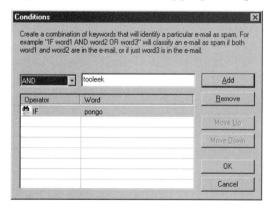

The Subject tab allows you to add subject keywords and conditions and operates exactly the same as the body keyword/condition function. The Actions tab operates the same as the Actions tabs on the other Properties windows in this section, allowing you to block e-mail that meets the conditions on the Keyword Checking Properties configuration and either delete the message, forward it to the user's spam folder, forward the message to an e-mail address, or move it to a local folder. You can also tag the message with a word or phrase, enable logging of keyword events, and generate a fake nondelivery message back to the spammer.

Other E-Mail Functions

MailEssentials contains several other e-mail management utilities, including Mail Archiving and Mail Monitoring, as well as Auto-Reply and Global Disclaimer generation. Although these functions are outside the scope of this chapter, be aware that GFI has packed this anti-spam tool with a lot of functionality. For more information about these functions, refer to the MailEssentials User Guide and other documentation on the GFI web site.

TREND MICRO SPAM PREVENTION SERVICE

Spam Prevention Service (SPS) is a feature-rich spam-fighting tool from Trend Micro. Although its spam-filtering process is similar to that of other tools covered in this chapter, its deployment strategy is different. SPS fights spam as a pass-through SMTP server, meaning that instead of applying rules to e-mail already received by the mail server, SPS filters mail before it ever touches the mail server.

How It Works

Deployed between the mail server and the Internet, SPS assigns a numeric value to incoming e-mail based on an equation formed by rules that apply a spam score or weight to the incoming message. The spam score is then compared to a global threshold and the mail is either forwarded on to the mail server, tagged as spam and forwarded on, held on the SPS server, or deleted entirely. SPS runs on its own machine and monitors port 25 (the SMTP port). In addition to its complex filter set, SPS also filters mail using the standard whitelist/blacklist features and limited header scanning.

Installing SPS

SPS is available via CD or as an installation archive from the Trend Micro web site at *http://www.trendmicro.com*. Though Trend Micro also distributes SPS for Linux and Solaris, we cover the Windows 2000 Server version in this chapter. SPS should be installed on its own machine with at least the following specifications:

- 1GHz Intel Pentium 4 processor
- 512MB RAM

- 100MB of hard disk space for software only (logging and reporting require more space, though how much space depends on the volume of e-mail you receive and your configuration choices)

While several different deployment options exist, especially in conjunction with other Trend Micro products, we cover only the most basic SPS setup in this chapter: one SPS server and one e-mail server.

Preinstall Checklist

Before you can install SPS, make sure that a port is available for SPS to listen on and that the port is reachable through the firewall. The default port is 25 (SMTP port). You'll also want to have Administrator access to the computer where SPS is to be installed, as well as the ability to change the mail exchanger (MX) records on the mail server. The MX records should be changed to point to the SPS server for mail exchange.

Once you have all this under control, you're ready to install Spam Prevention Services.

Installing

Log in to the Windows 2000 server as a user with Administrator rights and perform the following steps to install SPS:

1. Disable any services running on port 25, even if you plan to run SPS on a different port. By default, SPS installs listening to port 25, and if another service is running on that port the installation process fails.

2. Double-click the install archive and follow the prompts to install SPS. No complex configuration options are required during the install process. You will agree to a license agreement, set a destination folder, and that's it.

Initial Configuration

Once the install process completes, open the SPS configuration window, shown in Figure 11-15 by navigating to Start | Programs | Trend Micro | TrendSPS.

The following configuration tabs hold all the SPS goodness: Configuration, Spam Filters, Exception Filters, ActiveUpdate, Report, and Log. The two big icons in the upper-left corner of the Configuration window start and stop the SPS service. The big message that appears at the top of the window always tells you the state of the service.

Configuration The Configuration tab allows you to configure receiving e-mail servers, trusted domains, the whitelist and blacklist, the IPLOCK feature, as well as Advanced configuration options.

The Receiving Email Servers setting controls where SPS routes the incoming mail when it's through filtering it. Click the Edit button and enter either an IP address or the fully qualified domain name of your mail server.

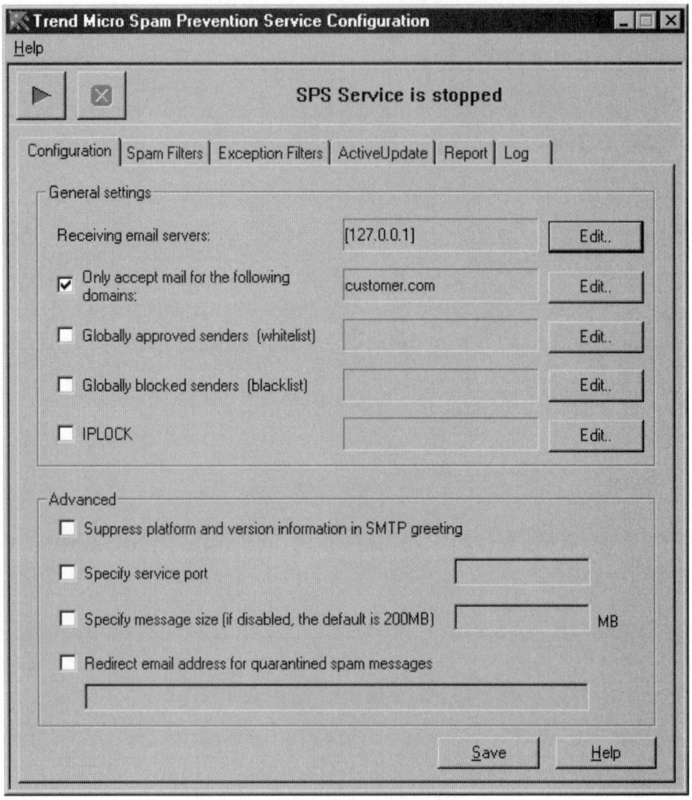

Anti-Spam Tool Kit

Figure 11-15. The SPS Configuration window

To enter an IP address, perform the following steps:

1. Click the Edit button.
2. In the field provided on the Receiving Email Servers window, enter the IP address enclosed in brackets (for example, [10.10.10.1]).
3. Click the Add button and the IP appears in the list provided.

To enter a domain name, perform the following steps:

1. Click the Edit button.

2. In the field provided on the Receiving Email Servers window, enter the full qualified domain name (with no brackets—for example, *mail.myserver.tld*).

3. Click the Add button and the domain name appears in the list provided.

If mail is being routed to multiple servers, multiple entries must be separated by commas. If you wish to deliver mail to a port other than 25, append the port number to the IP address or domain name, separated by a colon (:), as shown in the following examples:

- IP Address: [10.10.10.1]:2525
- Domain Name: mail.myserver.tld:2525

The Blacklist and Whitelist features allow you to add domains, IP addresses, and classless interdomain routing (CIDR) ranges of IP addresses in the formats shown next:

- Domain name: @spamhead.com
- IP address: [10.10.10.1]
- CIDR range: [10.10.10.0/12]

To include more than one entry, separate each with a comma. You can add up to 1500 blacklist and 1500 whitelist entries.

The IPLOCK feature prevents sender address spoofing (a common spammer tactic of low-grade identity theft). To enable IPLOCK, enter a domain name with an IP address or range. SPS then checks to see whether the IP address of the sender matches the range of IP addresses for the sender's domain. This setting is most useful if the spammer is attempting to spoof your domain name or one commonly used by legitimate senders to your mail server.

Other advanced features on this tab include these:

- **Specify Service Port**   Configures SPS to listen for incoming mail on an alternative port (other than 25, the default).
- **Redirect Email Address For Quarantine Spam Messages**   Lets you enter an e-mail address or addresses to which you will send quarantined messages.
- **Check Message Size**   Directs SPS to check the size of incoming e-mails and tag those that exceed the size threshold as spam.

Spam Filters   The Spam Filters tab, shown in Figure 11-16, allows you to configure (you guessed it) the SPS spam filters' sensitivity. Four category filters and one general spam level are available. These sliders control the actual thresholds to which SPS compares the weighted e-mail messages. To set the sensitivity level, simply slide the sliders on each filter left for less sensitive or right for more sensitive.

- **General Spam Level**   This threshold is the base or bulk filter for all e-mail that passes through SPS.
- **Sexual Conten**t   All word triggers associated with sexual content increase the message's Sexual Content value. This threshold controls whether a message is filtered or not.
- **"Make Money Fast"**   Another of the Big Four spam messages. This filter has the potential to keep you poor but also spam free.

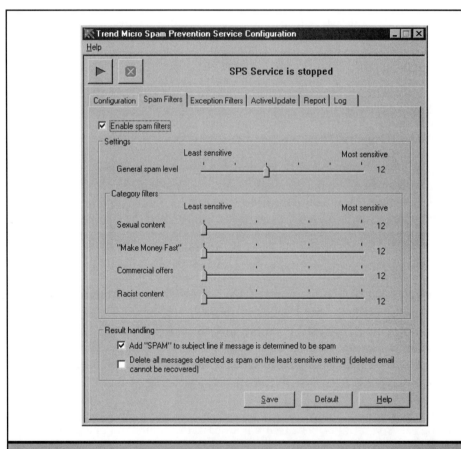

Figure 11-16.   The Spam Filters tab

- **Commercial Offers**   A catchall filter for advertisements of any kind other than the mentioned three. If you're a socialist, set this really high. To support capitalism, set this very low.
- **Racist Content**   Though not exactly a common spam criteria, racially charged spam could land an organization in deep legal trouble.

The Spam Filters configuration window also allows you to add the word *SPAM* to the subject line of messages determined to be spam and to delete all messages detected as spam, by simply checking the appropriate boxes.

> **NOTE**   The SPS documentation contains a lengthy description of filter sensitivity and a great testing methodology for balancing sensitivity to performance. Refer to the SPS User's Guide on the Trend Micro web site for more information.

Exception Filters   Exception filters allow you to configure filters to identify specific text strings (case-sensitive or insensitive) and immediately do something with that incoming message—be it delete, quarantine in a specific category, respond to the sender with an Error 50, or pass the message through. The most obvious use for this feature is as a "verification" method for legitimate e-mail. If your organization receives a lot of messages with the same text string (such as a disclaimer, message signature, and the like), configuring that string and setting the filter to pass-through diminishes the probability that the message will be misidentified as spam. Likewise, if you see spam messages that use the same string of text over and over and for some reason SPS is not catching these mails, simply set up an exception filter to find that string and automatically delete or quarantine the offending messages. It is important to note that using literal string matching with the body of a message can create numerous false negative scenarios.

To set up an exception filter, click the Exception Filters tab and click the New button. A text field appears for the name of the filter. Enter a name and click the OK button. The Exception Filter Editor window appears, as shown in Figure 11-17. Select an area of the message to scan for the string pattern (all the headers, various header areas, and areas of the body), enter the string to search for, and select either the Case Sensitive Match or Case Insensitive Match radio button. Then select an action for SPS to perform when it finds this string in a message. Once done, click the OK button and the exception filter is added to the list.

Updates, Logs, and Reports   SPS uses three main utilities to track, update, and report on its spam-fighting activities. To set up SPS for automatic updates, simply click the ActiveUpdate tab, enable the scheduled update process, and set a time and frequency to check for updates. If you're on a network with a proxy server, you can configure that from this window, as well.

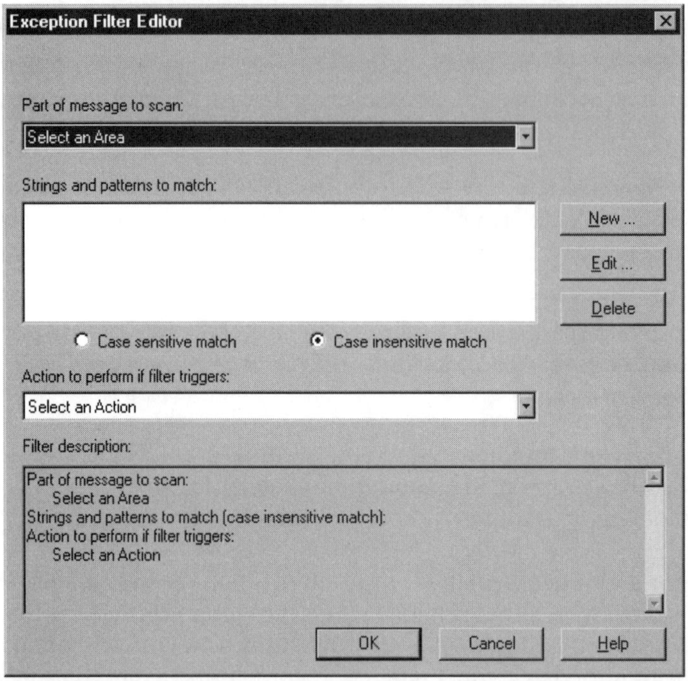

Figure 11-17. The Exception Filter Editor window

Finally, the Report tab allows you to construct various reports of SPS's activities over time and output that report either to text or HTML format. The Log tab provides a configuration interface to set up rotating log files of SPS's activities. You can either manually rotate logs by clicking the Rotate Now button or set up a schedule for SPS to rotate its log files automatically.

CHAPTER 12

ANTI-SPAM TOOLS FOR MACS

We've discussed client and server tools for Windows-based platforms, of which there are many. However, client tools for the Macintosh operating systems are relatively few. Gratefully, most UNIX-based implementations also compile on the OS X platform. For those wanting Mac-centric anti-spam clients, especially those still available for OS 9, we present four solutions.

POSTARMOR

PostArmor is a Java-based simple mail filter that runs as a Post Office Protocol (POP), Authenticated POP (APOP), or Internet Message Access Protocol (IMAP) proxy. The version we cover in this chapter is essentially the same across Windows, Linux/UNIX, and Mac OS 9 and X, although the installers are different for each platform. PostArmor is not open-source, but it is distributed for free if used as a single-machine client application. If used in the server mode, the application must be registered and a nominal fee paid, depending on the implementation.

How It Works

PostArmor acts as an e-mail proxy application, meaning that it connects to the server, scans the e-mail messages that are passed through the application, and blocks detected spam from within PostArmor. Your e-mail client checks mail through PostArmor and receives the messages cleared by that application.

PostArmor utilizes several common methods to detect spam messages, including DNSL Blacklist checking through SpamCop's open-relay database and OSIRUSOFT, word filtering, and sender/receiver validation. Hits on all of these methods combine to generate a spam score. You set the threshold, and PostArmor filters the mail.

PostArmor does all of its detection work in the header of the e-mail, starting with the sender's address and network. If either of these is on the Open Relay Database (ORDB) blacklist, the mail is automatically blocked. Then the program looks at the To field. If your e-mail address does not appear in this field, the message is automatically blocked (unless otherwise allowed by an address book entry). Next, PostArmor scans the subject of the message, matching and scoring words against its filter base. Finally, if the running spam score is high enough, PostArmor checks the sender's e-mail address for validity, which has the potential to be a time- and network-intensive process. If, during the above steps, the spam score reaches the threshold you've set, the message remains on the server for a set number of days (or it is deleted immediately if the spam score is high enough).

Installing

PostArmor is platform independent, although a separate distribution is available for the Windows, Linux, and each of the Macintosh platforms (essentially just a different installer for each). The Mac versions require the Macintosh Runtime for Java (MRJ) and

Swing (a Java GUI library) 1.1.1 or later to operate, both of which can be obtained from the Apple Developer web site at *http://developer.apple.com*. You can download PostArmor from the web site at *http://www.postarmor.com*. We cover the OS 9 version in this chapter.

Preinstall Checklist

Before installing PostArmor, ensure that both MRJ and Swing are properly installed on your system. To configure Swing, first ensure that the Swing libraries are present in the System Folder:Extensions:MRJ Libraries:MRJ Classes folder. If they are not there, locate your Swing installation—by default in the folder Applications (Mac OS 9):Swing X, where X is the version of Swing installed. Then select all the library files (those with the .jar extension), and make aliases by pressing COMMAND-M. Drag these alias files to the System Folder:Extensions:MRJ Libraries:MRJ Classes folder and remove the word *alias* from the filename of each. You can also drag the actual library files to the MRJ Classes folder, but the Swing uninstaller process fails if you ever have to uninstall the program.

After properly setting up Swing, you'll want to configure you e-mail client and record the pertinent information to set up PostArmor to check your mail. First, go to your e-mail client and record the following information: POP server and e-mail username (typically the name before the @ symbol in your e-mail address). Then, change the POP Server (also called Incoming Mail Server) field to localhost. (Note that if localhost does not properly resolve to your machine, type in the loopback IP address: 127.0.0.1.) For versions other than the Mac OS 9 distribution, you also must change the port number to 8110 (PostArmor's listening port). Since several e-mail clients for OS 9 do not allow the user to change the POP port number, this version of PostArmor listens on port 110.

Now you're ready to install.

Installing and Configuring PostArmor

To install PostArmor, double-click the compressed file (for OS 9 this file is called PostArmorMac_12.sit). The file then decompresses into a folder on your desktop called PostArmor_1.2.

To launch PostArmor, open the folder and double-click the PostArmor icon. Upon first launch, the program opens at its main interface, which is shown here.

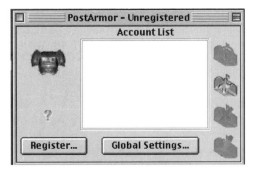

Anti-Spam Tool Kit

To add your e-mail information, follow these steps:

1. Click the blue mailbox icon with the green + sign on it. The Account Name window appears.

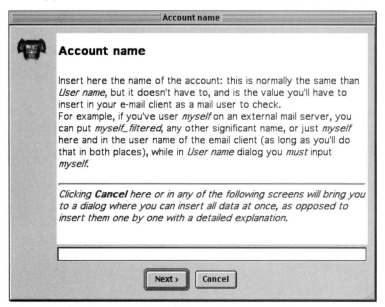

2. Type the desired name for this configuration and click the Next button. The User Name window appears.

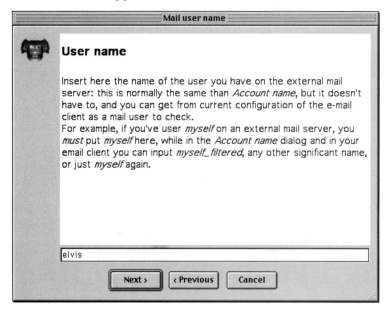

3. Type the username for your e-mail account (the name before the @ sign in your e-mail address) and click the Next button. The Mail Server Window appears.

4. Type the POP (incoming) mail server into the field provided and click the Next button. The Mail Server Type window appears.

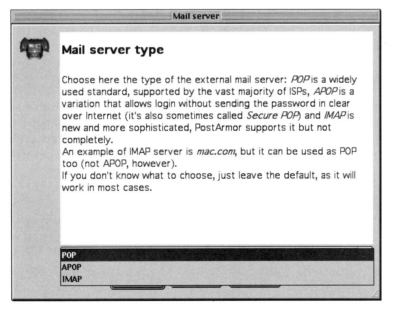

5. Select the mail server type from the drop-down list provided (the default is POP) and click the Next button. The E-mail Address window appears.

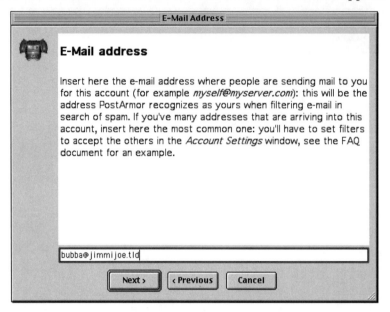

6. Type your e-mail address in the field provided and click the Next button. The SpamCop report address window appears.
7. If you use SpamCop, type that information in the field provided and click the Finish button. The PostArmor main interface opens, and your e-mail account appears in the Account List.

Use Your Armor!

PostArmor provides minimally accurate filtering on a fresh install (barely a 65 percent accuracy rate by our testing methods of 500 spams and 500 legitimate e-mails). As such, you should become familiar with the methods for increasing this accuracy. PostArmor provides two configuration screens that are accessed by clicking the Global Settings button on the main interface. From here, you can configure options and filters.

Thresholds, Accepted, and Blocked

The Options tab on the Settings dialog box, shown in Figure 12-1, provides configuration options for e-mail filtering score thresholds, reporting options, and automatically accepted and blocked senders.

The Settings area of the Options tab allows you to modify the "least score," the number of days to keep blocked spam, a setting for automatic deletion, and sender verification

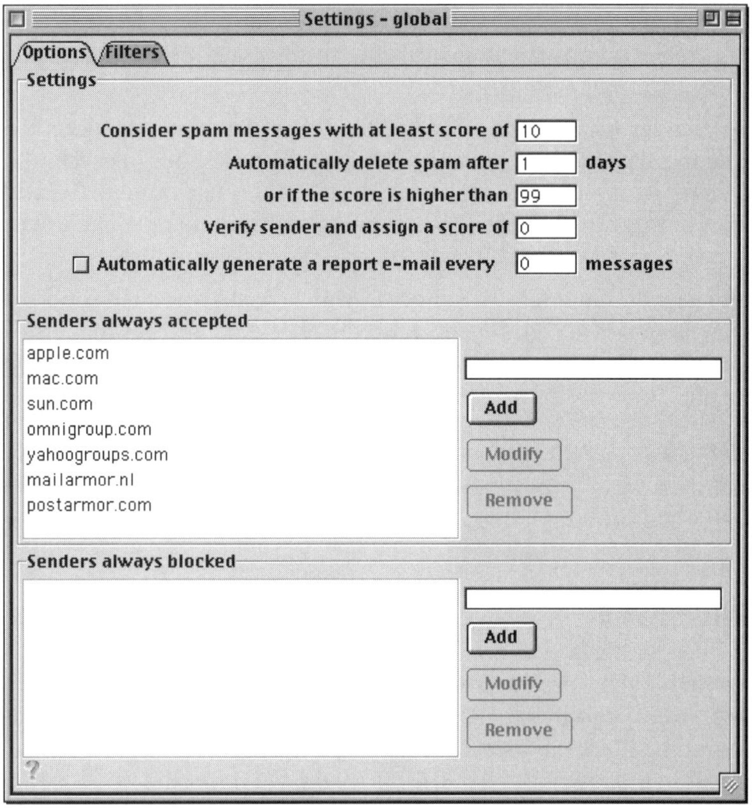

Chapter 12: Anti-Spam Tools for Macs

Figure 12-1. The Options tab

scoring. You may also have PostArmor send an e-mail report listing all mails it has blocked. Each function is described here:

- **Consider Spam Messages** This sets the lowest score a message can have and still be considered spam. Thus, if a message comes through with a score of 0–9, the message gets through without further checking. All other scores get fully checked and could be tagged as spam.

- **Automatically Delete Spam** PostArmor blocks messages it has tagged as spam for the number of days in this field. After that, the messages are deleted. If you set this to 0, PostArmor immediately deletes all messages it considers to be spam (this is not recommended).

- **Or If The Score Is Higher Than**   If PostArmor scores a message higher than the number in this field, the message is automatically deleted. The default setting is 99, and any message arriving from a blacklisted address or network receives a score of 100.

- **Verify Sender And Assign A Score Of**   If PostArmor cannot definitely determine that the message is spam, either by score or other methods, it checks the sender's mail server to validate the address. If PostArmor must validate the address, the number in this field is added to or subtracted from the message's overall score (depending on the results of the validation).

- **Automatically Generate A Report E-Mail**   PostArmor can send a report of all messages blocked. By checking the checkbox and setting a threshold (default is 1), PostArmor sends the report to your Inbox, listing the headers of the blocked messages.

The Senders Always Accepted and Senders Always Blocked areas function like any black/whitelist processes. You can add, modify, or remove an e-mail address or domain name by typing the desired text into the text box and clicking the appropriate button for each list.

Rulesets and Filters

PostArmor's ruleset interface on the Filters tab is the most extensible of any of the client tools we cover in this chapter. It's shown in Figure 12-2. The default rulesets are adequate, but as we said earlier, you'll want to evaluate your mail and add rulesets, as necessary. The top pane of the Filters tab lists all rulesets in place. When you click a ruleset, the actual rules appear in the lower pane of the tab. Next, we cover the options for adding and modifying rulesets.

Each ruleset contains the following parameters:

- **Name**   This option is user-configurable and does not affect the operation of the ruleset. The ruleset name that is entered appears in the PostArmor report when a message is blocked.

- **Relation**   The three parameters for this setting, *Or*, *And*, and *Sum*, control the combined score of all the rules under the ruleset. *Or* applies the Weight score to the message if any of the rules are true. *And* applies the Weight score only if all the rules are true. *Sum* adds the Weight of all the rules that apply to the message to the final Weight. Clicking the field opens a drop-down menu for easy selection.

- **Weight**   The score entered here is applied to the message as directed by the Relation setting.

- **Enabled**   Checking this box activates the ruleset for all messages.

To add a ruleset, click the New button, and a blank ruleset appears at the bottom of the list. To add rules to a ruleset, click the ruleset and then click the New button in the bottom pane of the tab. A blank rule appears in the list for modification.

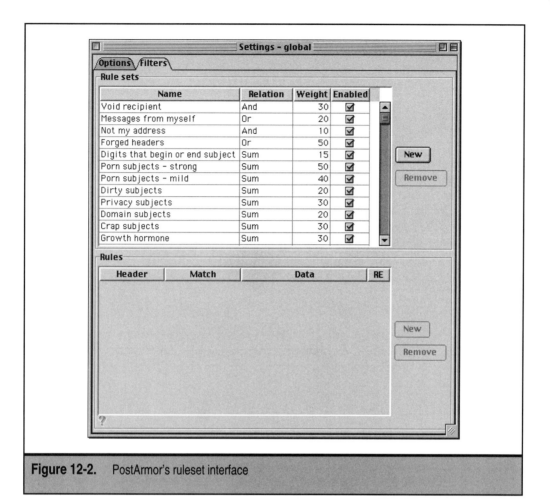

Figure 12-2. PostArmor's ruleset interface

Each rule has four fields that control its operation: Header, Match, Data, and Regular Expression (RE), as detailed next:

- **Header** This sets the part of the message header to which you want PostArmor to apply the rule, including the fields From, To, Cc, Bcc, Subject, Reply-To, Date, and Content-Type. The Any setting checks all of the above.
- **Match** PostArmor applies the match between the header and the given Data (see the next entry). The matches are Contains, Doesn't Contain, Is My Address, and Isn't My Address. No data is needed for the two address matches, as PostArmor pulls that from its configuration files. Contains fires the rule if the Data is contained in the Header field it's comparing. Doesn't Contain is the opposite.

- **Data** This is the string that PostArmor compares to the Header it's evaluating. This can be a simple string, where case is ignored, or a regular expression.
- **RE** By clicking this checkbox, PostArmor applies the Data as a regular expression.

POPMONITOR

POPmonitor is a simple e-mail management program that incorporates limited filtering, black/whitelisting and other anti-spam tool functions. As advertised, POPmonitor allows you to connect to your mailbox before mail downloads to your mail client and manually delete unwanted e-mails, run word filters against message headers and body, and apply black/whitelists to your mailbox. Of all the clients covered in this book, POPmonitor is the simplest in functionality and operation. We cover the Mac OS X version of POPmonitor, although a version for Mac OS 8/9 is also available. POPmonitor is distributed as shareware, limiting some functionality until the software is registered for a nominal fee.

How It Works

POPmonitor connects to your mailbox and downloads the headers of all the messages found there. From the main interface, you may then manually select individual messages to read, save, trust, block, bounce, or delete. Additionally, you can configure and apply simple word and black/whitelist filters to flag, block, or delete matching e-mails automatically.

Installing

POPmonitor is distributed for Mac OS X and OS 8/9 as a compressed file located at *http://www.vechtwijk.nl*. We cover installation and configuration of the OS X version in this chapter.

Installing and Configuring POPmonitor

After downloading the archive, double-click the file popmonitor_212x.hqx. The archive decompresses into a folder on your desktop. To launch POPmonitor, double-click the POPmonitor icon in this folder.

The initial configuration sequence begins when you launch the program for the first time. To configure POPmonitor, follow these steps:

1. At the bottom of the Welcome window, click the right arrow button to continue. The Account Information window appears.
2. Type in a descriptive name in the Account Name field, and then enter the username for your e-mail server (usually the half of your e-mail address before the @ sign) and your password.
3. Check the APOP box if your mail server uses the APOP protocol and check the Save Password box if you want POPmonitor to check e-mail automatically.

4. Type your POP mail server domain name in the POP Server field and the SMTP mail server domain name in the SMTP Server field (if you want POPmonitor to be able to send "bounce" messages). Click the right arrow button to continue. The Schedule And Filtering window appears, as shown here.

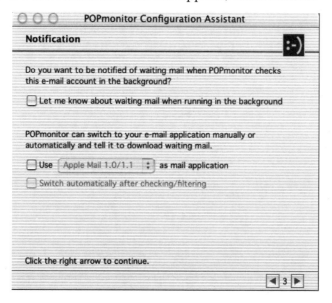

5. Read and check those options you want to enable, such as automatic mail checking and automatic deletion of tagged mail. Click the right arrow button to continue. The Notification window appears, as shown next.

6. Read and check those preferences you want to enable, such as notification of waiting mail and automatic mail client configuration. Click the right arrow button to proceed. The main POPmonitor program interface appears, as shown in Figure 12-3.

Figure 12-3. The main POPmonitor interface

Operating POPmonitor

With the exception of its message filters and black/whitelists, POPmonitor requires little maintenance. Unfortunately, the message filters and black/whitelists are the application's only defense against spam. While customizable, the message filters still match only whole words or regular expressions, applying minimal logic, and no message filters are included with the base installation. Blocked and Trusted senders (POPmonitor's verbiage for black/whitelists) function similar to blacklists and whitelists in any other anti-spam client. The most used tool with POPmonitor is the Delete button in your e-mail program, much as it was in the days before anti-spam tools.

Filters Galore

Filters can be used to tag, delete, or trust an incoming e-mail. POPmonitor scans incoming messages and applies its filters to each one. Thus, if you create a filter that deletes all e-mail with the word *Money* in the Subject line, POPmonitor scans each incoming message and attempts to match the word *Money* to each subject. Those that match get deleted, and all others pass through to its main interface. You can also use these filters in a kind of "password" mode, whereby you tell your friends to add a certain word or phrase in the subject or body of the message. Any mails that match that Trust filter pass on through.

To bring up the Filters window shown in the illustration, choose Edit | Filters. Filter names and descriptions appear in the center pane, with functional buttons on the right.

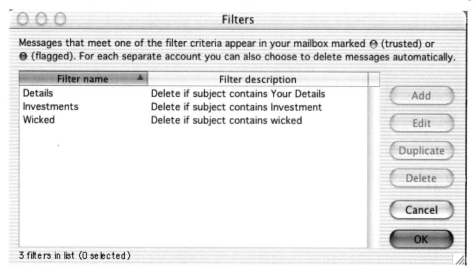

To add a filter, follow these steps:

1. Click the Add button. The Create Filter window appears, as shown in Figure 12-4.
2. Type a name into the Filter Name field and select an action (Flag, Delete, Flag/Delete, or Trust).

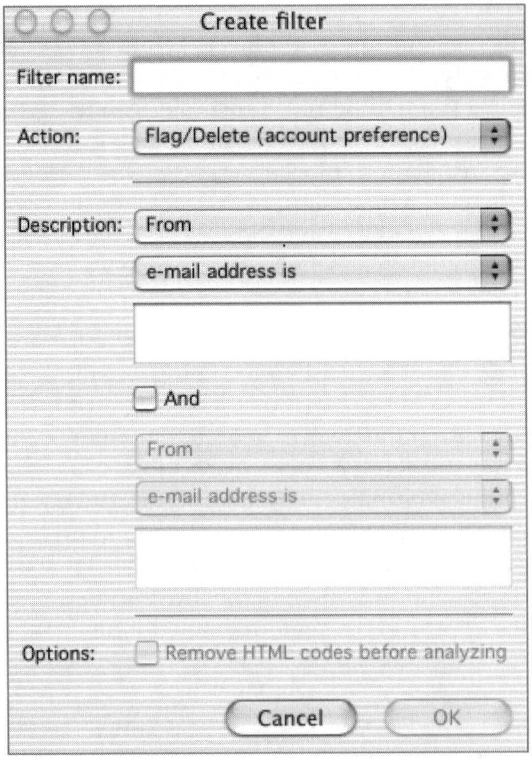

Figure 12-4. Create Filter window

3. In the Description block, select an area of the message to which the filter will apply (From, To, Any Recipient, Subject, Size, Header, Body, or Attachment).
4. Select a condition from the second drop-down window. For example, for a filter that matches a specific e-mail address, select E-mail Address Is.
5. In the field provided, type the string for the filter to match on, such as an e-mail address, a word or phrase in the subject or body of the message, or the like.
6. To add nominal logic to the filter, you can check the And box and add a second filter that must also apply to the message being filtered. You may also check the Remove HTML Codes Before Analyzing checkbox to have POPmonitor strip out all HTML code before scanning the message.
7. When the filter is complete, click the OK button. The filter name and description appear in the Filters window list.

You can also edit, duplicate, and delete filters by clicking the appropriate button in the button bar at the right of the Filters window.

Trusting and Blocking

POPmonitor utilizes standard blacklists and whitelists, as well. From these lists, you can block or allow specific e-mail addresses or entire domains. Essentially, you can perform the same action with filters, but the Approved/Blocked function is a bit easier to configure.

To access the Trusted Senders window shown in the illustration, choose Edit | Trusted Senders. As with filters, the Trusted Senders appear in a list format in the center pane, with functional buttons on the right. To add a Trusted Sender, click the Add button and type either the username and domain name in the appropriate fields or just the domain name. Then click the OK button. You can also add Trusted Senders by selecting a message in the main program interface and clicking the Trusted button. This function strips out the e-mail address and adds the sender to the list.

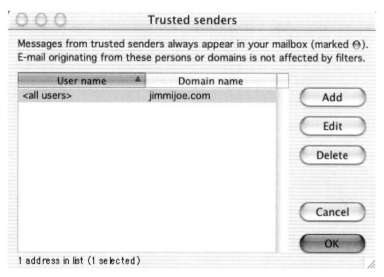

The Blocked Senders function works about the same as the Trusted Senders. Access the Blocked Senders window by choosing Edit | Blocked Senders. On the main interface, you can also add addresses (but not domains) to the Blocked Senders list by selecting the message and clicking the Block button.

SPAMFIRE

Spamfire is a filter-based POP/IMAP/Hotmail proxy for Mac OS 9 and OS X, distributed by Matterform Media. Using scored filters that search the headers and bodies of messages, Spamfire matches and flags incoming e-mail before it hits your Inbox. We cover the OS X version in this chapter.

How It Works

Spamfire downloads e-mail from your mail server and applies word-based filtering rules against the headers, body, and attachments. Each time a rule matches, Spamfire applies a weighted score, filtering those that score over its threshold. The program automatically updates filters from the Matterform server, and you can also add custom filters at any time. Additionally, you can add senders to a Friends or Spammers list to accept or block incoming mails automatically from e-mail addresses or domains. All of the incoming mail is managed from a central console before the messages download to your mail client.

Installing

Spamfire is distributed as an install package for Mac OS X and OS 9 from the Matterform web site at *http://www.matterform.com/*. Purchasing Spamfire entitles you to one year of free spam filter updates.

Installing and Configuring Spamfire

Once the install package downloads, double-click it and follow these steps:

1. At the software license agreement, click the Agree button. The Install window appears.
2. Drag the Spamfire icon to your Applications folder. The files copy to the selected folder.
3. Double-click the Spamfire icon. The About Spamfire window appears.
4. Click Enter Serial# and enter the product code. Click Continue.
5. At the Setup Assistant window, click the Next button. The E-mail Address window appears.
6. Type your full e-mail address and password, and then click the Next button. Spamfire tests the connection and password and the SMTP window appears.
7. Type in your SMTP (outgoing mail server) domain name or IP Address and a username and password, if your ISP requires one for sending mail. Then click the Next button. An e-mail window appears.
8. Type in any additional e-mail addresses that use the same account (such as e-mail forwards, group accounts, and the like), and then click the Next button. An e-mail client window appears.
9. Select your e-mail client from the drop-down box and click the Next button. A Friends list window appears.
10. If you have an address book or contacts list configured for your mail client, click the Import button to import the addresses to your Friends list. When complete, click the Next button. A threshold window appears.

11. Set Spamfire to the desired threshold setting by clicking the radio button next to the desired entry (Merciless, Vigilant, or Cautious). When complete, click the Next button.
12. Spamfire connects to Matterform.com to download and install the current mail filters, and then it displays an information window about the files installed. Click the Next button to continue.
13. Configure Spamfire to check mail automatically by selecting the Yes radio button. To check mail manually, click the No button. When complete, click the Next button. An information window appears.
14. Spamfire triggers your e-mail client to check messages after it has filtered the mailbox. You should turn off automatic checking on your mail client to prevent conflicts. Click the Next button.
15. The configuration completes. Click the Start button to start Spamfire. The main interface window is shown in Figure 12-5.
16. Click the Start Filtering button to begin the filtering process.

Firing Up the Spammers

For using word-based filters, Spamfire was very effective on a fresh install (90 percent accuracy rate at the Vigilant setting for us). To make the process more effective, you must

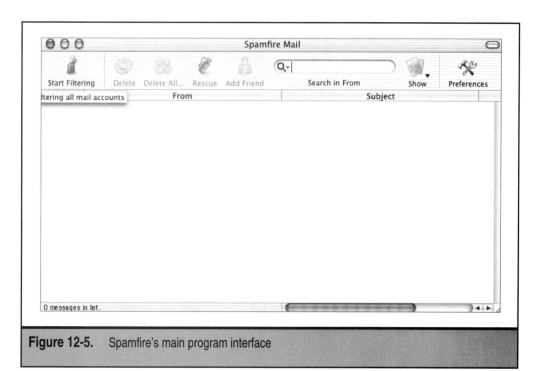

Figure 12-5. Spamfire's main program interface

add your own custom filters and Friends/Spammers lists. With so few messages inaccurately tagged as good, the process is simple. Additionally, you can report the spam messages to Matterform, allowing the company to improve the effectiveness of future filter releases. In the following sections, we talk about the program interface, filters, and Friends/Spammers lists.

Working with Fire

Spamfire's main interface allows you to access every major function of the program without searching through menus. When mail is processed, all messages appear in the main window. Each message can be categorized quickly by its status icon (Spam or Good), its overall spam score, as well as the sender, subject, receive date, and recipient e-mail address. Selecting an individual message allows you to delete the message, add the sender's address to your Friends list, or rescue it if it's been mistagged as spam.

The Show drop-down menu provides a filtered view of the messages processed, including all the spam messages, all the good messages, known spammer messages, and All Types. This is especially helpful if you receive large amounts of mixed mail to your account. The Preferences button gives you access to accounts configuration, Friends/Spammers lists, filters, and other configuration options.

Fueling Spamfire

Spamfire's Friends/Spammers list allows you to add e-mail addresses and domain names to allow or block automatically. You can access this list, shown in Figure 12-6, from the Preferences window after clicking the Preferences icon at the top of the main interface.

To add a friend or spammer to the list, click the Add Address button, and at the subsequent window select either From, To, or Reply-To from the drop-down list. Then type in the e-mail address or domain name and select either Friend, Spammer, or Mailing List from the drop-down list. When complete, click the OK button.

You can edit or delete entries by selecting the appropriate sender and clicking the Delete or Edit button. You can also import addresses from an e-mail client address book or contacts list by clicking the Import button. Finally, a checkbox at the bottom of the Senders Preferences window configures Spamfire to delete any mails received from known spammers (either from a filter or this list) automatically.

Flaming Filters

Filters add granularity to Spamfire's detection engine and can be created or modified either to block or allow certain types of mail. Matterform releases updated filters on a regular basis, and Spamfire can be configured to check for updates on a schedule or whenever the program is launched. Filters are stored in XML format, but they should be edited from the Spamfire interface to avoid errors. You can access the Filters interface, shown in Figure 12-7, from the Preferences window. Filters may be added, deleted, or edited from this window. Additionally, you can install Matterform's filter updates manually or automatically.

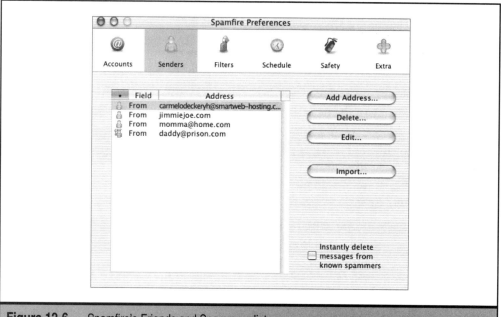

Figure 12-6. Spamfire's Friends and Spammers list

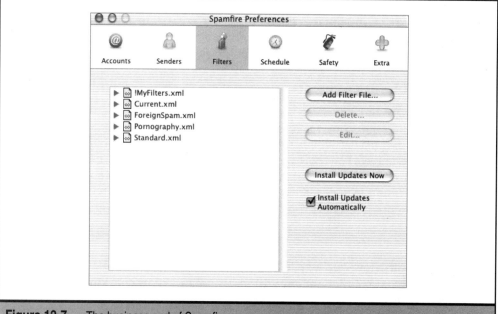

Figure 12-7. The business end of Spamfire

To add a filter, click the Add Filter File button and follow these steps:

1. Type in a filename for the filter in the File Name field. You may also add Author, Version, and About information in the appropriate fields. Click the OK button when you're ready to proceed. The filter file appears in the list.
2. Select the filter file and click the Add Filter Set button. A Name window appears.
3. Type the name of the Filter Set into the Name field and click OK. The Filter Set appears in the Filter file tree.
4. Select the Filter Set and click the Add Filter button. The New Filter window appears.
5. Type a descriptive name for the filter, and select Any or All from the drop-down list.
6. Type an appropriate score in the Score field (either a negative or positive number). This score is applied to messages that match this filter.
7. Select a location to match from the drop-down list (Body, Header Field, Attachment, or Size), and select a condition from the second drop-down list (Is/Not, Contains/Doesn't, Starts/Ends With, Is Greater Than, or Is Not My Address).
8. In the text field, enter the string on which the filter will match.
9. To add locations, conditions, and strings, click the More button. The dialog box shown in Figure 12-8 opens.
10. Click the red button in the upper-left corner to close the Filter window, and then you'll be prompted to save the filter.

MAILGOGOGO

Our last Mac entry is the POP proxy mail filter with little to configure or manage. Distributed by the Japanese company Maki Enterprise, MailGoGoGo is a mail filter that utilizes word matching and black/whitelists to manage incoming spam e-mail. MailGoGoGo runs best on OS 9 and earlier versions.

MailGoGoGo does not have the features and extensibility of other anti-spam tools for the Mac, but for a simple mail filter with black/whitelist functionality, it performs adequately. In our testing, MailGoGoGo caught about 75 percent of the spam we shot at it.

How It Works

MailGoGoGo comes complete with its own set of filters and black-box analysis methods. The program operates independently of your e-mail client, checking your mailbox and processing the messages either when you prompt it or on a scheduled basis.

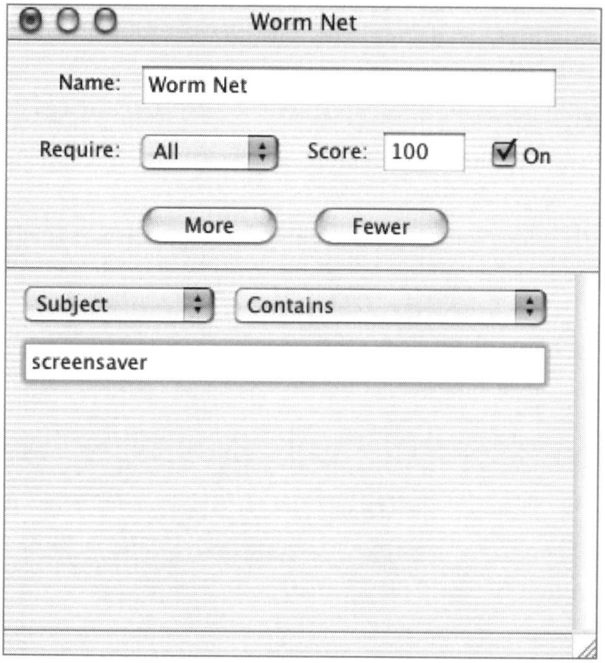

Chapter 12: Anti-Spam Tools for Macs

Figure 12-8. Setting up a filter

MailGoGoGo scans the body of the message and performs a context-sensitive analysis of the words and phrases found there, assigning a spam score to the message. If the score breaks MailGoGoGo's threshold, the message is deleted. Additionally, you can add e-mail addresses and domains to the white/blacklist for automatic approval or denial of messages that match these values. Additional functionality is provided with plug-ins, available at Maki's web site.

Installing

MailGoGoGo is distributed as a compressed archive containing an installer and documentation. Maki Enterprise also distributes a Windows 95/98 version of this program. MailGoGoGo can be purchased from the Maki Enterprise web site at *http://www.makienterprise.com*. The company also offers a free trial version of both Mac and Windows platforms.

Anti-Spam Tool Kit

Installing and Configuring MailGoGoGo

After downloading the archive, decompress the file and open the MailGoGoGo folder. To install and configure MailGoGoGo, follow these steps:

1. Double-click the installer icon. The Welcome window appears.
2. Click the Install button. The installer copies files to the appropriate directories and a confirmation message appears.
3. Click the OK button and at the MailGoGoGo splash screen, click the OK button again. The MailGoGoGo Basic Setting window appears, as shown here.

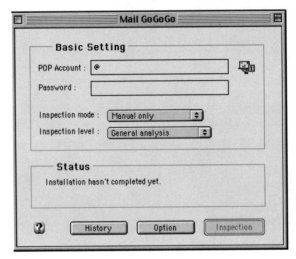

4. To configure MailGoGoGo, type your e-mail address in the POP Account field, your password in the Password field, and select your preferences for Inspection Mode and Inspection Level.
5. Click the Option button and set any preferences in the Options window.
6. Click the Select button in the Launch To section of the Options window, and browse to your mail client's executable file.
7. Click the Close button in the upper-right corner of the window and save your settings.
8. Press the Inspection button to start MailGoGoGo's filtering process.

Getting Spam to Go Go Go...

Once you start the Inspection process, MailGoGoGo scans your mailbox, applies its rules, and deletes anything it detects as spam. You can use a few options to control this process, including Analysis Level and white/blacklists. Additionally, MailGoGoGo provides a log file to check its spam-fighting progress.

To access the Analysis Setting window shown in Figure 12-9, choose Setting | Analysis. In the Sentence Analysis section of the window, you can select a Loose, Standard, or

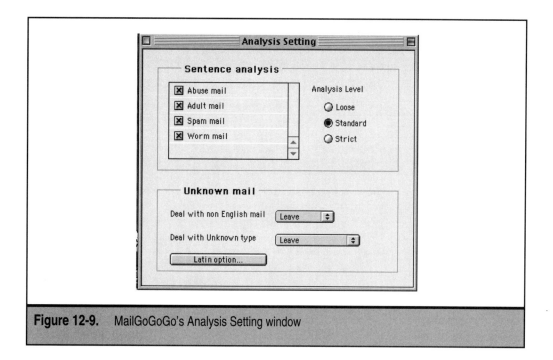

Figure 12-9. MailGoGoGo's Analysis Setting window

Strict analysis level and enable MailGoGoGo's four filtersets: Abuse Mail, Adult Mail, Spam Mail, and Worm Mail. These sets are black-box, meaning you cannot edit the rulesets directly or add additional rulesets. In the Unknown Mail section, you can configure MailGoGoGo to automatically delete non-English mail, as well as mail that is detected as spam but does not fall into MailGoGoGo's four rulesets. The Latin Option button allows you to add languages that use the same alphabet as English (such as French and Spanish), so that messages in these languages are not automatically filtered out.

Access the white/blacklist function by choosing Setting | Friend or Setting | Black List. Both lists work about the same. To add an entry to the Friend or Black List, click the Add button and type the domain name or full e-mail address into the text field provided in the list. Click the Close button in the upper-left corner of the window to close it and save your settings.

To view MailGoGoGo's log file History window, shown in Figure 12-10, click the History button on the Basic Setting window. The log displays in a separate window, giving you important information about the messages MailGoGoGo has deleted. The log can be exported to a text file by clicking the Export button.

Mail Gone, Gone, Gone

Overall, MailGo is fairly featureless, but it's quick and does catch a significant amount of spam. If you're stuck on a Macintosh OS earlier than 9, however, MailGo may be your

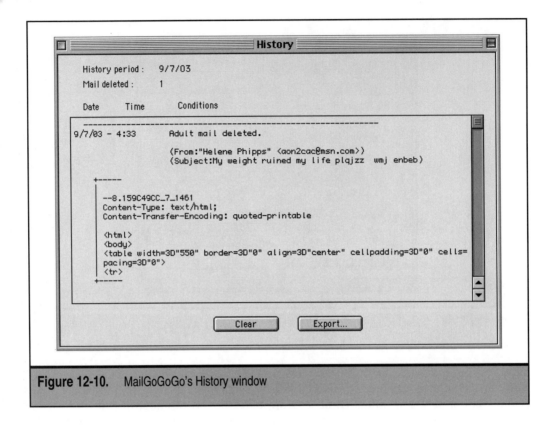

Figure 12-10. MailGoGoGo's History window

only option. The only problem is MailGo doesn't appear to be updated any longer, so do us and everyone else a favor: Upgrade your OS and get a real spam-fighting tool.

SUMMARY

The anti-spam client tools written specifically for the Mac maintain that Mac-centric look and feel and provide just as much functionality as Windows or Linux clients. While there are fewer spam tools specifically for the Macintosh, Mac OS X can compile and run any of the anti-spam tools for the Unix platform, such as POPMonitor and SpamBayes. If you're on an OS earlier than OS 9, your options are limited to software that won't be updated and lacks the features of modern spam-fighting tools.

CHAPTER 13

ANTI-SPAM TOOLS FOR LINUX

In Chapters 6, 7, and 8 we covered the granddaddy of anti-spam tools for Linux: SpamAssassin. Many, many more spam-fighting programs run on Linux, however. All of them tend to fill a specific niche that SpamAssassin may or may not already cover, and some interoperate with SpamAssassin. In this chapter, we look at six of these tools and give you specifics on how to bring them into your Linux mail environment. Two of the tools are distributed checksum matching networks, three are Bayesian classifiers, and one is a collection of Procmail recipes.

VIPUL'S RAZOR

Vipul's Razor (Razor for short) is both software and a collaborative, distributed anti-spam network. It is free, open source, and distributed under the Artistic License (like Perl).

When a user designates a piece of mail as spam, a "signature" is generated from it and is fed to the Razor network. From that point on, anyone who uses the Razor network has access to that signature. When a user receives a new e-mail message, it can be compared against the Razor database signatures to determine whether or not it's a message someone has already classified as spam. If so, a variety of actions can be performed: change the subject, add a header, move the message into a folder, or delete it outright. A certain amount of fuzziness is inherent in this matching, so that slight mutations in content are ignored (such as any random gibberish added at the end of a subject line).

The Razor network is the same network used by Cloudmark's Windows-based SpamNet software, which we covered in Chapter 10. It is made up of Razor Nominating

> ### Groking Procmail
>
> Many anti-spam tools for Linux require Procmail, the mail processor that runs after an e-mail has hit your mail server but before it's delivered to a user's mailbox. Fortunately, most Linux distributions come with Procmail as either a required or optional package. If yours doesn't include it, you can obtain Procmail at *http://www.procmail.org/*.
>
> The most important thing to understand about Procmail is that it uses what's called a *recipe* file, which is essentially a simplified script that Procmail understands and that instructs it on how to process the e-mail message. Too many options are available (and more than are needed to run most of these tools) to go into it in this chapter. If you're interested, the procmail.org web site has links to FAQs, How Tos, and sample recipe files. Procmail looks for an individual user's recipe file in his or her home directory as *.procmailrc*. The system-wide recipe file is called /etc/procmailrc.
>
> Unless otherwise noted, we suggest you run Procmail version 3.22 or later, as that version fixes a number of bugs.

The Importance of Being Human

Razor's creators discourage the network's users from using only other spam-detecting software (such as SpamAssassin or Bayesian classifiers) to decide automatically what is and is not spam, and then feed those messages into the Razor network. Only a human can truly differentiate between spam and ham, and the Razor network wants to know about only *true* spam to maintain a minimum of false positives. Razor does, however, allow you to report messages from "troll" e-mail accounts set up specifically to attract spam.

Servers (where new spam e-mails are processed) and Razor Catalogue Servers (which contain the distributed databases of signatures).

Razor was originally created by Vipul Ved Prakesh (cofounder of Cloudmark), and in the open-source spirit, many people are now contributing to the project, including Chad Norwood and Theo Van Dinter (one of SpamAssassin's developers).

More information on Razor and its licensing model can be found at *http://razor.sourceforge.net/*.

Examining the Razor

Razor is made up of several components, known as the *razor-agents*:

- **razor-admin**   Registers you with the Razor network.
- **razor-check**   The Razor filtering agent that checks mail against the network.
- **razor-report**   The Razor reporting agent that allows you to report an e-mail as spam to the Razor network.
- **razor-revoke**   A Razor reporting agent that lets you report an e-mail as not spam (that is, as ham) to the Razor network. This is useful if a message was incorrectly marked as spam by razor-check or if it was accidentally reported as spam.

The distribution is also made up of a couple of configuration files:

- **razor-agent.conf**   The configuration file for the various razor-agents, including razor-admin, razor-check, razor-report, and razor-revoke.
- **razor-whitelist**   A file that contains a list of e-mail addresses, domains, and body content that should be whitelisted. A mail containing entries in this file will not be reported or revoked, and it will automatically be classified as nonspam by razor-check.

In materials about Razor, references to Razor v1 and Razor v2 often appear. Razor v2 is a complete protocol redesign from Razor v1 and is much more effective. (For one thing, fewer false positives occur because it allows you to revoke messages.) Obviously, Razor v2 is the current version and the one we cover in this chapter.

Downloading and Installing Razor

Razor can be downloaded from *http://razor.sourceforge.net/*. It's distributed as two files:

- **razor-agents-2.*xx*.tar.gz**   This file contains the source code for the razor-agents. The *xx* is the minor version number (for instance, razor-agents-2.36.tar.gz).
- **razor-agents-sdk-2.*xx*.tar.gz**   This file contains a number of Perl modules that Razor requires.

Razor needs Perl 5 in order to run. It also requires the following Perl Modules:

- Net::Ping
- Net::DNS
- Time::HiRes
- Digest::SHA1
- Getopt::Long
- File::Copy
- Digest::Nilsimsa
- URI::Escape

These modules can be installed either from the razor-agents-sdk or directly from Comprehensive Perl Archive Network (CPAN). A few of them are modules also needed by SpamAssassin. Note that Razor itself is not available from CPAN.

The steps for installing Razor are as follows:

1. Download and un-tar razor-agents-sdk-2.*xx*.tar.gz:

   ```
   tar -xvf razor-agents-sdk-2.xx.tar.gz
   ```

2. Run the following commands to install the Perl modules:

   ```
   perl Makefile.PL
   make
   make test
   make install
   ```

   (Alternatively, you can install them using CPAN.)

3. Download and un-tar razor-agents-2.*xx*.tar.gz:

   ```
   tar -zxvf razor-agents-2.xx.tar.gz
   ```

4. Run the following commands to install the Razor agents:

```
perl Makefile.PL
make
make test
make install
```

If you're going to use SpamAssassin with Razor, install Razor first. If you've already installed SpamAssassin, go ahead and do it again. This will ensure that SpamAssassin detects Razor and is able to test it.

Using Razor

The first thing to do is run razor-client to create the necessary symbolic links for the razor-agents:

```
# razor-client
Creating symlink razor-client <== /usr/bin/razor-check
Creating symlink razor-client <== /usr/bin/razor-report
Creating symlink razor-client <== /usr/bin/razor-revoke
Creating symlink razor-client <== /usr/bin/razor-admin
```

Change from root to a user that you receive mail as and run the following command:

```
$ razor-admin -create
```

This builds a default configuration directory as ~/.razor (where the tilde is the path to your user's home directory). It also creates the following configuration files:

- razor-agent.conf
- servers.catalogue.lst
- servers.nomination.lst
- server.folly.cloudmark.com.conf
- servers.discovery.lst

If you plan on reporting spam to the Razor network, you need to register yourself with the network so that it can use statistics on your submissions to generate a "reputation" for you. You can do this in one of three ways:

- Generate your own username and password using the following command:
  ```
  razor-admin -register -user=<username> -pass=<password>
  ```
- Input an e-mail address but have it automatically generate a password using this command:
  ```
  razor-admin -register -user=<e-mail@addr.ess>
  ```

- Have the program automatically generate a random username and password: `razor-admin -register`

Any of these methods will suffice, so it's up to you which you use. The reputation you gain is based upon a Truth Evaluation System (TeS). The more real spam you report and the more nonspam you revoke, the better your rating. On the contrary, the more nonspam (such as legitimate mailing lists) you report, the lower your rating. Ratings are not currently published or available through a razor-agent (you can't even see your own).

Using razor-check

The next step is getting razor-check to run against your e-mail messages. The razor-check component can be run against one or more messages in UNIX mbox format, or against single messages in RFC 822 format. If an individual message tests positive for a presence in the Razor network, razor-check returns a 1; otherwise it returns a 0. If it's run against a mail file containing several messages, the message number (the serial number of the message in the mailbox, not the message ID) is returned.

You can either run razor-check offline against messages in a mailbox (for instance, against individual mailboxes in /var/spool/mail) or in real-time against incoming mail using Procmail. Another method (and the one we recommend) is to run it using SpamAssassin.

Running razor-check in Real-Time with Procmail

The most common way to run Razor is by invoking it with Procmail. The following recipe sends mail that tests positive for being in the Razor network into a folder called caughtspam.

```
:0 Wc
| razor-check
:0 Wa
$HOME/mail/caughtspam
```

You can also use the formail program that comes with the Procmail package to add a hidden X header for messages caught by Razor:

```
:0 Wc
| razor-check
:0 Waf
| formail -A "X-Razor-tag: SPAM"
```

You can then configure your e-mail client to look for this tag and move it into a folder. This is the best thing to do if you're using a site-wide recipe file and would rather the end users decide what to do with possible spam.

Running Razor Using SpamAssassin

Running Razor with SpamAssassin is relatively simple, especially if you installed Razor prior to installing SpamAssassin (the recommended way to do it). You should also make sure that `use_razor2` is set in your local.cf or user_prefs files. By default, Razor is used (set to 1).

```
use_razor2 ( 0 | 1 )
```

If you're using Razor and the message checksum is detected within the Razor network, the RAZOR2_CHECK test is flagged.

Razor Through a Firewall

Only outbound ports are needed to operate the razor-agents through a firewall. If you're using a stateful inspection firewall and allow all outbound traffic, you won't have to do anything. If your policy is to lock down all outbound traffic and allow only what's needed, you must open up TCP port 7 (echo, which Razor uses to find the server with the best response time) and TCP port 2703 (Razor2) for outbound traffic. Opening it up for all outbound traffic is the easiest thing to do, as servers might change. If your security policy is more restrictive, however, you need to allow only traffic destined to the IP addresses of the servers listed in the servers.catalogue.lst and servers.nomination.lst files.

DISTRIBUTED CHECKSUM CLEARINGHOUSE

The Distributed Checksum Clearinghouse (DCC), like Razor, is a distributed anti-spam network. It's also free and open source, distributed under its own licensing terms that simply say you cannot take credit for writing it. DCC is a project of Rhyolite Software and can be found at *http://www.rhyolite.com/anti-spam/dcc/*.

Mail designated by a user as spam will receive a checksum that is reported to the DCC network. The more checksums that are reported as spam, the higher the likelihood that that message is spam. A mail server or client will check against the DCC network using DCC tools and then compare the checksum of the message to that in the database. The DCC uses fuzzy checksums that "filter out" a certain amount of randomness and personalization in e-mail messages.

Unlike Razor, however, DCC is written in C and can be used in a variety of ways, from being called using Procmail or a .forward file, to being a Sendmail mail filter (milter), to running it using SpamAssassin.

Welcome to the Clearinghouse

DCC is made up of a server and several clients that are best geared toward different installations. The programs include these:

- **dccproc**   A DCC client that's used with Procmail, Mail/Message User Agents (MUAs), or Message Transfer Agents (MTAs) other than Sendmail. Using Procmail and dccproc is the fastest way to get DCC up and running, although it's also the slowest to use.

- **dccifd**   The client is actually a daemon. It provides a sort of local proxy that can be used as an interface to DCC for SpamAssassin and MTAs such as Postfix. It's faster than dccproc.

- **dccm** This is the Sendmail milter version of DCC. It's the fastest to use with Sendmail, although it's not as easy to set up as dccproc.
- **dccd** This is the DCC server daemon that makes you part of the DCC network checksum databases.
- **cdcc** This is a control program that modifies the control file for local DCC clients and also manages DCC servers remotely (with appropriate credentials).

You can either run your own DCC server or use someone else's with one of the clients. This is another way DCC is different from Razor: Not only can you participate in the network by reporting spam, but you can also become one of the distributed servers. The DCC team suggests that anyone who processes more than 100,000 messages per day benefits from running their own server, as it cuts down on the amount of network traffic and delays as a result of Internet latency.

If you set up your own server, you can configure it to require a password so that not just anyone can use it. Conversely, you can allow anonymous access to your server and let anyone use it. Currently about 18 public servers are listed on the DCC web site. Anyone who uses a DCC client but doesn't run their own server can use these, or they can find a private server to which someone is willing to give them access.

Downloading and Installing DCC

DCC is distributed in three source configurations:

- **dcc-dccd.tar.Z** The complete source package, including the server and all the clients and interface programs
- **dcc-dccproc.tar.Z** Includes dccproc and dccifd, which are used with mail clients
- **dcc-dccm.tar.Z** Includes the Sendmail milter interface (dccm) and the client programs (dccproc and dccifd)

Running a DCC server is beyond the scope of this section, so we focus on running the client programs. We also steer clear of running DCC as a milter, since that applies only to one MTA configuration (Sendmail) and is a complex process. For simply running the clients, any of the above packages will do, but we use dcc-dccproc.tar.gz here.

Download dcc-dccproc.tar.gz, gunzip it, and un-tar it in a source directory.

```
tar -zxvf dcc-dccproc.tar.gz
```

This will create a directory called ./dcc-dccproc-*x.xx* (where *x* represents the major and minor version numbers). Change into that directory and run the following:

```
./configure
make
make install
```

This builds and installs the DCC clients dccproc and dccifd. By default, they're installed in the /usr/local/bin directory.

Running DCC

To run the dccproc client, you must have Procmail installed. Then create a Procmail recipe that contains something like the following:

```
:0 f
| /usr/local/bin/dccproc -ERw -ccmn,5
:0 e
{
        EXITCODE=67
        :0
        $HOME/mail/spam
}
```

This script sends incoming mail through dccproc. It checks the most common DCC checksums (body, fuz1, and fuz2), and if the total value equals five or more, it will put the message in the user's spam folder.

DCC, in part or in whole, is extremely complex and has a multitude of configuration options. We've showed you only a quick and easy setup. Keep in mind that the suite is very flexible. Though documentation is sparse, check the FAQ on the DCC web site, and also join the DCC mailing list at *https://www.rhyolite.com/mailman/listinfo/dcc*.

BOGOFILTER

Bogofilter is a Bayesian classifier that uses advanced statistical methods and is written in C. It was originally created by Eric S. Raymond, noted programmer, author, and open-source software advocate. Now a number of other developers are assisting in the project. The *bogo* in Bogofilter stems from the word *bogus,* one of the meanings of which is "useless." In that sense, spam can be considered bogus e-mail, and it's Bogofilter's job to filter out this bogus e-mail based on a particular piece of spam's "bogosity" level. If all this sounds like jargon, you're right, because it is. You can visit Eric's Jargon File at *http://www.catb.org/~esr/jargon/* for more.

If you want to skip all that and go straight to Bogofilter, you can find it at *http://bogofilter.sourceforge.net/*.

Installing Bogofilter

Bogofilter is distributed as source code or as a package of binaries in RPM Package Manager (RPM) format. You have the option of downloading the most current version (bogofilter-current) or the most recent stable version (bogofilter-stable). The source is distributed as a gzipped tarball with the filename bogofilter-*x.xx.xx*.tar.gz, where the *x* represents the version numbers. As of this writing, the most current version is bogofilter-0.15.11.

The only requirement for Bogofilter (besides a C compiler if you're going to build it) is the Berkeley DB (usually just represented as *db*).

Download the source code and un-zip and un-tar it into a source directory:

```
tar -zxvf bogofilter-X.XX.XX.tar.gz
```

Then run the following:

```
sh ./configure
make
make install
```

This will build and install Bogofilter. The `configure` script will automatically detect the presence of any prerequisites. If it is having trouble finding something you know you have installed, you may be able to specify the location using one of the `configure` script's options. (To see the options, enter `sh ./configure --help`).

Running Bogofilter

After Bogofilter is installed, the first thing you need to do is train it to recognize both ham and spam. As with any Bayesian classifier, it may take 100 spam and ham messages each before the filter is trained well enough to catch a reasonable amount of spam and avoid false positives.

To train Bogofilter to recognize ham, point it to a mailbox that has no spam in it by running the following:

```
bogofilter -n < ham-mailbox
```

To train Bogofilter to recognize spam, point it to a mailbox that has nothing but spam by running the following:

```
bogofilter -s < spam-mailbox
```

Once Bogofilter is trained, you can set it up to filter your mail. To do this, you can add the following recipe to your .procmailrc file:

```
:0fw
| bogofilter -e -p
:0:
* ^X-Bogosity: Yes, tests=bogofilter
$HOME/mail/spam
```

The preceding recipe runs the mail through Bogofilter in a pass-through mode (the -p option), which adds the "X-Bogosity" header. The -e option tells Bogofilter that it's embedded in a Procmail recipe or some other mail filtering program. After the mail is run through, Procmail checks for the header "X-Bogosity: Yes, tests=bogofilter." If that header exists, it puts the mail in the spam folder. Otherwise, it delivers the mail normally.

You can retrain the database when it gets something wrong. Simply move any false positives from the spam folder back into your inbox and any false negatives from your inbox ham folder, and then rerun Bogofilter with the training options against those mail boxes.

SPAMBAYES

In Chapter 10 we looked at the Windows version of SpamBayes, which works as an Outlook plug-in. SpamBayes isn't just an Outlook plug-in, though; it's actually a whole suite of programs (including the plug-in) that make up the SpamBayes Project:

- **The Outlook plug-in**   Reviewed in Chapter 10
- **Pop3proxy**   A filter that analyzes mail as your POP client downloads it from the server
- **Imapfilter**   Works like Pop3proxy, but is used with the IMAP mail-reading protocol
- **Hammiefilter**   A filter that can be used with Procmail

Since we're writing a chapter on Linux anti-spam tools, we'll stick to using Procmail with SpamBayes.

All SpamBayes programs require that you have Python installed. Python is an open source, cross-platform, object-oriented scripting language and interpreter. Python packages come with many Linux distributions, and you can also obtain it at *http://www.python.org/*. SpamBayes requires Python 2.2 (the current version is 2.3.3) or later and can be found at *http://spambayes.sourceforge.net/*.

Installing SpamBayes

First, download the SpamBayes source from *http://spambayes.sourceforge.net/*. SpamBayes is distributed in a single gzipped tarball called spambayes-*x.y*.tar.gz, where *x* is the major and *y* is the minor version numbers. The current version as of this writing is 1.0a7.

Un-gzip and un-tar the package into a source directory:

```
tar -zxvf spambayes-x.y.tar.gz
```

It will create a directory called ./spambayes-x.y. Change into that directory.
Run the following command:

```
python ./setup.py install
```

This will install SpamBayes on your system (in /usr/bin by default). Relatively simple, right?

Using SpamBayes

After installing SpamBayes, you need to create the database that will store the Bayes tokens. You do this using the sb_filter.py script, specifying where you want to create the database by using the -d option and that it's a new database by using the -n option.

```
$ /usr/bin/sb_filter.py -d $HOME/.hammie.db -n
Created new database in /home/elvis/.hammie.db
```

Now you can optionally train SpamBayes based on the current contents of your mailbox. This is a good idea if you want SpamBayes to start filtering correctly from the get-go. It's important that you use the freshest messages possible, since they will most resemble your current definitions of spam and ham. You do this using the sb_mboxtrain.py script. After the -s option, put what you consider spam, and after the -g option, put what you consider ham.

```
$ /usr/bin/sb_mboxtrain.py -d $HOME/.hammie.db -s \
$HOME/mail/spam -g /var/spool/mail/elvis
Training ham (/var/spool/mail/elvis):
  Reading as Unix mbox
  Trained 20 out of 20 messages
Training spam (/home/elvis/mail/spam):
  Reading as Unix mbox
  Trained 7 out of 7 messages
```

Not many messages there, but it's a start.

Next we need to configure Procmail to run sb_filter.py against incoming messages. When sb_filter.py checks a message, it uses the Bayesian classifier to decide whether it's spam, ham, or unsure, and it adds an "X-Spambayes-Classfication" header to the message to that effect. Based on this, we'll create our Procmail script to look for those headers and sort messages into spam and unsure folders.

```
:0fw:hamlock
| /usr/bin/sb_filter.py -d $HOME/.hammie.db
:0
* ^X-Spambayes-Classification: spam
$HOME/mail/spam
:0
* ^X-Spambayes-Classification: unsure
$HOME/mail/unsure
```

NOTE Your folders might be different based on your configuration. Other examples are available within the SpamBayes documentation.

As for retraining the database when it gets something wrong, the easiest thing to do is simply move any false positives from the spam or unsure folder back into your inbox, and move any false negatives from your inbox or unsure folder to the spam folder. Then, rerun the sb_mboxtrain.py script we ran earlier with the same parameters. We can also have this script run nightly as a cron job.

QUICK SPAM FILTER

The Quick Spam Filter (QSF) is another Bayesian classifier. (Popular, aren't they?) It's designed to be simple to set up and use. QSF is written in C, and therefore it must be compiled on your system. If you're not interested in compiling, RPMs and even an experimental Windows binary are available. QSF is available from *http://www.ivarch.com/programs/qsf.shtml*.

One thing that sets QSF apart from some of the other Bayesian classifiers is its ability to use a MySQL backend database. This is useful if you're already running a MySQL server, as it will simplify database backups.

Downloading and Installing QSF

QSF's source code is distributed as a gzipped tarball called qsf-*x.x.x*.tar.gz, where the *x* is the major and minor version number. The current version as of this writing is qsf-0.9.9.tar.gz.

Installing QSF is easy. Simply un-zip and un-tar the tarball into a source directory:

```
tar -zxvf qsf-0.9.9.tar.gz
```

Then change into the newly created qsf-*x.x.x* directory and run the following:

```
sh ./configure
make
make install
```

The configure script will automatically detect prerequisites and whether you have MySQL installed on your system. If you're not running MySQL, have no worries: You can still use the GNU db format database, for which you'll need gdbm—if you don't have it for some reason, configure will tell you so.

Running QSF

After QSF is installed, you'll want to train it for the first time. As we did with Bogofilter and SpamBayes, move all your spam and nonspam into separate folders. Then run QSF in training mode with the following command:

```
qsf -T <spam-folder> <ham-folder>
```

So for our configuration we run this:

```
qsf -T ./mail/spam /var/spool/mail/elvis
Counting messages in folders... 35 3
```

```
round 1: checking spam...      reclassified [25.71%] 9/35
round 1: checking non-spam...  reclassified [66.67%] 2/3
round 2: checking spam...      reclassified [40.00%] 14/35
round 2: checking non-spam...  reclassified [33.33%] 1/3
etc....
round 29: checking spam...     reclassified [2.86%] 1/35
round 29: checking non-spam... reclassified [33.33%] 1/3
Several rounds with no improvement, ending training.
Optimising database... done
```

To run QSF against incoming mail, we'll once again use Procmail. The following Procmail recipe file can work for a site or an individual user:

```
:0 wf:$HOME/.qsflock
| qsf -ra

:0 H:
* X-Spam: YES
$HOME/mail/spam
```

With QSF, there is no unsure: A message is either spam or it isn't. If it is spam, QSF adds the header "X-Spam: YES," and that's what the Procmail recipe looks for after it's scanned. If it exists, it will move the spam into the spam folder.

You'll also notice that QSF is run with the options -ra. The -r tells QSF to add a header called "X-Spam-Rating" along with a score between 0 and 100. This is the message's "spamminess" based on Bayesian analysis. Anything 90 or higher is considered spam, anything lower than 90 isn't spam.

The -a option tells QSF to use an allow list (QSF's name for a whitelist). The whitelist isn't a text file, however. It's part of the database and therefore must be manipulated with the QSF program. A quick way to generate a whitelist is to add the -a option when you train your database the first time. This will put every From address in your nonspam folder into the allow list.

To retrain, you can either train the system as we did when we created the database for the first time or you can train on individual messages. To train on an individual message, save the message into a file. You can then train the system to see it as spam or nonspam:

```
cat message-file | qsf -m -a
```

The -m trains the system to see the message as spam. The addition of -a tells it to remove the user from the allow list (if it's in there). To train the system that a message is not spam, run the following:

```
cat message-file | qsf -M -a
```

If a message is mistagged, you can run one of the above lines for whichever classification the message should be reclassified as, but also add -w 2 as an option. This is the "weight" option, and setting the weight at 2 will double it, thus making it less likely the message (and similar ones) will be mistagged again.

THE SPAMBOUNCER

The SpamBouncer is a collection of Procmail recipes. While using Procmail exclusively is a rather "old-school" way of dealing with spam, some administrators still like the elegant simplicity of its regular expression matching. There's nothing hidden, no algorithms you have to have a major in mathematics to understand, and they're easy to modify—if you understand regular expressions, that is.

The SpamBouncer was created by Catherine A. Hampton and can be found at *http://www.spambouncer.org/*.

Installing and Configuring the SpamBouncer

First, make sure you have Procmail installed (see the "Groking Procmail" sidebar earlier in the chapter). The SpamBouncer also requires the nslookup or host programs to perform its DNSBL checks. One or both of these come with most Linux distributions.

The SpamBouncer is distributed as either a compressed tar file or a ZIP file. It's simply called sb.tar.Z or sb.zip. Once you get it, decompress and un-tar into a directory off of your home directory (creating a directory called something like *sb* should be fine):

```
mkdir sb
mv sb.tar.Z
cd sb
tar -Zxvf sb.tar.Z
```

What you end up with are a few dozen files with the *.rc* extension (the Procmail recipe files), plus a smattering of configuration files.

The SpamBouncer is unique among the products in this chapter in that it relies 100 percent on Procmail. To configure it, you must modify your .procmailrc file within your home directory.

 Many, many configuration options can be used for the SpamBouncer. We're going to cover only the most basic ones to get it up and running. You can also customize the procmail.rc file included with the SpamBouncer and use it as your .procmailrc file.

You need to set three variables within your .procmailrc file:

- **DEFAULT**   Specify your incoming e-mail box. On most UNIX systems, this will either be in /var/spool/mail or /var/mail, and the mailbox file has the same name as your username.
- **FORMAIL**   The formail utility is part of Procmail. Specify the location of formail here. It's usually stored in /usr/local/bin or /usr/bin.

- **SBDIR**   Specify the location of your SpamBouncer files. If you followed our earlier advice, they should be in your own directory under *sb*.

So, here's an example of what you might have in your .procmailrc file so far:

```
DEFAULT=/var/spool/mail/elvis
FORMAIL=/usr/bin/formail
SBDIR=$HOME/sb
```

Next, you need to create four hidden text files that the Spam Bouncer will use later. These are .legitlists, .localhostfile, .myemail, and .nobounce. The .legitlists file is a listing of your important mailing lists. The .localhostfile lists all the domains for which you accept mail. The .myemail file lists all the e-mail addresses you get mail for on the system. The .nobounce file is a list of e-mail addresses from which you accept mail. This is essentially a whitelist.

Next we set some specific variables that the SpamBouncer uses to deal with mail. Many can be used, but we're going to start with six to have a basic setup that minimizes false positives.

- **BLOCKFOLDER**   A mail folder where you want to put blocked mail.
- **SPAMFOLDER**   A mail folder where you want to put spam.
- **BLOCKREPLY and SPAMREPLY**   These variables are for the auto-reply levels for both spam and blocked messages. This is useful if you want to have the SpamBouncer automatically complain to the spammer's ISP. We don't want to do this for now, though, so both are set to SILENT.
- **PATTERNMATCHING**   This is another auto-reply setting, but it's for spam detected by pattern matching rather than known spammers. Set this to SILENT.
- **VIRUSFOLDER**   This is a folder where you want mails detected as having viruses saved. Note that the SpamBouncer is not a true virus scanner, in that it doesn't scan binary files for viral signatures. Instead it simply looks at mail messages for known virus text and filenames. The author of the SpamBouncer suggests just shunting viruses off to the purgatory of /dev/null, as the virus rules produce few false positives, and you don't want to take a chance of actually getting one.

> **NOTE**   The UNIX null device, represented in UNIX file systems as /dev/null, is a *data sink*, a black hole where data is sent when there's no desire to retrieve it later. It's a convenient place to send such things as logs or program output you don't care about or—in the case of e-mail—spam and viruses. It's also referred to as a *bit bucket*.

So, now our .procmailrc file should also have the following lines:

```
BLOCKFOLDER=$HOME/mail/blocked
SPAMFOLDER=$HOME/mail/spam
```

```
BLOCKREPLY=SILENT
SPAMREPLY=SILENT
PATTERNMATCHING=SILENT
VIRUSFOLDER=/dev/null
```

Finally, add the following line where you want to start filtering spam within your .procmailrc file:

```
INCLUDERC=$SBDIR/sb.rc
```

The next time you receive mail, it will run that message through the SpamBouncer's ruleset.

What You'll See

Like SpamAssassin, the SpamBouncer scores a message based on how many rules it trips. The SpamBouncer will add at least three headers to each e-mail that passes through it. The first header is the X-SpamBouncer header, which gives the version number of the SpamBouncer used. The second header is the X-SBSpamScore header, where the message's total score is shown. The third is the X-SBClass header, which labels the message according to the classification assigned to it by the SpamBouncer.

Here are the possibilities for the X-SBClass header:

- **X-SBClass: Admin**   E-mails with this tag are detected to have come from a mailer daemon (because they are bounces, for instance) and typically have the From address of root, admin, abuse, postmaster, and the like. You can also have these messages automatically delivered to a folder set in the ADMINFOLDER variable in your .procmailrc file.

Logging in Procmail

Because the SpamBouncer relies so heavily on Procmail, it may be difficult for you to tell whether it's doing anything at all. One way to keep an eye on it is to tell Procmail to log. To do this, add the following line to your .procmailrc file:

```
LOGFILE=$HOME/procmail.log
```

To get even more information out of the log, also turn on verbose logging:

```
VERBOSE=on
```

Verbose logging is going to generate a *lot* of information (a line for every rule within the SpamBouncer's recipe files), so it's best to leave it off unless you're debugging a problem.

- **X-SBClass: Blocked**   E-mails with this tag have received a spam score between 5 and 10. This means that the SpamBouncer thinks it might be spam, but it isn't definitely spam. You can set a specific blocked e-mail folder with the BLOCKFOLDER variable in .procmailrc.

- **X-SBClass: Bulk**   E-mails with this tag were not detected as spam but might be bulk e-mails from mailing lists. If you want to shunt these off into another folder (a good idea for prioritizing your e-mail) you can do so with the BULKFOLDER variable in .procmailrc.

- **X-SBClass: Ok**   This is the default tag for e-mails that aren't detected as admin, blocked, bulk, spam, or viruses. Messages with this tag are delivered normally to your e-mail folder.

- **X-SBClass: Spam**   E-mail with this tag has been classified as spam because it has a spam score of 10 or above. Spam can be sent into a specific folder with the SPAMFOLDER variable in your .procmailrc file.

- **X-SBClass: Virus**   E-mail with this tag has been classified as a virus. Infected e-mails can be sent to a specific folder with the VIRUSFOLDER variable in your .procmailrc file. The author of the SpamBouncer recommends just sending viruses to /dev/null because there are few false positives with these rules.

Instead of having Procmail shunt messages off into other folders, you can instead configure your e-mail client (such as Outlook, Mozilla, or Eudora) to look for these headers and do with them what you will.

A Pleasant Surprise

Honestly, we had our doubts about the SpamBouncer, but we were pleasantly surprised to find it extremely effective. It managed to tag 99 percent of incoming Unsolicited Commercial E-mails (UCEs) as either possible or definite spam with no false positives—and we were using it in its least restrictive configuration. It just goes to show you that while some of the sexy new anti-spam technologies have geek appeal, there's still something to be said about blacklists and pattern-matching rules that are updated on a regular basis by a dedicated programmer.

SUMMARY

If you're not interested in a full-blown SpamAssassin installation, the Linux anti-spam tools covered in this chapter are excellent alternatives. Vipul's Razor and DCC are distributed spam checksum databases that allow you to block spam others have already seen, and they can be used with SpamAssassin. Bogofilter, SpamBayes, and QSF are Bayesian classifiers that can be used by individual users on your Linux system. Finally, the SpamBouncer is a collection of Procmail rules that perform pattern matching and blacklist checking on incoming e-mail. Any of these Linux anti-spam tools are good for implementing specific anti-spam functionality on your Linux e-mail server or workstation.

PART IV

STOPPING SPAM IN THE LONG TERM

CHAPTER 14
KNOW YOUR ENEMY

Throughout this book, we have mentioned various spammer tactics, usually in relation to anti-spam rule creation. In this chapter, we discuss these tactics in depth and provide a "profile" of a typical spammer and his product: spam. Additionally, we discuss how to track the spammer back to his foul lair (though not usually a successful venture) and how to report when you've found a real-live "fathead" spammer.

PROFILE OF AN "E-MAIL DIRECT MARKETER"

Before we prompt a flood of hate mail and possible litigation, consider the following caveat: Not all direct marketers are scum-sucking, bottom-feeding spammers. Legitimate businesses do have real products to sell, and they responsibly market directly to people willing to receive direct solicitation of that real product. Although these businesses exist, they are drowning (or better yet, trapped) in the tidal wave of spammers posing as legitimate marketers. In this section we discuss the types of tools used by the spam gangs, how they cleverly construct e-mails to get past your filters, entice you to click, and then gather information on the backend. Finally, we discuss the back-alley information flow of the spam gangs. What happens when your e-mail address ends up on a list, and how do you save yourself from the coming spam flood?

Spam Tools

We realize this book is supposed to be about *anti*-spam tools, but to get the most out of your anti-spam tools, you must understand the tools that produce the spam in the first place. How do spammers manage to send all that e-mail and still remain relatively anonymous and unstoppable? As we discussed in earlier chapters, the architecture of the e-mail system is as much to blame as anything else. Within the confines of that architecture, spammers use classes of tools that have evolved as spam countermeasures have evolved. Here we discuss those tools and why they render certain countermeasures ineffective.

> **NOTE** Although this section covers tools for propagating spam, we didn't want to contribute to the problem by educating a new generation of spammers in specifics. Unfortunately, this means that this section is vague on details (such as specific products) but focuses on standard methodologies and base functionality for such tools.

The Spam Machine

First and foremost, the core spam program (sometimes a suite of programs) merges the two most important elements of a spammer's life: a list of victims and the message. Once combined, the application begins firing off spam to the intended targets. The less sophisticated of these tools utilize some lax system administrator's open mail relay to exchange the mail, since most ISPs enforce anti-spam policies for users on their networks. (Those that don't, risk ending up on blacklists.)

More advanced versions of the "ratware" (or software specifically designed to spew spam) actually have an SMTP mail exchanger built right into the suite, removing the need to piggyback off of someone else's MX. With a local MX, the spammer is free to open an ISP account for a few days (most ISPs have a free trial period), fire up the spam machine, and send off thousands of e-mails. Once done, the spammer closes out the account and moves on to the next ISP. This essentially makes centralized blacklists not only obsolete, but it also turns them into dangerous tools against unsuspecting ISPs. Once the spammer moves on, the ISP is stuck with either certain IP addresses or its entire domain is posted to a blacklist.

Additional core features for a good, albeit *bad*, spam machine include the following:

- **IP Spoofing**   Spammers that either want to stay with a certain Internet connection or otherwise want to cover their tracks obfuscate or falsify their IP address, making it difficult or impossible to trace a spam message back to a certain point. You can always find the mail exchanger (if the spammer uses a remote one), but beyond that, you're usually looking at a fake or temporary IP.

- **E-mail Address Management**   Spammers live and die by the validity of their e-mail lists. Some "direct e-mail marketing" applications verify e-mail addresses on the fly by using communication to the user's e-mail server (see Figure 14-1). Verified addresses can be organized by whatever criteria the spammer desires, and invalid addresses are deleted automatically.

- **Message Content Management**   These tools cover the gamut, and we discuss them in the section "Spam Content Management" in more detail. Management of the message content includes such practices as obfuscating certain anti-spam tool "trigger words" and inserting random lists of words to defeat Bayesian or other statistical filters.

- **Delivery/Read Confirmation**   E-mail clients, such as Eudora and Microsoft Outlook, include a feature called *read-receipt*. You've probably encountered it before. If an e-mail is sent with a read-receipt tag, the sender is notified when the receiver opens the e-mail. Spam tools have integrated this technology into their suites allowing for better address and message management. The spammer caveat to read-receipt is that no confirmation is needed by the recipient to send a read-receipt to the sender. It's an automatic, behind-the-scenes, invasion of your privacy.

- **Address Harvesting/Brute Force Spamming**   Though not all bulk mailers include these features, they are essential to the spammer's operation. Address harvesters are technically web spiders that gather e-mail addresses from web pages and newsgroups. A brute-force mailer sends e-mails to a specific domain with an incremental or dictionary change to the user field. Thus, the brute-force mailer might run through a list of common e-mail user names, such as john@domain.tld, paul@domain.tld, jane@domain.tld, looking for valid addresses within that domain. We discuss these topics in depth in Chapter 16.

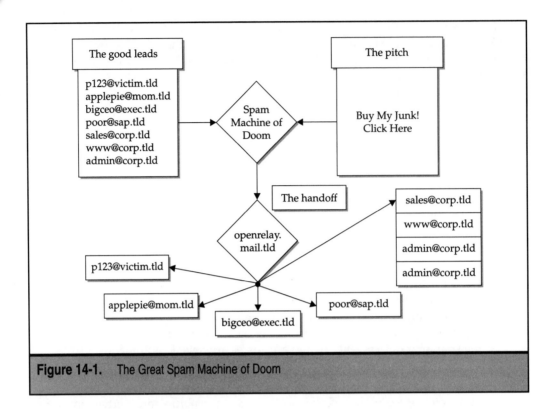

Figure 14-1. The Great Spam Machine of Doom

Spam Content Management

A full-featured content management tool is the second bread-and-butter item for a spammer. Depending on the countermeasure the message is trying to thwart, the content management component to a bulk e-mailer allows the spammer to construct a "silver bullet" that's sure to get in front of a potential customer. Here are a few of the common features:

- **Message Obfuscation** This class of tools changes the e-mail message in ways that are not noticeable to the reader, but with the intent of thwarting spam filters based solely on trigger words. By using dummy HTML tags, spammers can change the message as seen by the spam filter, while continuing to display the message that they want the recipient to see. The tool does it automatically based on settings available to the spammer. We discuss specific instances of message obfuscation in the "Getting to Know the Product (Spam)" section later in this chapter.

- **Personalization** This is a fairly simple function, but one that can be most annoying, especially if used in the subject line of the e-mail. This tool takes information from another source, either from the e-mail address, a collated database of user information, or other method, to insert the actual name of the recipient into the e-mail. Thus, if your e-mail address was janey@bigcomp.tld, the tool would take *janey* from the e-mail address, capitalize the first letter, and produce a subject line like this:

```
Subject: Janey, it was so good to see you...
```

Of course, this can also be a source of amusement if you monitor such e-mail addresses as support@, admin@, and the like.

- **Message Development** Though this has not always been the case, most modern spammers are not overly technical people in the same way that most modern hackers are not overly technical people, thus they do not have access to the skills to develop flashy e-mails using HTML and other code. Most modern bulk e-mail tools include an HTML editor (similar to Microsoft FrontPage) that allows the spammer to use templates or wizards to get its marketing message into a pleasing or flashy format. And speaking of flash, several on the horizon include development tools for animated e-mails (using Flash) and other scripting languages. Included in this are any "regulatory" statements or opt-out links that a spammer may have to attach to the subject or the end of the message.

- **Message Randomization** To thwart both peer-to-peer (P2P) anti-spam tools and Bayesian filters, message randomization tools change a single message in subtle ways. P2P anti-spam tools rely on a unique hash of a single message to communicate the spam to its users. To thwart both Bayesian and simple word filters, or at least make them less effective, randomization tools insert a long string of either nonsense characters or actual words at the end of the message. This practice either weights the message with normal words, balancing out the spam-identifying content, or it abnormally skews what the filter learns about words in a likely spam message. Additionally, it grows the word database for the filter, which could decrease its efficiency. Another similar practice is to insert random text from classic (public domain) literature. So, don't be surprised if a few lines of *Anna Karenina* appear at the end of your next spam message.

Victim Management

The final key piece in any spammer's toolkit is the ability to gather and manage e-mail addresses. Direct marketers receive e-mail addresses in many ways, from CDs distributed by legitimate opt-in sources to web page and newsgroup spiders that harvest addresses automatically. With many thousands of e-mail addresses, bulk mailers often use complex tools to sort, verify, add, delete, and remove duplicates. The following tools are considered standard:

- **Contact Management** A list manager allows the spammer to import e-mail addresses into their bulk mailer. Most accept e-mail addresses in a variety of formats from flat text files to comma-delimited lists to relational database tables. These functions also check for duplicates or "known-bad" addresses and integrate into other features for tracking responses, mail server bounces, and the like.

- **List Management** This class of functions manages the responses, bounce backs, and otherwise invalid e-mail addresses a spammer has in the victim list. This allows for a "clean" list of contacts the spammer can sell to other spammers.

The Purveyors of Spam

Spammers, and the companies that support them, run the gamut of businesses, from the shady basement scams to such well-known firms as Gateway Learning Corp (of Hooked on Phonics fame) and Ameriquest Mortgage Company. These organizations, like any company, are out to make money. How they make money tells as much about the spammers as you'll probably ever know.

Why Spam?

Companies spam for one reason: to make money. Spammers use the direct marketing approach to make their cash, although they have significant advantages over the old "paper-based" campaigns. In this section we dissect the direct marketing model and what it means to spammers.

Old-School Spammers The direct marketing approach is probably as old as marketing itself, whereby a company gains a list of prospects by soliciting them directly, either through mailers, cold calls, or other methods, to convince them to buy. In the days before e-mail, however, costs were associated with every point in the process. First, a product was needed, with all the capital that entails, and then a market was necessary, usually in the form of a list of prospects. The marketer could either generate this list from some ready source (depending on the business, this could be expensive) or purchase a list from another company that specialized in gathering contacts from magazine subscriptions, public records, and the like. The cost of the campaign, while fairly variable depending on the business and the campaign, usually comprised the bulk of the marketing costs. Developing printing and mailing marketing pieces and responding to "hits" all represented real costs before the company ever made a dime. And these costs grew exponentially, the larger the campaign grew. While there were some opportunities to make additional revenue by "validating" lists (that is, keeping data on respondents and selling this information),

---

Some Backup to Our Spam Claims

As a further disclaimer, we are not accusing Gateway Learning and Ameriquest of being spammers; however, referring to two Internet news articles, both companies are attributed to being either producers or consumers of e-mail lists that either ended up in a spammer's hands or originated in a spammer's e-mail harvester.

An article from MSNBC online describes a reporter's quest for the spammer at the other end of the spam message: see *http://msnbc.msn.com/id/3078642/*. Another article, from the online edition of the *Washington Post*, recounts the sordid story of Gateway Learning Corp's "change of policy" regarding selling or renting its users' private information; read it at *http://www.washingtonpost.com/ac2/wp-dyn/A54888-2003Jun30*.

for the most part the direct marketer was limited to the revenue generated from the product or service being peddled. This excludes the scams, of course. Then, and now, scams generate money directly only off of stupidity, greed, or naïveté.

The importance of the old model is that it takes money up front to make money down the line. This keeps the scam artists, poor products, and other chaff out of the wheat, at least by proportion from simple market force mechanics.

New Jack Direct Marketers   The e-mail direct marketer has taken this model and, through available technology, reduced the costs to a negligible amount in proportion to the volume of direct marketing pieces and, more importantly, figured out ways to *make* money at almost every stage of the process.

- **Product**   The most surprising fact of the spam business, even to us, is that most spammers don't even sell anything to their spam recipients. Most revenue from a spam-based business is generated through other means that only require the recipient's complicity. (See the following section, "Follow the Money Trail.") Those that do sell a product are technically at a disadvantage in this model, since they must have some capital associated with either wholesale buying or development of a product.

- **Prospects**   For a list of unvalidated prospects, the spammer needs only a few simple and generally cheap tools. E-mail addresses are everywhere and easily obtainable using existing web spider technology. (We speak more about e-mail spider harvesters in Chapter 16.) Additional tools can validate each address in turn, either before the spam is sent or by the user's actions after she receives the message. This gives the spammer another asset that can be sold and resold to other spammers, or even legitimate businesses.

- **Spam Tools**   The tools for generating and managing a spam business are inexpensive and easy-to-use, and they usually contain all the functions needed to gather and manage prospects, compose and manage content, and keep the spammer anonymous (as discussed earlier in this chapter). Additionally, for those spammers who develop in-house tools, these systems become another source of ready income by selling to other spammers.

- **The Campaign**   A spam campaign costs a miniscule fraction of its analog counterpart. Even now, a spammer can get an Internet account for a free evaluation period, hook up the spam machine, spew out thousands of messages, and then close up shop and move on to the next ISP. An important point to remember is that for a spammer to make money, he collects it up front from his client, the advertiser. Spam is the business of *transmitting* spam, not the ultimate response of the targets. The most compelling reason for anonymity is that the spammer wants the receiver of the spam to direct his interest (or flames, as the case may be) directly to the benefactor.

- **Other Cost Centers**   Responding to interested prospects probably represents the bulk of a spammer's costs. This usually entails setting up and managing a web page (since spammers do not want a direct response from their victims).

Still, the modern spammer's costs represent a fraction of a real-world direct marketing campaign with a sales force sitting on phones waiting for the customer to respond. As you'll see in the following section, though, the web site is generally the place where the spammer generates the most revenue, as well.

Follow the Money Trail

So, if everyone hates spam and almost no one responds and even fewer buy what the spammer is selling, how do spammers make money? The most fascinating fact to come out of our research for this book is that most spammers don't sell anything to the message recipients. In fact, the spammed almost always become unknowing revenue generators for the spammer. These are the most common ways that spammers make money:

- **Sell an actual product**   As we said, these spammers are in the minority, but they do exist. Small to large companies market and sell their products using unsolicited commercial e-mail. Usually, this is a somewhat indirect approach, like all marketing. A company sends a newsletter or other piece touting its products, which directs the user to the company's web site, where the product can be purchased and delivered to the customer. Of course, the web spin on this model is that the company could be selling a physical product, web content, software, or whatever. This method is most often used by pornography or online gambling web sites, or interestingly enough, to sell the spammers secondary products.

- **Generate web banner revenues**   Web banner advertising generates revenue for the spammer for every person that visits the spammer's web site. The "enhancements" to this scheme are web pop-up ads, browser spawns, and other annoying web push technologies. Ever gone to a web site only to have 20 windows pop up? You just made money for someone. How's that for an effortless revenue stream?

- **Validate contact information**   Spammers can validate that the e-mail addresses they spammed are real, are monitored by humans, and, more importantly, that humans read the spam messages and/or click the links in the messages. While this information is valuable to the spammer with regard to future spam opportunities, it's more valuable because now that information can be sold to other spammers.

- **Perpetrate a scam**   E-mail scams, like real-world scams, take many forms. Anything from multi-level marketing schemes to chain mails to outright theft of your credit card or other financial information is possible via e-mail. While scams are plentiful, the good news is that once money changes hands, especially electronically, the forensics trail becomes much clearer.

- **Sell the spam business model**   Talk about nepotism! One of the most interesting ways that spammers generate revenue is to recruit more spammers and sell them the contacts, tools, and methods. What did they teach us in business school? Sell what you know.

GETTING TO KNOW THE PRODUCT (SPAM)

If you delve into a well-constructed spam message, you'll realize that spammers, or at least the developers of their software, are ingenious. For almost every spam countermeasure, direct e-mail marketing software has an answer, and most often, spammers are proactively developing for the next countermeasure. In this section, we dissect a few spam messages and highlight the most common methods that spammers use to defeat your anti-spam tools. We also take a look at how spammers might thwart anti-spam tools of the future.

Anatomy of an E-Mail Header

To understand e-mail, and thus spam, you must understand the e-mail (or SMTP) header. Within the headers are the details of the pathway the mail took to get to you and certain information about the sender. The bad news is that almost everything that happens to the e-mail before it reaches your mail server can be forged. And if the message is spam, it probably is forged. In this section we discuss e-mail headers, what to look for, and how to determine whether the information contained there has been falsified.

Where Are the E-mail Headers?

If you use a desktop e-mail client, the headers are usually hiding. For those that use server-side clients, such as Pine, you may also have to enable headers to be able to view them. We discuss four e-mail clients next and how to find the headers on each.

Outlook Express   Of all the e-mail clients, Outlook Express is the least intuitive when it comes to finding e-mail headers (they're actually in the Properties field of the individual message). To read the headers on Outlook Express, perform these simple steps:

1. Open Outlook Express.
2. From the message list, right-click a message and select Properties. The Properties window appears.
3. Click the Details tab. There are your headers (Figure 14-2).

From this window, you can copy and paste the headers into your favorite text editor. You can also click the Message Source button to see the full source of the message, including headers and body.

Microsoft Outlook   For Outlook, the path is similar:

1. Open Outlook.
2. From the message list, right-click a message and choose Options. The Message Options window appears. The headers are at the bottom of that window (Figure 14-3).

Anti-Spam Tool Kit

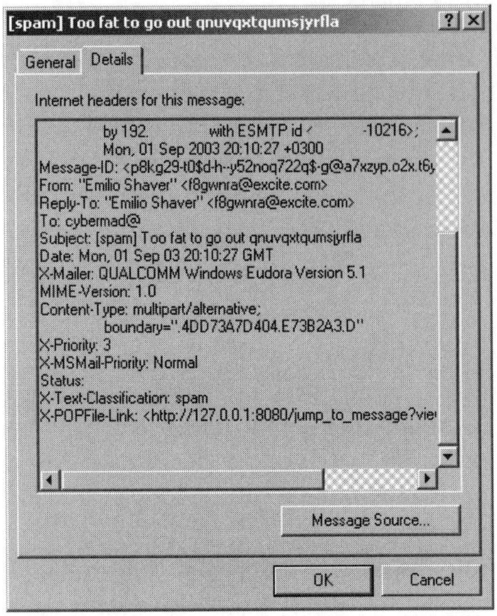

Figure 14-2. The Outlook Message Properties window

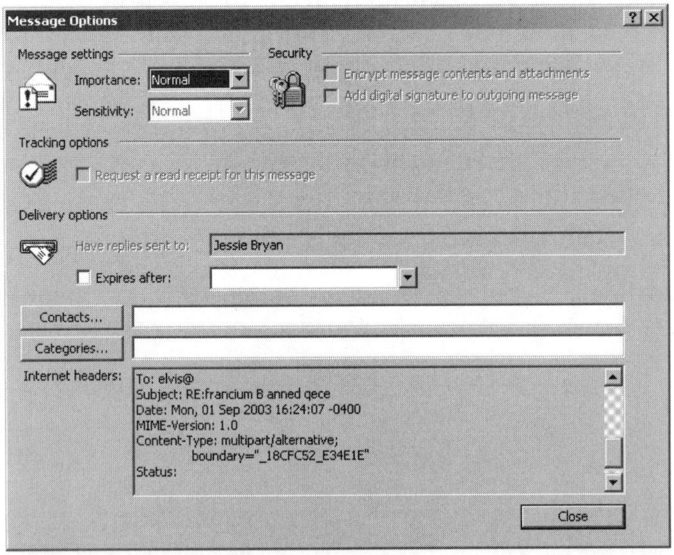

Figure 14-3. Outlook Message Options window with headers

To view the message source in Outlook, right-click anywhere in the message body and choose View Source. The source of the message opens in Notepad.

QUALCOMM Eudora Mail   Eudora is a little more intuitive.

1. Simply open the message and click the Blah Blah Blah button in the upper-left corner of the mail.
2. Click anywhere in the text field, hold down the SHIFT key, and click again to select the text.

Pine   Pine is not necessarily the most popular e-mail viewer out there, but we wanted to include a UNIX solution for those who might be ready to fire off hate mail. Personally, we know many people who use Pine, and they're all relatively sane and well adjusted.

1. Log in to your favorite UNIX host and run Pine.
2. Press the I key to get an index of your Inbox.
3. Select whichever message you want, and press the ENTER key to open the message. The message appears.
4. Press the H key. The full message with headers appears (Figure 14-4).

With the headers turned on, you also get the full source of the message, including HTML tags and the like.

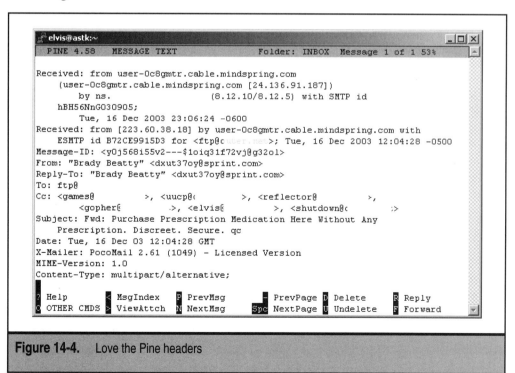

Figure 14-4.   Love the Pine headers

I've Got the Headers; Why Do I Care?

The headers can tell you, and more important, your full-featured spam tool, quite a lot about the mail you've received. Additionally, if you're reporting spam to your administrator, an anti-spam site, or trying to track down the culprit yourself, this is where you start.

Life of an E-mail Headers are added to an e-mail in three stages: Composition (by the mail client), Mail Exchange, and Mail Received. At each stage, specific information is added, and the spammer can easily forge the information in two of these stages.

When the mail is first composed, the mail client adds the following information:

- **From** The mail client inputs the e-mail address and real name of the sender directly from the mail client's configuration files. This information is configured by the sender and is easily forged. Many times, spammers put either your e-mail address or an address of someone else within your domain to attempt to thwart white/blacklists.

- **To** This is the user's mailbox to which the message is destined. Typically, this contains your e-mail address. Related to this is the CC: field, which includes anyone else the mail is copied to. If you receive a spam message and your e-mail address doesn't appear in the To: or CC: field, it's because the spammer used a blind carbon copy (BCC: field), which never appears in the headers.

- **Date** This field is taken directly from the sender's computer clock, which can be set to whatever time the sender wishes.

- **X Headers** These headers describe a variety of information from the mail client (X-Mailer) to priority (X-Priority) to read-receipt (X-Confirm-Reading-to). These fields are considered optional, user-defined fields and are generally used either to identify the sender or perform some other action on the mail. Some, like X-Priority, have become de-facto standards that are consistently understood by a variety of clients, while others are specific to a particular piece of software (such as mailing lists). By convention, all optional message fields start with an X. Note that these fields can be added at any stage of the e-mail's pathway to the receiver. In fact, many anti-spam tools use this field to list the spam score, anti-spam tool name, and the like.

- **Subject** The client also generates the Subject field of the message.

- **MIME Headers** The client program adds this class of headers to give the receiving client a heads-up as to the type of nontext elements contained in the message, such as image, sound, and other files. Typical MIME headers are MIME-Version, Content-Type, and Content-Transfer-Encoding.

Once the message leaves the client, it communicates first with the sender's mail exchanger. As discussed earlier, most spammer tools contain a SMTP mail gateway within the tool, allowing the spammer to forge all of the header information generated in this stage of the message as well. The following are some of the fields you might see that are generated by the mail exchanger.

- **Received: from**   This line describes the vitals of the mail transaction between the mail client and the SMTP exchanger. The full line typically reads like so:
  ```
  Received: from clienthostname.domain.tld (hostname.domain.tld [IP ADDRESS])
   by mailexchanger.domain.tld (mail server version information)
  ```
  If the spammer has used some unwitting site's open mail relay, half of this information could be correct. Additionally, a Received from line is added for every "hop" the mail takes between exchangers. The spammer can also add as many spurious Received from lines as desired to throw off the forensics trail. The first hostname and domain name (that is, the fully qualified domain name) are what the sender server gave when it gave its first SMTP handshake to the receiving server. This information is easy to forge. The hostname and IP address in the parentheses are reverse lookups done by the mail exchanger itself. While spoofing or falsifying this information is also possible, in most cases the spammer is either using an in-house temporary mail exchanger or the spammer's connection point is temporary, thus the real IP/hostname serves only to implicate the ISP that gave the spammer the account, especially if the spammer uses a public wireless Internet connection. See the sidebar, "Drive-by Spammers," for additional complications.

- **Other Headers**   The mail exchanger applies additional headers such as the Message-ID and date/time stamp. If these are on a real, live mail gateway and not something controlled by the spammer, these are real values and probably the only thread you have back to the originator of the spam.

The last step in the message life is the receiving mail server. Here additional headers are applied, depending on the communication with the mail exchanger:

- **Received: from**   The receiving mail host tacks on another Received line detailing the exchanger it received the mail from, a message ID (assigned by the receiving host), and a date/time stamp. Similar to the format described earlier, this line lists the "claimed" domain as well as a reverse lookup with IP addresses done by the receiving mail host.

- **Additional Headers**   Like the mail exchanger, the receiving mail server posts a message ID for identification purposes in the logs, and a date/time stamp. Other programs between the user and the message also add additional fields such as X-UIDL (added by the POP server) and X-Spam-Status (added by SpamAssassin).

Spam Examples

Okay, enough with the theoretical. In this section we go through the headers of two real, live spam messages, detailing the headers and the information we can (and can't) glean from them. Note that the examples we used have been altered to protect the authors and any possible victims of the spammer. None of the domain names are valid and all IP addresses are RFC 1918 "private address" space.

> ### Drive-by Spammers
>
> With the proliferation of unsecured or public wireless access to the Internet, a real danger of allowing spammers even easier anonymous access to free resources exists. Imagine a spammer with a laptop, wireless card, and full-featured spam tool with an SMTP gateway built in, sitting in a "wired" coffee shop (or outside your house!) sipping coffee and spewing spam through someone else's (or your) connection. Not only is it untraceable, but the owner of the connection could find her network resources on a blacklist very quickly. Can you say, "drive-by spamming?"

The Hijacked Mail Exchanger

The first illustrative spam we'll use is one that came through an open mail relay. Following are the mail headers listing the path the message took from sending client to received client. We've annotated the headers in the following section, which provide some forensics on the header information.

Gathering Data from the Header   The following spam message was actually received, but we've changed the IP addresses to RFC 1918 (Address Allocation for Private Internets) addresses and altered the domain names:

```
Received: from hijackedexchanger.exploited.tld (hijackedexchanger.exploited.tld
[10.1.1.2])
        by mail.astk.tld (8.12.10/8.12.5)
```

We received the mail from hijackedexchanger.exploited.tld at the IP (verified by our mail server with a reverse lookup). Note that our mail server added this portion of the header. At this time, we do not have absolute verification that the domain or IP address is correct—only that a communication from the host/domain was received and, on a reverse lookup, the IP address resolved to that host/domain. If the information had not matched, the actual domain returned would have appeared in the parenthesis with the IP address.

```
with SMTP id
     hBH6bwnG006849; for <elvis@trailerpark.tld>; Wed, 17 Dec 2003 01:42:50 -0600
```

Our mail server created an SMTP ID for the message, noting that it was destined for elvis's mail account at the specified time. The `for` field is the actual mailbox for which the message is destined and has little to no relation to the To field shown in a minute.

```
Received: from forgeddomain.tld by [10.1.1.2] by Tue, 16 Dec 2003 23:32:06 +0500
```

Before it reached our mail server, the message was transmitted from the IP address listed to the domain listed. Both of these could be forged. We'll see in the forensics. The timestamp is from the mail exchanger and is likewise suspect.

```
From: "Charlie Mckee" <sqqzq@forgeddomain.tld>
To: elvis@trailer.tld, emauro@trailer.tld
Subject: Re: NYZJR, entry into jerusalem
```

```
Mime-Version: 1.0
X-Mailer: mPOP Web-Mail 2.19
X-Originating-IP: [forgeddomain.tld]
Date: Tue, 16 Dec 2003 22:29:06 +0400
Reply-To: "Charlie" <sqqzq@forgeddomain.tld>
```

The sender's mail client generated all of this information and is suspect, at best. Note that the To field could have easily contained an e-mail address that had no relation to the From field earlier in the header. Likewise, a spammer often puts your own e-mail address in the From field to thwart black/whitelists.

Verifying the Information   We start by verifying that the domains used are real and that they resolve to the IP's listed. To do this, we use a few simple command line tools on a UNIX or Windows-based computer.

To verify the domain names, we use `whois`:

```
bash-2.04$ whois exploited.tld
Domain Name: EXPLOITED.TLD

   Administrative Contact, Technical Contact:
      Exploited Communications   (ID-OR)          Hostmaster@EXPLOITED.TLD
      1234 Need an Admin way
      St.Louis, MO 63132
      US
      (000) 555-1212 fax: (000) 555-1313

   Record expires on 03-Aug-2009.
   Record created on 04-Aug-1998.
   Database last updated on 17-Dec-2003 03:01:18 EST.

   Domain servers in listed order:

   NS1.EXPLOITED.TLD          172.31.255.3
   NS2.EXPLOITED.TLD          172.31.255.4
```

 The `whois` command is not available on the Windows platform. See the sidebar "Where is whois?" for more information on web-based domain lookup tools.

From this, we see that exploited.tld is a real domain, and since the nameserver is in the same IP range as the mail exchanger, we're pretty certain that's correct as well. To verify this, we use whois `nslookup` on the IP in the Received field of the header (172.31.255.1):

```
nslookup 172.31.255.1
Server:         172.31.255.3
Address:        172.31.255.1

1.255.31.172.in-addr.arpa       name = hijackedexchanger.exploited.tld.
```

> ### Where is whois?
>
> For those who don't have access to a UNIX system, you can also get "whois" information from the following web sites:
>
> - *http://www.internic.net*   Once the single domain authority, now you can navigate to individual domain registrars or pull up whois information on the Internic site.
> - *http://www.samspade.org*   You can look up domain information here and check popular black hole lists via downloadable software or a custom web portal page.
> - *http://www.geektools.com*   Geektools allows you to look up domain information and perform traceroutes to individual hosts from its web interface.

The addresses match! Since it is rare that a spammer uses an ISP's mail exchanger like everyone else, we're suspecting that this is an open relay. So, we go to *http://www.ordb.org* and enter the domain name or IP address into its database. Sure enough, it comes back as blocked for open relay. On other sites, such as SpamCop, we find that it's blocked as well. So, we know that much.

We know that the second level of the mail exchange (from the client to the mail exchanger) is patently false information, without even analyzing it further. The Received from field (forgeddomain.tld) doesn't even exist, and this entry should be in the format *host.domain.tld* with a validated IP address. Most likely the spammer connected from a free Internet account or other entry point and was able to fool the open mail relay successfully.

The Spammer Relay

Our second example most likely originates and was exchanged by a spam suite's built-in mail exchanger. What's troubling about this type of e-mail is that the spammer has a distinct advantage, no matter what. The point-of-entry can almost never be successfully blacklisted since the host/IP is probably in an ISP's dynamic host/IP pool for dial-up users. The spammer probably either has a free account or has connected through an unsecured or public source (such as a wireless access point). From an anti-spam analysis standpoint, only your content filters (Bayesian, P2P, or word-based) can successfully catch this spam.

```
Received: from fatboyspammer.tld (customer160-1.realdns.tld
[192.168.10.1]
    (may be forged))
```

The header added the "(may be forged)" line because fatheadspammer.tld is not a valid domain; however, the customer160-1.realdns.tld is a real domain and resolves to the IP address listed.

```
            by ourmail.bigcomp.tld (8.12.10/8.12.5) with ESMTP id
    hBH7vhnG013452
            for <elvis@banana.tld>; Wed, 17 Dec 2003 01:57:45 -0600
Message-Id: <200312170757.hBH7vhnG013452@ourmail.bigcomp.tld>
Received: from 10.1.1.32 by smtp.someferin.schanger.sch.tld;
            Wed, 17 Dec 2003 23:59:58 +0000
```

The first hop for this mail, from the client to the mail exchanger, has been totally forged. Neither the domain name nor the IP address exist, a sure sign that the spammer is running a mail exchanger locally.

We use `nslookup` or dig to confirm that both the IP address and domain name in the communication between our mail server and the spammer's mail exchanger is real. Since customer160-1.realdns.tld is obviously the remote access space of some ISP, and the mail went directly from that host to our mail server, we can assume that the spammer is running a mail exchanger. The good thing is that we have a record of a real point where the spammer connected. The bad news is that the spammer has probably already packed up and moved to another IP or another ISP. Checking *http://www.ordb.org*, the domain/IP is not listed, but if we check a few others, we find that the domain is listed as a known spammer. Using whois, we find that the domain belongs to a country in Argentina. Finally, pasting in the full header at *http://www.spamcop.com* gives us the admin at realdns.tld, where we can lodge a complaint. This may or may not be useful, since the ISP could be allowing spam to traffic on its network, or it may not have the resources to stop the spammer.

RED ALERT: REPORTING KNOWN SPAMMERS

So, you managed to track down the spam bear and trap it in its cave. What do you do now? Since it's still illegal to shoot spammers, your only recourse is to share information for the betterment of the Internet community. In this section, we cover the few ways you have to report spammers.

Direct E-mail

Your first, and probably least effective, way is to contact the administrator of the offending domain directly. Whether you've determined that the spammer was a remote-access client on an ISP's network, transiting through an open mail relay, or have otherwise found proof that a spammer originated on a given network, you can probably find the administrator responsible for following up.

The fastest way to find the point-of-contact is to take the header and go to *http://www.spamcop.com*. You'll find a handy tool that analyzes the headers and spits out the e-mail contact for the appropriate administrator. We discuss SpamCop in more detail in Chapter 5.

When you e-mail an administrator, be sure to include the full spam e-mail, including body and headers and any supporting information you have about the origin of the spam and the spammer. If you have multiple messages from the same spammer, include all headers for all the mails, if possible.

DNS Blacklists

If you fail to make headway with the administrator of the domain, you can report the information you've found to one of the DNS blacklists (discussed in more detail in Chapter 5). These sites usually require the full headers of the spam message and any other information you have on the spammer.

Update Your Own Anti-Spam Tool

If you are running one of the fine tools described in this book, ensure that the tool is updated with the spam message's information. Add the host or domain to your own blacklist, and ensure that keywords are entered or that the message is "learned" if you're using a Bayesian solution. If you use a P2P network solution, hash the message and send it up so others aren't affected by it. If you are a user on your organization's network or a customer of an ISP, be sure the administrators get that information as well. The only real way to fight spam is to spread the word. The spammers have the advantage, but we can reduce their effectiveness by communicating their actions far and wide.

SUMMARY

In this chapter, we covered the spammer's tools in addition to detailing the spam message itself. Most spammer tools contain a suite of programs and functions specifically designed to thwart anti-spam solutions. Built-in mail exchangers, message randomizers, the use of HTML, and random lists of words all target specific classes of anti-spam tools. Knowing spam tools and methods helps you to tweak your countermeasures to compensate. The spam message itself can also become a spam-fighting tool. Information in the message headers typically leads you as close to the spammer as you can get, and it usually gets you at least enough information to report the message and the sender. By sharing this information, you are helping others to fight spam, as well as helping yourself and your organization.

CHAPTER 15

ADVANCED TOPICS AND FINE TUNING

In this chapter we explore some advanced spamming topics, both from the defender's perspective as well as from the spammer's. Our objective is to delve into what really makes some of the technologies tick so that you will be well prepared on your mission of ridding your inbox of spam. Some of the items covered here are best described by using source code, but that by no means should dissuade you from diving right in. We promise to keep things at a topical and uncomplicated level.

We explore some of the finer facets of black/whitelisting and cover a new approach that splits the difference between the two, affectionately called *greylisting*. Next, we cover a group of defensive tactics with supporting examples, which are largely based on the methods and practices used by the spammers themselves. Lastly we explore some automation techniques for handling the ongoing operation of an anti-spam suite of tools and the problems you will likely encounter with their management.

THE BLACK, THE WHITE, AND THE GREY

One of the oldest and still most popular techniques for handling spam has been simple sender black/whitelisting. Although the clearest advancement in the science has been to centralize the management, testing and distribution of blacklisted sites using a network available server with subscribing mail servers worldwide, other developments are worth noting.

Roll-Your-Own Blacklist

For anyone who's been managing the spam problem for more than year, the temptation to erect your own blacklist (either implemented at a mail server level or even at your individual user level) has probably already occurred to you. Some organizations even make a common "baseline" blacklist available to its users, which they are free to adopt, modify, or ignore it as they see fit.

For example, we found a published blacklist that's remarkably long and complete, available for public download off of the Internet. This blacklist comprises many smaller personal blacklists, tied together with various comments and up-to-date findings provided by the persons who have contributed to it. You can retrieve the list from *http://www.stearns.org/sa-blacklist/sa-blacklist.current*.

Although you might be afraid of installing the entire thing (it's more than 10,000 lines long) without at least a casual look at its contents, we would certainly recommend spending a few minutes paging through it. A decent amount of information betraying how spammers organize their shops can be gleaned by a careful review of its contents.

Blacklisting with a Bite

Spam costs e-mail users and system administrators *real* money. There's no doubt about it. Often quoted in the press with huge intangible figures ranging in billions of dollars per year, analysts conjecture that the components of cost come largely from time wasted reading, deleting, performing administrative duties, and maintaining anti-spam software, just to name few.

With this in mind, a familiar and growing theme that we see approaching on the horizon is the concept of "recovery payments" directed at spammers for invading our lives. As we mentioned in Chapter 3, a movement has been sparked to charge all senders some fraction of a penny to send even a single message, which supporters hope would equalize things for the bulk mailers who would have to pay out of pocket to maintain their mail spigots. Of course, for that to work, a wholesale rebuild of the entire Internet would be required, a method of accounting for micro-payments and a mechanism to keep everyone honest would need to be built. Odds would say that this isn't going to happen anytime soon. Additionally, and somewhat discouragingly, even if that were to happen, the spammers would still probably find a clever way to circumvent the system so that their messages get distributed on someone else's nickel.

We still see all of the trappings of real money being used as ballast. Case in point: The blacklisting organizations have amassed big enough user bases and built strong enough influence to exert their own economic pressures when they want to be heard. As of the winter of 2003, we found that one DNS Blacklisting group had begun to charge for removal from one of their lists. Although the exact circumstances are somewhat vague, and their web site makes no mention of the policy, we see this as an illuminating sign of where we are headed. To give you an idea of scope, this DNSBL group wanted $50 to remove a marked IP address from its list.

Obviously, this opens the door to expanded litigation, accelerated arguments, and even the unusual circumstances that only money can bring to the table. Consider for a second if all of the networked blacklists had policies of removal for fees paid. We can see an obvious conflict of interest arising that would probably not result in behavior that was for the common good, that's for sure.

What in the World Is Greylisting

We've seen the term *greylisting* used to describe a variety of blocking techniques; however, a common element among them is that they all uniformly refer to an automated quarantine area where the traditional methods of spam classification produced results that were inconclusive. While in the quarantine, the proponents of greylisting suggest using additional techniques to help sort the spam from the ham.

In this section, we cover a particularly novel approach to greylisting as put forward by Evan Harris in his paper published online at *http://projects.puremagic.com/greylisting/*. Evan's approach is a blend of the quarantine zone and a traditional preemptive technique for reducing spam before it ever gets to your mailbox.

Evan's greylisting goals are consistent with those across the wider sphere of anti-spam filtering in general—namely, to incur as little processing as feasible while providing transparency to users, all while blocking what really is spam without blocking what isn't. His greylisting approach is targeted at the server or exchanger level, which is a bit different than how we've seen the term *greylisting* used with other packages, which operate at the desktop or client host level.

This approach operates by utilizing three pieces of key information: the IP address of the transmitting host, the sender's e-mail address, and the recipient's e-mail address (the latter two found in the e-mail header). Those three identifiers are taken together to form a *triplet*, a term used in this parlance of greylisting. From here, each triplet is indicative of a mail "relationship" and can be used to determine whether the sender and receiver have had prior communication.

Their basic theory states that spam comes from unknown sources about 99 percent of the time, and by using a well-formed, quick, and complete database of relationships specific to each user (or server), it should be trivial to discern whether a new communication proposed by a complete stranger should be accepted or not. What's unique about greylisting is that it doesn't just unilaterally dump mail, which would mean that all e-mail from strangers would be tossed without further regard.

Greylisting operates by identifying which relationships are "proposed" by the sender, checking against a local database, and stalling if they are unknown. Mail servers are sometimes unable to accept incoming mail for a variety of reasons (hard drive room is low, system load is high, configuration errors, and so on). The normal protocols for e-mail allow for this circumstance, and normal attempts at retransmission are conducted after waiting some period of time (anywhere from a few minutes to a few hours). Delaying or stalling e-mail in one of these circumstances is quite normal and happens millions of times day.

Customized spam-blasting software, however, rarely conforms to such rules of good communication conduct. This software's goals are to shovel as much out as they can in a limited amount of time, and then duck under the cover of darkness before they are seen. Since they are sending out millions upon millions of spams at a shot, their software ignores these "transient" network failures by aborting them without further consideration. Greylisting was designed to make use of this behavior and stall all mail that comes from an unknown source. Mail sent from a conforming mail server will be delayed, but only on its first communication with a new peer, and mail from spammers will be dropped by the spammers themselves.

Of course, the greylisting methods described here don't have a long shelf life if the spammers decide to devote their energies to working around them. The easiest thing that spammers can do would be to redesign their blaster applications around the logic of fully formed mail servers, supportive of all the communication nuances.

THE COMPLETE MX RELAY DEFENSE

Another strategy of a spam-blasting operation is to find unused, unprotected, or unregulated channels into a network. Usually through old or neglected mail exchangers (MX servers), spammers can get a foothold into your organization.

Be sure that all of your MX relays are set up with the same software and spam controls, including outsourced or infrequently used ones. In addition, many organizations apply spam filtering only at the main mail server, which can easily be determined by the spammers. Often third- or fourth-tier MX relays are easily identified by spam-bots and are used as primary transmission vehicles. Shuffling through MX entries is one of the best methods spammers have to circumvent all of your hard work in defeating their advances.

As a defensive posture, you could either choose to install your complement of spam-fighting solutions at all of your exposed mail servers, including the backup MX servers, or you could force a "re-forward" of e-mail back through the MX servers you have designated to the filtering.

DEFENSE BY DISGUISE

The harvesting of target addresses is largely done using web page scraping robots, or *bots* for short. To help contain the leakage of your addresses right at the source, only a few cheap and easy ways are available to use to protect yourself. By disguising e-mail addresses published on your web pages, you can avoid a big mountain of garbage collecting in your inbox.

First off, it would be a good idea to do some spot-checking of your addresses in Google or one of the other big Internet search engines. You should be able to find your own web pages cited, especially if you have linked references as part of your HTML files. This fact alone is one of the key reasons why spam-bots are quickly able to obtain a trajectory on your site and why you can't seem to shake them. This also makes for a good starting point so that you will be able to review the effectiveness of any countermeasures you have taken.

In the pages that follow, we cover four of the basic methods for reducing or even removing you from this worldwide target list.

Use Graphics Instead of Text

The simplest and most straightforward approach is to replace all of the e-mail addresses on your web site with graphical images of the same. For instance, the most common way to cite an e-mail address in HTML usually conforms to a variant of the following:

```
<A HREF="mailto:youraddress@yourorg.tld"> Mail us with this link</a>
```

This HTML code makes a URL link out of the address, which when clicked, will automatically open the browser's helper mail application and start a new message. Most people include these `mailto` links on their web sites, as it simplifies the web-to-mail transition for people interested in getting in touch with them.

E-mail addresses are even more frequently found on web pages without the `mailto` tag. We've seen countless e-mail addresses incorporated into web page footers, about us pages, and contact summaries. Both are equally easy to lift directly out of the HTML and place on a spammer's target list.

Use the HTML ASCII Equivalence

Another way to obfuscate a published e-mail address is to convert some or all of the characters into hexadecimal ASCII. Web servers will ignore the encoding, and web browsers will dutifully translate the numeric equivalents back into printable characters so that the user of the system won't know that anything at all has been changed. The following example and the prior example are exactly the same.

```
<A HREF="&#109;ail&#116;o:youraddress&#64;yourorg.&#116;&#108;&#100;">
 Mail us with this link
</a>
```

As you can see, inserting some ASCII translations into an HTML link does a pretty good job of scrambling the text into what appears to be nonsense, presumably making it difficult for the casual spam-bot to harvest the addresses. However, the protection afforded by this technique is not likely to last long, since newer, smarter spam-bots need only to do some preprocessing to bypass the defense. As a comparison to the image replacement defense, ASCII translation leaves much to be desired for continued protection; however, it does work quite effectively for right now.

To obfuscate your published e-mail addresses, having the full ASCII table around comes in most handy. Here is a web page that can be used as an excellent resource: *http://www.asciitable.com/*.

Use a Scripting Language (JavaScript)

A more advanced technique for foiling a spam harvester is to use a scripting language as an intermediary step prior to the delivery of the HTML code where the e-mail address is incorporated. JavaScript, for example, is an entirely client-side interpreted language, which would push the processing and interpretation responsibility of the translation to the spam-bot, which as we pointed out, is a slimmed-down blasting application without the brains to do advanced operations. In short, a spammer's harvester is a very limited vehicle, designed only with one thing in mind: to capture and retain as many addresses as possible. By having to process JavaScript or even translate raw embedded ASCII could slow it down as much as 10–50 times, an unacceptable overhead when so many other ripe opportunities are riddled throughout the Internet.

To simplify the creation of the JavaScript, and to provide you with a resource, we found an online conversion utility that produces the code for you, at *http://www.jmrosengard.com/SafeMailto/*.

Using the same example address that we used to illustrate the previous techniques, we generated an embedded JavaScript:

```
<script language='JavaScript'>
var v2="NUQXRRTUWSBW@IMQJ@IGGXA";
var v7=unescape("7%3A%24*360%272%201%179%268%23%252.i34%25");
var v5=v2.length;var v1="";
for (var v4=0;v4<v5;v4++){
     v1+=String.fromCharCode(v2.charCodeAt(v4)^v7.charCodeAt(v4));
}
document.write(
     '<a href="#" onclick= "window.location=\'mail\u0074o\u003a'+v1+'\'">
```

```
'v1.replace("@","\u0040")+'</a>');
</script>
```

As you can see, as we engage stronger and stronger methods for obfuscation, the denser and more garbled the output that is produced, which is exactly the point. By pushing the processing requirements toward the spammer, we gain a nice asymmetrical advantage ourselves, which is a bitter pill that the spammers should stomach for a change.

SPAM-BOTS AND HOW THEY WORK

In this section we don the hat of the enemy, as we analyze the operation of a spam-harvesting tool and explore some of the challenges spam-bots face when trying to collect and administer spam to a restless, aggravated, and retaliatory audience.

Let's start by writing our own short mail harvester to build a database of target e-mail addresses. Our application should be able to take a web page as a starting point and optionally follow any embedded web links that it finds along the way. It should also scan for `mailto:` tags anywhere it looks and output the address so that the operator can include them in the master database.

To keep things short, simple, and easy to follow, we didn't bother with a bunch of the niceties that would be the mark of a good, well-written application. The following is a complete code listing of our harvesting application, which we developed with the Perl programming language. If you'd like the latest electronic version, it's posted on our web site for download at *http://www.vorpalmedia.com/downloads/harvester.pl*.

```
#!/usr/bin/perl

#-----------------------------------------------------------
#
# E-Mail Address Harvester

#
#-----------------------------------------------------------

$totalsites = 0;

#-----------------------------------------------------------
# Scan Site
#-----------------------------------------------------------
sub scansite {
        $site_ = shift;

        $totalsites++;
        push (@scanned, $site_);
```

Anti-Spam Tool Kit

```perl
        print STDOUT "[$#unscanned,$totalsites]\nScanning $site_...\n\n";
        open (SCAN, "/usr/bin/wget -q -t1 -nh -O - '$site_' |");
        while (<SCAN>) {
            $scanline = $_;
            if ($scanline =~ /mailto:(.+)/) {
                $emailfound = $1;
                if ($emailfound =~ /([a-zA-Z0-9\-\.\_\%\@]+)/) {
                    print STDOUT "[$#unscanned,$totalsites]\t\t$1\n";
                }
            }
            if ($scanline =~ /((http|https|ftp)\:\/\/[a-zA-Z0-9\-\.]+\.[a-zA-Z0-9]{2,5})/) {
                $newsite = $1;

                #
                # This is quick and dirty (I'd advise using wget's command
                # line arguments to perform the same function)
                #
                if ($newsite =~ /cgi/ ||
                    $newsite =~ /\.gif/ ||
                    $newsite =~ /\.tif/ ||
                    $newsite =~ /\'/ ||
                    $newsite =~ /\.jpg/) {
                }
                else {
                    push (@unscanned, $newsite);
                }
            }
        }
        close (SCAN);
}

#----------------------------------------------------------
# Main Event Loop
#----------------------------------------------------------
{
    if ($#ARGV) {
        print STDOUT ("E-Mail Address Harvester\n");
        print STDOUT ("(c) Copyright 2003\n");
        print STDOUT ("Mike W. Erwin, Vorpal Media, Inc.\n\n");
        print STDOUT ("usage: harvester http://www.somewhere.xxx\n");
    }
    else {
        $site = $ARGV[0];
        if ($site =~ /^http:\/\//) {
        }
        else {
            $site = "http://".$site;
        }
        push (@unscanned, $site);
```

```perl
        #
        # Loop forever (ultimately the @scanned list will overflow)
        #
        while (1) {
                $found = 0;
                $site = pop @unscanned;

                for ($ct=0; $ct<=$#scanned; $ct++) {
                    if ($scanned[$ct] eq $site) {
                            $found = 1;
                    }
                }
                if (! $found) {
                    &scansite ($site);
                }

                # Prune the unscanned table so that it doesn't get too large
                if ($#unscanned > 500) {
                    $newsize = rand 200;
                    while ($#unscanned > (500 - $newsize)) {
                            $site = pop @unscanned;
                    }
                }
            }
        }
    }
}

#----------------------------------------------------------
# Notes and Debugging Comments
#
# A nice regular expression for parsing a full URI
#    ($scanline =~ /((http|https|ftp)\:\/\/[a-zA-Z0-9\-\.]+\.
# [a-zA-Z0-9]{2,5}(:[a-zA-Z0-9]*)?\/?([a-zA-Z0-9\-\._\?\,\'\/\\\+&%\$#\=~]
# )*)/) {
#
#
#----------------------------------------------------------
```

Harvesting with Our Perl Reaper

Now that we've got an application to use, let's give it a whirl around the block. The invocation of the harvester is straightforward. Just pass a web site to it on the command line and sit back to watch the mail addresses start popping up on the screen. Here's an example of the application operating for about 30 seconds, using a random web site as a starting point:

```
user@vorpalmedia.com % ./harvester.pl www.wherever.tld
[134,1]     nprhelp@npr.org
[216,2]     jorge@wfcr.org
[216,2]     jorge@wfcr.org
[251,7]     www@info.keio.ac.jp
```

```
[259,9]      k-ris.info@adst.keio.ac.jp
[259,9]      k-ris.info@adst.keio.ac.jp
[256,13]     office@ercim.org
[256,14]     kybele@escet.urjc.es
[259,15]     info@urjc.es
[266,18]     info@escet.urjc.es
[255,21]     mvaro@dlsi.ua.es
[264,24]     info@orbiteam.de
```

If you a career programmer, you'll notice a lot of stuff wrong with our example program. It does virtually no error checking, it's terrible at maintaining good internal data structures, and it's not very friendly on system resources. In short, if you are a nascent spammer looking for a starting point, this isn't it.

What we want to illustrate, however, is how quick and easy it was to develop a tool that automates the process of building a target list. That Perl script took us around an hour to write. Just image the resources and capabilities of the applications in use today by the *real* spamming organizations—five to ten years is a long time to make refinements.

Spam-bots Patented: the End of the World Must Be Near...

As the battle heats up and begins to involve lawyers, policy-makers, and real money, spammers are more frequently using the trappings of industry to protect themselves. To those ends, a patent on a spam harvesting robot was recently issued.

The following link describes the methods protected by the patent, which was issued in April 2002:

http://patft.uspto.gov/netacgi/nph-Parser?Sect1=PTO1&Sect2=HITOFF&d=PALL&p=1&u =/netahtml/srchnum.htm&r=1&f=G&l=50&s1=6,381,592.WKU.&OS=PN/6,381,592&RS= PN/6,381,592

What Is the Robots.txt File

Since harvesting is mainly directed at web pages, Usenet, mailing lists, bulletin boards, and chat rooms, many robotic scanners have been developed for a variety of purposes. For instance, we have the major Internet search engines to thank for their contribution to the arena, and with their advancements to the search technology, the benefits far outweigh the means. Using the web without Google is almost unthinkable.

Web-scraping robots that are operated for more ethical purposes also have built-in measures of control that are almost always absent in address-scroungers. Many sites publish a list of "off-limit" areas, where robots aren't welcomed. Proper etiquette dictates that passers-by should first read this file (robots.txt) before beginning a site-wide download. For obvious reasons, very few (if any), e-mail harvesters pay any attention to this file.

By way of example, we downloaded the robots.txt file from IBM, which is shown next. You'll see line after line of disallowed areas of the site that the administrators don't want spiders to crawl through.

Chapter 15: Advanced Topics and Fine Tuning

```
# $Id: robots.txt,v 1.18 2003/08/20 15:42:41 krusch Exp $
#
# This is a file retrieved by webwalkers a.k.a. spiders that
# conform to a defacto standard.
# See <URL:http://www.robotstxt.org/wc/exclusion.html#robotstxt>
#
# Comments to the webmaster should be posted at <URL:http://www.ibm.com/contact>
#
# Format is:
#       User-agent: <name of spider>
#       Disallow: <nothing> | <path>
# Flag  Date       By      Reason
# $l1-  19950130   epc     finally understood what the file was for!
# $L2=    19960909   epc     fixed url since mak moved to Webcrawler...
# $L3=    19970811   epc     drop /Stretch
# $L4=  19991102   krusch  fixed User-agent capitalization and contact info
# $L5=  20010327   krusch  Updated disallow rules
# ---------------------------------------------------------------------------
User-agent: *
Disallow: //
Disallow: /Admin
Disallow: /admin
Disallow: /zx
Disallow: /zz
Disallow: /common
Disallow: /cgi-bin
Disallow: /scripts
Disallow: /Scripts
Disallow: /i/
Disallow: /image
Disallow: /Search
Disallow: /search
Disallow: /link
Disallow: /perl
Disallow: /tmp
Disallow: /account/registration
Disallow: /webmaster

User-agent: Fast corporate crawler
Disallow: //
Disallow: /Admin
Disallow: /admin
Disallow: /zx
Disallow: /zz
Disallow: /common
Disallow: /cgi-bin
Disallow: /scripts
Disallow: /Scripts
Disallow: /i/
Disallow: /image
Disallow: /Search
```

```
Disallow: /search
Disallow: /link
Disallow: /perl
Disallow: /tmp
Disallow: /webmaster
```

Where Can I Get More Info on Robots?

Because quite a few different spiders and robots are prowling out there, diligently surfing for legitimate as well as nefarious purposes, we found a good online resource that can help you with identifying them. Robots and spidering applications will often leave a footprint in your weblogs, which can then be used to find the ultimate source of the snoop. Here are some excellent resources that can help you:

- http://www.robotstxt.org/wc/active.html
- http://www.siteware.ch/webresources/useragents/

SIPHONING A 55-GALLON DRUM OF SPAM

Once you've got spam filtering working reliably, and once you've built a system for updates that keeps your whole system in tune, all that's left are a few spams here and there, often as few as one per day (at least, that's what we can expect from a well-oiled system). What's curious is that we have to remind ourselves how *big* that iceberg of unseen spam actually is. In this section, we cover a few statistics of our spam corpus, which can help elucidate the elements that really matter to a system that's been around the block a few times and is essentially operating per its specification.

Consider the following distribution of the spaminess of our test mailbox. After collecting about ten days worth of mail, we were able to draw the following statistics:

- **Number of Spam Mails Received**   8014
- **Time Period Covered**   Sunday, 14 Dec 2003 20:03:20 to Thursday, 24 Dec 2003 14:18:09—about 10 days
- **Average spam received per hour**   33 (one every 2 minutes)
- **Number of links (http://)**   56,692
- **Number of secure links (https://)**   156

As you can see from the graphic in Figure 15-1, for the largest group of spam we received in the 10 days of our survey, fully 80 percent of them had SpamAssassin scores between 10 and 40. When taken as a measure of effectiveness, we were pleased to see that the grouping wasn't closer to a score of 5, which was our trigger for determining whether we should deliver it or not. Scores excessively close to 5 in our system represent a murky confidence interval, and they likely indicate that our system was issuing false negatives. Likewise, a grouping of mails that had high SpamAssassin scores would tend to lead us to believe that the weights associated with our junk mail filtering were too punitive and needed adjustment downward.

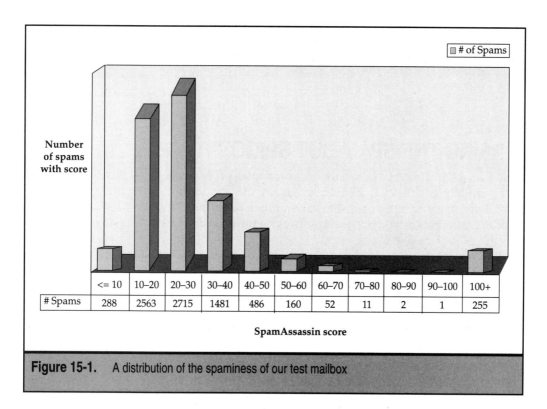

Figure 15-1. A distribution of the spaminess of our test mailbox

Another theory that we wanted to test was the premise that predominantly all spammers manufacture fictional and untraceable addresses made in a "one-off" fashion, one for each spam sent. We definitely found this to be case when we studied our corpus of 8000-odd spams. As a matter of fact, practically *every* spam had a "unique" From address, and we found that only about 200 of the 8000 had any duplicates at all, which we enumerate here:

```
30 saucyspecials@herewinner.com
29 pirtue01@the.kagos.com
24 phpromotions@hotmail.com
23 offers@consumertoday.dbhits.com
21 offers@branddirections.dbhits.com
20 lhx99030117@163.com
18 advancedmedicine@msn.com
16 youngdoctors@msn.com
15 microsale@gmx.net
14 buy.com_offers@buy.com
12 Sweepsgame@mail.apstarweb.com
11 getmyprize@getmyprize.com
 7 youask4it2@15.bluerocketonline.com
```

```
6 mikee@alcohol-sermon.com
3 help@camcontacts.net
3 gypsie@msn.com
2 freedom987ah@yahoo.com
2 cialis0@lycos.com
```

REVERSING THE SPAM-BOT SPIGOT

Now that we've covered the intricate architectures of how robotic automated collection agents troll for addresses 7×24×365, let's get to the fun part of how to incorporate a few other defensive measures against their assaults. The simplest and most logical tactic is to feed the spam bots what they want: addresses for their database. Who says the address they get need to be real ones?

The hard part is determining when you have a live spam-bot on the line with you. A few of the defensive techniques covered next can help determine this, usually through only empirical or traffic analysis in lieu of anything overt. As is their nature, the spam trafficking organizations do everything they can to minimize their footprint, their length of stay, and any indication that they were there at all. But they do leave a trace, and to get their messages sent, they need to make a connection at some point. It's by finding these traces that we can detect them best.

The Reverse Dictionary Defense

First, because we haven't discussed it in many chapters, we wanted to give you a brief on one method spammers use to test for known good accounts: the trolling method. By connecting to your mail server, a spam-testing tool can use a variety of means to guess the nature of the accounts found on your system. In short, a connection is made and after an initial handshake, the spam troller will attempt to iterate though a huge dictionary of short, simple names (such as Bob, Alice, Bill, Tom, Tim, John…, you get the idea) awaiting a response from the server on each. Some procedures glob all of the addresses in one giant header, others use separate connections, and still others operate by blending the two together.

These trolling reconnaissance attempts (also called *dictionary attacks*) can be defeated by checking for a common set of nonexistent usernames. For instance, let's say you establish five addresses as traps for the spammers—accounts that don't exist on your system, but could look like easy pickings to an automated spam-bot (say, Bill, Susan, Donna, Jerry, and Pat).

Once these addresses have been established, you would need to monitor their inboxes, which should be overflowing with spam in as little as a few weeks. The good thing about using a "spam trap" such as this one is that you can be 100 percent certain about its contents. There aren't going to be any false negatives or false positives for that matter. It's *all* spam and can be treated as such.

One good thing to do with collected spam is to process it using your Bayesian classifier. This process, too, can be automated using system-level tools, with a potentially good long-term payoff for little up-front work. By automating the refresh of machine learning systems on a weekly basis, you are able keep up with the twisting and turning of the spammers as they try to out-think your defenses.

Lastly, to make this strategy much more effective, you need to "publish" the spam addresses somewhere so that the spammers can obtain them during their normal scouring runs. These "honeypot" addresses are best hidden on web pages as HTML comments or in a similar obfuscated manner so that the spammer's pick it up with their automated address-harvesting bots, but your normal readership will ignore it.

For example, with this, we can almost ensure that spam will be forthcoming to our fake user Pat:

```
<!-- mailto:pat@whereever.tld -->
```

The DDoS Detection Defense

More often than not, the normal method of spamming (shot-gunning) is often regarded as a Distributed Denial of Service (DDoS) attack and is becoming easier and easier to identify by newer security analysis tools on the market today.

What's indicative of this approach is a lot of mail traffic originating from a group of hosts, sometimes even just a single host, with a high amount of parallel traffic being transmitted all within a short period of time. Additionally, by doing some content analysis, lots of little clues are present that support the theory that spammers are behind the traffic. For instance, by regarding only the header, some techniques can detect serialization with particular fields that can be a dead giveaway that a spam-blasting application is in use. Although spam developers have had years to refine them, we've found that spam-transmitting applications still have some glaring holes. One program in particular miscalculates the offset in hours of local time from GMT (Greenwich Mean Time), which is tantamount to shooting up a flare at midnight.

Advanced defenses such as Bayesian tools can sometimes detect this kind of pattern, but only through the use of mathematics and statistics. By studying the nature of their message, (much like they study the nature of your server) you can glean an insight into how spammers operate and thus thwart them before they make a move.

What to Send Once You've Identified Them

What we expect to see in the future are advancements based along the lines of what we have covered with this chapter. Although we have only scratched the surface, we see the capabilities of the next generation of the anti-spam armada to include a set of "real-time" detection tools, near-real-time countermeasures, and long-term statistical models that can more than tilt the balance of the war toward our favor.

However, the first step is to "know thy enemy," and right now, the enemy is cloaked in darkness and fleet of foot. As we covered in Chapter 3, many efforts are underway, chiseling away at the problem; we hope to see some early work in the field during 2004.

By confidently identifying a spam source *right at the time* that it connects to your server, you are given the fundamental ability to control the spammer's actions, enough even to balance up the scales. As they connect and you know *what* they are, you can then begin to discover *who* they are and *what* they are doing. You have to be able to catch both transactions as they happen and accurately identify them for who they are to extract the best intelligence on them. The first kind of connection is made by a spam-bot harvesting for addresses. The second is when a spam transmission is attempted. The state of the art with anti-spam filtering has no correlation between the two transactions and little in the way of managing or monitoring the first one.

Assuming that problem was solved, then what? What should you do next? The answer is to take evasive action and deploy a countermeasure. Currently very few options are available in that department. We've speculated that a class of countermeasures could certainly exist, even though they might be considered unethical by some and illegal by others.

One idea is to deny them service or provide them junk by using tactics of your own. On the lighter end of the spectrum, you could provide their harvester with lots and lots of fictional addresses that go nowhere. Even better, you could look up their ISP in real-time or surf around in their DNS and provide them with fictional addresses rooted with their own domain on their own network. On the spam transmission end, you could slow down their mail transmission to a glacial crawl by responding to them in byte-seconds or even slower. You could also do live log analysis and determine the sender's IP address, which would give you lots of scary retaliatory options.

SUMMARY

In this chapter we explored some advanced techniques used by the spammers, and we projected some of the more interesting features of where we think spam fighting is going in the next few years. We built a child's spam harvesting bot and investigated a handful of good defensive maneuvers that you could take to even up the playing field. Lastly we did a little sanity checking of the systems we erected and deployed with this book and found our strategies to be most effective.

CHAPTER 16

FIGHTING SPAM DEFENSIVELY

The art of defending against unwanted e-mail goes beyond simply installing a few anti-spam programs and updating the profiles. Spam e-mail is a security threat, in that it denies availability to resources, and with a combined attack such as a spam message with a virus attachment, this threat can quickly become very serious and expensive. As with any information security-related issue, a defense-in-depth posture is required. All of the tools we covered in the previous 15 chapters of this book do a great job of managing your spam-fighting energies, but additional, basic information security techniques could exponentially increase your success.

In earlier chapters, we discussed e-mail management organization and policy, but what other network and IT management-level strategies reduce the threat spam poses to the organization? In this chapter, we discuss these strategies. Some are extreme, but most are up-and-coming spam-fighting techniques that preclude current tools and methods.

WIN BEFORE FIGHTING

In addition to implementing tools, policies, and management schemes to deal with the spam that's hitting your mail server, you can prevent spam from ever reaching the server in the first place, or even reaching your network, in many ways. Three "points of exploitation" are discussed in this section: e-mail addresses, challenge/response, and future spam fighting.

E-mail Addresses

First off, how do spammers get your e-mail address in the first place? We've discussed this briefly in Chapter 2, but here we cover both the techniques the spammers use and the strategies you can implement (as a systems administrator or user) to thwart these tactics.

Devious Methods

The price of spamming is cheap and their tools are proven in other applications. We discuss three common methods developed from other, well-established technologies: brute force, spiders, and mailing lists.

One of the most common techniques for a spammer to hit your e-mail address is similar to methods hackers use to crack passwords on user accounts: a brute-force dictionary attack. The spammer gets a domain name (yourorg.com) and begins sending mail to a "dictionary" of possible usernames. Thus, the dictionary includes: tom@yourorg.com, jane@yourorg.com, betty@yourorg.com, and so on. Never mind that tom@yourorg.com doesn't exist as a valid e-mail address; Jane and Betty just got spammed. Spammer dictionaries contain thousands upon thousands of iterations of common e-mail usernames, including all the standard aliases such as webmaster@yourorg.com, sales@yourorg.com, and more. To prove it, set up an account called bsmith@yourorg.com. We'll bet you the price of this book that within 24 hours that e-mail account will begin to receive credit, body part enlargement, and other less savory offers without anyone ever knowing the e-mail address exists.

Spammers also get e-mail addresses from spiders, automated programs that cull through thousands of web sites, newsgroups, and message boards, cataloging and storing valid e-mail addresses for later exploitation. These spiders are adapted from the same technology that allows search engines such as Google and AltaVista to catalog web pages by examining the content. These valid e-mail lists are then fed into the Big Spam Machine and the spammer is off and running. Oftentimes these lists are circulated to groups of spammers, giving them more bang for their buck.

NOTE According to a Center for Democracy and Technology study, e-mail spiders (often affectionately referred to as web page scrapers) are the e-mail harvester of choice, by 95 percent of spammers. Read more about the center's study and findings on its web site at *http://www.cdt.org/speech/spam/030319spamreport.shtml*.

Finally, spammers utilize the old, tried-and-true method of sending junk snail mail, the dreaded mailing list. Any time you sign up for "free offers," subscribe to magazines, or otherwise give your e-mail address out for any commercial transaction, there's a risk that your information will be sold and eventually end up in the hands of a spammer. Additionally, spammers themselves compile findings from their spider and brute-force methods into lists for sale to other spammers, completing the Hateful Circle of Spam.

Protecting Your Information

How do you protect your e-mail address and still utilize this almost free, unlimited communication method? It's a fine line, but next we discuss three complementary methods for keeping your e-mail address out of the hands of the forces of spam.

E-mail Aliasing One method that seems to work well is the use of e-mail aliasing. E-mail aliases are essentially pointers that front for real e-mail addresses. We discussed them briefly in Chapter 1, but here, the application is somewhat different. Instead of a functional alias for a group of people or a role (such as webmaster@yourorg.com or support@yourorg.com), you can utilize aliases for your own e-mail address and filter or abandon it if the spammers find it. For example, Tom's real e-mail address is tom@yourorg.com. He does not want this address to go out to the greater Internet, though it does appear on "offline" content, such as his business card and letterhead. Tom uses e-mail for three rather distinct purposes: work-related communication, such as communications with co-workers, vendors, and partners; personal communications, such as notes to a few friends and relatives that e-mail him at work; and finally professional groups, such as the chamber of commerce, local charities, and the like. Tom has his mail administrator set up three aliases: tomsmith@yourorg.com, tommysmith@yourorg.com, and tsmith@yourorg.com. All three of these aliases point back to tom-smith445576@yourorg.com. Mr. Smith might subscribe to a professional mailing list with the tsmith address, a family web site with tommysmith, and he might provide the tomsmith address to several vendors at an online conference. If, suddenly, Tom begins receiving spam that hits the tommysmith address, he can either automatically filter all mail coming to that address to a specific folder for later review (provided his company doesn't use one of the fine tools outlined in this book), change the alias and communicate it to the few people that should know it, or remove the alias completely. Though somewhat cumbersome, changing e-mail aliases prevents changing or abandoning your *actual* e-mail address when spam becomes too much.

E-mail Obfuscation One common method on Usenet for thwarting spiders is e-mail obfuscation. This method entails changing how your e-mail address appears so that it fools a machine but not a human. Thus, if Elvis spends a lot of time posting to Usenet and web message boards, he would configure his e-mail address to appear as elvisREMOVE@ graceMEland.com. A person reading this would know to take out *REMOVE* and *ME* if he or she wishes to send Elvis an e-mail, while a spam spider would catalog the address, as is. Though it wastes only miniscule resources of the spammer, and somewhat burdens a person wishing to send you mail, it also adequately protects your e-mail address when it's sitting out there on a web message board for months (or years). It's also a good idea never to put an e-mail address link anywhere on your web site. Use a web form with a backend Common Gateway Interface (CGI) for transmitting messages to specific groups, such as sales@yourorg.com, support@yourorg.com, and so on. This keeps your e-mail addresses protected while still allowing your customers to communicate with you.

> **TIP** One improvement on this method is being implemented on a few of the savvy web boards we visit. On the fly, the web board's posting engine converts all e-mail addresses into a JPEG image. Not only does this effectively thwart spiders, but it removes the somewhat cumbersome practice of obfuscating your e-mail address every time you post, configuring your client with an invalid e-mail address, or forgetting altogether.

Server-Side Encoding A method that's gaining popularity within server-side programming languages to include PHP, Perl, ColdFusion, and ASP is the server-side encoding of e-mail addresses, especially those that appear on web pages, such as <a mailto:> web links, message boards, and newsgroups. The basic character conversion method is similar to e-mail obfuscation, but the e-mail address actually functions without the sender having to type the address manually into their mail client. The characters of both the `mailto` tag and the e-mail address are converted into decimal encoding, rather than plain text. Thus, the hyperlink *<a href=mailto"elvis@trailerpark.com">elvis@trailerpark.com</a>* becomes this:

```
<a href=mailto:&#101;&#108;&#118;&#105;&#115;&#64;&#116;&#114;&#97;&#105;&#108;
&#101;&#114;&#112;&#97;&#114;&#107;&#46;&#99;&#111;&#109;>&#101;&#108;&#118;
&#105;&#115;&#64;&#116;&#114;&#97;&#105;&#108;&#101;&#114;&#112;&#97;&#114;&
#107;&#46;&#99;&#111;&#109;</a>
```

The bad news is that this simplified character conversion technique fools only the least advanced e-mail harvesters. Most spammer tools actually already use these sneaky methods to conceal the spammer's e-mail address, web site, and other contact information from blacklists, spam filters, and other anti-spam tools.

The advanced version of the preceding example is to wrap that encoded e-mail address in a server-side encoder that generates the e-mail address on the fly, rather than display it on the web page or within the HTML code. For example, if Elvis wanted to be contacted from his web site, but he didn't want his e-mail address on every spam CD from here to Seoul, he'd use a server-side script to produce something like this:

```
<script type="text/javascript">
//<![CDATA[
function hiveware_enkoder(){var i,j,x,y,x=
"x=\"783d22793e23344f613e3132793c363e5d233733356c37624a6d6a3d5b79792f3a386d" +
"3735373637643e34385d5d5d23666f37356875373769353634346565365363567373c6a3438" +
"2c3e36643337333367383634363737652a7c37367a2c37373e33393837643683736663876" +
"6f35336674663564333331313838363437383862713833662937382839313638366433383835" +
"3a38262835372c7936332f333466631383736363833397476333363747437753164383664373" +
"3733364377329323336a2d313a3333383431383566353737392a2a38333c7e37357a5d2367" +
"353c6b31363e663637776237346d296534792f36316469353262733664427533332931373735" +
"2a2a65383c7935383e7965372f74323776633a33747537327329373a322a37643c7a38353e" +
"283737283c643767703638732967346a3e6237313c36336a3d3831792f37326d6637646f68" +
"3837756937383c6a33372c3e633332313a382a7c34357a2c31663e7937342f743767766338" +
"3574753833732937376a2d6534362a64333c7e323767703a37732964676a3e3732363c3466" +
"6a3d3736792f38336d6638336f68333375693a343c6a31372c3e3238323133632a7c34317a" +
"2c34633e7937632f7433667663375d5d74755d233c73297a3e6a2d2834362a37673c7e3765" +
"7a3e283c7a2f67707476733463746738757533438296b296a2a3c233c6b3e6677626d29792f" +
"64696273427529312a2a3c793e792f74766374757329322a3c7a3e28283c677073296a3e31" +
"3c6a3d792f6d666f6875693c6a2c3e352a7c7a2c3e792f747663747573296a2d332a3c7e67" +
"7073296a3e333c6a3d792f6d666f6875693c6a2c3e352a7c7a2c3e792f747663747573296a" +
"2d332a3c7e3a7e7a2f747663747573296b2a3c223b793d27273b783d756e65736361706528" +
"78293b666f7228693d303b693c782e6c656e6774683b692b2b297b6a3d782e63686172436f" +
"646541742869292d313b6966286a3c3332296a2b3d39343b792b3d537472696e672e66726f" +
"6d43686172436f6465286a297d79\";y='';for(i=0;i<x.length;i+=2){y+=unescape('" +
"%'+x.substr(i,2));}y";
while(x=eval(x));}hiveware_enkoder();
//]]>
</script>
```

The rendered HTML from all that coding looks like this:

```
Test your link: elvisNO@SPAMmcgrawhill.com
```

Server-side encoding provides you with the ability to, or not to, obfuscate the display e-mail address on the page, while still protecting your address with script-wrapped encoding on the backend. See the sidebar "Server-side E-mail Encoding" for more information on server-side encoding.

Server-side E-mail Encoding

Some fine spamfighters out there have taken it upon themselves to keep the anti-spam side of the spam war one step ahead. Here are a few sites that might be of use to you if you wish to implement server-side e-mail address encoding on your web site:

- *http://jamesthornton.com/software/redirect-mailto.html*   James Thorton has several script examples on his web site, including one in Perl, OpenACS, Cold Fusion, PHP, and ASP scripting languages.

- *http://www.hiveware.com/enkoder_form.php*   We used the encoding application on the Hiveware web site to generate the JavaScript example in this chapter. Go to this link and input an e-mail address to see more of this example. Hiveware also distributes a Macintosh OS X application that does the same thing (called the Hiveware Enkoder).

- *http://www.tdavisconsulting.com/characterset.html* and *http://www.tdavisconsulting.com/spam.html*   Tony Davis maintains a web site with a partial decimal character set (the first link) and a simple e-mail link encoding form that does not wrap the encoded link in a script (the second link).

And if you doubted for a second that the spam war was an escalating arms race, we offer the following web link. It's a handy e-mail address encoder that e-mails you the encoded address and a newsletter of "the weekly Internet and e-commerce news." You'll find it at *http://www.siteup.com/encoder.html*. *Do not put your real e-mail address in this form!* Though we cannot claim for certain that this is a spammer's site, the products offered are of that "dual-use" variety that tends to set off our spam warning bells.

Nonalphabetic E-mail Addresses   The final method for protecting your e-mail address is meant to thwart the brute-force dictionary spammers and is definitely an extreme measure. Although most e-mail accounts are derived from a person's name to make the address easy to remember, some organizations and individuals are opting to change their addresses to nonsensical letter combinations or even numbers. Older netizens may remember that the online service CompuServe did this with usernames from its inception. While this may prevent legitimate senders from reaching you, in this era of smart address books and e-mail aliasing, one extreme measure may significantly reduce the amount of spam that ever touches your network.

Extreme E-mail Methods

Several somewhat extreme but common sense methods are available for protecting your e-mail address. The first is *never* to give out you address to anyone from which you do not want to receive e-mail. This advice is difficult to follow, and it does not necessarily protect your address from brute-force spamming, but it is effective, at least for a while. Alternatively, you may maintain a "pre-email" presence on one of the many free e-mail services available through such places as Yahoo! and Hotmail. These throwaway accounts can either be used as masking accounts, whereby you give out that address freely until a sender becomes "trusted," and then give out your real address, or simply used as a valid e-mail address for web and UseNet posting, registrations for web services, and the like.

Challenge/Response: The Next Weird Thing

One of the methods discussed seriously in Internet mail development circles is the use of a challenge/response system for authenticating e-mail. In Chapters 3 and 10, we discussed a product that incorporates this system. While this system can be exceedingly cumbersome to new senders, a challenge/response mail system (or some variation on the theme) may become the best and only solution to the growing spam problem, at least until the e-mail system as a whole is re-architected.

The Problem It Solves

We've spoken about how broken the e-mail system is today. Anyone can send anyone anything by simply obtaining (or guessing) someone's e-mail address. While in a snail-mail world, this is rarely dangerous and usually just annoying, the "free and open" e-mail system has cost organizations hundreds of millions of dollars in lost time and equipment to spam, viruses, worms, and other such attacks. To close this loop, the challenge/response system was developed.

Why Challenge/Response?

Going on the notion that spam comes from spammers and good e-mail only comes from legitimate senders, the challenge/response system requires initial interaction by an unknown sender with an automated system before the sender's e-mail is "verified." The simplified process works similar to this example:

1. An old school chum, Jerry, sends a mail to Tom at his e-mail address tom@yourorg.tld.
2. Tom's e-mail server receives the mail, compares the From field of the message to a list of known-good senders (essentially a whitelist).

3. Jerry's e-mail address does not appear in the whitelist, so the system sends an automated reply to Jerry directing him to a web site.
4. Jerry receives the message, goes to the web site, and has to validate that he is an actual human and not a Gigantic SpamBot Machine of Doom. Usually this entails looking at an image of numbers or a word and typing what he sees into an entry field.
5. Once confirmed, Jerry's message goes on to Tom's Inbox and Jerry is added to the whitelist.

If this were a spammer, the reply message from the server would either never register or drift off to whatever bit-bucket the spammer claims as a real e-mail address. Messages that aren't replied to are either dumped, the e-mail addresses added to a blacklist, or both. With this system, you are almost guaranteed to never receive bulk unsolicited spam—although there is one glaring hole and a few annoyances with challenge/response.

The first glaring hole is the spoofed known-good address in the From field. Often, spammers put a real address in the From field, and quite often it's a known good address. Either they spoof another address internal to your mail system (root@yourorg.com) or they actually put *your own* e-mail address in the From field. In these cases (without further configuration options), challenge/response fails. Most often, these systems are configured to whitelist all internal addresses (and possibly whole domains), as well as domains and addresses from common vendors and mail or web services (such as yahoo.com, msn.com, and others). Though most can be configured however the systems administrator sees fit, this adds to the system's overhead, considerably.

The minor annoyances are numerous. First of all, you're adding complication to a process that has been easy for several years (decades, for some of us). You enter someone's e-mail address into the To field, add a subject, type a message, and off the mail goes to its destination. Add to that the need to verify yourself, and some people won't bother (especially sales prospects, customers coming from unknown addresses, and the like). Second, as all complex systems have their hiccups, challenge/response adds another failure point to an e-mail system that is far from bug-free. Imagine a favored customer receiving hundreds of verification messages because your challenge/response system experienced a glitch. It's not something that would happen often, but is definitely a consideration. Likewise, imagine two companies that have implemented such a system trying to communicate with each other for the first time. Tom at The Weird Company sends mail to Jerry at The Happy Company. Happy's mail server sends a challenge back to Weird's that responds with a challenge message. Though most of the systems we've seen automatically add outgoing To addresses to the whitelist, this could be a possibility. Finally, an issue that has not seen a valid solution: accessibility for the disabled. Many programs for the sight-impaired user read text aloud to the user but do not interpret images. If a sight-impaired sender receives a challenge message to a sent mail, that person wouldn't be able to be verified as a legitimate sender without assistance.

While challenge/response shows some promise for a robust system, frankly Internet users aren't ready for it yet. The main problem is that most users don't understand the overall problems that spam presents to the e-mail world. Sure, they receive spam to their inboxes and it's annoying, but they don't see the big picture of billions of unwanted messages soaking up resources worldwide (and costing lots of money to control). For users on a well-developed filtered network, such as SpamBayes or SpamAssassin, they may see only a fraction of the spam that's sent to them, further adding to the perception that spam is not a problem for them and that challenge/response is a draconian measure.

Future Spam-Fighting

To address the problem of the open mail system, engineers are hard at work to develop a fully verifiable, trusted system that not only legitimizes incoming senders, but also makes bulk spammers a thing of the past. Though this seems pie-in-the-sky to those of us that are in the trenches every day tweaking filter rules, tracking down and reporting spammers, the future of spam-fighting is trusted authentication. We have high hopes for IPv6 and other efforts that fundamentally change the way the underlying network operates. A common refrain with all of them is security, first and foremost.

KEEPING YOUR OWN HOUSE CLEAN

While the spam-fighting tools presented in this book are powerful and feature-rich, the first step to fighting spam is ensuring that you are not adding to the problem. In this section we cover the four simple rules for preventing your resources from being used by spammers: closing your open relays, hardening all hosts and servers, restricting access, and sniffing out spyware.

Open Relays

The main problem to the ongoing spam-fighting campaign is the open e-mail relay. In earlier chapters, we discussed DNSBLs that track and block mail from open relays, but how do you close your mail exchanger to spammers? In this section, we discuss how to secure mail relaying for Sendmail 8.12 and Microsoft Exchange 2000. Both of these mail servers deny relaying by default; however, certain configuration options allow some flexibility for mail exchange that may be required in your environment.

Sendmail

We chose Sendmail 8.12 for this chapter because this release was the first to deny relaying by default. All versions since 8.9 also deny relaying out-of-the-box. Although previous releases could be hacked to deny relays, the process was cumbersome and a bit arcane. For more information on Sendmail versions and anti-spam features, refer to *http://www.sendmail.org*.

Sendmail added several relaying features to its configuration files and rulesets to allow a mail administrator very specific or very general relaying practices. We cover a generic setup here, but for complex setups, such as for an ISP or other site where multiple offsite or off-domain relaying occurs, consult the sendmail web site or documentation.

With sendmail, you can relay an entire domain, relay based on mail exchanger records, relay messages based on the local or mail From field or based on an access-approved database that you configure. We cover the access-approved database in this chapter.

 Note that implementing custom anti-relaying rules could tie up resources both on your network and mail server as well as others. Many of these rules rely on domain or user lookups and may create additional communications traffic between mail servers, DNS servers, firewalls, and the like. Be sure you understand your own configuration and the configurations of other mail servers before you implement these types of rules.

For our purposes, we're going to stick with the blanket default deny relay feature for all networks outside ours. To micro-manage the senders, hosts, domains, and networks that we allow or deny to relay through our exchanger, we used the access_db feature. Though the access_db is akin to a standard white/blacklist feature available on most anti-spam tools, the importance of sendmail's implementation is that messages are accepted or rejected *before* the mail exchanger processes the mail. Sendmail checks the information provided by the sender during the connection session, applies its access database rules to the envelope and connection information, and then relays, denies, or otherwise dispositions the mail as directed by the access database.

Setting Up Your Access Database   To set up an access database for sendmail, you must create a flat text file in your favorite editor listing the users, hosts, e-mail addresses, domains, and/or networks you wish to check and the actions you wish the access_db feature to take when it finds a match. Then you must use makemap to create a database map used by the keyed map lookups, essentially allowing sendmail to interpret the data in the database. Keep in mind that, by default, all users, hosts, domains, and networks outside your own are denied relay, unless you've implemented other features or configuration options.

First create the text file of triggers or keys and actions. The format for each line is KEY<whitespace>ACTION. We've created an example file here to illustrate the formatting and permutations of the various options and actions:

```
elvis@bigcheeseman.tld RELAY
fatheadspammer.tld REJECT
niceguy.fatheadspammer.tld OK
IPv6:4:5:6:7:8:9:10 OK
192.168.200 DISCARD
192.168.150.22 ERROR:"550 Get out of here you UBERSPAMMER"
```

In this example, the following occurs:

- Any mail from elvis@bigcheeseman.tld is automatically relayed.
- Any mail from the fatheadspammer.tld domain is rejected and sendmail replies to the sender with a general-purpose message.

- Any mail from the host niceguy.fatheadspammer.tld is deemed okay, even if the host is rejected by other rules in the running ruleset. Thus, this rule excepts the previous rule to reject all mail from fatheadspammer.tld.
- All messages from the IPv6 network 4:5:6:7:8:9:10:* are OK.
- All e-mail traffic for the network 192.168.200.* is not only denied relay, it's discarded without a reply.
- Mail from the host 192.168.150.22 is denied relay, and a reply with the indicated message is sent.

Once you've created your access database, you must create a map file using `makemap`. Using our example, this command creates the map_access file in /etc/mail/:

```
makemap hash /etc/mail/access < /etc/mail/access
```

When your access_db file is ready, you're next step is to configure sendmail to use it.

Configuring Sendmail To set up the access_db feature, edit the sendmail.mc file (or the .mc file for your sendmail implementation) and add the following line before the MAILER section:

```
FEATURE(`access_db', `has -T<TMPF> /etc/mail/access_map')
```

Note that the single quote before `access_db` is the grave accent or backward apostrophe (`) located in the upper-left corner of your keyboard (it shares the tilde key).

Once this line is added, make your sendmail.cf file by typing:

```
# m4 sendmail.mc > sendmail.cf
```

If this command is successful, you'll be returned to the command prompt with no messages. Restart sendmail using the new config file and you're off and running. For more information about using m4 and other sendmail features, check out *http://www.sendmail.org*.

Microsoft Exchange

Microsoft Exchange 5.0 and earlier versions have no provision for preventing unauthorized relay of e-mail through the SMTP gateway. Starting with version 5.5, Exchange allows you to allow or deny networks and hosts (by domain name or IP) to relay mail through the gateway. We cover Exchange 2000 in this section, but these methods also work for Exchange 2003. For more information about securing mail relays on Microsoft Exchange, refer to the Microsoft TechNet site at *http://www.microsoft.com/technet/*.

NOTE Though we don't cover Exchange 5.5 here, an excellent article giving step-by-step instructions for configuring and testing Exchange mail relays by Joseph Neubauer is on the Windows Network web site at *http://www.winnetmag.com/MicrosoftExchangeOutlook/Article/ArticleID/7696/MicrosoftExchangeOutlook_7696.html*.

Securing Mail Relays on Microsoft Exchange 2000 Exchange 2000 allows for a flexible SMTP mail relaying configuration, accepting or denying e-mail based on IP address, network, and/or domain name. Authenticated users can override these restrictions, reducing the effects of a misconfiguration.

To access the Relay Restrictions configuration, open the Exchange System Manager and navigate to your SMTP virtual server in the Administrative Groups/*AdminGroup*, where *AdminGroup* is your administrative group. Right-click the virtual server and choose Properties.

Under the Access tab, you may allow connections to the SMTP virtual server by clicking the Connections button or restrict connections to the mail server by clicking the Relaying button.

The Relay Restrictions window allows you to allow or deny relay access to networks or hosts by IP address or domain name. Simply click the Only The List Below radio button, and then click the Add button to add allowed hosts. Click the Allow All Computers That Successfully Authenticate radio button to ensure that all known-good hosts on your network are allowed relay access, regardless of the restrictions configured.

Securing Your Resources

Any computer connected to the Internet is a potential spam target, and not just on the receiving end. Even if you've secured your open e-mail relays, individual hosts on your network pose an inviting and free resource for potential spammers. With the advanced payloads currently carried by virus-spam combinations and spyware, it would not take much innovation to embed a web or mail server kit, allowing the spammer to serve up illicit web pages or exchange a flood of spam bound for victims elsewhere. In this section we discuss three areas to consider when securing your resources from spammer exploitation.

Hardening Your Hosts

Individual computers present an inviting target for computer criminals, especially spammers. Not only do they offer ready resources to further the criminal's processing needs, they also present a wealth of information about the user, the organization, and other, more attractive resources, on the organization's network. All of this information represents real value to the spammer. In the following sections, we present a few common sense methods to prevent or deter spammers from using your host computers as spam machines.

Secure A host computer runs a myriad of programs and services, each with its own associated vulnerabilities. Chief among these is the standard operating system services and kernel. While we leave debates about the most secure operating system to other, more flammable forums, the following common sense hardening methods should apply to any computer running any operating system.

- **Disable unneeded services** All operating systems and many applications run services in the background that the user never sees. While many of them are legitimate, such as those controlling local sharing protocols and the like, most are unneeded and often insecure. Review the OS configuration of your host computers and disable or remove unneeded services. This includes any and all "server" services, such as personal web servers, file transfer services, and any service that could be available to the Internet.

- **Control application installation**   Users want to install applications. Often there is a productivity need to have an application, but sometimes the user installs an application on his local host to test something he's working on, to evaluate the program, or just for fun. Create definitive policies concerning installation of applications that may allow outside users to exploit vulnerabilities. Back up these policies with access control tools on the host itself and through your network security posture.

- **Scan for open ports**   Every network available service requires a port to facilitate communication between the server application and the client connecting to the service. For example, a web server commonly listens for web browser connections on port 80 and 443 (HTTPS.) Individual client computers should rarely (if ever) need to run any application that requires a listening port for communications (exceptions to this rule include Microsoft networking). All computers that host such services should be secured in your network DMZ. Use port-scanning tools such as Nmap to check your host computers regularly for unauthorized listening services.

- **Store data securely**   Data is the lifeblood of anyone using a computer, whether it's pictures of your grandchildren or a report for work. Your personal and organizational data has value to you and to potential intruders, including spammers. While spammers rarely go to the trouble of hacking into systems for e-mail addresses, virus trojan payloads, spyware, and the like are specifically created to shuttle your data to criminals that use it for their own ends. As a best-practices policy, store all data on a file server within a secure network. In this manner, when a trojan or similar exploit gains access to your host, there is nothing to steal. If storing data on a server is not possible, consider encrypting all data or sensitive data on your hard drive, accessible only by password. While this can be a cumbersome process, it is the best way to thwart a potential breach. Also in support of this objective of availability, keep regular backups. Identify what data is important, back it up to archive media and circulate that to an offsite facility in the event of a catastrophe. The old saw "no backup, no restore" is now more critical than ever.

- **Keep a base configuration**   Finally, when you've built a secure installation of an operating system, install this base configuration to all hosts on your network. You can accomplish this in many ways, from step-by-step installation guides to a single host operating system image (using Ghost or DriveImage or similar utilities) used on all host computers.

- **Remove any programs you aren't using**   Especially sample CGI programs that come with web servers. The sample form mail script that came with your web server might include a bug that allows spammers to use your web server to send their mail.

Monitor   As any security expert will tell you, you can't protect anything if you don't know where it is, what it's supposed to do, and what it's actually doing. Monitoring network and host activity is a broad subject, quite beyond the scope of this spam book, but these few simple guidelines (and a lot more reading) can give you the edge on spammers.

- **Intrusion detection/prevention systems**   Many network and host intrusion detection/prevention systems are available to combat not only general attacks to your resources, but also specific threats, such as those used by spammers. While every individual host does not require its own monitoring, consider a network intrusion system that constantly monitors incoming and outgoing traffic. All of these systems provide configuration for alerts based on anomalous outgoing network traffic. If you know that all of your mail services should originate from your DMZ, a network intrusion detection system could be your first line of reporting when a host has been compromised and has an illicit mail server running on it. Host-based intrusion detection (usually in concert with a centralized reporting system) can alert you to unauthorized access, services, and other compromises, usually in real-time. Snort is an example of a network intrusion detection system, and Tripwire is an example of a host-based intrusion detection system.

- **Firewalls**   Network and host firewalls prevent and allow network traffic to and from your networks and hosts. A proper firewall configuration, along with definitive network segmenting, can prevent illicit services, such as a spammer's rootkit, from turning your resources into free processing for computer criminals.

- **The human factor**   While often disregarded, the person who sits in front of the computer for eight (or more!) hours a day is usually the best indicator that all is not well. Implement an organization-wide incident response procedure and advertise it to all users. When a user knows that her computer is not "acting right," she can do the monitoring work for you.

Respond   The most successful exploits are those that are allowed to happen, even with all the best prevention and monitoring procedures and tools in place. Develop and use a rigorous response procedure for all incidents on your computing resources, including automated responses available with many information security tools and a manual procedure for stopping exploits in their tracks. There is no quicker way to find your network on a real-time black hole list than to allow a spammer a few hours of intimate control of your information resources.

SPYWARE: ANOTHER SPAM PATHWAY

Spyware consists of programs that are installed on a computer without the user's explicit permission that monitor and report on activity or other data on the computer. Spyware is also known as adware, trojan horses, and $%#$$#@ web pop-ups. While many spyware programs are truly illicit, several legitimate programs, such as Microsoft Media Player, Real Media Player, and others, also collect information on user actions (DVD movies watched, MP3 music files opened, and so on) and surreptitiously report this information to a remote server. While this may be an innocuous exchange of information for the benefit of the user, it is still network communication that the user did not specifically allow and the vendor did not explicitly disclose (or perhaps it did, hidden in the fine print of the license agreement you clicked past). In most security profiles, this is a trojan horse program. In this section we cover the illicit version of these programs, their operation, potential exploits, and methods for preventing them from contributing to the spam problem.

Pop-ups: The New Spam

In the early days of the web, considerable energy was paid to developing "push" technology. The power of the web at that time was that a user saw only information that was specifically clicked. Those golden days of the web are far behind us, of course. Now when you open a web site, even one as legitimate as CNN, you can expect at least one web pop-up to appear. The best of them appear behind your main web browser. The nightmare pop-ups continue ad infinitum and may just install a handy trojan on your system so that you can receive these "important messages" even when you aren't browsing the web.

Several programs exist to stop pop-ups of all kinds and range from free host-based squashers to quite expensive enterprise-level applications. Most modern browsers have features that can be turned on to squelch those noisy pop-ups. While most virus-scanning programs do not stop "adware" programs such as Gator from installing on your system, you can configure your web browser to deny downloading automatically the Java-based cookies these trojans use to install on your system.

Another form of pop-up spam has recently been plaguing Windows users who connect their systems directly to the Internet. This one uses the Windows Messenger Service that's a standard part of Windows Networking. (Note that this is not the same thing as Windows Messenger or MSN Messenger instant messaging clients.) On most Windows networks, this text-based pop-up service is of benefit because it lets you know that your print job is done or that backups have been completed, or it lets a systems administrator send a network-wide notice (for example, that a server is about to go offline). Unfortunately, it also requires no authentication and is anonymous over the Internet, so spammers have started using it to get their messages across.

To prevent abuse of the Messenger Service, you can either use a firewall that blocks the port used by Windows Messenger Service (port 135), disable the service completely, or do both. We recommend both, unless you're on a corporate network and disabling the service would impact the support of your network in a negative way, in which case you should block the port on your perimeter. In fact, given the vulnerabilities exploited by the Blaster worm and others, we recommend that you block all Windows Networking ports (ports 135 through 139) at your perimeter. You shouldn't need to use Windows Networking over the Internet. If you do, use a virtual private network (VPN) instead.

Disabling the Messenger Service in Windows 2000 and Windows XP

You can learn how to disable the Messenger service in Windows 2000 by consulting the following web site: *http://www.microsoft.com/windows2000/techinfo/administration/communications/msgrspam.asp*.

And in Windows XP, consult *http://www.microsoft.com/windowsxp/pro/using/howto/communicate/stopspam.asp*.

If you're running Windows 98 or ME, you're out of luck: The Messenger Service cannot be disabled on these versions of Windows.

Using Internet Connection Firewall to Stop Messenger Service Spam

Windows XP comes with Internet Connection Firewall (ICF), which can be used to prevent incoming Messenger Service spam or attacks. Starting with Windows XP Service Pack 1, ICF blocks all incoming unicast, multicast, and UDP traffic on specific network connections that have ICF turned on.

Various implementations and considerations are covered in the following article on the Microsoft support web site: *http://support.microsoft.com/?kbid=330904*.

True Spyware

Actual spyware is used as a marketing tool for those Internet leech companies that can't figure out a more legitimate way to make a buck. While you surf the Web, these programs monitor the sites you visit and report back to a central server what pages you viewed and how long you spent there. Many, like Gator, also pop up mini-advertisements related to the sites you visit, as you visit them. While no confirmed spyware programs actually pick up your e-mail address, once such a program is on your system, it doesn't take a huge jump in functionality to snag both your address and all those others in your address book. Most anti–pop-up programs disable or remove spyware, as well, and most anti-virus programs detect and quarantine or delete true trojan horse programs (spyware's more evil twin). If you have become infected with these programs, the only other solution is to wipe your hard drive clean and reinstall from scratch.

Anti-Spyware Tools

Anti-spyware tools scan your browser cache, memory, system registry, hard drives, and removable drives for various spyware. Most of these programs also block web and spyware pop-up adds that we all love so much. Most also function similar to anti-virus packages that should be familiar, operating either in a passive/manual mode, whereby you initiate a scan on your system, or in "active" mode, where the software actually detects the spyware in-flight, stops it, and asks you to decide whether to install it or not. After detecting the spyware components, all anti-spyware systems delete or quarantine the offending programs.

Ad-aware 6.0 from Lavasoft

We cover only one of a sea of anti-spyware systems out there: Ad-aware from Lavasoft. This program is available from the Lavasoft web site for free (noncommercial use), though the anti–pop-up feature is available only if you pay for it. Download the current version of Ad-aware from *http://www.lavasoftusa.com*.

Installing Ad-aware 6.0   Perform these steps for Ad-aware installation success:

1. Double-click aaw6.exe. The Ad-aware 6 Personal window appears.
2. Click Next, read and agree to the license agreement, and click Next, again. The Destination Location window appears.
3. Choose a destination on your hard drive and click the Next button. The Start Installation window appears.
4. Click the Next button, and Ad-aware begins installation.
5. Once installation is done, the Ad-aware main window appears, as shown in Figure 16-1.

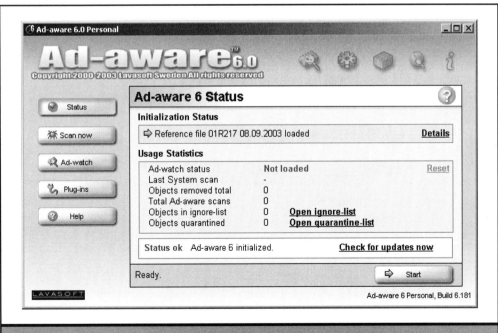

Figure 16-1.   The Ad-aware main window

Using Ad-aware   Ad-aware's use is pretty straightforward. The main window defaults to a status report, showing you the initialization status and usage statistics, including last system scan, objects removed total, total ad-aware scans, objects in ignore-list, and objects quarantined.

From the main screen, you can view and use the following features:

- **Initialization status details**   Click the Details link to view the current reference file loaded (Figure 16-2). The reference file contains the profiles of spyware in the wild that Ad-aware detects and quarantines. This file can be updated from the main screen by clicking the Check For Updates Now link.

- **Open Quarantine List**   Clicking this link allows you to view, delete, or restore any quarantined spyware (Figure 16-3). If you click an auto-quarantine file from the Quarantined Objects window, you can view the individual files in the quarantine group, as shown here.

- **Check for Updates Now**   Clicking this link allows you to check Lavasoft for updated profiles for Ad-aware, as shown next. Click the Connect button, and Ad-aware alerts you if there are updates available and gives you the option to install them.

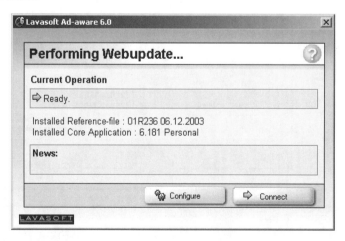

Chapter 16: Fighting Spam Defensively

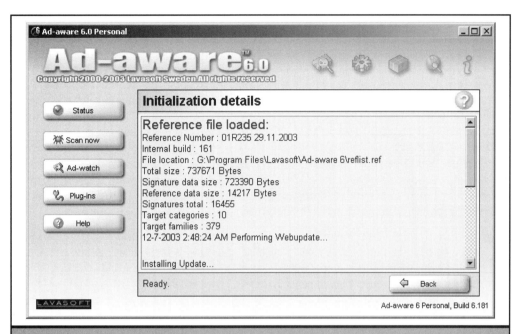

Figure 16-2. Details of the reference files installed on your software

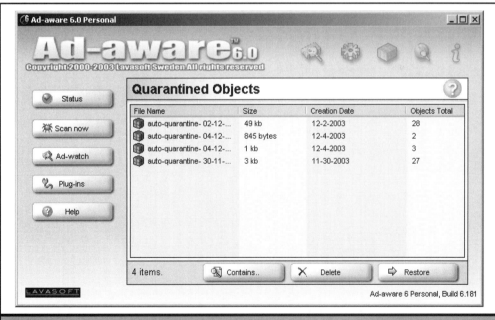

Figure 16-3. View the quarantined items and delete or restore them.

- **Scan Now** This is the meat and potatoes of Ad-aware. Click the Scan Now button and you're presented with a few options. You can perform a smart scan, a custom scan, or select individual files or folders to scan. Click the Next button to start your scan, and you'll see a window showing you what Ad-aware is doing.

Handling Detected Objects Once Ad-aware finishes its scan, you have to tell it what to do with the evil it's detected on your system. The program displays a flashing red spider and the number of objects detected (see Figure 16-4).

Click the Next button to view the objects (see Figure 16-5). Each item lists the vendor, type, category, object, and a brief description if available. To quarantine the objects, place a check mark next to the desired objects and then click the Next button. All items are quarantined.

NOTE When Ad-aware finishes its scan, it emits a horrible noise when it has detected spyware on your system. If you have heart problems or are easily startled, be sure to disable the sound by clicking the gear icon (Settings) in the upper-right corner of the main window, and then click the Tweak settings button and the Misc. Settings tree. Click Play Sound If Scan Produced A Result to change the green checkmark to a red X. Then click the Proceed button.

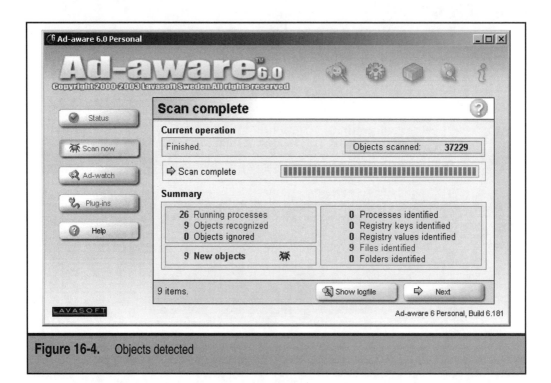

Figure 16-4. Objects detected

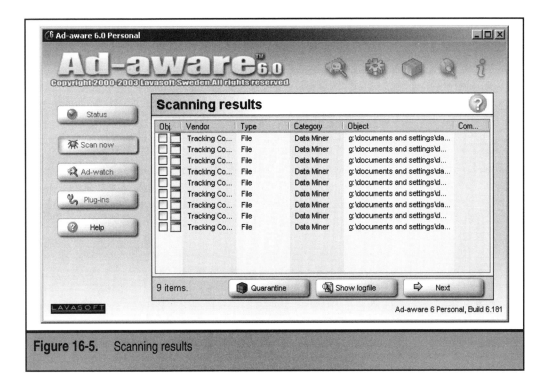

Figure 16-5. Scanning results

SUMMARY

In this chapter, we talked about various strategies, outside of your anti-spam tools, for combating spam before it actually reaches you, including protecting your e-mail addresses, keeping your own mail server resources out of the hands of the spammers, and protecting your hosts and other computers on your network from becoming zombie spam-spewers. Finally, we discussed spyware, its new convergence with spammer tools, and anti-spyware programs that protect you from that threat.

GLOSSARY

DEFINITIONS AND ACRONYMS

adware   Programs installed on a computer, often surreptitiously, that generate pop-up ads. Adware is often bundled with *spyware*.

Bayesian analysis   A probability-based statistical theory and method invented in the eighteenth century by the Reverend Thomas Bayes. It started being used in anti-spam tools after Paul Graham released his August 2002 article, "A Plan for Spam."

Bayesian classifier   An anti-spam tool that uses Bayesian analysis to classify e-mail as either spam or nonspam. It does this based on probabilities after learning what spam and nonspam look like.

blacklist   A group of e-mail addresses from which you never want to accept mail.

challenge/response anti-spam tools   These tools automatically reply back to an unknown sender's e-mail message, asking the sender to reply to the message, fill out a web page, or do any other number of tasks to prove they are a real person and not an automated bulk e-mailer. Once the sender replies, the e-mail will go through.

checksum   An alphanumeric value generated by running a message through a hashing algorithm. The value generated is smaller than the original message and is one-way (that is, the content of the original message cannot be gleaned from the hash). Small changes in the message will produce different checksums, so hashes are often used in authentication to determine whether a file or message has changed. Popular hashing algorithms are MD5 and SHA1.

CVS   The Concurrent Versioning System (CVS) is the file tree that developers use to write code and make changes to programming projects. It allows them to check-in and check-out of modified code.

DNS   The Domain Name Service (DNS) maps IP addresses to host and domain names, and vice versa. DNS servers run DNS software to perform this translation and make up the Internet's DNS architecture.

DNSBL   A DNS Blacklist (DNSBL) is an IP or domain blacklist of known spammers, suspected spammers, or open relays and open proxies. The blacklist uses the DNS (Domain Name Service) architecture, allowing for a distributed model that multiple clients can use.

FQDN   A Fully Qualified Domain Name (FQDN) is a host's complete domain name address, including the hostname and domain name—for example, *hostname.mydomain.tld*.

headers   The part of an e-mail message, usually at its beginning, that contains the routing information for the message, the sender and recipient, the subject, and any extra application-specific flags or tags (priority, Mail/Message User Agents, and so on). Users normally see only a few of these headers unless they configure their mail client to reveal them.

IMAP   The Internet Message Access Protocol (IMAP) is a protocol used by mail clients to read e-mail from a mail server. It's a newer protocol than POP (Post Office Protocol) and supports additional features. As with POP, the version number is appended, so you'll often see the latest version referred to as IMAP4.

malware   For *malevolent software*, a general term for programs that intentionally cause harm to a computer system. Viruses, worms, and Trojans are examples. Recently the definition has expanded to include spyware.

MIME   Multipurpose Internet Mail Extensions (MIME) is a standard that states how nontext messages are to be formatted when sent over the Internet. E-mail attachments, for instance, are sent using MIME. MIME is also commonly used by web browsers to display nontext or HTML parts of web pages.

MTA   Mail Transfer Agent (MTA) is the mail server software that transfers e-mail between servers and delivers it to the user's mailbox. MTAs include sendmail, postfix, and Exchange.

MUA   Mail User Agent (MUA) is the mail client software that allows an individual user to send and receive mail. MUAs include Outlook, Eudora, and Pine.

MX   A mail exchanger (MX) record is a record in DNS that lists to which server e-mail for a particular domain should be delivered.

open proxy   A *proxy* is a network device or server that makes a connection to a network resource for an end user, rather than the end user making the connection directly to the resource. Correctly configured proxies limit who can connect to them. Open proxies, however, allow any user to connect to them from anywhere and go to any resource. Spammers use this because it allows them to hide behind the proxy server.

open relay   A mail server that allows an anonymous third-party to relay or send messages through it—that is, neither the sender nor the receiver is a local user on the mail server. Spammers often use open relays to hide where they're coming from.

POP   Post Office Protocol (POP) is a protocol used by mail clients to read e-mail from a mail server. Sometimes the version number is appended. The latest version, for instance, is referred to as POP3.

RFC   Request for Comments (RFCs) are Internet Engineering Task Force (IETF) papers that make up the policies and procedures for the Internet at large. RFCs can apply to protocols, sysadmin procedures, system or router configurations, or user behavior. They're not "laws" and are therefore not mandatory, but following them is considered a best practice and good behavior.

SMTP   Simple Mail Transfer Protocol (SMTP) is the protocol used by mail servers to send mail to each other. It's also used by mail clients to send mail to mail servers.

spam   A common term for unsolicited commercial bulk e-mail. Named *spam* for its repetitive, loud, nonsensical nature, which is drawn from a Monty Python comedy skit in which people drown out conversation by singing "spam, spam, spam, spam, spammity spam...." Not to be confused with the trademarked canned meat product from Hormel.

spyware   Programs installed on a computer, often surreptitiously, that monitor and report on web surfing activity or other data on the computer. Spyware is often bundled with *adware*.

SSL   Secure Sockets Layer (SSL) is a common method of encrypting connections between computers at the application layer—for instance, between a web server and web browser, or a mail server and a mail client.

tarball   UNIX lingo for a file or directory archive created by the *tar* utility.

TLD   Top Level Domain (TLD) is the part of the domain name that appears farthest to the right; for example, *.com*, *.net*, *.org*, *.us*, and *.info*. TLDs are controlled by TLD registrars.

UBE   Unsolicited bulk e-mail (UBE) are e-mails, typically sent in bulk, that the recipient did not request. Sometimes UBE is used synonymously with UCE (unsolicited commercial e-mail), but some people make the distinction that UBE might not necessarily contain advertisements.

UCE   Unsolicited commercial e-mail (UCE) are e-mail advertisements typically sent in bulk that the recipient did not request. In other words, UCE is junk mail.

USENET   Also called Internet newsgroups, USENET is a large, distributed collection of forums covering a multitude of topics—such as computers (*comp.**), science (*sci.**), and everything else (*alt.**). USENET is widely credited as being the birthplace of the term *spam* to mean commercial postings. Unfortunately, USENET has waned in popularity (in part due to the proliferation of spam), though it still remains a viable information resource.

whitelist   A group of trusted e-mail addresses from which you always want to accept mail.

APPENDIX A

SELECTED ANTI-SPAM RESOURCES

E-MAIL AND SPAM-RELATED RFCS

A Request for Comments (RFC) is a loose Internet standard as set forth by the Internet Engineering Task Force (IETF). RFCs govern the way the Internet works and the way people behave on the Internet. RFCs are generally considered to be guidelines and best-practices rather than rules, though adhering to them helps ensure the smooth flow of communication on the Internet. The following table details the RFCs related to spam and e-mail.

RFC Number	URL	Description
RFC 821	http://www.faqs.org/rfcs/rfc821.html	Simple Mail Transfer Protocol (SMTP) Older version of the SMTP RFC, but often referred to
RFC 954	http://www.faqs.org/rfcs/rfc954.html	NICNAME/WHOIS
RFC 2142	http://www.faqs.org/rfcs/rfc2142.html	Mailbox Names for Common Services, Roles, and Functions
RFC 2505	http://www.faqs.org/rfcs/rfc2505.html	Anti-Spam Recommendations for SMTP MTAs
RFC 2635	http://www.faqs.org/rfcs/rfc2635.html	DON'T SPEW: A Set of Guidelines for Mass Unsolicited Mailings and Postings (spam)
RFC 2821	http://www.faqs.org/rfcs/rfc2821.html	Simple Mail Transfer Protocol (SMTP) Replaces RFC 821
RFC 3098	http://www.faqs.org/rfcs/rfc3098.html	How to Advertise Responsibly Using E-Mail and Newsgroups

PAPERS, WHITEPAPERS, AND TREATISES

The following table lists papers, whitepapers, and treatises dealing with the theory of spam-fighting. Some of these theories have made their way into actual practice.

Title	URL	Description
The Next Step in the Spam Control War: Greylisting	http://projects.puremagic.com/greylisting/	Evan Harris' paper on greylisting, a cross between blacklisting and whitelisting.
A Plan for Spam	http://www.paulgraham.com/spam.html	Paul Graham's forward-thinking paper on fighting spam using Bayesian analysis. This paper is widely credited with starting the Bayesian revolution in anti-spam tools.

SPAM AND THE LAW

This next table details resources for not only fighting spam but also for bulk e-mailers who wish to follow the law.

Legal Resource	URL	Description
Spam Laws Web Site	http://www.spamlaws.com/	A collection of spam legislation from the U.S. and around the globe, compiled by Internet privacy lawyer David E. Sorkin
Spam Legislation Likely to Pass; Will It Work?	http://maccentral.macworld.com/news/2003/05/26/spamlegislation/	MacCentral, 05/26/2003, an article on the effectiveness of anti-spam legislation
The Harris Poll® #75, December 10, 2003—Spam Keeps on Growing	http://www.harrisinteractive.com/harris_poll/index.asp?PID=424	A poll on public attitudes towards spam, spammers, and spam laws

DNS BLACKLISTS

DNS Blacklists (DNSBLs) are a collaborative spam-fighting tool. Blacklists include the IP addresses and domains of known spammers, open relays, and open proxies and are accessed via the DNS protocol by e-mail clients and servers. This table lists the DNSBLs covered in this book.

Blacklist	URL
Open Relay Database (ORDB)	http://www.ordb.org/
Mail-Abuse Prevention System (MAPS)	http://www.mail-abuse.org/
SpamCop	http://www.spamcop.net/
Distributed Server Boycott List (DSBL)	http://www.dsbl.org/
SpamHaus	http://www.spamhaus.org/
Not Just Another Bogus List (NJABL)	http://www.njabl.org/
RFC Ignorant (RFCI)	http://www.rfc-ignorant.org/

SPAMASSASSIN RESOURCES

The following table lists some of the available SpamAssassin resources.

SpamAssassin Resource	URL	Description
SpamAssassin	http://www.spamassassin.org/	Home page for the open-source distribution of SpamAssassin.
	http://news.spamassassin.org/	News site.
Rule Writing HOWTO	http://mywebpages.comcast.net/mkettler/sa/SA-rules-howto.txt	Matthew Kettler's SpamAssassin rule writing HOWTO.
Exit0 SpamAssassin Wiki	http://www.exit0.us/index.php	A site where SpamAssassin users can add their own custom rules for others to use. A great place to look for rules that might not exist in the SpamAssassin base ruleset. Provides links to other rules sites as well.
William Stearn's SpamAssassin Blacklist	http://www.stearns.org/sa-blacklist/	William Stearns manually updates a blacklist for use with SpamAssassin.

E-MAIL CLIENTS

E-mail clients—also called Mail User Agents (MUAs)—are what many users think about when they think about e-mail. The following table describes the e-mail clients covered in this book.

E-Mail Client	URL	Description
Microsoft Outlook	http://office.microsoft.com/home/default.aspx	Outlook comes with Microsoft Office and is generally considered an anti-spam solution for corporate or power users.
Microsoft Outlook Express	http://www.microsoft.com/windows/ie/default.asp	OE comes with Internet Explorer and is generally considered an anti-spam solution for home users.
Eudora	http://www.eudora.com/	Eudora is a classic e-mail client for Windows and Macintosh computers. It comes in full (paid), sponsored (free, with ads), and light (free, but limited features) versions.
Mozilla Mail	http://www.mozilla.org/products/mozilla1.x/	Mozilla Mail is part of the Mozilla browser suite.

E-Mail Client	URL	Description
Mozilla Thunderbird	http://www.mozilla.org/products/thunderbird/	Mozilla Thunderbird is a stand-alone e-mail client (that is, you don't have to download the Mozilla browser) available from the Mozilla folks.

E-MAIL SERVERS

E-Mail Servers—also called Mail Transfer Agents (MTAs)—are the way e-mail is routed on the Internet. The following table describes the more popular e-mail servers.

E-mail Server	URL	Description
Sendmail	http://www.senmdail.org/	The venerable and ubiquitous SMTP server for Unix and Linux systems
Postfix	http://www.postfix.org/	A modern SMTP server for Unix and Linux systems, seen as an easy-to-use alternative to Sendmail
Qmail	http://www.qmail.org/ or http://cr.yp.to/qmail.html	An SMTP server for Unix and Linux systems built for speed and security
Microsoft Exchange	http://www.microsoft.com/exchange/	Microsoft's enterprise e-mail solution for Windows servers

ANTI-SPAM CLIENT TOOLS FOR WINDOWS

The following table describes anti-spam client tools for Windows users.

Windows Client Tool	URL	Description
SpamBayes	http://spambayes.sourceforge.net	SpamBayes is a powerful open source spam filter for the Windows and Linux platforms that uses Bayesian analysis to quantify incoming messages as spam, ham (legitimate mail), or unknown.
SpamPal	http://www.spampal.org	SpamPal is an anti-spam proxy program that relies on DNS blacklist/banlist information to tag and sort suspected spam. SpamPal is available for Windows 9x/2000/XP and is compatible with any standard Post Office Protocol 3 (POP3) e-mail client, such as Eudora, Outlook/Outlook Express, and Pegasus Mail.

Windows Client Tool	URL	Description
SpamCatcher	http://www.mailshell.com/spamcatcher/download.html	Mailshell SpamCatcher is a complex e-mail filtering plug-in for Microsoft Outlook 2000/2002/XP as well as for POP3 clients, such as Eudora, Netscape Messenger, and the like. Thwarting spam by utilizing both approve and block lists and a remote algorithmic rules engine, SpamCatcher identifies, tags, and filters incoming spam. In addition to the POP client version, a SpamCatcher service is also available for web-based e-mail sites, such as Yahoo!, Hotmail, and America Online.
Lyris MailShield Desktop	http://www.mailshield.com/products/mailshield/desktop/index.html	Lyris MailShield Desktop is an e-mail proxy application that uses filtering rules, "fuzzy logic," and e-mail lists to filter incoming spam before it reaches your Inbox. Supporting POP, IMAP, and MAPI protocols as well as msn.com and Hotmail's HTML interfaces, Lyris MailShield Desktop also integrates a spam-reporting system with numerous configuration options. MailShield Desktop runs on Windows 98, Me, 2000, and XP and supports any POP3, IMAP, or MAPI e-mail client.
SPAMfighter	http://www.spamfighter.com	SPAMfighter is a distributed anti-spam solution that relies on individual users to update a central server with known spam messages. SPAMfighter is available for Windows 98/Me/2000/XP and functions as a plug-in for Microsoft Outlook 2000/2002/2003 and with Outlook Express.
SpamButcher	http://www.spambutcher.com	SpamButcher is a POP3 proxy anti-spam tool that uses an unconfigurable "fuzzy logic" system to filter suspected spam. Available for Windows 95 and up, SpamButcher functions with any POP3 client application, including Outlook, Outlook Express, Eudora, Pegasus, and the like.

Windows Client Tool	URL	Description
iHateSpam	*http://www.sunbelt-software.com/product.cfm?id=930*	iHateSpam from Sunbelt Software uses heuristic processing, rules-based engines, and block/unblock lists to identify incoming spam messages. Running as an Outlook or Outlook Express plug-in, iHateSpam processes e-mail and quarantines spam outside of the mail client for further review.
SpamNet	*http://www.cloudmark.com*	Cloudmark bills SpamNet as "collaborative spamfighting." Operating as a P2P network application, users running SpamNet contribute to the anti-spam community just by deleting spam from their Inbox. Once deleted, other SpamNet users can tag these unwanted e-mails as spam. SpamNet operates on Windows 98/NT/2000/XP and works with Outlook 2000/2002/XP.
KnockKnock	*http://www.knockmail.com*	KnockKnock is a POP3 e-mail filter that manages spam using approved and denied lists with a twist. The program incorporates a challenge-password system to prevent nonsolicited e-mail from reaching you at all. KnockKnock is available for Windows $9x$/2000/XP and works with most POP3 clients, including Netscape, Outlook Express, and Eudora.
POPFile	*http://POPFile.sourceforge.net/*	POPFile is a free, open-source anti-spam tool that uses word and logic filters to classify e-mail and sort it into buckets (folders) as directed by you. POPFile is compatible with any POP e-mail client and the Windows version operates on Windows $9x$/NT/2000/XP/2003. The cross-platform version operates with any operating system that runs the Perl programming environment.

ANTI-SPAM SERVERS FOR WINDOWS

The following table describes anti-spam server solutions.

Windows Server Tool	URL	Description
iHateSpam Server Edition	*http://www.sunbelt-software.com*	iHateSpam Server Edition runs on Windows 2000 Server with Service Pack 3 or later and MS Exchange 2000 with Service Pack 3 or later and uses semantic and rules-based filtering and black/whitelists to block spam at the mail gateway.
GFI MailEssentials	*http://www.gfi.com/mes/*	MailEssentials is a Bayesian filter-based anti-spam server solution available from GFI, Inc. In addition to spam filtering, MailEssentials adds server-based e-mail tools such as global disclaimer signatures, reporting, mail archiving, and auto-replies.
Trend Micro Spam Prevention Service	*http://www.trendmicro.com*	Spam Prevention Service (SPS) is a feature-rich spam-fighting tool from Trend Micro that fights spam as a pass-through SMTP server. Instead of applying rules to e-mail already received by the mail server, SPS filters mail before it ever gets to the mail server.

ANTI-SPAM TOOLS FOR THE MACINTOSH

The following table describes anti-spam tools available for the Macintosh.

Macintosh Tool	URL	Description
PostArmor	*http://www.postarmor.com*	PostArmor is a Java-based simple mail filter that runs as a Post Office Protocol (POP), Authenticated POP (APOP), or Internet Message Access Protocol (IMAP) proxy. PostArmor is not open-source, but it is distributed for free if used as a single-machine client application.

Macintosh Tool	URL	Description
POPmonitor	http://www.vechtwijk.nl	POPmonitor is a simple e-mail management program that incorporates limited filtering, black/whitelisting and other anti-spam tool functions.
Spamfire	http://www.matterform.com/	Spamfire is a filter-based POP/IMAP/Hotmail proxy for Mac OS 9 and OS X, distributed by Matterform Media. Using scored filters that search the headers and body of messages, Spamfire matches and flags incoming e-mail before it hits your inbox.
MailGoGoGo	http://www.makienterprise.com	Our last Mac entry is the POP proxy mail filter with little to configure or manage. Distributed by the Japanese company Maki Enterprise, MailGoGoGo is a mail filter that utilizes word matching and black/whitelists to manage incoming spam e-mail. MailGoGoGo runs best on OS 9 and earlier versions.

ANTI-SPAM TOOLS FOR LINUX

The following table details the collection of Linux tools covered in this book.

Linux Tool	URL	Description
Procmail	http://www.procmail.org	The ubiquitous e-mail processor for Unix systems
Vipul's Razor	http://razor.sourceforge.net/	A collaborative, distributed anti-spam network.
Distributed Checksum Clearinghouse (DCC)	http://www.rhyolite.com/anti-spam/dcc/	A distributed anti-spam network
Bogofilter	http://bogofilter.sourceforge.net/	A Bayesian e-mail classifier for Unix systems
SpamBayes	http://spambayes.sourceforge.net/	A Bayesian e-mail classifier for Unix systems

Linux Tool	URL	Description
Quick Spam Filter (QSF)	http://www.ivarch.com/programs/qsf.shtml	A Bayesian e-mail classifier for Unix systems
The SpamBouncer	http://www.spambouncer.org/	A collection of Procmail recipes for fighting spam

OTHER TACTICS AND TOOLS

The following table lists additional tools used not only for fighting spam but also for sending spam.

Resource	URL	Description
E-mail address harvesting	http://www.cdt.org/speech/spam/030319spamreport.shtml	A Center for Democracy & Technology study about the methods used to harvest e-mail addresses.
Server-side encoding	http://www.hiveware.com/enkoder_form.php or http://jamesthornton.com/software/redirect-mailto.html	These two sites have example e-mail encoders that you can try.
	http://www.tdavisconsulting.com/characterset.html or http://www.tdavisconsulting.com/spam.html	Tony Davis's site containing more information about e-mail encoding.
Securing your mail relay	http://www.winnetmag.com/MicrosoftExchangeOutlook/Article/ArticleID/7696/MicrosoftExchangeOutlook_7696.html	This site covers securing Microsoft Exchange 5.5.
	http://www.microsoft.com/technet/	TechNet covers other versions of Microsoft Exchange.
	http://www.sendmail.org	SendMail's site contains information on the built-in anti-relaying tools in SendMail.
Anti-spyware tools and strategies	http://www.microsoft.com/windows2000/techinfo/administration/communications/msgrspam.asp	Microsoft's site tells you how to disable Windows Messenger Service, a spyware/pop-up pathway, on Windows 2000.
	http://www.microsoft.com/windowsxp/pro/using/howto/communicate/stopspam.asp	This Microsoft site tells you how to disable Windows Messenger Service on Windows XP.

Resource	URL	Description
	http://support.microsoft.com/?kbid=330904	This Microsoft site tells you how to use Internet Connection Firewall to stop Messenger Service attacks.
	http://www.lavasoftusa.com	Ad-aware from Lavasoft is a great anti-spyware tool.
Spammer tactics and tools	http://msnbc.msn.com/id/3078642/	An MSNBC article about how spammers get your e-mail addresses from legitimate businesses.
	http://www.washingtonpost.com/ac2/wp-dyn/A54888-2003Jun30	A *Washington Post* article about Gateway Learning's change of privacy protection.
	http://www.geektools.com or http://www.samspade.org	On these sites, you can look up domain information and perform traceroutes.
	http://www.spamcop.com	From this site, you can analyze e-mail headers.

U.S. GOVERNMENT SITES CONCERNING SPAM

Web Site	URL	Description
Spam E-mail: Harvesting Your E-mail Address	http://www.ftc.gov/bcp/conline/edcams/spam/index.html	The Federal Trade Commission (FTC) site for spam education and reporting.
Internet Fraud Complaint Center	http://www.ifccfbi.gov/index.asp	Run by the FBI, this center investigates fraud committed over the Internet and through e-mail.

APPENDIX B
ABOUT THE CD-ROM

For those of you who want to work along with the book, we have compiled a CD-ROM that contains

- A selection of the top anti-spam tools ready to install on your computer
- Live links to the web sites where you can access the latest versions of all the anti-spam tools mentioned in the book

HOW TO USE THE CD-ROM

After you launch the CD, you will need to agree to the terms in the End User License Agreement. Once you agree, you will see the GNU Public License. After reading the GNU Public License, click the OK button. You will then see the Python Public License. After reading the Python Public License, click the OK button, and an interface similar to the book's cover will appear within Adobe Acrobat Reader. Clicking the authors' names will take you to a page with more information about the lead authors.

In the center of the cover are two live buttons. The Tools On The CD button will take you to the tools on the CD; the Links To Additional Tools button takes you to the links to the additional tools discussed in the book. To the left of the cover, you will find bookmarks, which you can use to navigate to the different components on the CD. There, you will find information on how to use the CD and Adobe Acrobat Reader.

ANTI-SPAM TOOLS ON THE CD

We assembled a selection of the anti-spam tools discussed in the book and placed them on the CD-ROM to provide easy access for administrators who wish to download these tools directly from the CD to their system. The tools are used to prevent SPAM.

Several of the tools available on the CD are free under the GNU Public License, which is located on the CD for your review.

The Tools On The CD page includes a list of the tools on the CD, along with the latest URL for each tool, in case you need more information on how to install the tool or you want to download the most recent version online. When you click the tool name you may see a dialog that reads:

"The file D:\OPENE~14.EXE is set to be launched by this PDF file. The file may contain programs, macros, or viruses that could potentially harm your computer. Only open the file if you are sure it is safe. If this file was placed by a trusted person or program then click Open to view this file."

Click the box that reads: Do Not Show This Message Again, and click the Open button. Then, Acrobat will take you to the folder where all of the tools are located. There you will find folders for each of the tools. Double-click the tool you want to access and then you will see the actual tool file ready for you to install on your system.

Some of the programs can be used to gain unauthorized access to vulnerable systems. Our suggestion is to set up a couple of default NT, Novell, and UNIX systems in a lab and to walk through the techniques discussed in this book.

LINKS TO ADDITIONAL TOOLS

When you click the Links To Additional Tools button, it takes you to the live links for the additional tools listed in the book.

 NOTE The links contained on the CD are the latest links available at the time the book went to press.

PROBLEMS WITH THE CD

If you can not get the CD to work, you may have a defective drive or a defective CD. Be sure the CD is inserted properly in the drive. (Test the drive with other CDs to see if they run.)

If you live in the U.S. and the CD included in your book has defects in materials or workmanship, please call McGraw-Hill at 1-800-217-0059, 9 A.M. to 5 P.M. Monday through Friday, Eastern Standard Time, and McGraw-Hill will replace the defective disc. If you live outside the U.S., please contact your local McGraw-Hill office. You can find contact information for most offices on the International Contact Information page immediately following the index of this book, or you can send an e-mail to *omg_international@mcgraw-hill.com*.

Index

See Glossary for a list of definitions and acronyms.

Symbols
/ (forward slash), using with folders in iHateSpam Server Edition, 264
: (colon), using with SPS server, 279
~ (tilde)
    in Razor default configuration directory, 311
    in SpamAssassin installations, 103

Numbers
23_bayes.cf file, contents of, 115
2505 (SMTP and MTA Best Practices), RFC associated with, 28–29

abuse-related list in RFCI, features of, 77
access_db feature, configuring for sendmail, 371
access privileges policy, establishing for e-mail, 11
Ad-aware 6.0
    handling detected objects with, 380–381
    installing, 377
    using, 378–380

address harvesting component of spam machine *See also* e-mail harvester
    explanation of, 329
    resource for, 396
Adult Content Senders list in Outlook, adding senders to, 162–166
Adult e-mail filters in Outlook, configuring, 159–166
AI (artificial intelligence), fighting spam with, 7–8
all_spam_to setting in SpamAssassin, description of, 133
amavisd-new, using with SpamAssassin, 138–140
AMaViS project, origin of, 138
Ameriquest Mortgage Company, obtaining information about, 332
Analysis Setting window in MailGoGoGo, accessing, 304–305
anti-spam controls
    criteria for, 23
    strategic placement of, 21
anti-spam tools. *See also* defense by disguise techniques; DDoS detection defense; reverse dictionary defense; spam
    assessing ease of use of, 26
    assessing stability of, 25
    breadth of, 23
    depth of, 23–24
    impact of, 24
    interoperability of, 26

operation of, 24
resource for, 396–397
selecting, 22
updating, 344
anti-spyware tools, using, 376–381
Apple Developer web site, accessing, 285
application installation, controlling, 373
ASCII table, accessing, 350
ASRG (Anti-Spam Research Group), web address for, 4
AUPs (Acceptable Use Policies)
establishing for e-mail, 11
reading and reviewing, 50
authentication, explanation of, 19
authorization policy, establishing for e-mail, 11
automated learning feature of SpamAssassin, overview of, 116–117
automatic updates
configuring SPS server for, 281
scheduling with Windows Scheduled Tasks, 260–261

Bad Words, managing with MailShield Desktop, 208
Ban on Deceptive Unsolicited Bulk Electronic Mail Act of 2003, introduction of, 9
bayes_* configuration settings in SpamAssassin Bayesian classifier, descriptions of, 119–120
bayes_* files in SpamAssassin Bayesian classifier, descriptions of, 114–115
bayes_path configuration, setting, 122
Bayesian analysis, performing with SpamAssassin, 90
Bayesian Analysis Properties window in MailEssentials server, accessing, 271–272
Bayesian classifier in SpamAssassin. *See also* Bogofilter Bayesian classifier; QSF (Quick Spam Filter) Bayesian classifier; rules in SpamAssassin; SpamAssassin
automated learning feature of, 116–117
correcting mistakes with, 118
examining files in, 114–115
expiring database entries in, 119–121
guidelines for use of, 123
implementing, 114
implementing systemwide, 122
reclassifying learned messages with, 119
retraining systems with, 119
sa-learn utility in, 117
training, 117–122
training with ham messages, 118
training with spam, 118

Bayesian filtering, features of, 32–34
Bayesian learning, considerations related to, 123
Bayes statistics, getting with SpamAssassin, 121–122
benefactors, targeting, 39–41
BindMail provider-based system, features of, 56
blacklists. *See also* DNSBLs (DNS Blacklists)
configuring in MailEssentials server, 269–271
configuring with MailShield Desktop, 207
creating, 346
drawbacks of, 35
managing, 34–35
managing with iHateSpam Server Edition, 261
managing with MailGoGoGo, 305
managing with SpamAssassin, 131–133
managing with SpamCatcher, 202
managing with SPAMFighter, 215–217
managing with SpamPal, 188–189
managing with SPS server, 279
relationship to recovery payments, 347
relationship to spam, 6–7
types of, 35
using with Outlook Express, 153–156
blacklist services, comparison of, 51–52
Blocked Character Sets, configuring in iHateSpam Server Edition, 261–262
blocked senders list in Outlook Express, advantage of, 156
Blocked Senders window in POPmonitor, accessing, 297
blocked words, adding in KnockKnock, 240
BLOCKFOLDER variable in .procmailrc file, setting for SpamBouncer, 322
BLOCKREPLY variable in .procmailrc file, setting for SpamBouncer, 322
body analysis, performing with SpamAssassin, 90
body rule type in SpamAssassin, description of, 128
Bogofilter Bayesian classifier. *See also* Bayesian classifier in SpamAssassin; QSF (Quick Spam Filter) Bayesisan classifier; rules in SpamAssassin; SpamAssassin
features of, 315
installing, 315–316
resource for, 395
training and running, 316–317
Bounce Message Filtering flag in iHateSpam Server Edition, configuring, 260
Brightmail gateway-based system, benefits of, 55–56
brute-force dictionary attack, explanation of, 362
brute force spamming component of spam machine, explanation of, 329
buckets, managing with POPFile, 246

Index 405

CAN-SPAM Act of 2003, introduction of, 8, 41
CDO (Collaboration Data Objects), obtaining
    information about, 253
CD-ROM
    anti-spam tools on, 400–401
    linking to additional tools from, 401
    troubleshooting problems with, 401
    using, 400
challenge/response approaches, implementing,
    36–37, 367–369
character set blocks
    configuring in iHateSpam Server Edition, 262
    configuring in MailEssentials server, 274
checksum databases, SpamAssassin support for,
    90–91
CIDR (classless interdomain routing) notation,
    example of, 132
client-based spam filters, overview of, 52–53
client mailbox systems, examples of, 18
codes, configuring in KnockKnock, 240
colon (:), using with SPS server, 279
Conditions window in MailEssentials server,
    accessing, 265
confidentiality policy, establishing for e-mail, 10
Configuration window in SpamButcher,
    displaying, 223
contact management, explanation of, 331
content analysis, overview of, 30–34
CPAN (Comprehensive Perl Archive Network)
    installing SpamAssassin from, 99–100
    installing SpamAssassin with, 94
Custom Filters window in SpamButcher,
    displaying, 225, 227
CVS (Concurrent Versioning System), installing
    SpamAssassin from, 94, 104

data, storing securely, 373
Date information in e-mail messages, significance
    of, 338
DB_File Perl module, using with SpamAssassin, 97
DCC (Distributed Checksum Clearinghouse)
    downloading and installing, 314–315
    features of, 313–314
    resource for, 395
    running, 315
DCC Perl module, using with SpamAssassin, 97

DDoS detection defense, overview of, 359. See also
    anti-spam tools; defense by disguise techniques;
    reverse dictionary defense; spam
DDoS (Distributed Denial of Service), relationship
    of FFBs to, 39–40
Debian packages, installing SpamAssassin from,
    104–105
Declude, web address for, 66
DEFAULT variable in .procmailrc file, setting for
    SpamBouncer, 321
defense by disguise techniques. See also anti-spam
    tools; DDoS detection defense; reverse
    dictionary defense; spam
    using graphics instead of text, 349
    using HTML ASCII equivalence, 349–350
    using scripting languages, 350–351
Delivery Status Notification (DSN)-Related list in
    RFCI, features of, 76
describe tag in SpamAssassin, explanation of, 129
dial-up user lists, relationship to DNSBLs, 65
Digest::SHA1 Perl module, using with
    SpamAssassin, 98
direct e-mail
    approaches to, 332–334
    combating, 343
direct user accounts, managing for small
    office/home office, 12. See also e-mail accounts;
    role accounts
"dirty dozen" FTC scams, list of, 14–15
DNS, segregating inbound versus outbound e-mail
    with, 46
DNSBLs (DNS Blacklists). See also blacklists
    adding or removing entries from, 65
    choosing, 66
    configuring in iHateSpam Server
        Edition, 270
    configuring in SpamPal, 189–190
    criteria for, 64–65
    DSBL (Distributed Server Boycott List),
        72–73
    implementing within sendmail, 78–80
    implementing with Microsoft Exchange,
        81–88
    implementing with Postfix, 80–81
    MAPS (Mail Abuse Prevention Systems),
        66–69
    NJABL (Not Just Another Bogus List), 74–75
    ORDB (Open Relay Database), 71–72
    reporting spammers to, 344
    resources for, 385
    RFCI (RFC Ignorant), 75–78
    SpamAssassin support for, 90–91
    SpamCop, 69–71
    Spamhaus, 73–74
    types of, 62–64

documentation policy, establishing for e-mail, 11
domain-based DNSBLs
    configuring Postfix for, 80–81
    configuring sendmail for, 79–80
    features of, 63–64
Domain Configuration window in iHateSpam Server Edition, displaying, 259
domain names, entering in SPS server, 278
domains
    blocking with SpamPal, 190
    including in WHOIS-related RFCI list, 77
    verifying, 341
"drive-by-spamming," explanation of, 42
DSBL (Distributed Server Boycott List)
    accessing, 389
    features of, 72–73
    subscribing to, 73
DUL (Dial-up User List) in MAPS, features of, 67–68
--dump expire switch, using with SpamAssassin's Bayesian classifier, 121

E

Edit Sender window in Outlook Express, displaying, 155
e-mail
    archiving, 49
    blocking with SpamPal, 190–191
    methods for checking of, 13–14
    RFCs related to, 388
e-mail accounts. *See also* direct user accounts; role accounts
    configuring with SpamButcher, 223
    organizing, 10
e-mail address encoder, obtaining, 366
e-mail addresses
    adding headers to, 338
    adding in Exchange 2003, 84
    extreme methods for protection of, 366
    gathering and managing, 331–332
    managing with KnockKnock, 238–239
    obfuscating, 349–350
    obtaining, 362–366
    protecting, 363–366
    role in greylisting, 348
    using nonalphabetic e-mail addresses, 366
e-mail address management component of spam machine, explanation of, 329
e-mail aliasing, explanation of, 363–364
E-Mail Bouncer provider-based system, features of, 57–58
e-mail client resources, accessing, 390–391

e-mail control components
    breadth considerations, 23
    depth considerations, 23–24
    impact considerations, 24
    operational considerations, 24
e-mail control systems, goals of, 20–21
e-mail filters, strategic placement of, 21
e-mail flow architecture, overview of, 18–19
e-mail harvester, example of, 351–353. *See also* address harvesting component of spam machine
e-mail headers
    anatomy of, 335–337
    gathering data from, 340–341
    significance of, 338–339
e-mail identities, restricting access to, 20–21
e-mail message content, targeting for analysis, 30–34
e-mail messages, managing with KnockKnock, 238–239
e-mail obfuscation, explanation of, 364
e-mail policies
    developing, 9–14
    for small office/home office, 12–13
    testing and refining, 14
e-mail protocols, diagram of, 19
e-mail servers, resources for, 391
e-mail systems, compartmentalizing, 13
e-mail transaction systems, types of, 18
Enable Spam Score Timeout setting in SpamCatcher, configuring, 200–201
end-user mailbox systems, examples of, 18
Eric's Jargon File, web site for, 315
error messages, adding in Exchange 2003, 83
Eudora
    configuring for SpamCatcher, 195–196
    configuring spam filters on, 144–146
    finding e-mail headers in, 337
    modes of, 144
    resource for, 390
Eudora's SpamWatch
    training, 146
    tweaking, 145–146
    watching for spam with, 144–145
exception filters, configuring in SPS server, 281–282
Exchange, resource for, 391
Exchange SMTP OnArrival Sink, using with iHateSpam Server Edition, 253
Exchange 2000
    combating open relays with, 371–372
    implementing DNSBLs with, 81–82
Exchange 2000/2003 server, installing MailEssentials server on, 268
Exchange 2003, implementing DNSBLs with, 82–88

Index 407

expungement window policy, establishing for e-mail, 11
ExtUtils::MakeMaker Perl module, using with SpamAssassin, 96

false negatives and positives, troubleshooting with SpamBayes, 181
FFBs (Filters that Fight Back), features of, 39–40
Field Chooser window in SpamBayes, displaying, 182
File::Spec Perl module, using with SpamAssassin, 96
filter configuration files, editing with MailShield, 211
Filter Now dialog box in SpamBayes, displaying, 179–180
Filter Rules dialog box in SpamBayes, displaying, 178
filters. *See also* spam filtering
    adding in POPmonitor, 295–297
    applying to virtual SMTP servers in Exchange 2003, 86–87
    applying with SPAMFighter, 218
    applying with Spamfire, 300–302
    configuring in SpamButcher, 224
filtersets in MailGoGoGo, enabling, 305
filter triggers, managing with MailShield Desktop, 207–209
Firebird browser, relationship to Mozilla, 147
firewalls
    operating razor-agents through, 313
    using, 374
folders
    adding to SpamNet's filtering, 235
    creating in SpamBayes, 179
--force expire switch, using with SpamAssassin's Bayesian classifier, 120–121
--forget switch, using with SpamAssassin's Bayesian classifier, 119
formail program, using with Razor, 312
FORMAIL variable in .procmailrc file, setting for SpamBouncer, 321
forwarding and redirection policy, establishing for e-mail, 11
forward slash (/), using with folders in iHateSpam Server Edition, 264
Friends and Enemies list in iHateSpam, managing, 230–231
Friends and Good Words feature in MailShield, configuring, 209

Friends/Spammers list in Spamfire, features of, 300
From information in e-mail messages, significance of, 338
FTC (Federal Trade Commission), web address for, 14

gateway-based solutions, features of, 44–45, 54–56
Gateway Learning Corp., obtaining information about, 332
gateway systems, examples of, 18
GCC, using with SpamAssassin, 95
Gentoo Linux, installing SpamAssassin from, 105
global filters, configuring with iHateSpam Server Edition, 261–263
GNU Make, using with SpamAssassin, 95
Good Words, managing with MailShield Desktop, 209–210
graphics, using instead of text, 349
greylisting
    overview of, 347–348
    resource for, 388
guidelines, developing for e-mail policies, 9

ham folders, selecting with SpamBayes Manager, 176–177
ham messages, training SpamAssassin's Bayesian classifier with, 118
ham versus spam, 8
Harris Interactive, web address for, 8
hash-based filters, features of, 31–32
header analysis, performing with SpamAssassin, 90
Header Checking Properties window in MailEssentials server, accessing, 272–274
header rule type in SpamAssassin, description of, 128
headers. *See* e-mail headers
heuristic versus keyword filtering and pattern matching, 31
hosts, hardening, 372–374
HTML::Parser Perl module, using with SpamAssassin, 96
HTML ASCII equivalence, using, 349–350

I

ICF (Internet Connection Firewall), stopping Messenger Service spam with, 376
Ignore Lists option in SpamPal, explanation of, 191–192
iHateSpam client
    checking Quarantine management interface in, 229–230
    configuring, 228–229
    features of, 228
    installing, 228
    managing Friends and Enemies lists in, 230–231
    resource for, 393
iHateSpam filters, features of, 53–54
iHateSpam Server Edition
    configuring, 254–259
    features of, 250
    filtering spam with, 259–266
    installing, 250–253
    resource for, 394
    troubleshooting, 259
inbound versus outbound e-mail, segregating by means of DNS, 46
inboxes, configuring in SpamNet, 235
incidents, developing response procedures for, 374
Incoming Listening Port setting, configuring in SpamCatcher, 198–199
Internet advertising, RFC associated with, 29
Internet Fraud Complaint Center web site, accessing, 397
intrusion detection/prevention systems, using, 374
IP addresses
    entering in SPS server, 278
    role in greylisting, 348
IP-based DNSBLs
    configuring sendmail for, 79
    features of, 62–63
    using Exchange 2003 with, 82–88
IPLOCK feature in SPS server, configuring, 279
IP spoofing component of spam machine, explanation of, 329
IPWHOIS-related list in RFCI, features of, 78

J

JavaScript, using as defense by disguise, 350–351
journals, setting size in SpamAssassin's Bayesian classifier, 120

Junk And Address Books section in SpamWatch, options in, 146
Junk e-mail filters in Outlook, configuring, 159–166
Junk Mailbox section in SpamWatch, options in, 146
junk mail controls in Mozilla, turning on, 148–149
Junk Threshold slider in SpamWatch, setting, 145

K

Keyword Checking function in MailEssentials server, configuring, 274–276
keyword filters
    versus pattern matching and heuristic filtering, 31
    pros and cons of, 30
    using, 6
keywords and conditions, adding in MailEssentials server, 276
KnockKnock client-based filter
    accepting and denying pending messages with, 238–239
    configuring, 237
    configuring secret codes in, 240
    disadvantages of, 241
    features of, 53, 236
    installing, 236–237
    resource for, 393
known good phrases, adding to SpamButcher, 225
Known Senders tab in SpamButcher, options on, 224
known spammer lists, relationship to DNSBLs, 65

L

language settings in SpamAssassin, overview of, 133–135
learn tflag in SpamAssassin, description of, 128–129
legal resources, list of, 389
lint functionality in SpamAssassin, example of, 131
Linux server-based filters, comparing, 54–55
Linux tools. *See* Bogofilter Bayesian classifier; DCC (Distributed Checksum Clearinghouse); QSF (Quick Spam Filter) Bayesian classifier; Razor network; SpamBayes open-source anti-spam tool; SpamBouncer Procmail recipes
list management, explanation of, 332
lists in DSBL, features of, 72
local.cf configuration file in SpamAssassin, features of, 107–108

localizing SpamAssassin, 133–135
log file History window in MailGoGoGo, viewing, 305
log information, auditing and reviewing, 49–50
Lyris MailShield, web address for, 204

M

Macintosh spam-filtering clients, comparison of, 53
Mac tools, 302–306. *See* POPmonitor; PostArmor mail filter; Spamfire
magic tokens, dumping with SpamAssassin's Bayesian classifier, 121. *See also* tokens
magnets, managing with POPFile, 246
mail. *See* e-mail
Mail::Audit Perl module, using with SpamAssassin, 97
MailCircuit provider-based system, features of, 57
MailEssentials server
    configuring, 269–276
    downloading for use with Exchange 2000, 81
    features of, 54, 266–267
    installing, 267–268
    resource for, 394
mail exchanger hijacking example, 340–342
MailGoGoGo
    features of, 53, 302–303
    installing and configuring, 303–304
    resource for, 395
MailShield Desktop client
    configuring, 205–206
    configuring blacklists with, 207
    configuring Friends and Good Words feature in, 209–210
    editing filter configuration files with, 211
    features of, 52, 204
    installing, 204–205
    interface for, 207–212
    managing Bad Words with, 208
    resource for, 392
Manage Address window in KnockKnock, displaying, 238–239
Management group in iHateSpam Server Edition, configuring, 254
MAPS DNSBL, accessing, 389
MAPS (Mail Abuse Prevention Systems)
    features of, 66–68
    subscribing to, 69
mbox format in Unix, using with SpamAssassin's Bayesian classifier, 117, 119
MD5 hash algorithm, obtaining information about, 32

message content, targeting for analysis, 30–34
message content management component of spam machine, explanation of, 329
Message Delivery Properties window in Exchange 2003, options in, 84
message development, role in spam content management, 331
message obfuscation, role in spam content management, 330
message randomization, role in spam content management, 331
Message Rules. *See also* rules in SpamAssassin
    in Outlook, 166–168
    in Outlook Express, 156–158
Message Rules window in Outlook Express, displaying, 155
messages. *See* e-mail messages
message weighting system in iHateSpam Server Edition, features of, 263
Messenger Service, preventing abuse of, 375–376
meta rule type in SpamAssassin, description of, 128
micro-payments, pros and cons of, 38–39
Microsoft Exchange, implementing DNSBLs with, 81–88
Microsoft Outlook. *See* Outlook
MIMEDefang
    location in mail flow, 136
    requirements for, 136–138
    subscribing to mailing list for, 137
    using with SpamAssassin, 135–138, 140
MIME fields, checking with MailEssentials server, 272, 274
MIME headers information in e-mail messages, significance of, 338
more_spam_to setting in SpamAssassin, description of, 132
Mozilla Mail
    configuring spam filters on, 147–152
    dealing with false positives in, 149
    resource for, 390
    training, 149
Mozilla message filters, using with SpamAssassin, 149–152
MRJ (Macintosh Runtime for Java), obtaining, 284–285
MTA servers, running SpamAssassin as gateway to, 140
MTAs (Mail Transfer Agents)
    RFC associated with, 28–29
    using with SpamAssassin, 95
MUAs (mail user agents), scoring in SpamAssassin, 126–131
multihop lists in DSBL, features of, 73

MX (mail exchanger), using with DNS, 46
MX relay defense, overview of, 348–349

N

Net::DNS Perl module, using with
    SpamAssassin, 97
net tflag in SpamAssassin, description of, 129
network activity, monitoring, 374
"The Next Step in the Spam Control War:
    Greylisting," accessing, 388
nice tflag in SpamAssassin, description of, 129
NJABL (Not Just Another Bogus List)
    accessing, 389
    features of, 74–75
    subscribing to, 75
NML (Non-conforming Mailing List) in MAPS,
    features of, 67
nonrepudiation, explanation of, 20

O

OE (Outlook Express)
    blocking senders in, 153–156
    configuring spam filters in, 152–158
    finding e-mail headers in, 335
    preparing for SpamPal installation, 185–186
    resource for, 390
    using Message Rules with SpamAssassin,
        156–158
    using POPFile with, 242–243
ok_locales setting in SpamAssassin, description of,
    133–134
open e-mail relays
    resource for, 396
    vulnerability of, 369–372
open proxy lists, relationship to DNSBLs, 65
Open Relay Database, web address for, 15
open-relay lists, relationship to DNSBLs, 64
open-relay mode, relationship to spam, 6–7
OPM (Open Proxy Monitor) in MAPS, purpose, 68
opt-out clause of Senate bill 1052, significance of, 9
ORDB (Open Relay Database)
    accessing, 389
    example of, 79
    features of, 71–72
    subscribing to, 72
ORFilter, downloading for use with Exchange
    2000, 81

organization size, impact on choosing spam
    solutions, 46–47
Outlook
    configuring Adult and Junk e-mail filters in,
        159–166
    configuring spam filters on, 158–168
    finding e-mail headers in, 335–337
    resource for, 390
    using SpamNet with, 233
Outlook folders, using SpamCatcher with, 201
Outlook Message Rules, using with SpamAssassin,
    166–168

P

PATTERNMATCHING variable in .procmailrc file,
    setting for SpamBouncer, 322
pattern matching versus keyword and heuristic
    filtering, 31
Perl modules
    using with amavisd-new, 139
    using with MIMEDefang, 137
    using with Razor, 310
    using with SpamAssassin, 95–98
Perl reaper, harvesting e-mail with, 353–354
Perl scripting language, accessing, 90, 95
personalization, role in spam content management,
    330–331
personal use installations of SpamAssassin,
    performing, 103
per-user SpamAssassin configuration, performing,
    109–110
phrases and words, configuring in
    KnockKnock, 240
Pine, finding e-mail headers in, 337
"A Plan for Spam" paper, accessing, 114, 388
Pod::Usage Perl module, using with
    SpamAssasin, 96
policies, configuring in iHateSpam Server Edition,
    263–266
policy recommendations, making for spam
    solutions, 48–50
POPFile client
    configuring, 244, 247
    configuring Remote Authentication servers
        with, 247
    features of, 242
    installing, 242–244
    managing buckets and magnets with, 246
    resource for, 393
    training, 244–246

POP mailbox defaults, checking with SpamButcher, 221
POPmonitor
    features of, 292
    installing, 292–294
    operating, 295–297
    resource for, 395
POPMonitorX client-based spam filter, features of, 53
pop-ups, overview of, 375–376
ports, scanning for open status of, 373
Post Armor client-based spam filter, features of, 53
PostArmor mail filter
    configuring, 288–292
    features of, 284
    installing, 284–288
    resource for, 394
Postfix
    implementing DNSBLs with, 80–81
    resource for, 391
    using amavisd-new with, 138–139
Postmaster-related list in RFCI, features of, 76
procedures, developing for e-mail policies, 9
Procmail. *See also* recipe files in Procmail; SpamBouncer Procmail recipes
    logging when used with SpamBouncer, 323
    obtaining, 308
    resource for, 395
    running razor-check in real-time with, 312
    using recipe files with, 110
    using with QSF, 320
    using with SpamAssassin, 95
.procmail.rc file, configuring for SpamBouncer, 321–323
programs, removing when unused, 374
provider-based solutions, features of, 44–45
Providers option in SpamPal, explanation of, 191–192
proxies, using with DNSBLs, 65
proxy settings, configuring in SpamCatcher, 201
publication restrictions, establishing for e-mail policies, 10
Public Blacklists, configuring in SpamPal, 189–190
PureMessage, web address for, 93
Python, obtaining, 317
Pyzor Perl module, using with SpamAssassin, 97

Q

Qmail, resource for, 391
QSF (Quick Spam Filter) Bayesian classifier. *See also* Bayesian classifier in SpamAssassin; Bogofilter Bayesian classifier; rules in SpamAssassin; SpamAssassin
    downloading and installing, 319
    features of, 319
    resource for, 396
    running, 319–320
QUALCOMM Eudora Mail, finding-email headers in, 337
quarantined items, viewing in Ad-aware 6.0, 378–379
Quarantine folders, managing in iHateSpam Server Edition, 265
Quarantine management interface in iHateSpam, checking, 229–230

R

rawbody rule type in SpamAssassin, description of, 128
razor-agents
    creating symbolic links for, 311
    operating through firewalls, 313
razor-check, running against e-mail messages, 312
Razor network
    advisory about, 309
    downloading and installing, 310–311
    features of, 308–310
    registering with, 311–312
    resource for, 395
    running with SpamAssassin, 312–313
Razor Perl module, using with SpamAssassin, 97
RBL+ (Realtime Blackhole List+) in MAPS, features of, 68–69
RBL (Realtime Blackhole List) in MAPS
    features of, 68–69
    using sendmail with, 79
Received: from information in e-mail messages, significance of, 339
Receiving Email Servers setting, configuring in SPS server, 277
recipe files in Procmail. *See also* Procmail; SpamBouncer Procmail recipes
    creating for DCC, 315
    purpose of, 308
    using with SpamAssassin configuration, 110
"recovery payments," relationship to blacklists, 347
Red Hat RPMs, installing SpamAssassin from, 104
Redirection Mailbox function in iHateSpam Server Edition, configuring, 265
relays. *See* open e-mail relays
Remote Authentication servers, configuring with POPFile, 247
Replication Server window in iHateSpam Server Edition, displaying, 257–258

report_safe option in SpamAssassin, effect of, 107–108
Reporting Settings window in iHateSpam Server Edition, displaying, 256–257
Reporting tool in iHateSpam Server Edition, accessing, 266
reports
    creating with PostArmor mail filter, 289–290
    creating with SPS server, 282
RE (Regular Expressions), configuring in PostArmor, 291–292
resource plans, establishing, 13–14
resources, securing, 372–374
return status codes, modifying in Exchange 2003, 83, 85
reverse dictionary defense, overview of, 358–360. *See also* anti-spam tools; defense by disguise techniques; DDoS detection defense; spam
rewrite_subject option in SpamAssassin, effect of, 107
RFCI DNSBL, accessing, 389
RFCI (RFC Ignorant)
    Abuse-related list in, 77
    Delivery Status Notification (DSN)-Related list in, 76
    IPWHOIS-related list in, 78
    overview of, 75–76
    Postmaster-Related list in, 76
    subscribing to, 78
    WHOIS-related list in, 77
RFCs (Requests for Comment)
    2505 (SMTP and MTA Best Practices), 28–29
    2635 (An Explanation for Why Spam Is Harmful), 29
    3098 (A Discussion of Responsible Internet Advertising), 29
    for e-mail and spam, 388
    overview of, 28
RHSBLs (right-hand side blacklists), features of, 63–64
Roaring Penguin Software Inc., web address for, 136
role accounts, managing for small office/home office, 12. *See also* direct user accounts; e-mail accounts
rotots.txt file from IBM, examining, 354–356
RSS (Relay Spam Stopper) in MAPS, features of, 68
rule-based versus keyword filtering and pattern matching, 31
rules, customizing in iHateSpam Server Edition, 262–263
rulesets, configuring in PostArmor mail filter, 290–292
rules in SpamAssassin. *See also* Bayesian classifier in SpamAssassin; Bogofilter Bayesian classifier;
QSF (Quick Spam Filter) Bayesian classifier; rules in SpamAssassin; SpamAssassin
    building, 129–131
    creating and modifying, 127
    location of, 127
    rule type component of, 127–129
    storing, 130
    testing, 131
rule type tag in SpamAssassin, explanation of, 127–129

sa-learn utility in SpamAssassin's Bayesian classifier
    getting statistics with, 121–122
    using, 117–119
sb_filter.py script, using, 318
sb_mboxtrain.py script, using, 318
SBDIR variable in .procmailrc file, setting for SpamBouncer, 322
SBL (Spamhaus Blacklist), web address for, 73
scores
    assigning to rules in SpamAssassin, 91–92, 130
    checking for distribution of spaminess, 356–357
    configuring in PostArmor mail filter, 288–289
    using with Bayesian analysis, 116–117
score tag in SpamAssassin, explanation of, 129
scripting languages, using as defense by disguise, 350–351
secret codes, configuring in KnockKnock, 240
secret words and phrases, configuring in KnockKnock, 240
security policy, establishing for e-mail, 10
Senate bill 1052, introduction of, 9
senders
    adding to Adult Content Senders list in Outlook, 162–166
    blocking in Outlook Express, 153–156
    blocking with KnockKnock, 239
    managing in POPmonitor, 297
    managing with iHateSpam Server Edition, 261
    managing with SpamCatcher, 202–203
sendmail
    combating open relays with, 369–371
    configuring for domain-based RHSBLs, 79–80
    configuring for IP-based DNSBLs, 79
    implementing DNSBLs within, 78–80
    resource for, 391

Index

server-based spam filters, overview of, 53–54
server platforms, organizing, 13
server-side encoding
    explanation of, 364–366
    resource for, 396
server systems, examples of, 18
services, disabling when unneeded, 372–373
SHA-1 hash algorithm, obtaining information about, 32
signature-based filters, features of, 31–32
site-wide installations of SpamAssassin, performing, 102–103
site-wide SpamAssassin configuration, performing, 110
SkyScan provider-based system, features of, 57
SLAs (Service Level Agreements), reading and reviewing, 50
small office/home office, e-mail policy for, 12–13
Smart Caching feature in iHateSpam Server Edition, configuring, 256–257
SMTP Events Management window in iHateSpam Server Edition, displaying, 259
SMTP fields, checking with MailEssentials server, 272
SMTP headers, anatomy of, 335–339
SMTP/NNTP sinks, obtaining information about, 253
SMTP (Simple Mail Transport Protocol) servers, examples of, 18
Sourceforge, web address for, 173, 242
spam. *See also* anti-spam tools; defense by disguise techniques; DDoS detection defense; reverse dictionary defense
    becoming familiar with, 335–343
    and blacklists, 6–7
    developing strategy for, 9
    example of, 339–343
    filtering by keywords, 6
    first example of, 4–5
    versus ham, 8
    history of, 4–5
    identifying, 21
    legal resources for, 389
    managing with MailShield Desktop, 209
    managing with SpamBayes, 181–183
    methods and tools for fighting of, 7–8
    and open-relay mode, 6–7
    origin of, 5
    ratio for receipt of, 4
    RFC associated with, 29
    RFCs related to, 388
    training SpamAssassin's Bayesian classifier with, 118
    U.S government sites related to, 397
    using Eudora's SpamWatch for, 144–145

spam analysis techniques
    challenge/response approaches, 36–37
    overview of, 29–30
    targeting benefactors, 39–41
    targeting message content, 30–34
    targeting senders or intermediaries, 34–39
SpamAssassin. *See also* Bayesian classifier in SpamAssassin; Bogofilter Bayesian classifier; QSF (Quick Spam Filter) Bayesian classifier; rules in SpamAssassin
    blacklisting features in, 131–133
    in commercial products, 93
    creating rules in, 126–131
    data flow in, 92
    examining Bayesian-related files in, 114–115
    examining output from, 111–112
    features of, 90–91
    as gateway to other e-mail servers, 140
    hardware requirements for, 98
    implementing Bayesian classifier in, 114
    installing from CPAN, 99–100
    killer features of, 93
    lint functionality in, 131
    localizing, 133–135
    preparing for installation of, 98–99
    resource for, 390
    rules used by, 91
    running Razor with, 312–313
    scores assigned to rules in, 91–92
    software requirements for, 94–95
    using amavisd-new with, 138–139
    using MIMEdefang with, 135–138
    using Mozilla message filters with, 149–152
    using Outlook Express Message Rules with, 156–158
    using Outlook Message Rules with, 166–168
    whitelisting features in, 131–133
SpamAssassin components
    local.cf configuration file, 107–108
    spamassassin utility, 105
    spamc client, 106–107
    spamd daemon, 106
    user_prefs configuration file, 108–109
SpamAssassin configurations
    per-user, 109–110
    site-wide, 110
    spamd, 110–111
SpamAssassin installation
    from CVS, 104
    from Debian packages, 104–105
    from Gentoo Linux, 105
    from Red Hat RPMs, 104
    from tarball, 101–103
SpamAssassin's Bayes rules, overview of, 115–116
spamassassin utility, features of, 105

SpamBayes client
    creating folders in, 179
    enabling filtering in, 178–180
    features of, 172–173
    installing, 173–174
    operating and managing spam with, 181–183
    training, 175–178
SpamBayes Manager, launching, 175–176
SpamBayes open-source anti-spam tool
    installing, 317
    resource for, 391, 395
    using, 318–319
    using with Procmail, 317–319
spam-bots
    functionality of, 351–356
    obtaining information about, 356
SpamBouncer Procmail recipes
    features of, 321
    installing and configuring, 321–323
    resource for, 396
SpamButcher client
    authentication methods supported by, 221
    checking default POP mailboxes with, 221
    configuring accounts with, 223
    disadvantages of, 226
    features of, 218
    installing, 219–220
    resource for, 392
SpamCatcher client
    enabling scanning for Outlook folders with, 201
    features of, 194
    installing, 194–198
SpamCatcher client network configuration
    of automatic rule updates, 199
    of Flagging and Modification functions, 200
    of Lenient setting, 200
    of ports and updates, 198–199
    of proxy settings, 201
    resource for, 392
    of timeouts and custom settings, 200–202
spamc client in SpamAssassin, features of, 106–107
spam content management, overview of, 330–331
SpamCop DNSBL
    accessing, 389
    features of, 69–71, 343
    subscribing to, 71
spamd daemon in SpamAssassin, features of, 106
Spam Definitions tool in iHateSpam Server Edition, configuring, 260
spamd SpamAssassin configuration, performing, 110

Spam E-mail: Harvesting Your E-Mail Address web site, accessing, 397
SPAMfighter client
    configuring, 214–218
    features of, 213
    installing, 213–214
    obtaining, 213
    resource for, 392
spam-fighting
    future of, 369
    papers, whitepapers, and treatises related to, 388
spam filtering. *See also* filters
    circumventing, 41–42
    configuring in iHateSpam Server Edition, 256, 259–266
    configuring in Outlook Express, 152–158
    configuring in POPmonitor, 295–297
    configuring in PostArmor, 290–292
    configuring in SPS server, 279–281
    configuring on Eudora, 144–146
    configuring on Outlook, 158–168
    configuring on SpamNet, 235
    on Mozilla Mail, 147–152
    in SpamBayes, 178–180
spam-filtering clients, comparing, 52–53
Spamfire
    features of, 298, 300
    installing and configuring, 298–299
    resource for, 395
SPAMFOLDER variable in .procmailrc file, setting for SpamBouncer, 322
Spam Handling and Detection window in MailShield, displaying, 210–211
Spamhaus
    accessing, 389
    features of, 73–74
    subscribing to, 74
spaminess, distribution of, 356–358
SpamKiller for Microsoft Exchange Small Business, web address for, 93
Spam Laws web site, accessing, 389
spam legislation, trends forming around, 8–9, 40–41
Spam Legislation Likely to Pass; Will It Work? resource, accessing, 389
spam machine
    characteristics of, 328–329
    diagram of, 330
spammer relay example, 342–343
spammers
    identifying, 21
    profitability of, 334
    reporting to authorities, 48–49, 343–344

resources related to, 397
slowing down, 37–38
types of, 332–334
untraceable addresses used by, 357–358
spam messages, typical words used in, 33
SpamNet client
configuring, 233–235
features of, 232
installing, 232–233
resource for, 393
spam-fighting options in, 235–236
Spamnix, web address for, 93
SpamPal client
Connections, Ports, and Protocols screen in, 193
features of, 183–184
Ignore Lists option in, 191–192
installing, 185–187
Interface screen in, 193
Message Tagging screen in, 193
plug-ins for, 193–194
resource for, 391
using blacklists with, 189–191
using whitelists with, 188–189
SPAMREPLY variable in .procmailrc file, setting for SpamBouncer, 322
spam reports, configuring with SpamButcher, 223–224
spam scams, list of, 14–15
SpamShark provider-based system, features of, 57
spam solutions
architectural considerations, 48
organization size considerations, 46–47
policy recommendations for, 48–50
support and maintenance considerations, 47
technical recommendations for, 50–51
spam sources, immediate identification of, 359–360
spamtraps in SpamCop, purpose of, 70–71
SpamWatch. *See* Eudora's SpamWatch
spiders, characteristics of, 363
SPS (Spam Prevention Service) server
configuring, 277–282
features of, 276
installing, 276–277
resource for, 394
spyware, overview of, 375–381
standards, developing for e-mail policies, 9
statistical filtering, features of, 32–34
storage requirements, analyzing for logging, 49
Subject information in e-mail messages, significance of, 338
Swing, obtaining, 284–285
Sys::Syslog Perl module, using with SpamAssassin, 96

System Management tool in iHateSpam Server Edition, configuring, 256–259
systems, identifying for e-mail policies, 13–14

tarballs, installing SpamAssassin from, 94, 101–103
tflags rule type in SpamAssassin, description of, 128–129
The Harris Poll #75–Spam Keeps Growing resource, accessing, 389
Thunderbird mail and news client
relationship to Mozilla, 147
resource for, 391
tilde (~)
in Razor default configuration directory, 311
in SpamAssassin installations, 103
To information in e-mail messages, significance of, 338
tokens. *See also* magic tokens
analyzing in SpamAssassin Bayesian classifier, 114–115
expiring in SpamAssassin's Bayesian classifier, 119
setting size in SpamAssassin's Bayesian classifier, 120
Tom and Jerry's CPA Service, example setup of e-mail server for, 11–13
Tracing Mode in iHateSpam Server Edition, configuring, 256
Trend Spam Prevention server-based filter, features of, 54
Trimming Junk Mailbox section in SpamWatch, options in, 146
triplets in greylisting, significance of, 348
trusted_networks setting in SpamAssassin, description of, 131–132
Trusted Senders window in POPmonitor, accessing, 297

unconfirmed lists in DSBL, features of, 73
Unix mbox format, using with SpamAssassin's Bayesian classifier, 117, 119
UNIX server-based filters, comparing, 54–55
"unknown" feature in SpamBayes, purpose of, 181
updates accounts, managing for small office/home office, 13
url rule type in SpamAssassin, description of, 128
USENET, relationship to spam, 5

user_prefs configuration file in SpamAssassin, features of, 108–109
userconf tflag in SpamAssassin, description of, 129
user groups, managing for small office/home office, 12
User Management tool in iHateSpam Server Edition, configuring, 254–255

victim management, overview of, 331–332
Vipul's Razor. *See* Razor network
VIRUSFOLDER variable in .procmailrc file, setting for SpamBouncer, 322

web sites
    Ad-aware 6.0, 377
    amavisd-new, 139
    Ameriquest information, 332
    Apple Developer, 285
    ASRG (Anti-Spam Research Group), 4
    BindMail provider-based system, 56
    blacklists, 346
    Bogofilter Bayesian classifier, 315
    CPAN (Comprehensive Perl Archive Network), 94
    CPAN.pm, 99
    DCC (Distributed Checksum Clearinghouse), 313–314
    DCC Perl module, 97
    DNSBLs (DNS Blacklists), 66
    E-Mail Bouncer provider-based system, features of, 57–58
    Eric's Jargon File, 315
    Eudora, 144
    Exchange mail relay configuration and testing, 371
    Firebird browser, 147
    FTC (Federal Trade Commission), 14
    Gateway Learning information, 332
    GCC and GNU Make, 95
    GFI Mail Essentials, 81
    greylisting, 347
    Harris Interactive, 8
    JavaScript conversion tool, 350–351
    Lyris MailShield, 204
    MailCircuit provider-based system, 57
    MailEssentials server, 267
    MailGoGoGo, 303

MAPS (Mail Abuse Prevention Systems), 67
MD5 hash algorithm, 32
Messenger Service, 376
Microsoft TechNet, 371
MIMEDefang, 135, 137
Mozilla, 147
Open Relay Database, 15
ORDB (Open Relay Database), 71
ORFilter, 81
patent for spam harvesting robot, 354
"A Plan for Spam" paper, 114, 388
POPFile open-source anti-spam tool, 242
POPmonitor, 292
Postfix, 80
Procmail, 95
PureMessage, 93
Python, 317
Pyzor Perl module, 97
QSF (Quick Spam Filter) Bayesian classifier, 319
Razor network information, 309
Razor Perl module, 97
RFCI (RFC Ignorant), 76
RFC 2505 (SMTP and MTA Best Practices), 28
RFC 2635 (An Explanation for Why Spam Is Harmful), 29
RFC 3098 (A Discussion of Responsible Internet Advertising), 29
rhbl.m4 file by Derk J. Balling, 79
Roaring Penguin Software Inc., 136
SBL (Spamhaus Blacklist), 73
sendmail, 78, 369
server-side encoding, 366
SHA-1 hash algorithm, 32
SkyScan provider-based system, 57
Sourceforge, 173, 242
SpamAssassin project, 90
spam-bot information, 356
SpamBouncer Procmail recipes, 321
SpamCop DNSBL, 343
SPAMFighter, 213
Spamfire, 298
SpamKiller for Microsoft Exchange Small Business, 93
spam legislation efforts, 9
SpamNet, 232
Spamnix, 93
SpamPal anti-spam proxy program, 185
SpamShark provider-based system, 57
SPS (Spam Prevention Service) server, 276
Thunderbird mail and news client, 147
whois information, 342

whitelist_to setting in SpamAssassin, description of, 132
whitelists
  configuring in MailEssentials server, 269–271
  implementing, 35–36
  managing with iHateSpam Server Edition, 261
  managing with MailGoGoGo, 305
  managing with SpamCatcher, 202
  managing with SPAMFighter, 215–217
  managing with SPS server, 279
  using with SpamAssassin, 131–133
  using with SpamPal, 188–189
whois command, verifying domain names with, 341–342
WHOIS-related list in RFCI, features of, 77
Windows clients. *See* iHateSpam client; KnockKnock client-based filter; MailShield Desktop client; POPFile client; SpamBayes client; SpamButcher client; SpamCatcher client network configuration; SPAMfighter client; SpamNet client; SpamPal client

Windows Scheduled Tasks, scheduling automatic updates with, 260–261
Windows servers. *See* iHateSpam Server Edition; MailEssentials server; SPS (Spam Prevention Service) server
Windows 2000 and XP, disabling Messenger Service in, 376
words and phrases, configuring in KnockKnock, 240

X headers information in e-mail messages, significance of, 338
X-SBClass header in SpamBouncer, options for, 323–324
X-Spam-Flag header, configuring Mozilla Mail to filter on, 150–152

INTERNATIONAL CONTACT INFORMATION

AUSTRALIA
McGraw-Hill Book Company
Australia Pty. Ltd.
TEL +61-2-9900-1800
FAX +61-2-9878-8881
http://www.mcgraw-hill.com.au
books-it_sydney@mcgraw-hill.com

CANADA
McGraw-Hill Ryerson Ltd.
TEL +905-430-5000
FAX +905-430-5020
http://www.mcgraw-hill.ca

**GREECE, MIDDLE EAST, & AFRICA
(Excluding South Africa)**
McGraw-Hill Hellas
TEL +30-210-6560-990
TEL +30-210-6560-993
TEL +30-210-6560-994
FAX +30-210-6545-525

MEXICO (Also serving Latin America)
McGraw-Hill Interamericana Editores
S.A. de C.V.
TEL +525-1500-5108
FAX +525-117-1589
http://www.mcgraw-hill.com.mx
carlos_ruiz@mcgraw-hill.com

SINGAPORE (Serving Asia)
McGraw-Hill Book Company
TEL +65-6863-1580
FAX +65-6862-3354
http://www.mcgraw-hill.com.sg
mghasia@mcgraw-hill.com

SOUTH AFRICA
McGraw-Hill South Africa
TEL +27-11-622-7512
FAX +27-11-622-9045
robyn_swanepoel@mcgraw-hill.com

SPAIN
McGraw-Hill/
Interamericana de España, S.A.U.
TEL +34-91-180-3000
FAX +34-91-372-8513
http://www.mcgraw-hill.es
professional@mcgraw-hill.es

**UNITED KINGDOM, NORTHERN,
EASTERN, & CENTRAL EUROPE**
McGraw-Hill Education Europe
TEL +44-1-628-502500
FAX +44-1-628-770224
http://www.mcgraw-hill.co.uk
emea_queries@mcgraw-hill.com

ALL OTHER INQUIRIES Contact:
McGraw-Hill/Osborne
TEL +1-510-420-7700
FAX +1-510-420-7703
http://www.osborne.com
omg_international@mcgraw-hill.com

Protect Your Network

The tools are out there—learn the best ways to use them!

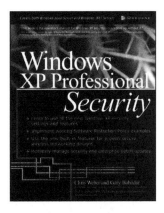

Also available: SQL Server Security   Web Services Security
0-07-222515-7   0-07-222471-1

OSBORNE DELIVERS RESULTS!

www.osborne.com

[Sound Off!

Visit us at **www.osborne.com/bookregistration** and let us know what you thought of this book. While you're online you'll have the opportunity to register for newsletters and special offers from McGraw-Hill/Osborne.

We want to hear from you!

[Sneak Peek

Visit us today at **www.betabooks.com** and see what's coming from McGraw-Hill/Osborne tomorrow!

Based on the successful software paradigm, Bet@Books™ allows computing professionals to view partial and sometimes complete text versions of selected titles online. Bet@Books™ viewing is free, invites comments and feedback, and allows you to "test drive" books in progress on the subjects that interest you the most.

OSBORNE DELIVERS RESULTS!]

The GNU License

Linux is written and distributed under the GNU General Public License which means that its source code is freely-distributed and available to the general public.

GNU GENERAL PUBLIC LICENSE
Version 2, June 1991

Copyright (C) 1989, 1991 Free Software Foundation, Inc.
675 Mass Ave, Cambridge, MA 02139, USA
Everyone is permitted to copy and distribute verbatim copies of this license document, but changing it is not allowed.

Preamble

The licenses for most software are designed to take away your freedom to share and change it. By contrast, the GNU General Public License is intended to guarantee your freedom to share and change free software—to make sure the software is free for all its users. This General Public License applies to most of the Free Software Foundation's software and to any other program whose authors commit to using it. (Some other Free Software Foundation software is covered by the GNU Library General Public License instead.) You can apply it to your programs, too.

When we speak of free software, we are referring to freedom, not price. Our General Public Licenses are designed to make sure that you have the freedom to distribute copies of free software (and charge for this service if you wish), that you receive source code or can get it if you want it, that you can change the software or use pieces of it in new free programs; and that you know you can do these things.

To protect your rights, we need to make restrictions that forbid anyone to deny you these rights or to ask you to surrender the rights. These restrictions translate to certain responsibilities for you if you distribute copies of the software, or if you modify it.

For example, if you distribute copies of such a program, whether gratis or for a fee, you must give the recipients all the rights that you have. You must make sure that they, too, receive or can get the source code. And you must show them these terms so they know their rights.

We protect your rights with two steps: (1) copyright the software, and (2) offer you this license which gives you legal permission to copy, distribute and/or modify the software.

Also, for each author's protection and ours, we want to make certain that everyone understands that there is no warranty for this free software. If the software is modified by someone else and passed on, we want its recipients to know that what they have is not the original, so that any problems introduced by others will not reflect on the original authors' reputations.

Finally, any free program is threatened constantly by software patents. We wish to avoid the danger that redistributors of a free program will individually obtain patent licenses, in effect making the program proprietary. To prevent this, we have made it clear that any patent must be licensed for everyone's free use or not licensed at all.

The precise terms and conditions for copying, distribution and modification follow.

GNU GENERAL PUBLIC LICENSE TERMS AND CONDITIONS FOR COPYING, DISTRIBUTION AND MODIFICATION

0. This License applies to any program or other work which contains a notice placed by the copyright holder saying it may be distributed under the terms of this General Public License. The "Program", below, refers to any such program or work, and a "work based on the Program" means either the Program or any derivative work under copyright law: that is to say, a work containing the Program or a portion of it, either verbatim or with modifications and/or translated into another language. (Hereinafter, translation is included without limitation in the term "modification".) Each licensee is addressed as "you".

Activities other than copying, distribution and modification are not covered by this License; they are outside its scope. The act of running the Program is not restricted, and the output from the Program is covered only if its contents constitute a work based on the Program (independent of having been made by running the Program). Whether that is true depends on what the Program does.

1. You may copy and distribute verbatim copies of the Program's source code as you receive it, in any medium, provided that you conspicuously and appropriately publish on each copy an appropriate copyright notice and disclaimer of warranty; keep intact all the notices that refer to this License and to the absence of any warranty; and give any other recipients of the Program a copy of this License along with the Program.

You may charge a fee for the physical act of transferring a copy, and you may at your option offer warranty protection in exchange for a fee.

2. You may modify your copy or copies of the Program or any portion of it, thus forming a work based on the Program, and copy and distribute such modifications or work under the terms of Section 1 above, provided that you also meet all of these conditions:

a) You must cause the modified files to carry prominent notices stating that you changed the files and the date of any change.

b) You must cause any work that you distribute or publish, that in whole or in part contains or is derived from the Program or any part thereof, to be licensed as a whole at no charge to all third parties under the terms of this License.

c) If the modified program normally reads commands interactively when run, you must cause it, when started running for such interactive use in the most ordinary way, to print or display an announcement including an appropriate copyright notice and a notice that there is no warranty (or else, saying that you provide a warranty) and that users may redistribute the program under these conditions, and telling the user how to view a copy of this License. (Exception: if the Program itself is interactive but does not normally print such an announcement, your work based on the Program is not required to print an announcement.)

These requirements apply to the modified work as a whole. If identifiable sections of that work are not derived from the Program, and can be reasonably considered independent and separate works in themselves, then this License, and its terms, do not apply to those sections when you distribute them as separate works. But when you distribute the same sections as part of a whole which is a work based on the Program, the distribution of the whole must be on the terms of this License, whose permissions for other licensees extend to the entire whole, and thus to each and every part regardless of who wrote it. Thus, it is not the intent of this section to claim rights or contest your rights to work written entirely by you; rather, the intent is to exercise the right to control the distribution of derivative or collective works based on the Program.

In addition, mere aggregation of another work not based on the Program with the Program (or with a work based on the Program) on a volume of a storage or distribution medium does not bring the other work under the scope of this License.

3. You may copy and distribute the Program (or a work based on it, under Section 2) in object code or executable form under the terms of Sections 1 and 2 above provided that you also do one of the following:

a) Accompany it with the complete corresponding machine-readable source code, which must be distributed under the terms of Sections 1 and 2 above on a medium customarily used for software interchange; or,

b) Accompany it with a written offer, valid for at least three years, to give any third party, for a charge no more than your cost of physically performing source distribution, a complete machine-readable copy of the corresponding source code, to be distributed under the terms of Sections 1 and 2 above on a medium customarily used for software interchange; or,

c) Accompany it with the information you received as to the offer to distribute corresponding source code. (This alternative is allowed only for noncommercial distribution and only if you received the program in object code or executable form with such an offer, in accord with Subsection b above.)

The source code for a work means the preferred form of the work for making modifications to it. For an executable work, complete source code means all the source code for all modules it contains, plus any associated interface definition files, plus the scripts used to control compilation and installation of the executable. However, as a special exception, the source code distributed need not include anything that is normally distributed (in either source or binary form) with the major components (compiler, kernel, and so on) of the operating system on which the executable runs, unless that component itself accompanies the executable.

If distribution of executable or object code is made by offering access to copy from a designated place, then offering equivalent access to copy the source code from the same place counts as distribution of the source code, even though third parties are not compelled to copy the source along with the object code.

4. You may not copy, modify, sublicense, or distribute the Program except as expressly provided under this License. Any attempt otherwise to copy, modify, sublicense or distribute the Program is void, and will automatically terminate your rights under this License. However, parties who have received copies, or rights, from you under this License will not have their licenses terminated so long as such parties remain in full compliance.

5. You are not required to accept this License, since you have not signed it. However, nothing else grants you permission to modify or distribute the Program or its derivative works. These actions are prohibited by law if you do not accept this License. Therefore, by modifying or distributing the Program (or any work based on the Program), you indicate your acceptance of this License to do so, and all its terms and conditions for copying, distributing or modifying the Program or works based on it.

6. Each time you redistribute the Program (or any work based on the Program), the recipient automatically receives a license from the original licensor to copy, distribute or modify the Program subject to these terms and conditions. You may

not impose any further restrictions on the recipients' exercise of the rights granted herein. You are not responsible for enforcing compliance by third parties to this License.

7. If, as a consequence of a court judgment or allegation of patent infringement or for any other reason (not limited to patent issues), conditions are imposed on you (whether by court order, agreement or otherwise) that contradict the conditions of this License, they do not excuse you from the conditions of this License. If you cannot distribute so as to satisfy simultaneously your obligations under this License and any other pertinent obligations, then as a consequence you may not distribute the Program at all. For example, if a patent license would not permit royalty-free redistribution of the Program by all those who receive copies directly or indirectly through you, then the only way you could satisfy both it and this License would be to refrain entirely from distribution of the Program.

If any portion of this section is held invalid or unenforceable under any particular circumstance, the balance of the section is intended to apply and the section as a whole is intended to apply in other circumstances.

It is not the purpose of this section to induce you to infringe any patents or other property right claims or to contest validity of any such claims; this section has the sole purpose of protecting the integrity of the free software distribution system, which is implemented by public license practices. Many people have made generous contributions to the wide range of software distributed through that system in reliance on consistent application of that system; it is up to the author/donor to decide if he or she is willing to distribute software through any other system and a licensee cannot impose that choice.

This section is intended to make thoroughly clear what is believed to be a consequence of the rest of this License.

8. If the distribution and/or use of the Program is restricted in certain countries either by patents or by copyrighted interfaces, the original copyright holder who places the Program under this License may add an explicit geographical distribution limitation excluding those countries, so that distribution is permitted only in or among countries not thus excluded. In such case, this License incorporates the limitation as if written in the body of this License.

9. The Free Software Foundation may publish revised and/or new versions of the General Public License from time to time. Such new versions will be similar in spirit to the present version, but may differ in detail to address new problems or concerns.

Each version is given a distinguishing version number. If the Program specifies a version number of this License which applies to it and "any later version", you have the option of following the terms and conditions either of that version or of any later version published by the Free Software Foundation. If the Program does not specify a version number of this License, you may choose any version ever published by the Free Software Foundation.

10. If you wish to incorporate parts of the Program into other free programs whose distribution conditions are different, write to the author to ask for permission. For software which is copyrighted by the Free Software Foundation, write to the Free Software Foundation; we sometimes make exceptions for this. Our decision will be guided by the two goals of preserving the free status of all derivatives of our free software and of promoting the sharing and reuse of software generally.

NO WARRANTY

11. BECAUSE THE PROGRAM IS LICENSED FREE OF CHARGE, THERE IS NO WARRANTY FOR THE PROGRAM, TO THE EXTENT PERMITTED BY APPLICABLE LAW. EXCEPT WHEN OTHERWISE STATED IN WRITING THE COPYRIGHT HOLDERS AND/OR OTHER PARTIES PROVIDE THE PROGRAM "AS IS" WITHOUT WARRANTY OF ANY KIND, EITHER EXPRESSED OR IMPLIED, INCLUDING, BUT NOT LIMITED TO, THE IMPLIED WARRANTIES OF MERCHANTABILITY AND FITNESS FOR A PARTICULAR PURPOSE. THE ENTIRE RISK AS TO THE QUALITY AND PERFORMANCE OF THE PROGRAM IS WITH YOU. SHOULD THE PROGRAM PROVE DEFECTIVE, YOU ASSUME THE COST OF ALL NECESSARY SERVICING, REPAIR OR CORRECTION.

12. IN NO EVENT UNLESS REQUIRED BY APPLICABLE LAW OR AGREED TO IN WRITING WILL ANY COPYRIGHT HOLDER, OR ANY OTHER PARTY WHO MAY MODIFY AND/OR REDISTRIBUTE THE PROGRAM AS PERMITTED ABOVE, BE LIABLE TO YOU FOR DAMAGES, INCLUDING ANY GENERAL, SPECIAL, INCIDENTAL OR CONSEQUENTIAL DAMAGES ARISING OUT OF THE USE OR INABILITY TO USE THE PROGRAM (INCLUDING BUT NOT LIMITED TO LOSS OF DATA OR DATA BEING RENDERED INACCURATE OR LOSSES SUSTAINED BY YOU OR THIRD PARTIES OR A FAILURE OF THE PROGRAM TO OPERATE WITH ANY OTHER PROGRAMS), EVEN IF SUCH HOLDER OR OTHER PARTY HAS BEEN ADVISED OF THE POSSIBILITY OF SUCH DAMAGES.

END OF TERMS AND CONDITIONS

Appendix: How to Apply These Terms to Your New Programs

If you develop a new program, and you want it to be of the greatest possible use to the public, the best way to achieve this is to make it free software which everyone can redistribute and change under these terms.

To do so, attach the following notices to the program. It is safest to attach them to the start of each source file to most effectively convey the exclusion of warranty; and each file should have at least the "copyright" line and a pointer to where the full notice is found.

<one line to give the program's name and a brief idea of what it does.> Copyright (C) 19yy <name of author>
This program is free software; you can redistribute it and/or modify it under the terms of the GNU General Public License as published by the Free Software Foundation; either version 2 of the License, or (at your option) any later version.

This program is distributed in the hope that it will be useful, but WITHOUT ANY WARRANTY; without even the implied warranty of MERCHANTABILITY or FITNESS FOR A PARTICULAR PURPOSE. See the GNU General Public License for more details.

You should have received a copy of the GNU General Public License along with this program; if not, write to the Free Software Foundation, Inc., 675 Mass Ave, Cambridge, MA 02139, USA.

Also add information on how to contact you by electronic and paper mail.

If the program is interactive, make it output a short notice like this when it starts in an interactive mode:

Gnomovision version 69, Copyright (C) 19yy name of author Gnomovision comes with ABSOLUTELY NO WARRANTY; for details type `show w'. This is free software, and you are welcome to redistribute it under certain conditions; type `show c' for details.

The hypothetical commands `show w' and `show c' should show the appropriate parts of the General Public License. Of course, the commands you use may be called something other than `show w' and `show c'; they could even be mouse-clicks or menu items—whatever suits your program.

You should also get your employer (if you work as a programmer) or your school, if any, to sign a "copyright disclaimer" for the program, if necessary. Here is a sample; alter the names:

Yoyodyne, Inc., hereby disclaims all copyright interest in the program `Gnomovision' (which makes passes at compilers) written by James Hacker.

<signature of Ty Coon>, 1 April 1989
Ty Coon, President of Vice

This General Public License does not permit incorporating your program into proprietary programs. If your program is a subroutine library, you may consider it more useful to permit linking proprietary applications with the library. If this is what you want to do, use the GNU Library General Public License instead of this License.

Python Software Foundation License
Python 2.1.1 license

This is the official license for the Python 2.1.1 release:

A. HISTORY OF THE SOFTWARE
==========================

Python was created in the early 1990s by Guido van Rossum at Stichting Mathematisch Centrum (CWI) in the Netherlands as a successor of a language called ABC. Guido is Python's principal author, although it includes many contributions from others. The last version released from CWI was Python 1.2. In 1995, Guido continued his work on Python at the Corporation for National Research Initiatives (CNRI) in Reston, Virginia where he released several versions of the software. Python 1.6 was the last of the versions released by CNRI. In 2000, Guido and the Python core development team moved to BeOpen.com to form the BeOpen PythonLabs team. Python 2.0 was the first and only release from BeOpen.com.

Following the release of Python 1.6, and after Guido van Rossum left CNRI to work with commercial software developers, it became clear that the ability to use Python with software available under the GNU Public License (GPL) was very desirable. CNRI and the Free Software Foundation (FSF) interacted to develop enabling wording changes to the Python license. Python 1.6.1 is essentially the same as Python 1.6, with a few minor bug fixes, and with a different license that enables later versions to be GPL-compatible. Python 2.1 is a derivative work of Python 1.6.1, as well as of Python 2.0.

After Python 2.0 was released by BeOpen.com, Guido van Rossum and the other PythonLabs developers joined Digital Creations. All intellectual property added from this point on, starting with Python 2.1 and its alpha and beta releases, is owned by the Python Software Foundation (PSF), a non-profit modeled after the Apache Software Foundation. See http://www.python.org/psf/ for more information about the PSF.

Thanks to the many outside volunteers who have worked under Guido's direction to make these releases possible.

B. TERMS AND CONDITIONS FOR ACCESSING OR OTHERWISE USING PYTHON
===

PSF LICENSE AGREEMENT
----

1. This LICENSE AGREEMENT is between the Python Software Foundation ("PSF"), and the Individual or Organization ("Licensee") accessing and otherwise using Python 2.1.1 software in source or binary form and its associated documentation.

2. Subject to the terms and conditions of this License Agreement, PSF hereby grants Licensee a nonexclusive, royalty-free, world-wide license to reproduce, analyze, test, perform and/or display publicly, prepare derivative works, distribute, and otherwise use Python 2.1.1 alone or in any derivative version, provided, however, that PSF's License Agreement and PSF's notice of copyright, i.e., "Copyright (c) 2001 Python Software Foundation; All Rights Reserved" are retained in Python 2.1.1 alone or in any derivative version prepared by Licensee.

3. In the event Licensee prepares a derivative work that is based on or incorporates Python 2.1.1 or any part thereof, and wants to make the derivative work available to others as provided herein, then Licensee hereby agrees to include in any such work a brief summary of the changes made to Python 2.1.1.

4. PSF is making Python 2.1.1 available to Licensee on an "AS IS" basis. PSF MAKES NO REPRESENTATIONS OR WARRANTIES, EXPRESS OR IMPLIED. BY WAY OF EXAMPLE, BUT NOT LIMITATION, PSF MAKES NO AND DISCLAIMS ANY REPRESENTATION OR WARRANTY OF MERCHANTABILITY OR FITNESS FOR ANY PARTICULAR PURPOSE OR THAT THE USE OF PYTHON 2.1.1 WILL NOT INFRINGE ANY THIRD PARTY RIGHTS.

5. PSF SHALL NOT BE LIABLE TO LICENSEE OR ANY OTHER USERS OF PYTHON 2.1.1 FOR ANY INCIDENTAL, SPECIAL, OR CONSEQUENTIAL DAMAGES OR LOSS AS A RESULT OF MODIFYING, DISTRIBUTING, OR OTHERWISE USING PYTHON 2.1.1, OR ANY DERIVATIVE THEREOF, EVEN IF ADVISED OF THE POSSIBILITY THEREOF.

6. This License Agreement will automatically terminate upon a material breach of its terms and conditions.

7. Nothing in this License Agreement shall be deemed to create any relationship of agency, partnership, or joint venture between PSF and Licensee. This License Agreement does not grant permission to use PSF trademarks or trade name in a trademark sense to endorse or promote products or services of Licensee, or any third party.

8. By copying, installing or otherwise using Python 2.1.1, Licensee agrees to be bound by the terms and conditions of this License Agreement.

BEOPEN.COM TERMS AND CONDITIONS FOR PYTHON 2.0

BEOPEN PYTHON OPEN SOURCE LICENSE AGREEMENT VERSION 1

1. This LICENSE AGREEMENT is between BeOpen.com ("BeOpen"), having an office at 160 Saratoga Avenue, Santa Clara, CA 95051, and the Individual or Organization ("Licensee") accessing and otherwise using this software in source or binary form and its associated documentation ("the Software").

2. Subject to the terms and conditions of this BeOpen Python License Agreement, BeOpen hereby grants Licensee a non-exclusive, royalty-free, world-wide license to reproduce, analyze, test, perform and/or display publicly, prepare derivative works, distribute, and otherwise use the Software alone or in any derivative version, provided, however, that the BeOpen Python License is retained in the Software, alone or in any derivative version prepared by Licensee.

3. BeOpen is making the Software available to Licensee on an "AS IS" basis. BEOPEN MAKES NO REPRESENTATIONS OR WARRANTIES, EXPRESS OR IMPLIED. BY WAY OF EXAMPLE, BUT NOT LIMITATION, BEOPEN MAKES NO AND DISCLAIMS ANY REPRESENTATION OR WARRANTY OF MERCHANTABILITY OR FITNESS FOR ANY PARTICULAR PURPOSE OR THAT THE USE OF THE SOFTWARE WILL NOT INFRINGE ANY THIRD PARTY RIGHTS.

4. BEOPEN SHALL NOT BE LIABLE TO LICENSEE OR ANY OTHER USERS OF THE SOFTWARE FOR ANY INCIDENTAL, SPECIAL, OR CONSEQUENTIAL DAMAGES OR LOSS AS A RESULT OF USING, MODIFYING OR DISTRIBUTING THE SOFTWARE, OR ANY DERIVATIVE THEREOF, EVEN IF ADVISED OF THE POSSIBILITY THEREOF.

5. This License Agreement will automatically terminate upon a material breach of its terms and conditions.

6. This License Agreement shall be governed by and interpreted in all respects by the law of the State of California, excluding conflict of law provisions. Nothing in this License Agreement shall be deemed to create any relationship of agency, partnership, or joint venture between BeOpen and Licensee. This License Agreement does not grant permission to use BeOpen trademarks or trade names in a trademark sense to endorse or promote products or services of Licensee, or any third party. As an exception, the "BeOpen Python" logos available at http://www.pythonlabs.com/logos.html may be used according to the permissions granted on that web page.

7. By copying, installing or otherwise using the software, Licensee agrees to be bound by the terms and conditions of this

License Agreement.

CNRI OPEN SOURCE GPL-COMPATIBLE LICENSE AGREEMENT
----

1. This LICENSE AGREEMENT is between the Corporation for National Research Initiatives, having an office at 1895 Preston White Drive, Reston, VA 20191 ("CNRI"), and the Individual or Organization ("Licensee") accessing and otherwise using Python 1.6.1 software in source or binary form and its associated documentation.

2. Subject to the terms and conditions of this License Agreement, CNRI hereby grants Licensee a nonexclusive, royalty-free, world-wide license to reproduce, analyze, test, perform and/or display publicly, prepare derivative works, distribute, and otherwise use Python 1.6.1 alone or in any derivative version, provided, however, that CNRI's License Agreement and CNRI's notice of copyright, i.e., "Copyright (c) 1995-2001 Corporation for National Research Initiatives; All Rights Reserved" are retained in Python 1.6.1 alone or in any derivative version prepared by Licensee. Alternately, in lieu of CNRI's License Agreement, Licensee may substitute the following text (omitting the quotes): "Python 1.6.1 is made available subject to the terms and conditions in CNRI's License Agreement. This Agreement together with Python 1.6.1 may be located on the Internet using the following unique, persistent identifier (known as a handle): 1895.22/1013. This

Agreement may also be obtained from a proxy server on the Internet using the following URL: http://hdl.handle.net/1895.22/1013".

3. In the event Licensee prepares a derivative work that is based on or incorporates Python 1.6.1 or any part thereof, and wants to make the derivative work available to others as provided herein, then Licensee hereby agrees to include in any such work a brief summary of the changes made to Python 1.6.1.

4. CNRI is making Python 1.6.1 available to Licensee on an "AS IS" basis. CNRI MAKES NO REPRESENTATIONS OR WARRANTIES, EXPRESS OR IMPLIED. BY WAY OF EXAMPLE, BUT NOT LIMITATION, CNRI MAKES NO AND DISCLAIMS ANY REPRESENTATION OR WARRANTY OF MERCHANTABILITY OR FITNESS FOR ANY PARTICULAR PURPOSE OR THAT THE USE OF PYTHON 1.6.1 WILL NOT INFRINGE ANY THIRD PARTY RIGHTS.

5. CNRI SHALL NOT BE LIABLE TO LICENSEE OR ANY OTHER USERS OF PYTHON 1.6.1 FOR ANY INCIDENTAL, SPECIAL, OR CONSEQUENTIAL DAMAGES OR LOSS AS A RESULT OF MODIFYING, DISTRIBUTING, OR OTHERWISE USING PYTHON 1.6.1, OR ANY DERIVATIVE THEREOF, EVEN IF ADVISED OF THE POSSIBILITY THEREOF.

6. This License Agreement will automatically terminate upon a material breach of its terms and conditions.

7. This License Agreement shall be governed by the federal intellectual property law of the United States, including without limitation the federal copyright law, and, to the extent such U.S. federal law does not apply, by the law of the Commonwealth of Virginia, excluding Virginia's conflict of law provisions. Notwithstanding the foregoing, with regard to derivative works based on Python 1.6.1 that incorporate non-separable material that was previously distributed under the GNU General Public License (GPL), the law of the Commonwealth of Virginia shall govern this License Agreement only as to issues arising under or with respect to Paragraphs 4, 5, and 7 of this License Agreement. Nothing in this License Agreement shall be deemed to create any relationship of agency, partnership, or joint venture between CNRI and Licensee. This License Agreement does not grant permission to use CNRI trademarks or trade name in a trademark sense to endorse or promote products or services of Licensee, or any third party.

8. By clicking on the "ACCEPT" button where indicated, or by copying, installing or otherwise using Python 1.6.1, Licensee agrees to be bound by the terms and conditions of this License Agreement.
    ACCEPT

CWI PERMISSIONS STATEMENT AND DISCLAIMER

Copyright (c) 1991 - 1995, Stichting Mathematisch Centrum Amsterdam, The Netherlands. All rights reserved.

Permission to use, copy, modify, and distribute this software and its documentation for any purpose and without fee is hereby granted, provided that the above copyright notice appear in all copies and that both that copyright notice and this permission notice appear in supporting documentation, and that the name of Stichting Mathematisch Centrum or CWI not be used in advertising or publicity pertaining to distribution of the software without specific, written prior permission.

STICHTING MATHEMATISCH CENTRUM DISCLAIMS ALL WARRANTIES WITH REGARD TO THIS SOFTWARE, INCLUDING ALL IMPLIED WARRANTIES OF MERCHANTABILITY AND FITNESS, IN NO EVENT SHALL STICHTING MATHEMATISCH CENTRUM BE LIABLE FOR ANY SPECIAL, INDIRECT OR CONSEQUENTIAL DAMAGES OR ANY DAMAGES WHATSOEVER RESULTING FROM LOSS OF USE, DATA OR PROFITS, WHETHER IN AN ACTION OF CONTRACT, NEGLIGENCE OR OTHER TORTIOUS ACTION, ARISING OUT OF OR IN CONNECTION WITH THE USE OR PERFORMANCE OF THIS SOFTWARE.

LICENSE AGREEMENT

THIS PRODUCT (THE "PRODUCT") CONTAINS PROPRIETARY SOFTWARE, DATA AND INFORMATION (INCLUDING DOCUMENTATION) OWNED BY THE McGRAW-HILL COMPANIES, INC. ("McGRAW-HILL") AND ITS LICENSORS. YOUR RIGHT TO USE THE PRODUCT IS GOVERNED BY THE TERMS AND CONDITIONS OF THIS AGREEMENT.

LICENSE: Throughout this License Agreement, "you" shall mean either the individual or the entity whose agent opens this package. You are granted a non-exclusive and non-transferable license to use the Product subject to the following terms:

(i) If you have licensed a single user version of the Product, the Product may only be used on a single computer (i.e., a single CPU). If you licensed and paid the fee applicable to a local area network or wide area network version of the Product, you are subject to the terms of the following subparagraph (ii).

(ii) If you have licensed a local area network version, you may use the Product on unlimited workstations located in one single building selected by you that is served by such local area network. If you have licensed a wide area network version, you may use the Product on unlimited workstations located in multiple buildings on the same site selected by you that is served by such wide area network; provided, however, that any building will not be considered located in the same site if it is more than five (5) miles away from any building included in such site. In addition, you may only use a local area or wide area network version of the Product on one single server. If you wish to use the Product on more than one server, you must obtain written authorization from McGraw-Hill and pay additional fees.

(iii) You may make one copy of the Product for back-up purposes only and you must maintain an accurate record as to the location of the back-up at all times.

COPYRIGHT; RESTRICTIONS ON USE AND TRANSFER: All rights (including copyright) in and to the Product are owned by McGraw-Hill and its licensors. You are the owner of the enclosed disc on which the Product is recorded. You may not use, copy, decompile, disassemble, reverse engineer, modify, reproduce, create derivative works, transmit, distribute, sublicense, store in a database or retrieval system of any kind, rent or transfer the Product, or any portion thereof, in any form or by any means (including electronically or otherwise) except as expressly provided for in this License Agreement. You must reproduce the copyright notices, trademark notices, legends and logos of McGraw-Hill and its licensors that appear on the Product on the back-up copy of the Product which you are permitted to make hereunder. All rights in the Product not expressly granted herein are reserved by McGraw-Hill and its licensors.

TERM: This License Agreement is effective until terminated. It will terminate if you fail to comply with any term or condition of this License Agreement. Upon termination, you are obligated to return to McGraw-Hill the Product together with all copies thereof and to purge all copies of the Product included in any and all servers and computer facilities.

DISCLAIMER OF WARRANTY: THE PRODUCT AND THE BACK-UP COPY ARE LICENSED "AS IS." McGRAW-HILL, ITS LICENSORS AND THE AUTHORS MAKE NO WARRANTIES, EXPRESS OR IMPLIED, AS TO THE RESULTS TO BE OBTAINED BY ANY PERSON OR ENTITY FROM USE OF THE PRODUCT, ANY INFORMATION OR DATA INCLUDED THEREIN AND/OR ANY TECHNICAL SUPPORT SERVICES PROVIDED HEREUNDER, IF ANY ("TECHNICAL SUPPORT SERVICES"). McGRAW-HILL, ITS LICENSORS AND THE AUTHORS MAKE NO EXPRESS OR IMPLIED WARRANTIES OF MERCHANTABILITY OR FITNESS FOR A PARTICULAR PURPOSE OR USE WITH RESPECT TO THE PRODUCT. McGRAW-HILL, ITS LICENSORS, AND THE AUTHORS MAKE NO GUARANTEE THAT YOU WILL PASS ANY CERTIFICATION EXAM WHATSOEVER BY USING THIS PRODUCT. NEITHER McGRAW-HILL, ANY OF ITS LICENSORS NOR THE AUTHORS WARRANT THAT THE FUNCTIONS CONTAINED IN THE PRODUCT WILL MEET YOUR REQUIREMENTS OR THAT THE OPERATION OF THE PRODUCT WILL BE UNINTERRUPTED OR ERROR FREE. YOU ASSUME THE ENTIRE RISK WITH RESPECT TO THE QUALITY AND PERFORMANCE OF THE PRODUCT.

LIMITED WARRANTY FOR DISC: To the original licensee only, McGraw-Hill warrants that the enclosed disc on which the Product is recorded is free from defects in materials and workmanship under normal use and service for a period of ninety (90) days from the date of purchase. In the event of a defect in the disc covered by the foregoing warranty, McGraw-Hill will replace the disc.

LIMITATION OF LIABILITY: NEITHER McGRAW-HILL, ITS LICENSORS NOR THE AUTHORS SHALL BE LIABLE FOR ANY INDIRECT, SPECIAL OR CONSEQUENTIAL DAMAGES, SUCH AS BUT NOT LIMITED TO, LOSS OF ANTICIPATED PROFITS OR BENEFITS, RESULTING FROM THE USE OR INABILITY TO USE THE PRODUCT EVEN IF ANY OF THEM HAS BEEN ADVISED OF THE POSSIBILITY OF SUCH DAMAGES. THIS LIMITATION OF LIABILITY SHALL APPLY TO ANY CLAIM OR CAUSE WHATSOEVER WHETHER SUCH CLAIM OR CAUSE ARISES IN CONTRACT, TORT, OR OTHERWISE. Some states do not allow the exclusion or limitation of indirect, special or consequential damages, so the above limitation may not apply to you.

U.S. GOVERNMENT RESTRICTED RIGHTS: Any software included in the Product is provided with restricted rights subject to subparagraphs (c), (1) and (2) of the Commercial Computer Software-Restricted Rights clause at 48 C.F.R. 52.227-19. The terms of this Agreement applicable to the use of the data in the Product are those under which the data are generally made available to the general public by McGraw-Hill. Except as provided herein, no reproduction, use, or disclosure rights are granted with respect to the data included in the Product and no right to modify or create derivative works from any such data is hereby granted.

GENERAL: This License Agreement constitutes the entire agreement between the parties relating to the Product. The terms of any Purchase Order shall have no effect on the terms of this License Agreement. Failure of McGraw-Hill to insist at any time on strict compliance with this License Agreement shall not constitute a waiver of any rights under this License Agreement. This License Agreement shall be construed and governed in accordance with the laws of the State of New York. If any provision of this License Agreement is held to be contrary to law, that provision will be enforced to the maximum extent permissible and the remaining provisions will remain in full force and effect.